ALASTAIR SAWDAY'S
SPECIAL PLACES TO STAY

SPAIN

JOSE NAVARRO

Design:	Caroline King
Maps & Mapping:	Bartholomew Mapping, a division of HarperCollins, Glasgow
Printing:	Canale, Italy
UK Distribution:	Portfolio, Greenford, Middlesex
US Distribution:	The Globe Pequot Press, Guilford, Connecticut

Published in February 2003

Alastair Sawday Publishing Co. Ltd
The Home Farm Stables, Barrow Gurney, Bristol BS48 3RW
Tel: +44 (0)1275 464891 Fax: +44 (0)1275 464887
E-mail: info@specialplacestostay.com Web: www.specialplacestostay.com

The Globe Pequot Press
P. O. Box 480, Guilford, Connecticut 06437, USA
Tel: +1 203 458 4500 Fax: +1 203 458 4601
E-mail: info@globe-pequot.com Web: www.globe-pequot.com

Fifth edition

ISBN 1-901970-80-9 in the UK
ISBN 0-7627-2552-4 in the US

Printed in Italy

ALASTAIR SAWDAY'S
SPECIAL PLACES TO STAY

SPAIN

A wonderful book – it opens the door
to more than 340 remarkable places.

The
Globe
Pequot
Press

Guilford
Connecticut, USA

ALASTAIR
SAWDAY
PUBLISHING

Alastair Sawday Publishing
Bristol, UK

JOSE NAVARRO

CONTENTS

Acknowledgements • A word from Alastair Sawday •
Introduction • General map • Maps

CONTENTS

CONTENTS

CONTENTS

See the back of the book for:

- What is Alastair Sawday Publishing?
- www.specialplacestostay.com
- Alastair Sawday's Special Places to Stay series
- The Little Earth Book
- The Little Food Book
- Booking form
- Report form
- Quick reference indices
- Index by property name
- Index by place name
- Exchange rates
- Explanation of symbols

ACKNOWLEDGEMENTS

When Guy Hunter-Watts finally succumbed to 'paperitis', having edited four editions of this guide, and opted for a life carousing and exploring the hills of Andalucia, we sympathised. It is hard to juggle competing balls, and those hills are irresistible. But we miss him and were relieved to have been able to lure him back to a little gentle inspecting and grateful for his continued support having passed on the main baton.

Who better to take it over than a Spaniard living in Bristol? Jose Navarro is a freelance photographer and writer with a passion for cultural and environmental issues, books and bicycles. He writes and speaks excellent English and, most importantly, understands what makes a place 'special'. He has managed the Spanish inspectors and the demanding administrative load of this project with real determination, skill and commitment and we are hugely grateful to him. Jo Boissevain pulled together the final pieces of the complicated jigsaw, and Rose Shawe-Taylor and Vivien Cripps brought their flair and vision to the writing.

Barry Birch and Rob Paterson are the other people to whom we owe much, for they buzzed about Spain with humour and great good will, inspecting places for us. The fact that an Irish balloonist became one of our main inspectors must say something about our eclecticism – or his!

Alastair Sawday

Series Editor:	Alastair Sawday
Project Manager:	Jose Navarro
Editorial Director:	Annie Shillito
Production Manager:	Julia Richardson
Web Producer:	Russell Wilkinson
Production Assistants:	Rachel Coe, Paul Groom
Editorial Assistants:	Jo Boissevain, Roanne Finch
Additional writing	Jo Boissevain, Vivien Cripps, Rose Shawe-Taylor
Inspections:	Barry Birch, Guy Hunter-Watts, Rob Paterson

Thank you, too, to other inspectors who saw just one or two houses for us.

And from Jose: Special thanks to Meg, because she's always there for me.

A WORD FROM ALASTAIR SAWDAY

Not since the heady days of the 50s and 60s have so many
people poured over the Pyrenees in pursuit of pleasure.
Back then there was the added excitement of the constant
risk of imprisonment by the Guardia Civil. Their three-
cornered hats were either loved or feared. Travel too, of
course, was more colourful. According to Anthony Carson
"there was never any doubt that one had arrived in Spain.
There was a faint sound of drums, a smell of crude olive oil,
and currents of strong, leaking electricity." My own early
memories of Spain are of donkeys, silence, old men and
disabled ex-soldiers from the Civil War selling lottery
tickets and matches.

Nowadays Spain is easy on the traveller. Many of you who
go there are doing so to explore the interior, a vast area as
fascinating as anywhere in Europe. Although we have places
to stay throughout the country we are especially proud of
the rural ones. For those who want to walk deep into the
countryside, penetrate the heart of old Spain, see wildlife
that is the richest in Europe – there are places here where
you can lay your head in peace and comfort.

So do treat this book as a valuable resource. Whatever you
wish to do there is probably somewhere to do it, and someone
to show you how. Look up the indices at the back of the book
and you will see where to stay if you want to go riding or
walking, where to find vineyards and wheelchair access.
Above all you will find friends wherever you go, for the
Spaniards (and non-Spaniards) in this remarkable book are
all chosen because we like them. They are lovely people.

Alastair Sawday

INTRODUCTION

How we choose our Special Places?

We look for owners, homes and hotels that we like – and we are fiercely subjective in our choices. 'Special' for us is not a measure of the number of creature comforts you get but relates to many different elements that make a place 'work'. Certainly the way guests are treated comes as high on our list as the setting, the architecture and the food. We are not necessarily impressed by high star ratings.

In this fifth edition we are delighted to include properties belonging to the Pazos de Galicia association. These are usually manor houses, of historical and architectural importance, which dot the Galician landscape. We are again including members of Rusticae, an association of hotels that have kept their character and personal service. Expect this book to lead you to places that are original, individual and welcoming. We hope it will bring you closer to the Spain that we love, a country whose people are vibrant and spontaneous, incredibly friendly and – yes, the cliché is true – different.

So how how does this square with the foreign-run places in this book? We don't search out ex-pats. But some of them have created marvellous places to stay and those we include have a proven track-record of commitment to their adopted land and people.

What to expect

The Spanish 'way of being' is hugely different from the British or the American one. One small scene illustrates the point. Imagine that you are standing at the counter of a bar in, say, the old town of Ronda. Two working men enter the bar, and one shouts at the barman. "*Oiga! Una cerveza,*" – literally, "Here, give me a beer". The barman doesn't bat an eyelid and a beer is thumped down on the bar: not a 'please' nor a 'thank you' from either party. You might think that the two men are about to come to blows: why else would they be shouting at each other when standing just one foot apart? It gradually dawns on you from the smiles and laughter that this is simply a lively discussion and that daggers will not be drawn. Meanwhile, just behind the two men, an unwatched TV screams at full volume. You are both irritated and deafened. So you pluck up courage and ask the barman if he could just turn it down '*un poquito*'. "Of course, amigo", he replies, and turns it off, clearly bemused because he had not even noticed it was switched on. The whole scene shows that you can't judge Spain by your own cultural

INTRODUCTION

yardsticks. So in hotels, bars and restaurants be quick to pardon what might at first seem a brash or an abrupt way of being. The Spanish language can be as rich and convoluted as it is economical, almost austere. Don't be suprised or put off by how rarely the words 'please' and 'thank you' are used in daily conversations. It seems to be a language convention to avoid complex rhetoric and be direct; no rudeness is meant at all.

Mañana, mañana

Yes, we all know that the Spanish conception of time can be fairly loose. It makes me think of Salvador Dali's painting of a melting watch dripping from a table onto the floor. However, frustrating at first, it encompasses a different approach to life from the one we are used to in more northern latitudes. Spaniards firmly believe they determine the course of time and not the other way round. You will have to take this on board and relax about time when in Spain. Enjoy all those 'little' things that can make life so enjoyable, with which the Spaniards regularly indulge themselves. The *sobremesa*, the ubiquitous chat over coffee after lunch; a *siesta* to cope with the rigours of the hot summers; or *el paseo*, the aimless stroll down the main avenue at dusk with no specific purpose in mind.

Finding the right place for you

We have sought out beautiful homes and hotels throughout Spain. But, occasionally, the 'charm' factor can be low: form often follows function and the Spanish like to get together in (very) large groups. Choose your hotel on looks alone and you will miss out on some remarkable places. Don't be too put off by, say, a cavernous looking restaurant. The food may well be tremendous. And, likewise, be prepared to tolerate a 'sugary' taste in decoration. The rooms will be comfortable and come with a reasonable price tag.

We want you to spend your time in places that you will like. We aim to write honest descriptions. Hotels, like people, are never perfect. So read the descriptions carefully!

How to use this book

Maps

Look at the map at the front of the book, find your area, then look for the places which are mapped. Note their numbers and look up the same entry number which you will find at the bottom of the page.

INTRODUCTION

Rooms

We tell you the range of accommodation in single, double, twin, triple or quadruple rooms or in apartments, suites, cottages or houses. Extra beds can often be added for children. Check when booking.

Prices

The prices that we quote for rooms are exclusive of VAT at 7%. Prices are given for the room unless otherwise specified. When VAT and/or breakfast is included we let you know. The same applies to prices that we quote for meals.

The prices we quote were applicable at the time that this book went to press. We publish every two years so expect prices to be higher if you are using this book in 2004 or early 2005.

A word about the Balearic & the Canary Islands

Expect to pay about 50% more here than in the rest of Spain. We promise that we haven't sought out expensive places — that's just the way it is.

Symbols

There is an explanation of our symbols on the last page of the book. Use these as a guide, not as a statement of fact.

Phones & phone codes

From Spain to another country: dial 00 then add the country code and then the area code without the first 0. E.g. ASP in England, from Spain:
UK No. 01275 464891 becomes 00 44 1275 464891

Within Spain: All nine digits are needed whether intra or inter-provincial.

Calling Spain from another country:
From the USA: 011 34 then the nine-digit number.
From the UK: 00 34 then the nine-digit number.

Most mobile numbers begin with a 6. This is your best clue as to when you're dialling an (expensive) mobile number.
Buy telephone cards from tobacconists or post offices (coin operated boxes are few). The cheapest starts at about €6 (£4, US$6).

INTRODUCTION

Abbreviations

C/ — *calle* — street   Ctra — *carretera* — road

s/n — *sin número* — un-numbered   Pts — *pesetas*

Types of properties

Expect to find.

Can	A farmhouse in Catalonia or the Balearic Islands. Often isolated.
Casita	A cottage or small house.
Casona	A grand house in Asturias (many were built by returning émigrés).
Cortijo	A free-standing farmhouse, generally in the south.
Finca	A farm; most of those included here are on working farms.
Fonda	A simple inn which may or may nor serve food.
Hacienda	A large estate. Originally a South American term.
Hostal	Another type of simple inn where food may or may not be served.
Hostería	A simple inn which tends to serve food.
Hostelería	Another term for an inn which may or may not serve food.
Mas	Another term for a farmhouse in the north-east of Spain.
Masía	Another term for a farmhouse in the east of Spain.
Posada	Originally it meant a coaching inn. Beds and food available.
Palacio	A grand mansion house.
Palacete	A slightly less grand version of the above.
Pazo	A grand country or village manor in Galicia.
Venta	A simple restaurant; rooms have often come later.

The spelling of proper names in Spain

Where there are two official languages (as in Galicia, the Basque Country or Catalonia) place names will often have two spellings. Orense will be Ourense in Galicia. Lerida will be spelt Lleida on road signs in Catalonia. In the Basque Country

INTRODUCTION

regional spellings usually accompany the Spanish one e.g. Vitoria will be signposted Vitoria-Gasteiz. We try to use the ones that you are most likely to see in each instance: this may mean one version in the address, another in the directions on how to get there. We have no political agenda!

Meals

Times The Spanish eat much later than we do: breakfast often doesn't get going until 9am, lunch is generally eaten from 2pm and dinner is rarely served before 8.30pm.

Breakfast The 'Continental' in larger hotels tends to be uninspired: coffee, toast (perhaps cakes), butter and jam. Marmalade is a rare sight and freshly squeezed juice the exception. But few places would object if you supplement your meal with your own fruit.

Many Spaniards breakfast on pâtés and olive oil, perhaps with garlic and certainly with tomato in Catalonia. Your hotelier may assume that you prefer a blander, more northern-European offering. So do check.

Tea tends to be poor so take a few tea bags with you and ask for hot water. *Té* in Spain is normally served without milk. Ask for it *con leche* if you like it with milk or *con limón* for a slice of lemon. Bars nearly always serve camomile tea (*manzanilla*) – it can be a useful evening drink because coffee is nearly always very strong.

Lunch and dinner The daily set meal – *el menú del día* – is normally available at both lunch and dinner although waiters will often simply present you with the à la carte menu. But do ask for it; it tends to be great value and will often have fresher ingredients. Many restaurants serve only à la carte at weekends.

Tapas and *raciones* A *tapa* is a small plate of hot or cold food served with an aperitif before lunch or dinner: it remains an essential part of eating out in Spain. It could be a plate of olives, anchovies, cheese, spicy chorizo sausage, fried fish... portions vary as does the choice. It is a delicious way to try out local specialities and don't worry if your Spanish is poor – *tapas* are often laid out along the bar for you to point at. If you would like a plateful of any particular *tapa* then ask for *una ración de queso* (cheese), for example. Most bars will also serve you a half portion – *una media ración*.

INTRODUCTION

Some historians attribute the Spanish 'obsession' with meat dishes to the rationing that followed the Spanish Civil War. The truth is that meat is an ubiquitous element in the Spanish daily diet. This means that outside main towns it might be difficult to arrange for vegetarian meals. Be prepared to find salads the only vegetarian alternative on offer.

Tipping

Leaving a tip is the norm in Spain. In bars you are given your change on a small saucer; leave a couple of small coins. For lunch or dinner 5%-10% is fine but you would rarely be made to feel embarrassed if you don't tip. Taxi drivers don't all expect a tip.

Bathrooms

It seems that Spaniards do not fully appreciate the benefits of a long soak in a foaming bath. Hence the plug may be missing from your bathroom. Just in case, pack one of those handy universal bath plugs you can buy.

Seasons

When we give a price range the lower is the Low Season, the higher the High Season. There may also be a Mid Season price. In most of Spain, High Season includes Easter, Christmas, public holidays and the summer. Some hotels (especially those in the big cities) classify weekends as High and weekdays as Low.

Public Holidays

Spain being the religious country that it is, there are, apart from the public holidays nationwide, a whole array of local festivities in the honour of one Saint or another in every town and village in Spain. You may find this terribly frustrating – for shops and restaurants might be shut – or you may enjoy joining the locals in the celebration. Either way it will be difficult for you to find out beforehand when the local holiday for the village you are heading for will be. As a rule August tends to be filled with festivities. January 1st, January 6th, Good Friday, Easter Monday, May 1st, Corpus Christi (usually early June), June 24th, July 25th, August 15th, October 12th, November 1st, December 6th, December 8th, December 25th.

INTRODUCTION

Booking

Try to book well ahead if you plan to be in Spain during
holidays. August is best avoided unless you are heading
somewhere remote. Many hotels will ask you for a credit card
number when you book. And remember to let smaller hotels
and B&Bs know if you want dinner.

There's a bilingual booking form at the back of the book.
Hotels often send back a signed or stamped copy as
confirmation. Hotels don't necessarily assume that you
are expecting a speedy reply (this includes e-mails)!

Arrival/Registration/Checking out times

Many city hotels will only hold a reservation until the early
evening, even though you might have booked months in
advance. So ring ahead if you are planning to arrive late.
(It remains law that you should register on arrival in a hotel.
Hotels have no right to keep your passport.)

Payment

The most commonly accepted credit cards are Visa, MasterCard
and Eurocard. Many smaller places don't take plastic because of
high bank charges. But there is nearly always a cash dispenser
(ATM) close at hand; again Visa, MasterCard and Eurocard are
the most useful.

Euros

The euro became the official currency at the beginning of 2002.
However, you will find that many Spaniards still refer
to the old peseta, the former currency, particularly if talking
about large sums of money. At the time of publication of
this guide, just over a year after the new currency started
to exchange hands in the Spanish streets, the peseta is still
very much alive in people's minds. It might take a few years
for people to feel comfortable with the new European system,
so be prepared to make some calculations in the much loved
and lamented peseta.

Plugs

Virtually all sockets now have 220/240 AC voltage
(usually two-pin). Pack an adaptor if you travel with
electrical appliances.

INTRODUCTION

Driving and car hire

Foreign number plates attract attention in the big cities so never leave your car with valuables inside. Use a public car park; they are cheap and safe.

It is compulsory to have in the car: a spare set of bulbs, a warning triangle and a basic first aid kit. (Spain has good terms for car hire – for a small one from £100, or $140 US, for a week.)

Public transport

Trains, buses and taxis are very cheap in Spain. You meet people, and get much more of a feel for the country by travelling this way. Spain has a high-speed rail link between Madrid and Seville which gets you down south in under two and a half hours and a high speed link will soon be in place between Catalonia and Madrid. Some regional lines would bring a tear to any rail buff's eye, the journey between Ronda and Algeciras particularly.

Look out for the national coach company if you want to travel by public transport. ENATCAR (Empresa Nacional de Transportes por Carretera) underwent a massive restructuring some years ago and established concessions in every major town. As a result of this it has some of the most modern and comfortable coaches you will find in Europe. And it is cheap too. The rarity of roundabouts in the road network and the existence of motorway tolls – which deter drivers from using the faster roads – mean that coach journeys tend to be shorter compared to in the UK.

The Alhambra

A visit is a highlight of any trip to Spain. But tickets must be booked in advance.

Subscriptions

Owners pay to go into this guide. Their fee goes some way towards covering the inspection and production costs of an all-colour book. It is not possible however, for people to buy their way into the book – whatever our rivals may suggest!

INTRODUCTION

Environment   We try to be as 'green' as possible. We lend bicycles to staff and provide a pool car. We celebrate the use of organic, home-grown and locally produced food. We are working to establish an organic standard for B&Bs and run an Environmental Business Trust to stimulate business interest in the environment.

We also publish *The Little Earth Book*, a collection of essays on environmental issues. A new title, *The Little Food Book*, is another hard-hitting analysis – this time of the food industry. To try to reduce our impact on the environment we plant trees: the emissions directly related to our office, paper production, printing and distribution have been 'neutralised' through the planting of indigenous woodlands with Future Forests. We are, officially, Carbon Neutral.

Internet   Our web site www.specialplacestostay.com has online pages for all the places featured here and in our other books. For more details see the back of the book.

Disclaimer   We make no claims to be objective in choosing our *Special Places To Stay*. They are here because we like them. Our opinions and tastes are ours alone and this book is a statement of them; we hope that you share them.

We have done our utmost to get our facts right but apologise unreservedly for any mistakes that may have crept in. Sometimes, too, prices shift, usually upwards, and 'things' change. Please tell us about any errors or changes.

And finally   Thank you to all those who have taken the time to share your opinions with us. You have helped make this edition of the book even better than the last!

Please let us have your comments; there is a report form at the back of this book. Or e-mail us at spain@sawdays.co.uk

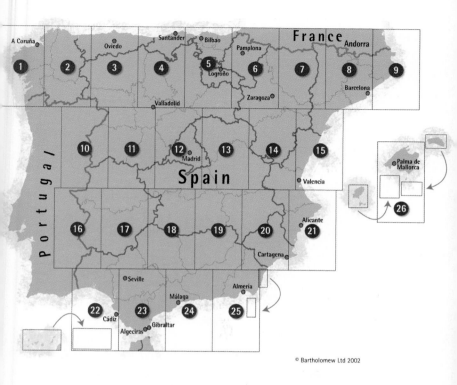

A guide to our map page numbers

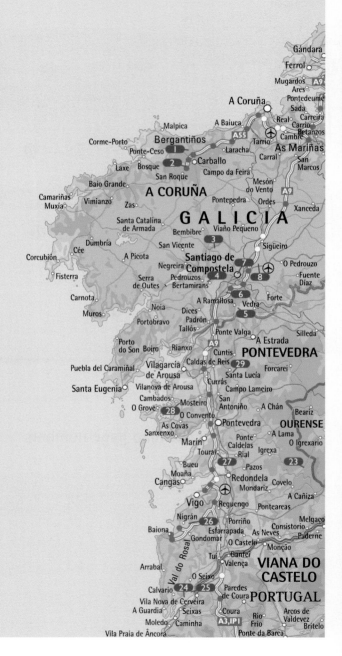

Map 1

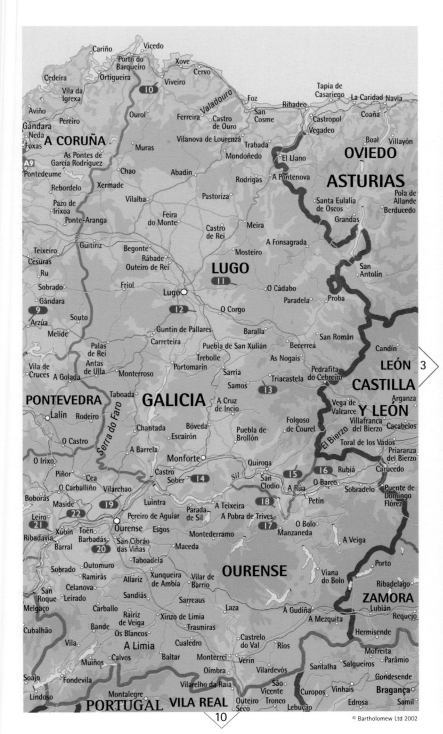

© Bartholomew Ltd 2002

Map 2

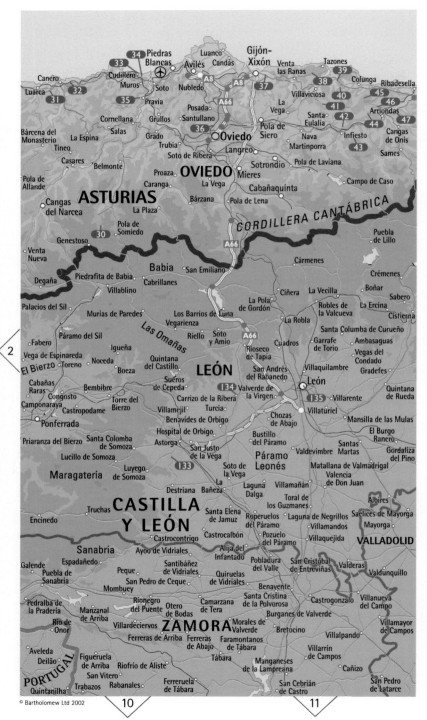

Map 3

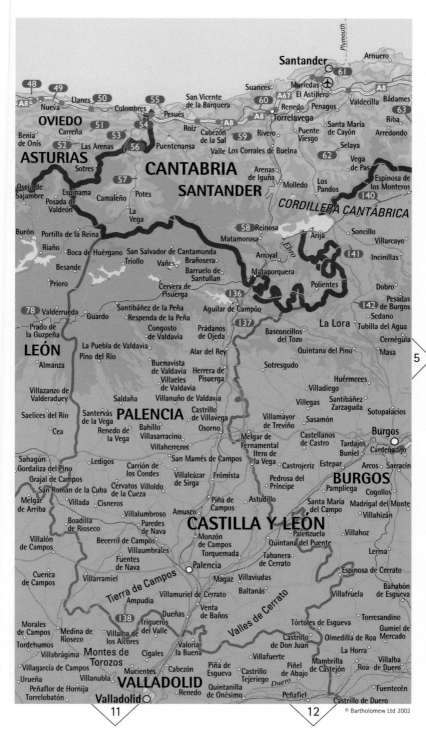

Map 4

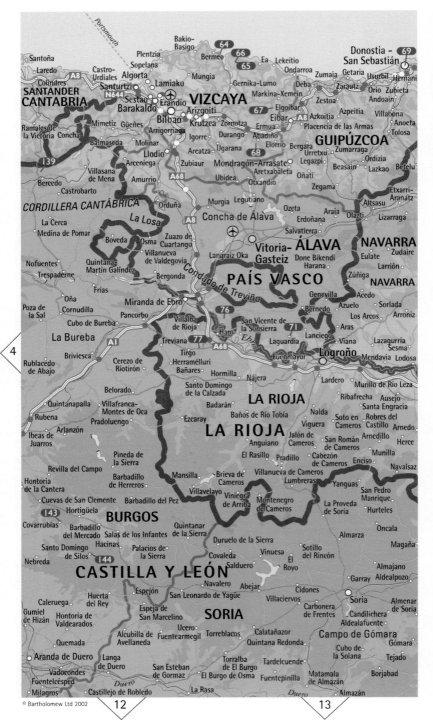

Map 5

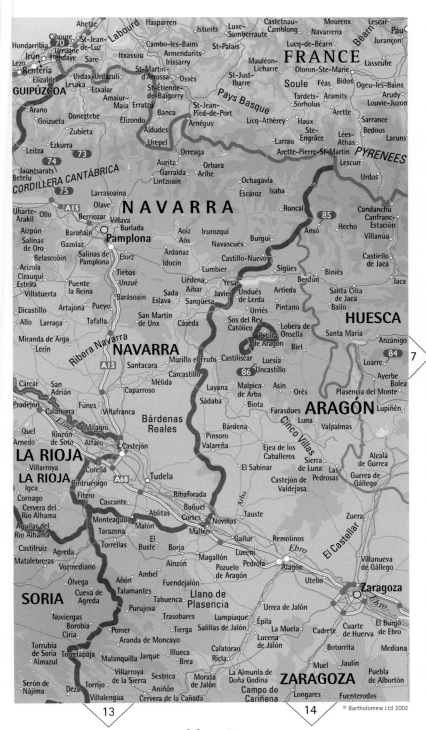

Map 6

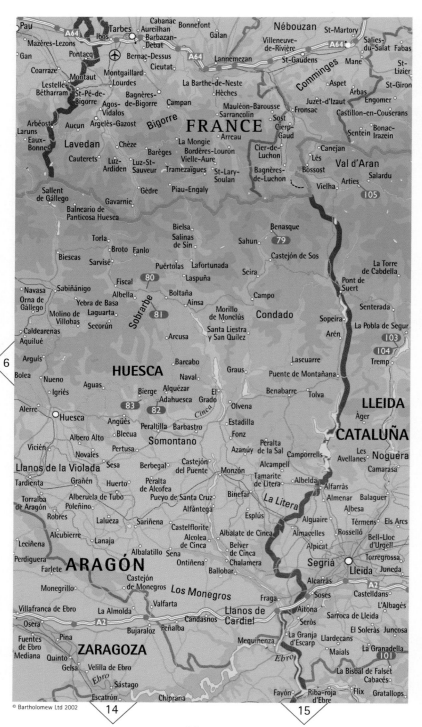

Map 7

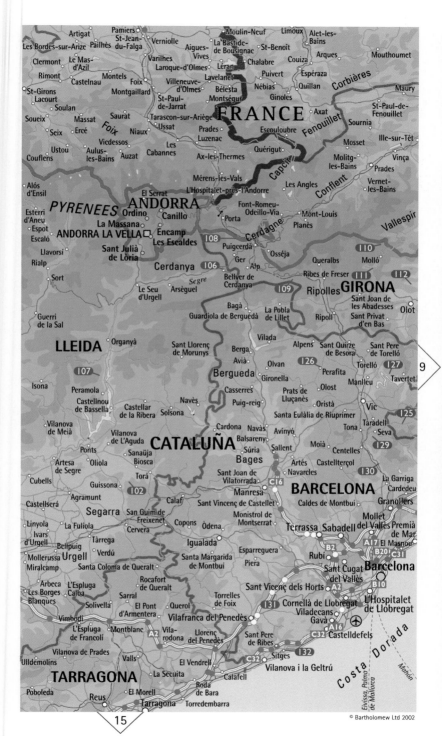

© Bartholomew Ltd 2002

Map 8

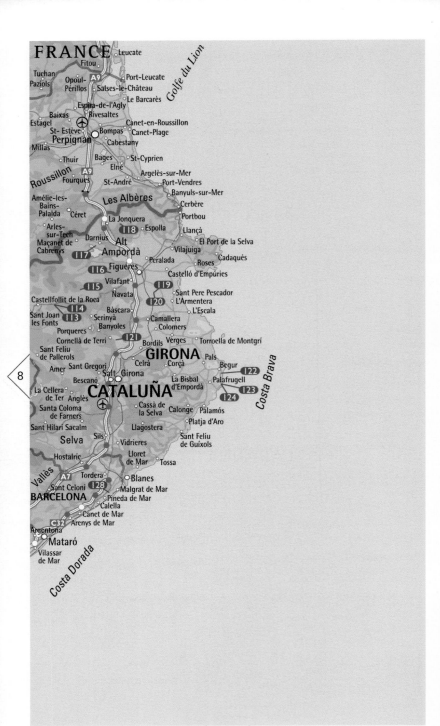

FRANCE · Leucate
Fitou
Tuchan
Paziols
Opoul-
Périllos
A9
Port-Leucate
Salses-le-Château
Le Barcarès
Espira-de-l'Agly
Baixas · Rivesaltes
Estagel
St- Estève
Bompas · Canet-Plage
Perpignan · Cabestany
Millas
Thuir · Bages · St-Cyprien
Elne
Argelès-sur-Mer
Roussillon · Fourques · St-André · Port-Vendres
Banyuls-sur-Mer
Amélie-les-Bains-Palalda · Céret · Les Albères · Cerbère
Arles-sur-Tech · La Jonquera · Portbou
Maçanet de Cabrenys · Darnius · 118 · Espolla · Llançà
117 · Alt Empordà · El Port de la Selva
Vilajuïga · Cadaqués
Peralada · Roses
116 · Figueres
Castelló d'Empúries
115 · Vilafant
Navata · 119 · Sant Pere Pescador
Castellfollit de la Roca · 120 · L'Armentera
114 · Bàscara · L'Escala
Sant Joan les Fonts · 113 · Serinyà · Camallera
Porqueres · Banyoles · Colomers
Cornellà de Terri · 121 · Bordils · Verges · Torroella de Montgrí
Sant Feliu de Pallerols
Amer · Sant Gregori · Celrà · Pals
GIRONA
Salt · Girona · Corçà · Begur
Bescanó · La Bisbal · Palafrugell · 122
CATALUÑA · d'Empordà · 123
La Cellera de Ter · Anglès · 124 · Costa Brava
Santa Coloma de Farners · Cassà de la Selva · Calonge · Palamós
Sant Hilari Sacalm · Llagostera · Platja d'Aro
Selva · Sils · Sant Feliu de Guíxols
Vidrieres
Hostalric · Lloret de Mar · Tossa
Vallès · A7 · Tordera · Blanes
Sant Celoni · 128 · Malgrat de Mar
BARCELONA · Pineda de Mar
Calella
C32 · Canet de Mar
Argentona · Arenys de Mar
Mataró
Vilassar de Mar
Costa Dorada

Golfe du Lion

Canet-en-Roussillon

8

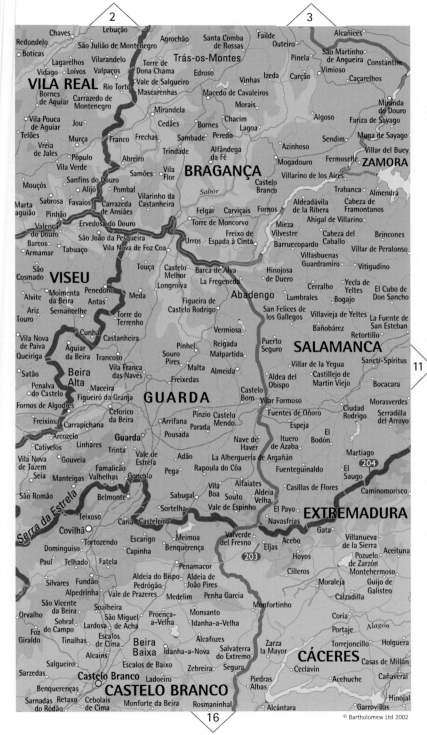

© Bartholomew Ltd 2002

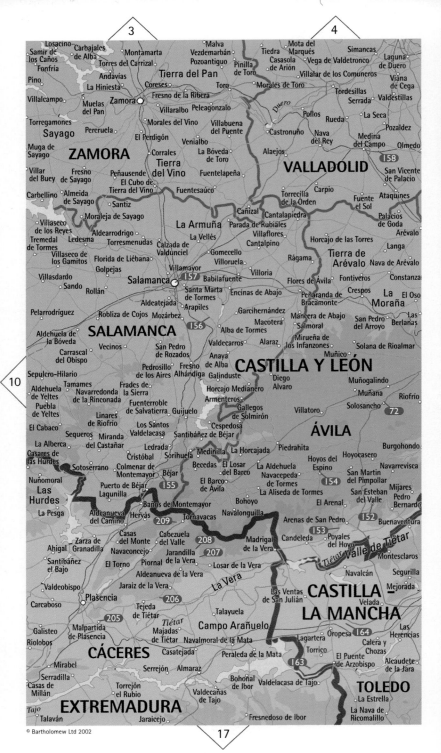

Map 11

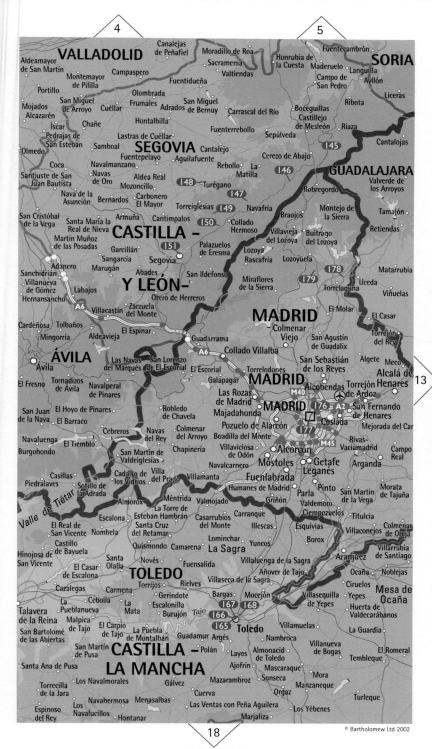

VALLADOLID

Aldeamayor
de San Martín
Montemayor
de Pililla
Campaspero
Canalejas
de Peñafiel
Moradillo de Roa
Sacramenia
Valtiendas
Honrubia de
la Cuesta
Maderuelo
Fuentecambrón
Campo de
San Pedro
Languilla
Ayllón

SORIA

Portillo
Mojados
Alcazarén
San Miguel
de Arroyo
Cuéllar
Fuentidueña
Olombrada
Frumales
Adrados
San Miguel
de Bernuy
Carrascal del Río
Boceguillas
Castillejo
de Mesleón
Riaza
Ribota
Liceras

Íscar
Pedrajas de
San Esteban
Olmedo
Chañe
Hontalbilla
Fuenterrebollo
Sepúlveda
Cantalojas

Coca
Navalmanzano
Samboal
Lastras de Cuéllar
SEGOVIA
Cantalejo
Cerezo de Abajo
145

Santiuste de San
Juan Bautista
Navas
de Oro
Fuentepelayo
Aguilafuente
Rebollo
La
Matilla
146

GUADALAJARA

Nava de la
Asunción
Bernardos
Mozoncillo
Aldea Real
Carbonero
el Mayor
148
Turégano
147
Navafría
Robregordo
Valverde de
los Arroyos

San Cristóbal
de la Vega
Santa María la
Real de Nieva
Armuña
Cantimpalos
Torreiglesias
149
150
Collado
Hermoso
Braojos
Montejo de
la Sierra
Tamajón
Retiendas

Martín Muñoz
de las Posadas
Garcillán
151
Palazuelos
de Eresma
Villavieja
del Lozoya
Buitrago
del Lozoya

Adanero
Sanchidrián
Villanueva
de Gómez
Hernansancho
Sangarcía
Marugán
Abades
Segovia
San Ildefonso
Lozoya
Rascafría
Lozoyuela
178
Matarrubia
Uceda
Viñuelas

A6
Labajos
Otero de Herreros
Miraflores
de la Sierra
179
Torrelaguna

Cardeñosa
Mingorría
Tolbaños
Aldeavieja
Zarzuela
del Monte
Villacastín
El Espinar
Guadarrama
A6
Collado Villalba
MADRID
Colmenar
Viejo
San Agustín
de Guadalix
El Molar
El Casar
Torrejón
del Rey
Meco

ÁVILA

Ávila
Tornadizos
de Ávila
Las Navas
del Marqués
San Lorenzo
de El Escorial
El Escorial
Torrelodones
San Sebastián
de los Reyes
Algete
Alcalá de
Henares
13

El Fresno
Navalperal
de Pinares
Galapagar
MADRID
Alcobendas
Torrejón
de Ardoz
San Fernando
de Henares

San Juan
de la Nava
El Hoyo de Pinares
El Barraco
Las Rozas
de Madrid
M40
MADRID
176
A2

Navaluenga
Burgohondo
El Tiemblo
Cebreros
Robledo
de Chavela
Navas
del Rey
Colmenar
del Arroyo
Majadahonda
Pozuelo de Alarcón
Boadilla del Monte
Coslada
177
Mejorada del Car

San Martín de
Valdeiglesias
Chapinería
Villaviciosa
de Odón
Alcorcón
Móstoles
M45
Rivas-
Vaciamadrid
Campo
Real

Casillas
Piedralaves
Sotillo de
la Adrada
Cadalso de
los Vidrios
Villa
del Prado
Navalcarnero
Getafe
Leganés
Arganda

Valle de Tiétar
Almorox
Méntrida
Villamanta
Fuenlabrada
Humanes de Madrid
Parla
Pinto
San Martín
de la Vega
Morata
de Tajuña

El Real de
San Vicente
Nombela
Escalona
La Torre de
Esteban Hambrán
Santa Cruz
del Retamar
Valmojado
Casarrubios
del Monte
Carranque
Illescas
Griñón
Valdemoro
Ciempozuelos
Esquivias
Titulcia
Colmenar
de Oreja

Hinojosa de
San Vicente
Castillo
de Bayuela
El Casar
de Escalona
Quismondo
Camarena
Lominchar
La Sagra
Yuncos
Borox
Villaconejos
Aranjuez
Villarrubia
de Santiago

Santa Ana de Pusa
Santa
Olalla
Novés
Fuensalida
Villaluenga de la Sagra
Añover de Tajo
Ocaña
Noblejas

TOLEDO

Cazalegas
Carmena
Torrijos
Rielves
Villaseca de la Sagra
Ciruelos
Yepes
Mesa de
Ocaña

Talavera
de la Reina
La
Pueblanueva
Cebolla
La
Mata
Gerindote
Escalonilla
Bargas
Mocejón
Villasequilla
de Yepes
Huerta de
Valdecarábanos

San Bartolomé
de las Abiertas
Malpica
de Tajo
El Carpio
de Tajo
Burujón
167
166
168
Tajo
165
Villamuelas
La Guardia

San Martín
de Pusa
La Puebla
de Montalbán
Guadamur
Argés
Toledo
Nambroca

Los Navalmorales
CASTILLA –
LA MANCHA
Polán
Layos
Ajofrín
Almonacid
de Toledo
Mascaraque
Villanueva
de Bogas
El Romeral
Tembleque

Torrecilla
de la Jara
Gálvez
Mazarambroz
Sonseca
Mora
Manzaneque

Espinoso
del Rey
Los
Navalucillos
Navahermosa
Menasalbas
Hontanar
Cuerva
Las Ventas con Peña Aguilera
Orgaz
Los Yébenes
Marjaliza
Turleque

© Bartholomew Ltd 2002

Map 12

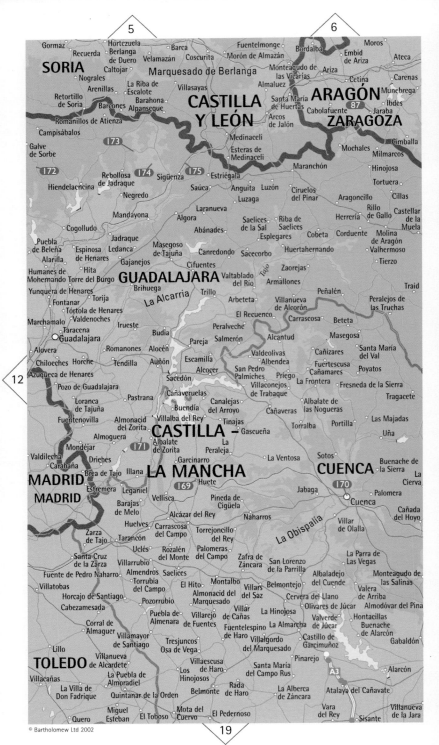

Gormaz · Recuerda · Hortezuela · Barca · Fuentelmonge · Bordalba · Moros · Ateca
Berlanga · Velamazán · Coscurita · Morón de Almazán · Embid · de Ariza
SORIA · de Duero · Caltojar · Marquesado de Berlanga · Monteagudo de · Ariza · Cetina · Carenas
Nógrales · La Riba de · Villasayas · las Vicarías · Almaluez · Santa María · Cabolafuente · Munebrega · **ARAGÓN**
Retortillo · Arenillas · Escalote · Barahona · Alpanseque · de Huertas · Arcos · 87 · Ibdes · Jaraba
de Soria · Barcones · Romanillos de Atienza · de Jalón · **ZARAGOZA**
Campisábalos
Galve · 173 · Medinaceli · Mochales · Cimballa
de Sorbe · Esteras de · Milmarcos
172 · Rebollosa · 174 · Sigüenza · 175 · Estriégala · Marancón · Hinojosa
Hiendelaencina · de Jadraque · Saúca · Anguita · Luzón · Ciruelos · Tortuera
Negredo · Luzaga · del Pinar · Aragoncillo · Cillas
Mandayona · Laranueva · Rillo · Castellar
Cogolludo · Algora · Saelices · Riba de · Herrería · de Gallo · de la
Puebla · Jadraque · Ledanca · Abánades · de la Sal · Saelices · Cobeta · Corduente · Muela
de Beleña · Espinosa · Masegoso · Esplegares · Huertahernando · Molina · Valhermoso
Alarilla · de Henares · Gajanejos · de Tajuña · Canredondo · Sacecorbo · de Aragón
Humanes de · Hita · Cifuentes · Tajo · Zaorejas · Tierzo
Mohernando Torre del Burgo · **GUADALAJARA** · Valtablado · Armallones
Yunquera de Henares · Brihuega · del Río · Peñalén · Traid
Fontanar · Torija · La Alcarria · Trillo · Arbeteta · Villanueva · Peralejos de
Tórtola de Henares · de Alcorón · Carrascosa · Beteta · las Truchas
Marchamalo · Valdenoches · Irueste · El Recuenco · Masegosa
Taracena · Budia · Peralveche · Santa María
○Guadalajara · Pareja · Salmerón · Alcantud · Cañizares · del Val
Alovera · Romanones · Aloc én · Valdeolivas · Fuertescusa · Poyatos
Chiloeches · Horche · Téndilla · Auñón · Escamilla · Albendea · Cañamares
Azuqueca de Henares · Alcocer · San Pedro · Priego · La · Fresneda de la Sierra
Pozo de Guadalajara · Sacedón · Palmiches · Frontera · Tragacete
Cañaveruelas · Villaconejos · Albalate de · Uña
Loranca · Pastrana · Buendía · Canalejas · de Trabaque · las Noguéras
de Tajuña · del Arroyo · Cañaveras · Torralba · Portilla · Las Majadas
Fuentenovilla · Almonacid · Villalba del Rey · Tinajas · Gascueña
del Zorita · Albalate · La · La Ventosa · Sotos · Buenache de
Almoguera · **CASTILLA** · la Cierva · La
Mondéjar · 171 · de Zorita · Peraleja · Garcinarro · **CUENCA** · Cierva
Valdilecha · Driebes · Illana · **LA MANCHA** · 170 · Palomera
Carabaña · Brea de Tajo · Huete · Jabaga · ○Cuenca · Cañada
MADRID · Estremera · Leganiel · 169 · Pineda de · Villar · del Hoyo
MADRID · Barajas · Vellisca · Cigüela · Naharros · de Olalla
de Melo · Alcázar del Rey · La Obispalía · La Parra de
Zarza · Huelves · Carrascosa · Torrejoncillo · Las Vegas
de Tajo · Tarancón · del Campo · del Rey · Zafra de · San Lorenzo · Albaladejo · Monteagudo de
Santa Cruz · Uclés · Rozalén · Palomeras · Záncara · de la Parrilla · del Cuende · las Salinas
de la Zarza · Villarrubio · del Monte · del Campo · Valera
Fuente de Pedro Naharro · Almendros · Saelices · El Hito · Montalbo · Villars · Belmontejo · Cervera del Llano · de Arriba
Villatobas · Torrubia · Almonacid del · del Saz · La Hinojosa · Olivares de Júcar · Almodóvar del Pinar
Horcajo de Santiago · del Campo · Pozorrubio · Marquesado · Villar · La Almarcha · Valverde · Hontacillas
Cabezamesada · Puebla de · Villarejo · de Cañas · de Júcar · Buenache
Corral de · Almenara · de Fuentes · Fuentelespino · Castillo de · de Alarcón · Gabaldón
Almaguer · Villamayor · Tresjuncos · de Haro · Villalgordo · Garcimuñoz
Lillo · de Santiago · Osa de Vega · del Marquesado · Pinarejo · Alarcón
Villanueva · Villaescusa · Santa María · A3
TOLEDO · de Alcardete · Los · de Haro · del Campo Rus
Villacañas · La Puebla de · Hinojosos · Rada · La Alberca · Atalaya del Cañavate
La Villa de · Almoradiel · Belmonte · de Haro · de Záncara · Villanueva
Don Fadrique · Quintanar de la Orden · Vara · de la Jara
Miguel · Mota del · El Pedernoso · del Rey
Quero · Esteban · El Toboso · Cuervo · Sisante

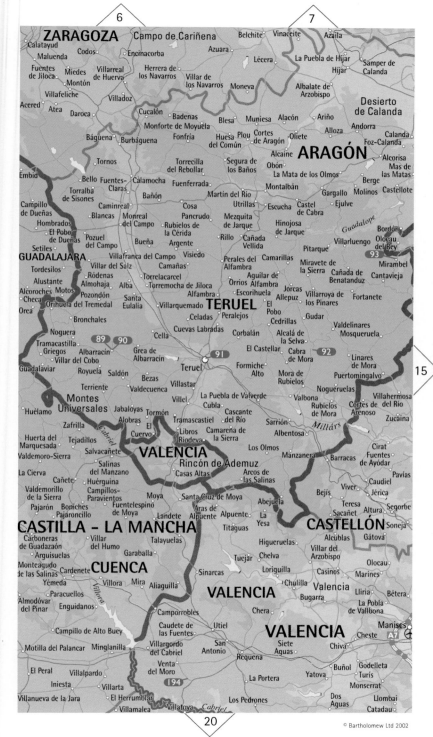

ZARAGOZA
Calatayud
Maluenda · Codos
Fuentes · Miedes
de Jiloca · Montón · Villarreal
de Huerva
Villafeliche
Acered · Atea · Villadoz
Daroca
Báguena · Burbáguena
Tornos
Embid
Bello · Fuentes-Claras · Cálamocha
Torralba · de Sisones
Campillo · Caminreal
de Dueñas · Blancas · Monreal
Hombrados · del Campo
El Pobo · Pozuel · Bueña
de Dueñas · del Campo
Setiles
GUADALAJARA · Villafranca del Campo
Tordesilos · Villar del Salz
Alustante · Almohaja · Alba
Alcoroches · Motos · Pozondón
Checa · Orihuela del Tremedal · Santa
Orea · Eulalia
Bronchales
Noguera
Tramacastilla
Griegos · Albarracín
Villar del Cobo
Guadalaviar · Royuela · Saldón
Terriente · Valdecuenca
Montes · Villastar
Universales · Jabaloyas
Huélamo · Alobras
Zafrilla · El
Cuervo
Huerta del · Tejadillos · Salvacañete
Marquesada
Valdemoro-Sierra
La Cierva
Cañete · Huérguina
Valdemorillo · Campillos-
de la Sierra · Paraviento
Pajarón · Boniches · Fuentelespino
Pajaroncillo · de Moya
CASTILLA - LA MANCHA
Carboneras
de Guadazaón · Villar
Arguisuelas · del Humo
Monteagudo · Cardenete
de las Salinas
Yémeda
Paracuellos · Víllora · Mira · Aliaguilla
Almodóvar · Enguídanos
del Pinar
Campillo de Alto Buey
Motilla del Palancar · Minglanilla
El Peral · Villalpardo
Iniesta · Villarta
Villanueva de la Jara · El Herrumblar
Villamalea

Campo de Cariñena · Belchite · Vinaceite · Azaila
Azuara
Lécera · La Puebla de Híjar · Sámper de
Encinacorba · Calanda
Herrera de · Híjar
los Navarros · Villar de · Moneva
los Navarros · Albalate de
Arzobispo
Desierto
de Calanda
Cucalón · Badenas · Blesa · Muniesa · Alacón · Ariño
Monforte de Moyuela · Alloza · Andorra
Fonfría · Huesa · Plou · Cortes · Oliete · Calanda
del Común · de Aragón · Foz-Calanda
Torrecilla · Segura de · Alcaine · ARAGÓN · Alcorisa
del Rebollar · los Baños · Obón · Mas de
La Mata de los Olmos · las Matas
Fuenferrada · Montalbán · Berge
Bañón · Gargallo · Molinos · Castellote
Cosa · Martín del Río · Ejulve
Pancrudo · Utrillas · Escucha · Castel
Rubielos de · Mezquita · de Cabra
la Cérida · de Jarque · Hinojosa · Guadalope
Rillo · Cañada · de Jarque · Bordón
Argente · Vellida · Pitarque · Villarluengo · Olocau
del Rey
Visiedo · Perales del · Camarillas · Miravete de · Mirambel
Camañas · Alfambra · la Sierra · Cañada de · Cantavieja
Torrelacárcel · Aguilar de · Benatanduz
Torremocha de Jiloca · Orrios · Alfambra · Jorcas
Alfambra · Escorihuela · Allepuz · Villarroya de · Fortanete
Villarquemado · El · los Pinares
TERUEL · Pobo · Gudar
Celadas · Peralejos · Cedrillas
Cuevas Labradas · Corbalán · Valdelinares
Cella · Alcalá de · Mosqueruela
la Selva
89 90 · El Castellar · Cabra
Grea de · de Mora · 92
Albarracín · Teruel · Formiche · Mora de · Linares
91 · Alto · Rubielos · de Mora
Bezas · Puertomingalvo
Villel · La Puebla de Valverde · Noguerualas · Villahermosa
Cubla · Valbona · Rubielos · del Río
Tormón · Cascante · de Mora · Cortes de
Tramascastiel · del Río · Sarrión · Arenoso · Zucaina
Libros · Camareña de · Millárs
Riodeva · la Sierra · Albentosa · Cirat
VALENCIA · Los Olmos · Manzanera · Fuentes
Rincón de Ademuz · Barracas · de Ayódar
Casas Altas · Arcos de · Pavías
Salinas · las Salinas · Viver · Caudiel
del Manzano · Bejís · Jérica
Moya · Abejuela · Teresa · Segorbe
Santa Cruz de Moya · Sacañet · Altura
Aras de · Alpuente · La · Soneja
Landete · Alpuente · Yesa · CASTELLÓN
Talayuelas · Titaguas · Alcúblas · Gátova
Higueruelas · Villar del
Garaballa · Tuejar · Chelva · Arzobispo · Olocau
Sinarcas · Loriguilla · Casinos · Marines
Chulilla · Valencia · Lliria · Bétera
Camporrobles · Chera · Bugarra · La Pobla
de Vallbona
Caudete de · Utiel · VALENCIA · Manises
las Fuentes · Siete · Cheste · A7
Villargordo · San · Aguas · Chiva
del Cabriel · Antonio
Venta · Requena · Buñol · Godelleta
del Moro · La Portera · Yatova · Turís
194 · Monserrat
Dos · Llombai
Villatoya · Cabriel · Los Pedrones · Aguas · Catadau

© Bartholomew Ltd 2002

15

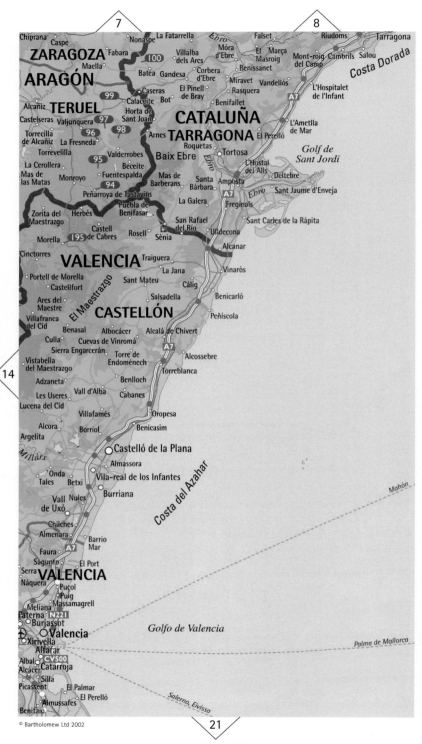

Chiprana
Caspe
Nonaspe
La Fatarrella
Ebro
Falset
Riudoms
Tarragona
ZARAGOZA
Fabara
100
Villalba
dels Arcs
Móra
d'Ebre
El
Marça
Masroig
Mont-roig
del Camp
Cambrils
Salou
Maella
Corbera
d'Ebre
Benissanet
Costa Dorada
ARAGÓN
Batea
Gandesa
Miravet
Vandellós
99
Caseras
El Pinell
de Bray
Rasquera
L'Hospitalet
de l'Infant
A7
Alcañiz
TERUEL
Calaceite
Bot
Benifallet
Castelseras
Valjunquera
97
Horta de
Sant Joan
CATALUÑA
L'Ametlla
de Mar
Torrecilla
de Alcañiz
La Fresneda
96
98
Arnes
TARRAGONA
El Perelló
Valderrobes
Roquetas
Tortosa
Golf de
Sant Jordi
Torrevelilla
95
Baix Ebre
Ebro
La Cerollera
Beceite
L'Hostal
del Alls
Deltebre
Mas de
las Matas
Monroyo
Fuentespalda
Mas de
Barberans
Santa
Bàrbara
Amposta
A7
Ebro
Sant Jaume d'Enveja
Peñarroya de Tastavins
La Galera
Freginals
Zorita del
Maestrazgo
Herbés
Puebla de
Benifasar
San Rafael
del Rio
Sant Carles de la Ràpita
Morella
195
Castell
de Cabres
Rosell
La
Sènia
Ulldecona
Cinctorres
Alcanar
VALENCIA
Traiguera
Portell de Morella
La Jana
Vinaròs
Castellfort
Sant Mateu
Cálig
Ares del
Maestre
Salsadella
Benicarló
El Maestrazgo
CASTELLÓN
Peñíscola
Villafranca
del Cid
Benasal
Albocácer
Alcalá de Chivert
Culla
Cuevas de Vinromá
A7
Sierra Engarcerán
Torre de
Endoménech
Alcossebre
Vistabella
del Maestrazgo
Benlloch
Torreblanca
Adzaneta
Vall d'Alba
Les Useres
Cabanes
Lucena del Cid
Villafamés
Oropesa
Alcora
Borriol
Benicasim
Argelita
Millárs
Castelló de la Plana
Almassora
Onda
Tales
Betxi
Vila-real de los Infantes
Costa del Azahar
Mahón
Nules
Burriana
Vall
de Uxó
Chilches
Almenara
Barrio
Mar
Faura
A7
El Port
Sagunto
Serra
VALENCIA
Nàquera
Puçol
Puig
Meliana
Massamagrell
Paterna
N221
Burjassot
Golfo de Valencia
Valencia
Palma de Mallorca
Xirivella
Alfafar
Albal
CV500
Alcácer
Catarroja
Silla
Picassent
El Palmar
El Perelló
Salerno, Eivissa
Almussafes
Benifaió

© Bartholomew Ltd 2002

Map 15

Proença-a-Nova

LEIRIA
Malpica
do Tejo
Perais

Vila Velha de Ródão
Fratel

Cedillo

Navas del
Madroño

Brozas
202

SANTARÉM
Mação

Montalvão

Santiago de Alcántara

CÁCERES

Envendos
Monte Claro

Membrio

Arroyo de la Luz

Amieira
do Tejo
Nisa

Nossa Senhora da Graça
de Póvoa e Meadas

Salorino

Herreruela

Gavião
Arez

201

Atalaia

Beirã

Aliseda

Comenda
Gáfete
Alpalhão
Castelo

Valência de
Alcántara

Sierra de San Pedro

São
Bartolomeu
Monte da Pedra
de Vide
Marvão

Aldeia
da Mata
Vale
do Peso
Alagoa
San Vicente
de Alcántara

Torre das
Vargens
Cunheira
Fortios
Portalegre

Crato

Alegrete

Alburquerque

Vale de Açor

PORTALEGRE

Barulho
La Codosera

Puebla de Obando

Ponte
de Sor
Valongo
Seda
Alter
do Chão

Esperança

Galveias

Assumar

Arronches

Villar
del Rey
La Roca
de la Sierra

Benavila
Cabeço
de Vide
Vaiamonte

Senhora do Rosário

Aldeia
Velha
Ervedal
Fronteira

Monforte

Ouguela

Avis
Vale de Maceiras

Santa Eulália

Nossa Senhora da Graça dos Degolados

Maranhão
Casa
Cano
Santo Amaro

Barbacena
São Vicente
Caia

Campo
Maior

Branca
Sousel
Veiros

Vila Fernando

Montijo

Pavia
Santa Vitória
do Ameixial
Orada
Santo
Aleixo

Talavera
la Real
Puebla de
la Calzada

São
Gregório
Estremoz
Arcos
Vila Boim
Terrugém

Elvas
Badajoz

Vimieiro
Rio de
Moinhos
A6,IP7

Gafanhoeira
Vale do Pereiro
Évora-Monte
Bencatel
Borba
São Romão

BADAJOZ

A6,IP2,IP7

Vila Viçosa
Juromenha

La Albuera
Etrín
Bajo
Corte de
Peleas

Arraiolos
Azaruja
ÉVORA
Alandroal
Pardais

Olivenza
Valverde
de Leganés

Santa
Marta

Mina do Bugalho

San Jorge
de Alor

17

A6,IP7
Redondo
Terena

Torre de
Miguel Sesmero
Nogales

Bairro dos Canaviais
PORTUGAL
Aldeia dos
Mármelos

Llanos de
Olivenza
Táliga
196
La Morera

Évora
Santa
Susana
Aldeia de
Ferreira
Alconchel
Barcarrota
Salvaleón

Casas Novas
de Mares
Cheles
EXTREMADURA
Salvatierra
de los Barros

Montoito
Vendinha
Caridade
Monsaraz

São Brás do
Regedouro
São
Manços
Reguengos
de Monsaraz
São Pedro
do Corval

Higuera
de Vargas

Campinho
Mourão

Villanueva del Fresno
Valle de
Santa Ana

Aguiar
Torre de
Coelheiros
Monte do Trigo

Luz

Zahinos
Jerez de los
Caballeros

Viana do Alentejo
Portel
São Marcos do Campo

Vila Nova
da Baronia
Oriola

Amieira

Valencia
del Mombuey
Oliva de
la Frontera

Ardila

Alvito
Santana
Vera
Cruz
Alqueva
Estrela
Granja

Vila
Alva
Póvoa de
São Miguel
Amareleja

Higuera la Real

Vila
Ruiva
Vidigueira
Marmelar
Santo
Amador

Barrancos
Encinasola

Alentejo
Cuba
Selmes
Pedrógão
Moura

Safara

Trigaches
São
Matias
Machados

São
Brissos
Brinches

Sobral
da Adiça

Beringel
Nossa Senhora
das Neves
Pias

La Nava

Santa
Vitória
Beja

Penedo
Gordo
Quintos
Vale de
Vargo
Rosal de la Frontera
Aroche
Cortegana
Jabugo

Ervidel
Cabeça Gorda
Salvada
Serpa

210
211

Trindade
São
Brás
Santa
Iria
Vila Nova
de São Bento
Vila Verde
de Ficalho

HUELVA
San
Telmo
Almonaster
la Real

Albernoa
BEJA
Vales Mortos

Santa Bárbara
de Casa

Entradas
Vale
de Açor
Mosteiro
Amendoeira

ANDALUCÍA
El Cerro de Andévalo
Valdelamusa

Algodor
Corte Gafo de Cima
Corte
do Pinto
Paymogo
Cabezas
Rubias
Silos de
Calañas

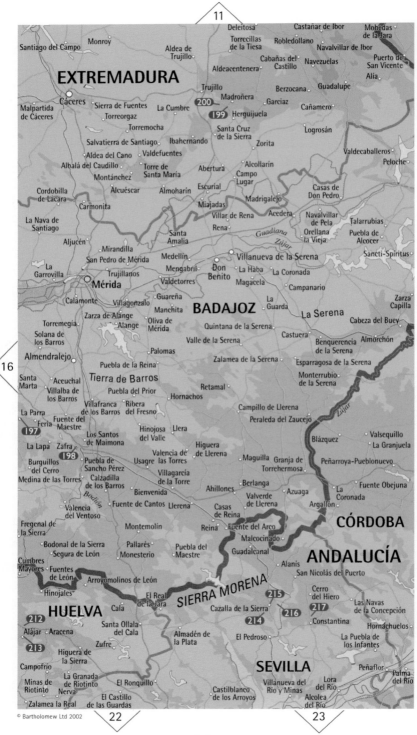

Santiago del Campo   Monroy   Aldea de   Deleitosa   Castañar de Ibor   Mohedas
                                      Trujillo   Robledollano   Navalvillar de Ibor   de la Jara
                                                         Torrecillas
                                                         de la Tiesa   Puerto de
EXTREMADURA   Aldeacentenera Cabañas del   Navezuelas   San Vicente
                                                                   Castillo   Alía
                                      Trujillo   Berzocana   Guadalupe
Malpartida   Cáceres   Sierra de Fuentes La Cumbre   Madroñera
de Cáceres   Torreorgaz   **200**   Garciaz   Cañamero
                                               199 Herguijuela
                    Torremocha
                                          Santa Cruz   Logrosán
         Salvatierra de Santiago Ibahernando de la Sierra
                          Valdefuentes   Zorita   Valdecaballeros
   Aldea del Cano   Peloche
Albalá del Caudillo   Torre de   Abertura   Alcollarín
            Montánchez Santa María   Campo
                                      Escurial   Lugar
Cordobilla   Alcuéscar Almoharín   Casas de
de Lácara   Madrigalejo   Don Pedro
       Carmonita   Miajadas
La Nava de   Villar de Rena   Acedera   Navalvillar
Santiago   Santa   Rena   de Pela   Talarrubias
                           Amalia   _Guadiana_   Orellana   Puebla de
     Aljucén   _Zújar_ la Vieja   Alcocer
          Mirandilla   Sancti-Spiritus
   La   San Pedro de Mérida Medellín   Villanueva de la Serena
   Garrovilla   Mengabril Don   La Haba La Coronada
          Trujillanos   Valdetorres Benito Magacela
      ○ **Mérida**   Campanario
    Calamonte   Guareña   La   Zarza
           Villagonzalo Manchita   Guarda   Capilla
        Zarza de Alange   Oliva de   **BADAJOZ**   La Serena
Torremegia   Alange Mérida   Cabeza del Buey
Solana de   Quintana de la Serena
los Barros   Valle de la Serena   Castuera
  Almendralejo   Palomas   Benquerencia Almôrchón
           Puebla de la Reina   Zalamea de la Serena   de la Serena
                                                      Esparragosa de la Serena
Santa   Aceuchal **Tierra de Barros** Retamal   Monterrubio
Marta Villalba de   de la Serena
       los Barros   Puebla del Prior Hornachos
La Parra   Fuente del   Campillo de Llerena
  Feria   Maestre Villafranca Ribera   Peraleda del Zaucejo
  197   de los Barros del Fresno
La Lapa Zafra   Hinojosa Llera   Blázquez Valsequillo
  198   del Valle   La Granjuela
Burguillos Puebla de Valencia de Higuera Maguilla Granja de Peñarroya-Pueblonuevo
del Cerro Sancho Pérez Usagre las Torres de Llerena   Torrehermosa
Medina de las Torres Calzadilla Villagarcía   Berlanga   Fuente Obejuna
            de los Barros de la Torre Ahillones   Azuaga   La
   Bodión   Bienvenida   Valverde   Coronada
      Valencia Fuente de Cantos Llerena   de Llerena Argallón
      del Ventoso   Casas   **CÓRDOBA**
Fregenal de   de Reina Fuente del Arco
la Sierra   Montemolin   Reina   Malcocinado
   Bodonal de la Sierra Pallarés Puebla del Guadalcanal   **ANDALUCÍA**
    Segura de León Monesterio Maestre   Alanís
Cumbres   San Nicolás del Puerto
Mayores Fuentes   Cerro
   de León Arroyomolinos de León   **215**   del Hiero Las Navas
Hinojales   El Real   **SIERRA MORENA**   de la Concepción
    HUELVA Calá de la Jara   Cazalla de la Sierra **217**
212   **214** **216** Constantina Hornáchuelos
Alájar Aracena Santa Ollala   La Puebla de
213   del Cala   Almadén de   El Pedroso   los Infantes
      Higuera de Zufre   la Plata
Campofrío la Sierra   Peñaflor
Minas de La Granada   **SEVILLA**   Lora Palma
Riotinto de Riotinto El Ronquillo   Villanueva del del Río del Río
  Nerva   Castilblanco Río y Minas Alcolea
Zalamea la Real El Castillo de los Arroyos   del Río
         de las Guardas

Map 17

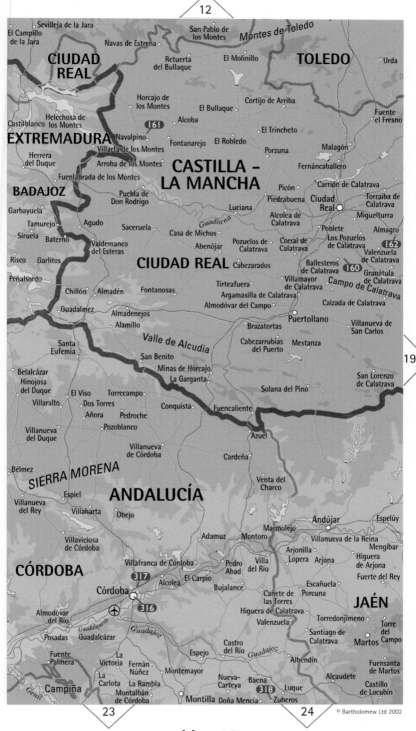

Sevilleja de la Jara
El Campillo de la Jara
Navas de Estrena
San Pablo de los Montes
Montes de Toledo
CIUDAD REAL
Retuerta del Bullaque
El Molinillo
TOLEDO
Urda

Horcajo de los Montes
Cortijo de Arriba
Fuente el Fresno

Helechosa de los Montes
Castilblanco
Alcoba
El Bullaque
161
EXTREMADURA
Navalpino
Fontanarejo
El Robledo
El Trincheto
Malagón
Villarta de los Montes

Herrera del Duque
Arroba de los Montes
Porzuna
Fernáncaballero

Fuenlabrada de los Montes
CASTILLA – LA MANCHA

BADAJOZ
Puebla de Don Rodrigo
Picón
Carrión de Calatrava
Torraiba de Calatrava
Piedrabuena
Ciudad Real

Garbayuela
Luciana
Miguelturra

Tamurejo
Agudo
Sacerruela
Guadiana
Alcolea de Calatrava
Poblete
Almagro

Siruela
Baterno
Casa de Michos
Pozuelos de Calatrava
Corral de Calatrava
Los Pozuelos de Calatrava
162

Risco
Garlitos
Valdemanco del Esteras
Abenójar
Ballesteros de Calatrava
Valenzuela de Calatrava

Peñalsordo
CIUDAD REAL
Cabezarados
Granátula de Calatrava
160

Chillón
Almadén
Fontanosas
Tirteafuera
Villamayor de Calatrava
Campo de Calatrava

Guadalmez
Almadenejos
Argamasilla de Calatrava
Almodóvar del Campo
Calzada de Calatrava

Alamillo
Valle de Alcudia
Brazatortas
Puertollano
Villanueva de San Carlos

Santa Eufemia
San Benito
Cabezarrubias del Puerto
Mestanza

Belalcázar
Minas de Horcajo
La Garganta
Solana del Pino
San Lorenzo de Calatrava

Hinojosa del Duque
El Viso
Torrecampo
Conquista
Fuencaliente

Villaralto
Dos Torres
Añora
Pedroche

Villanueva del Duque
Pozoblanco
Azuel

Villanueva de Córdoba
Cardeña

Bélmez
SIERRA MORENA
Venta del Charco

Espiel
ANDALUCÍA

Villanueva del Rey
Villaharta
Obejo
Andújar
Espelúy

Villaviciosa de Córdoba
Adamuz
Montoro
Marmolejo
Villanueva de la Reina
Mengíbar

CÓRDOBA
Villafranca de Córdoba
Pedro Abad
Villa del Río
Arjonilla
Lopera
Arjona
Higuera de Arjona
Fuerte del Rey

317
Alcolea
El Carpio
Escañuela
Porcuna

Córdoba
Bujalance
Cañete de las Torres
JAÉN

Almodóvar del Río
316
Higuera de Calatrava
Torredonjimeno
Torre del Campo

Posadas
Guadalcázar
Guadalquivir
Valenzuela
Santiago de Calatrava
Martos

Fuente Palmera
La Victoria
Fernán Núñez
Montemayor
Castro del Río
Guadajoz
Albéndin
Fuensanta de Martos

La Carlota
La Rambla
Espejo
Alcaudete
Castillo de Locubín

Campiña
Montalbán de Córdoba
Nueva-Carteya
Baena
Luque

Genil
Montilla
Doña Mencía
Zuheros
318

© Bartholomew Ltd 2002

Map 18

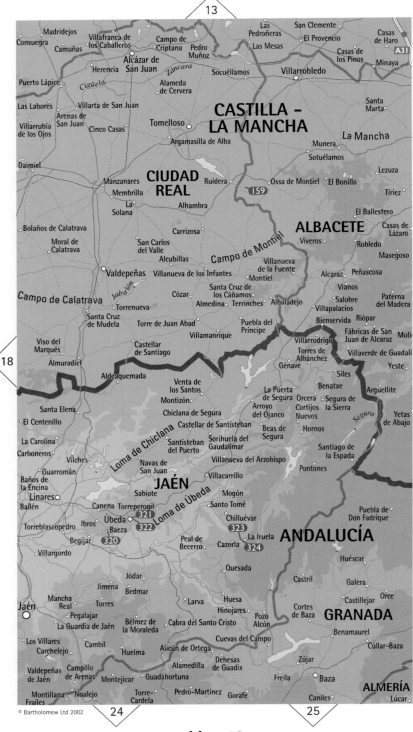

Madridejos
Consuegra
Camuñas
Villafranca de los Caballeros
Campo de Criptana
Pedro Muñoz
Las Pedroñeras
San Clemente
El Provencio
Casas de Haro
A31
Alcázar de San Juan
Herencia
Záncara
Socuéllamos
Villarrobledo
Casas de los Pinos
Minaya
Puerto Lápice
Cigüela
Alameda de Cervera
Santa Marta
Las Labores
Villarta de San Juan
Arenas de San Juan
Cinco Casas
Tomelloso
CASTILLA – LA MANCHA
Villarrubia de los Ojos
Argamasilla de Alba
La Mancha
Daimiel
Manzanares
Membrilla
La Solana
CIUDAD REAL
Ruidera
Alhambra
Munera
Sotuélamos
Ossa de Montiel
El Bonillo
Lezuza
159
Tiriez
Bolaños de Calatrava
Carrizosa
El Ballestero
ALBACETE
Casas de Lázaro
Moral de Calatrava
San Carlos del Valle
Alcubillas
Campo de Montiel
Viveros
Robledo
Masegoso
Valdepeñas
Villanueva de los Infantes
Villanueva de la Fuente
Montiel
Alcaraz
Peñascosa
Viaños
Paterna del Madera
Jabalón
Cózar
Santa Cruz de los Cáñamos
Almedina
Terrinches
Albaladejo
Salobre
Villapalacios
Campo de Calatrava
Torrenueva
Santa Cruz de Mudela
Torre de Juan Abad
Villamanrique
Puebla del Príncipe
Bienservida
Riópar
Viso del Marqués
Castellar de Santiago
Villarrodrigo
Torres de Albánchez
Fábricas de San Juan de Alcaraz
Moli
Villaverde de Guadali
Álmuradiel
Génave
Yeste
Aldeaquemada
Venta de los Santos
Montizón
Siles
Benatae
Arguellite
Santa Elena
Chiclana de Segura
Castellar de Santisteban
La Puerta de Segura
Arroyo del Ojanco
Orcera
Cortijos Nuevos
Segura de la Sierra
El Centenillo
Yetas de Abajo
La Carolina
Carboneros
Vilches
Santisteban del Puerto
Sorihuela del Guadalimar
Beas de Segura
Hornos
Segura
Loma de Chiclana
Navas de San Juan
Villanueva del Arzobispo
Santiago de la Espada
Guarromán
Baños de la Encina
Linares
Bailén
Sabiote
JAÉN
Villacarrillo
Pontones
Canena
Torreperogil
321
Mogón
Torreblascopedro
Ibros
Úbeda
322
Loma de Úbeda
Santo Tomé
Chillúevar
Puebla de Don Fadrique
Begíjar
Baeza
320
Peal de Becerro
Cazorla
La Iruela
324
323
ANDALUCÍA
Villargordo
Quesada
Huéscar
Castril
Galera
Orce
Jódar
Jimena
Bedmar
Larva
Huesa
Hinojares
Pozo Alcón
Cortes de Baza
Castillejar
Jaén
Mancha Real
Torres
GRANADA
Pegalajar
La Guardia de Jaén
Bélmez de la Moraleda
Cabra del Santo Cristo
Benamaurel
Los Villares
Carchelejo
Cambil
Huelma
Alicún de Ortega
Cuevas del Campo
Cúllar-Baza
Valdepeñas de Jaén
Campillo de Arenas
Montejicar
Guadahortuna
Alamedilla
Dehesas de Guadix
Zújar
Freila
Baza
ALMERÍA
Montillana
Frailes
Noalejo
Torre-Cardela
Pedro-Martínez
Gorafe
Caniles
Lúcar

Map 19

Casas de Benitez
Quintanar del Rey
Ledaña
Villagarcía del Llano
Cenizate
Casas-Ibáñez
Casas de Ves
Balsa de Ves
Cabriel
Cortes de Pallás
Millares
Navas de Jorquera
Madrigueras
Fuentealbilla
Villa de Ves
Cofrentes
A31
Tarazona de la Mancha
Mahora
Abengibre
Alcalá del Júcar
Jalance
Jarafuel
Quesa
La Roda
Motilleja
Júcar
Casas de Juan Núñez
Carcelén
Casas de Juan Gil
Zarra
VALENCIA
Valdeganga
Alatoz
Ayora
VALENCIA
La Gineta
La Felipa
Pozo-Lorente
ALBACETE
Albacete
Hoya Gonzalo
Higueruela
Alpera
La Herrera
Santa Ana
Chinchilla de Monte-Aragón
Villar de Chinchilla
Bonete
Corral-Rubio
Almansa
La Font de la Figuera
Balazote
Argamasón
El Salobral
Pozo Cañada
Pétrola
La Higuera
Montealegre del Castillo
La Encina
Pozuelo
San Pedro
CASTILLA -
Fuente-Álamo
Caudete
Cañada
Casas de Lázaro
Pozohondo
LA MANCHA
Yecla
Villena
Peñas de San Pedro
Ontur
Alcadozo
Tobarra
Albatana
Salinas
Bogarra
Liétor
Hellín
Monóvar
Ayna
Isso
Minateda
Jumilla
Casas del Puerto
ALICANTE
Pinoso
La Romana
Molinicos
Elche de la Sierra
Agramón
Cancarix
182
Algueña
Peñarrubia
Letur
Férez
Socovos
Moharqué
Barinas
Segura
Taibilla
Cieza
Abanilla
Yetas de Abajo
Benizar y la Tercia
Calasparra
Abarán
Blanca
Fortuna
A7
Cox
El Sabinar
Moratalla
Ricote
Archena
Lorquí
Molina de Segura
Orihuela
Santomera
MURCIA
Ceutí
Alguazas
Beniel
Nerpio
Caravaca de la Cruz
Cehegín
Las Torres de Cotillas
Murcia
Archivel
Barranda
180
Bullas
Mula
Alcantarilla
El Palmar
La Alberca
Almudema
Pliego
Barqueros
Sucina
El Moral
Zarzadilla de Totana
MURCIA
Librilla
Los Martínez
Balsicas
Los Royos
Zarcilla de Ramos
Alhama de Murcia
Corvera
Valladolises
Torre-Pacheco
Topares
La Paca
Las Terreras
Aledo
Totana
Los Maldonados
Balsa Pintada
Albujón
ALMERÍA
Fuensanta
Cánovas
Fuente Álamo
La Palma
GRANADA
María
Vélez-Blanco
Lorca
Los Cantareros
La Pinilla
Los Dolores
Las Palas
Barrio del Peral
Cartagena
Vélez-Rubio
El Portús
181
Puerto Lumbreras
Mazarrón
Isla Plana
La Azohía
Chirivel
ANDALUCÍA
Almendricos
El Cabildo y la Campana
Cope
Calabardina
Oria
Taberno
Santa María de Nieva
Pulpí
Águilas
Partaloa
Somontín
Albox
Huércal-Overa
Olula del Río
Arboleas
Zúrgena

Map 20

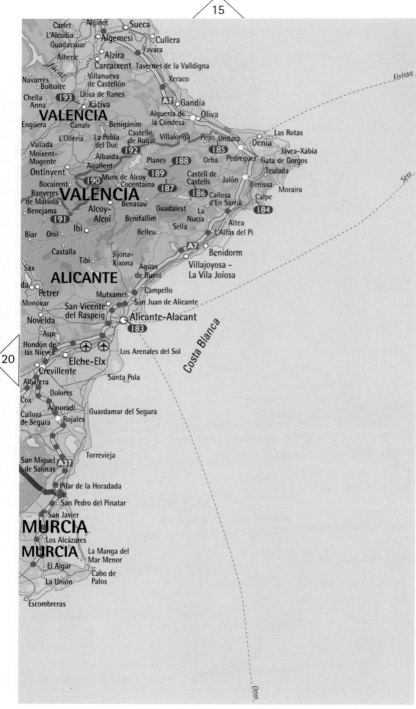

Carlet
L'Alcudia
Guadassuar
Alberic
Alginet
Algemesí
Sueca
Cullera
Alzira
Favara
Carcaixent
Tavernes de la Valldigna
Navarrés
Bolbaite
Villanueva
de Castellón
Xeraco
Chella
Anna
193
Llosa de Ranes
A7
Gandía
VALENCIA
Xàtiva
Alqueria de
la Condesa
Oliva
Enguera
Canals
Benigánim
Vallada
L'Olleria
La Pobla
del Duc
Castelló
de Rugat
Villalonga
Pego
Ondara
Las Rotas
192
Denia
Moixent-
Mogente
Albaida
Agullent
Planes
188
Orba
Pedreguer
Jávea-Xàbia
Gata de Gorgos
Ontinyent
Muro de Alcoy
Cocentaina
189
Castell de
Castells
Teulada
190
Jalón
Benissa
Moraira
Bocairent
Banyeres
de Mariola
VALENCIA
187
186
Callosa
d'En Sarrià
Calpe
184
Benasau
Guadalest
Alcoy-
Alcoi
Benejama
Benifallim
La
Nucía
191
Sella
Altea
Biar
Onil
Ibi
Relleu
L'Alfàs del Pi
Castalla
Jijona-
Xixona
A7
Benidorm
Tibi
Aguas
de Busot
Villajoyosa -
La Vila Joíosa
Sax
ALICANTE
da
Petrer
Mutxamel
Campello
Monóvar
San Vicente
del Raspeig
San Juan de Alicante
Novelda
Aspe
Alicante-Alacant
Hondón de
las Nieves
183
Los Arenales del Sol
Elche-Elx
Crevillente
Santa Pola
Albatera
Cox
Dolores
Callosa
de Segura
Almoradí
Rojales
Guardamar del Segura
San Miguel
de Salinas
A37
Torrevieja
Pilar de la Horadada
San Pedro del Pinatar
San Javier
MURCIA
Los Alcázares
MURCIA
La Manga del
Mar Menor
El Algar
Cabo de
Palos
La Unión
Escombreras

Costa Blanca

Eivissa

Sète

Orán

Map 21

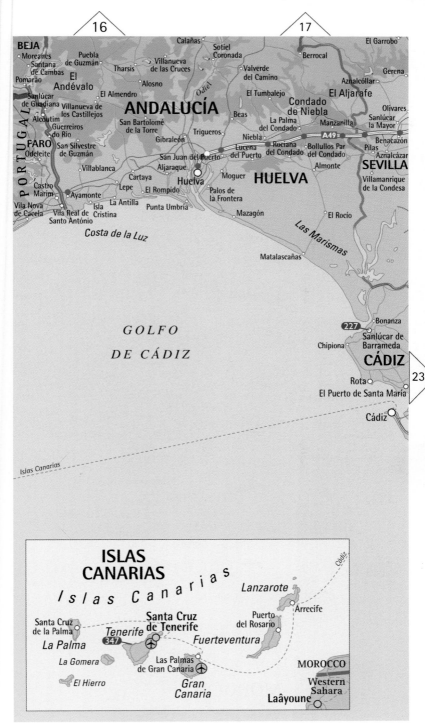

BEJA
Moreanes
Santana
de Cambas
Pomarão
Sanlúcar
de Guadiana
Alcoutim
Guerreiros
do Rio
FARO
Odeleite
Castro
Marim
Vila Nova
de Cacela
Vila Real de
Santo António

Puebla
de Guzmán
El
Andévalo
El Almendro
Villanueva de
los Castillejos
San Silvestre
de Guzmán
Villablanca

Tharsis
Alosno

Calañas
Sotiel
Coronada
Villanueva
de las Cruces

ANDALUCÍA

San Bartolomé
de la Torre
Trigueros
Gibraleón
San Juan del Puerto
Aljaraque
Huelva
Cartaya
Lepe
El Rompido
La Antilla
Isla
Cristina
Punta Umbria

Moguer
Palos de
la Frontera

Mazagón

El Garrobo

Berrocal

Valverde
del Camino

El Tumbalejo
Beas

La Palma
del Condado
Niebla
Lucena
del Puerto
Rociana
del Condado

HUELVA

Gerena

Aznalcóllar

Condado
de Niebla
Manzanilla

A49

Bollullos Par
del Condado
Almonte

El Rocío

Olivares
Sanlúcar
la Mayor
Benacazón
Pilas
Aznalcázar

SEVILLA

Villamanrique
de la Condesa

Costa de la Luz

Las Marismas

Matalascañas

PORTUGAL

Ayamonte

GOLFO
DE CÁDIZ

Bonanza
227
Chipiona
Sanlúcar de
Barrameda

CÁDIZ

Rota
El Puerto de Santa María

Cádiz

Islas Canarias

ISLAS
CANARIAS
Islas Canarias

Santa Cruz
de la Palma
La Palma
La Gomera
El Hierro

Tenerife
347
Santa Cruz
de Tenerife

Las Palmas
de Gran Canaria
Gran
Canaria

Fuerteventura

Lanzarote

Puerto
del Rosario
Arrecife

Cádiz

MOROCCO
Western
Sahara
Laâyoune

© Bartholomew Ltd 2002

Map 22

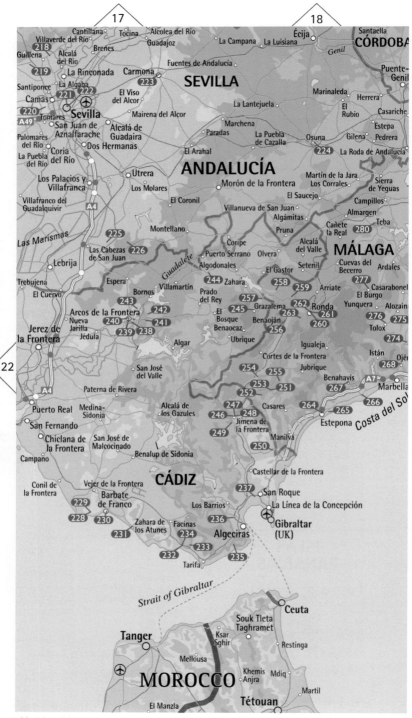

Map 23

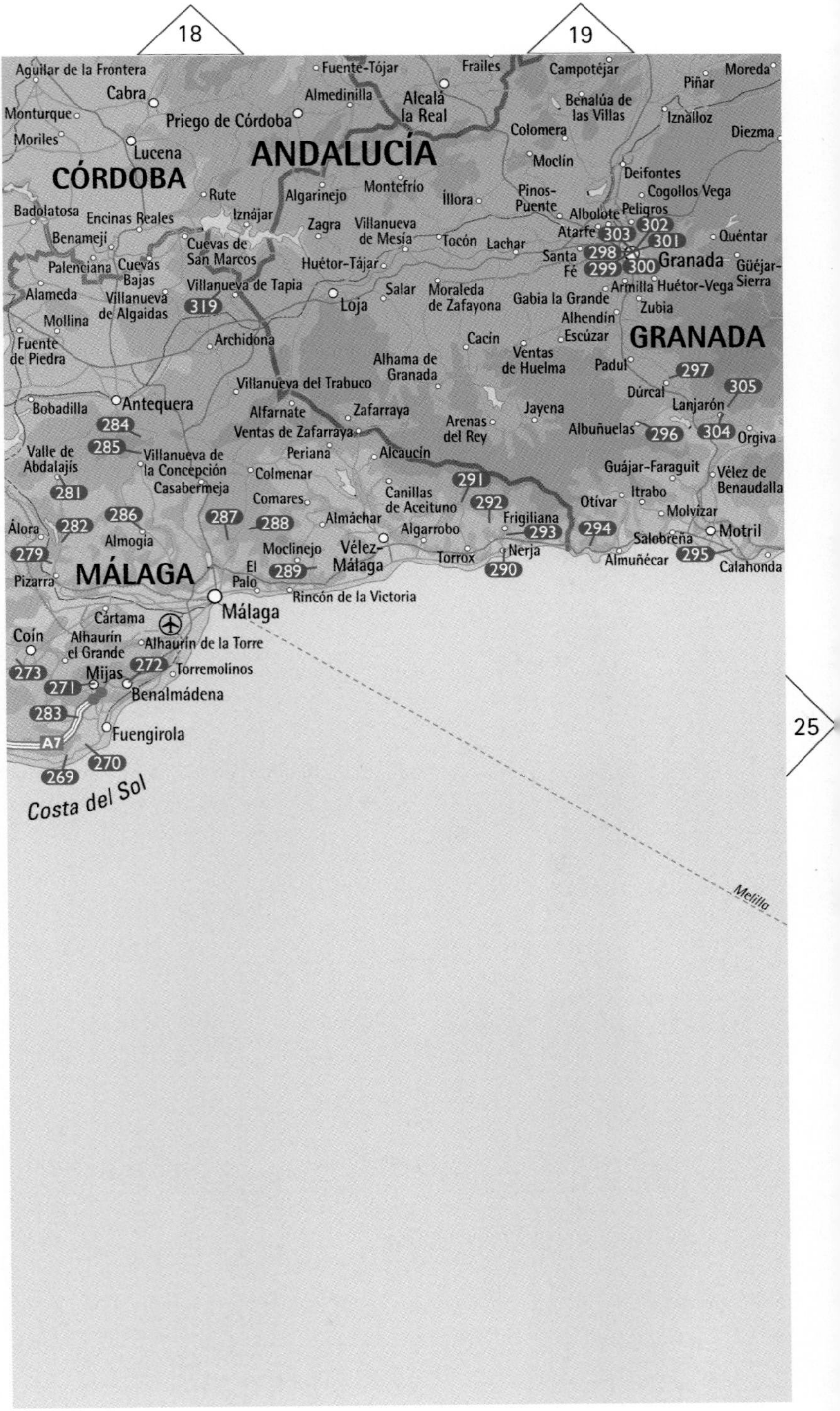

Aguilar de la Frontera
Fuente-Tójar
Frailes
Campotéjar
Moreda
Piñar

Cabra
Almedinilla
Benalúa de
las Villas
Iználloz

Monturque
Priego de Córdoba
Alcalá
la Real
Colomera
Diezma

Moriles
ANDALUCÍA
Moclín
Deifontes

Lucena
Montefrío
Íllora
Pinos-
Puente
Cogollos Vega
Peligros

CÓRDOBA
Rute
Algarinejo
Albolote
302
301

Badolatosa
Encinas Reales
Iznájar
Zagra
Villanueva
de Mesía
Tocón
Lachar
Atarfe
303
Quéntar

Benamejí
Cuevas de
San Marcos
Huétor-Tájar
Santa
Fé
298
299
300
Granada
Güéjar-
Sierra

Palenciana
Cuevas
Bajas
Villanueva de Tapia
Salar
Moraleda
de Zafayona
Gabia la Grande
Armilla
Huétor-Vega

Alameda
Villanueva
de Algaidas
319
Loja
Alhendín
Escúzar
Zubia

Mollina
Archidona
Cacín
Ventas
de Huelma
Padul
GRANADA

Fuente
de Piedra
Alhama de
Granada
297
305

Bobadilla
Villanueva del Trabuco
Dúrcal
Lanjarón

Antequera
284
Alfarnate
Zafarraya
Jayena
Albuñuelas
296
304
Órgiva

Valle de
Abdalajís
285
Ventas de Zafarraya
Arenas
del Rey

Villanueva de
la Concepción
Periana
Alcaucín
Guájar-Faraguit
Vélez de
Benaudalla

281
Casabermeja
Colmenar
291
Otívar
Itrabo

Álora
282
286
287
Comares
288
Canillas
de Aceituno
292
Frigiliana
293
294
Molvízar
Salobreña
Motril

279
Almogía
Almáchar
Algarrobo
Nerja
Almuñécar
295
Calahonda

Pizarra
MÁLAGA
Moclinejo
289
Vélez-
Málaga
Torrox
290

El
Palo
Rincón de la Victoria

Coín
Cártama
Málaga
Alhaurín de la Torre

Alhaurín
el Grande
272
Torremolinos

273
271
Mijas
Benalmádena

283
Fuengirola

A7

269
270
Costa del Sol

Melilla

Map 24

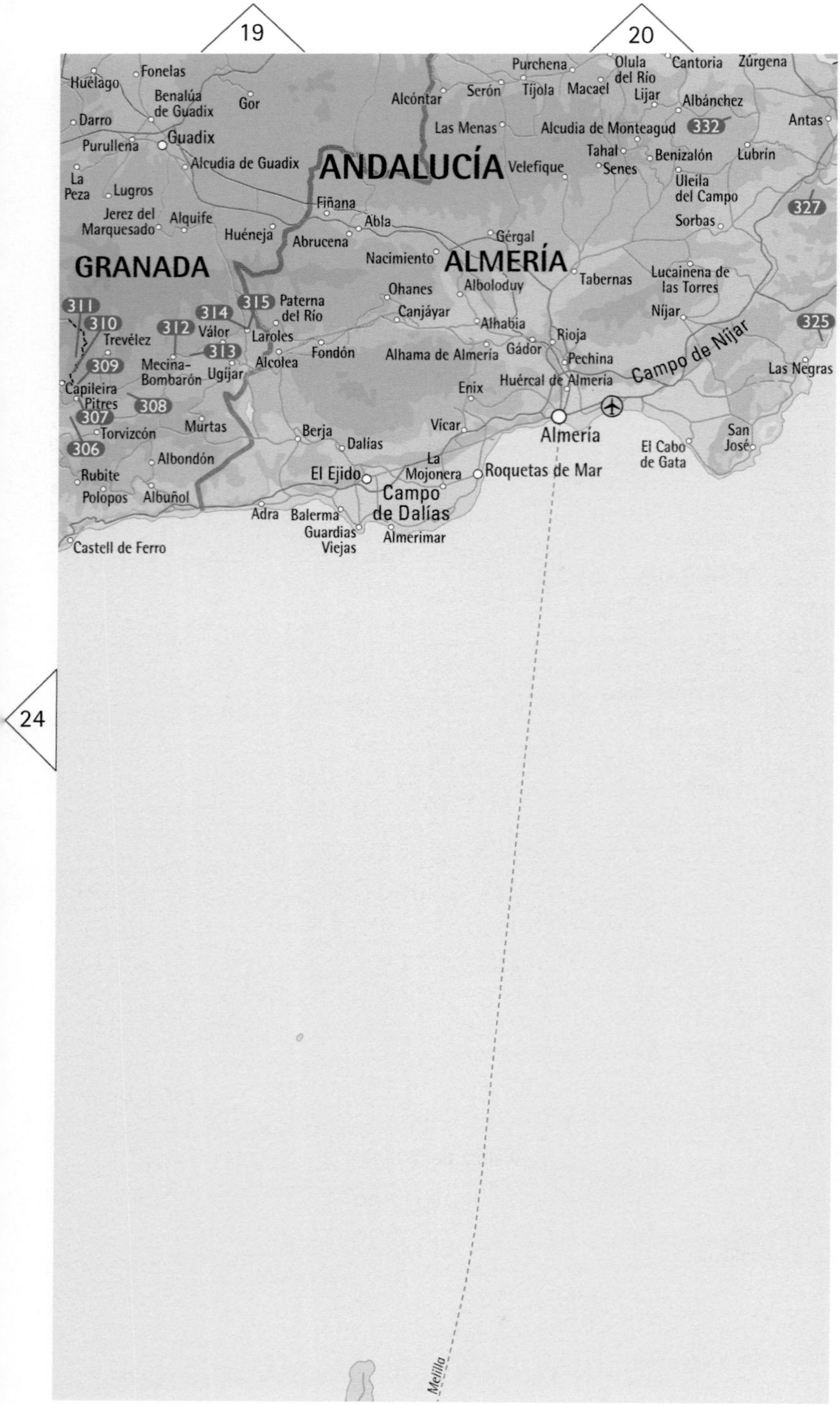

Huélago
Fonelas
Purchena
Olula del Río
Cantoria
Zúrgena
Benalúa de Guadix
Gor
Alcóntar
Serón
Tijola
Macael
Lijar
Albánchez
Darro
Alcudia de Monteagud
332
Antas
Purullena
Guadix
Las Menas
Alcudia de Guadix
ANDALUCÍA
Velefique
Tahal
Benizalón
Lubrín
La Peza
Lugros
Fiñana
Senes
Uleila del Campo
327
Jerez del Marquesado
Alquife
Abla
Gérgal
Sorbas
Huéneja
Abrucena
Nacimiento
ALMERÍA
Tabernas
Lucainena de las Torres
GRANADA
Ohanes
Alboloduy
311
315
Paterna del Río
Canjáyar
Níjar
325
310
312
Valor
Laroles
Alhabia
Trevélez
313
Alcolea
Fondón
Alhama de Almería
Gádor
Rioja
Campo de Níjar
Las Negras
309
Mecina-Bombarón
Ugíjar
Pechina
Capileira
Pitres
308
Huércal de Almería
307
Torvizcón
Murtas
Enix
306
Albondón
Berja
Vícar
San José
Rubite
Dalías
El Cabo de Gata
Polopos
Albuñol
La Mojonera
Almería
El Ejido
Roquetas de Mar
Adra
Balerma
Campo de Dalías
Castell de Ferro
Guardias Viejas
Almerimar

Meliilla

© Bartholomew Ltd 2002

Map 25

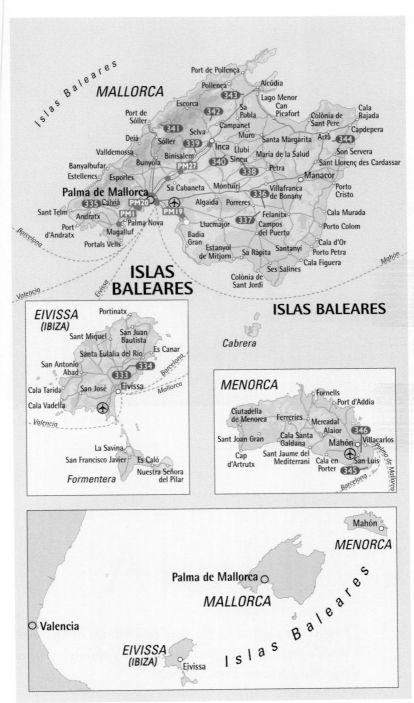

Islas Baleares

MALLORCA

Port de Pollença
Pollença
Alcúdia
Escorca
343
Lago Menor
Can
Picafort
Sa
Pobla
Port de
Sóller
342
Colònia de
Sant Pere
Cala
Rajada
341
Campanet
Muro
Capdepera
Selva
Santa Margarita
Artà
344
Deià
Sóller
339
Inca
Son Servera
Valldemossa
Binisalem
340
Llubí
Maria de la Salud
Sant Llorenç des Cardassar
Banyalbufar
Bunyola
PM27
Sineu
Petra
338
Estellencs
Esporles
Manacor
Palma de Mallorca
Sa Cabaneta
Montuïri
336
Villafranca
de Bonany
Porto
Cristo
335
Calvià
PM20
Algaida
Porreres
Cala Murada
Sant Telm
PM1
PM19
Felanitx
Porto Colom
Andratx
Palma Nova
Llucmajor
337
Campos
del Puerto
Port
d'Andratx
Magalluf
Badia
Gran
Cala d'Or
Porto Petra
Portals Vells
Estanyol
de Mitjorn
Sa Ràpita
Santanyi
Cala Figuera

Barcelona

Mahón

ISLAS
BALEARES

Valencia

Eivissa

Ses Salines
Colònia de
Sant Jordi

ISLAS BALEARES

EIVISSA
(IBIZA)
Portinatx

Cabrera

Sant Miquel
San Juan
Bautista
Santa Eulalia del Río
Es Canar
334
San Antonio
Abad
333
Cala Tarida
San José
Eivissa
Cala Vadella

Barcelona
Mallorca
Valencia

MENORCA
Fornells
Port d'Addia
Ciutadella
de Menorca
Ferreries
Mercadal
Alaior
346
Sant Joan Gran
Cala Santa
Galdana
Mahón
Villacarlos
Cap
d'Artrutx
Sant Jaume del
Mediterrani
Cala en
Porter
San Luis
345

La Savina
San Francisco Javier
Es Caló
Nuestra Señora
del Pilar
Formentera

Palma de Mallorca

Barcelona

Mahón
MENORCA

Palma de Mallorca

MALLORCA

Valencia

EIVISSA
(IBIZA)
Eivissa

Islas Baleares

© Bartholomew Ltd 2002

Map 26

GALICIA

"A reflective pilgrim on the road to Santiago always makes a double journey...the backward journey through time and the forward journey through space."
WALTER STARKIE

Casa Entremuros

Cances Grandes 77, 15107 Carballo, La Coruña

Here are long stretches of fine, sandy beaches, hidden coves and a number of old fishing villages where the seafood is among the best in Spain. Santiago and Rosa will help to unlock the region's secrets for you if you stay at their solid old granite house. You approach through the pretty, old stable yard, with annexe to one side, lawns and flowers. There are four bedrooms, not huge, but handsome, with shining parquet-clad floors, fitted wardrobes, carefully restored antique beds and good (though somewhat small) bathrooms. No. 3 is the best, we felt, with its antique trunk and two large wardrobes. There is a large, light-filled lounge with a dresser and a wood-burner in the huge *lareira*. Rosa makes fresh fruit juices and there is local cheese and honey and cake. No meals apart from breakfast but Casa Elias is only a mile away – you can have a memorable meal there at any time of year. This is a warm, quiet and unassuming place to stay on the wild, indented coastline of the Rías Altas, little known beyond Galicia. *No smoking.*

rooms	4 doubles.
price	€41–€51. Single €33–€41. VAT included.
meals	Breakfast €4.
closed	15 December–15 January.
directions	From Santiago de Compostela, by Alameda, road for 'Hospital General'. Continue to Carballo, then towards Malpica to Cances; house signed by petrol station.

Santiago Luaces de La-Herrán

tel	+34 981 757099
fax	+34 981 703877
e-mail	casaentremuros@finisterrae.com
web	www.casaentremuros.com

map 1   entry 1

Pazo de Souto

Lugar de la Torre 1, 15106 Sisamo-Carballo, La Coruña

Since Carlos and his father José opened their fine old manor to guests they have gradually established a reputation for being one of the best places to stay in this little-known corner of Galicia. The house has stood here near the rugged north coast for 300 years, lost among fields of maize and wooded glades. The vast sitting room has a *lareira* (inglenook), exposed granite and heavy old beams. The dining area, similarly designed, has tables up on a gallery; all is subtly-lit, and there is a very cosy bar area. Outside is a large garden, and, from the terrace, fine views across the surrounding farmland. A splendid granite staircase leads to the guest rooms; we preferred those on the first floor, attractively furnished with Twenties beds and dressers to the smaller attic ones. It is all very spick and span. Plenty of local folk were dining here when we visited (fresh fish daily from the nearby fishing village of Malpica) — a good sign. Carlos is most helpful and has impeccable English; it would be hard to find more charming hosts. All this and the wild beauty of the north coast. *A Pazos de Galicia Hotel.*

rooms	11 doubles.
price	€45–€75; single €36–€48.
meals	Lunch/dinner €12 set menu, €22 à la carte.
closed	Rarely.
directions	From Santiago C-545 for Santa Comba to Portomouro. Here, signs to Carballo; in village centre at Plaza de Galicia, signs for Malpica. After petrol sation, left for Sisamo. Continue past church. Souto signed to right.

José Taibo Suárez

tel	+34 981 756065
fax	+34 981 756191
e-mail	reservas@pazodosouto.com
web	www.pazodosouto.com

Casa Grande do Bachao

Monte Bachao s/n, Sta. Cristina de Fecha, 15820 Santiago de Compostela, La Coruña

In a clearing in a wood you find – not a gingerbread cottage nor the home of Red Riding Hood's grandmother, but an elegant stone house. Arrive at the right time of day and lunch or dinner will be in full swing, the dining room packed with people of all ages. The house has been stylishly furnished without eclipsing the original bones of the place. Bedrooms are elegant and simple, each one distinct. The dining room is huge and light, with a high beamed ceiling, stone floor and sculptures dotted about; as if to emphasise the importance of food here, a huge stone feeding-trough has been placed next door. If you enjoy splendid isolation, you won't need to venture far (though Santiago *is* only a 15-minute drive): here are sauna, gym, library (many books on flora and fauna) and bikes for hire. A spot of trout fishing can also be arranged. The setting, with its storybook appeal, will please the children, as will such enticements as the telescope, the games room and the swimming pool. And the freedom to explore, which is all of a sudden possible when parents are distracted by fine food. Excellent value. *A Pazos de Galicia Hotel.*

rooms	10: 9 doubles, 1 twin.
price	€30–€72.
meals	Breakfast €5; lunch/dinner €13.
closed	Christmas & New Year.
directions	From Santiago, CP-0701, Santa Comba road. Pazo signed on right before village. Follow path & track for approx. 5km, signed.

Javier Goyanes

tel	+34 981 194118
fax	+34 981 192028
e-mail	bachao@pazosdegalicia.com
web	www.pazosdegalicia.com

map 1   entry 3

Hostel Casa Rosalía

Soigrexa 19, 15280 Os Anxeles-Brión, La Coruña

Named after Galicia's most famous poetess, the *posada* Rosalía was opened for Holy Year in 1993, since when it has established its reputation as a reliable and friendly staging-post. The hotel is basically an old granite farmhouse with a modern extension that houses most of the bedrooms. You enter by a rather grand wrought-iron gate, then through to the patio bounded by a series of intimate eating areas — wonderfully snug for dining in the colder months. Meals are served in the courtyard in summer. The food — lots of regional fare, especially roasts — is good value and there are often barbecues. Pride of place in the restaurant goes to the ubiquitous *lareira*, the vast inglenook fireplace typical of old Galician farmhouses. New owners, the Román brothers, are attentive English-speaking hosts who always find time for a chat. Most of the rooms are smallish, with modern prints, wooden or tiled floors and stained pine furniture; bathrooms are roomy. The décor is modern, generally greens and pinks; we particularly liked those in the old part of the building. There's a pool in the garden, and horse-riding can be arranged.

rooms	29 doubles/twins.
price	€ 34–€ 53; single € 26–€ 41.
meals	Breakfast € 3.60; lunch/dinner € 12.
closed	22 December–21 January.
directions	From Santiago, N–650 for Pontevedra. Before leaving city, right on C-543 for Noía. After Bertamirans, hotel signed to left.

Alberto & Javier Román

tel	+34 981 887580
fax	+34 981 887557
e-mail	romanulloa@interbook.net
web	www.hotelcasarosalia.com

Pazo Cibran

San Xulian de Sales , 15885 Santiago de Compostela, La Coruña

We could tell you about the 18th-century history and period furniture of this house, its glorious big garden, its vine-covered walkways and bamboo woods, its entwined camellias and 200-year-old trees, its delightful chapel and library filled with ancient books. We could mention, too, the paintings, the converted stables, the vases of fresh flowers. But the true spirit of this elegant house is personified by Carmen herself (Maica to those who know her), a relaxed and wonderful hostess who shares her family home with people who come as strangers and leave as friends. Her enthusiasm for Cibran and its surroundings is underpinned by a true love of the history and beauty of this area, and she has excellent local information on the heart of nearby Santiago, Pazo de Oca (the 'Versailles' of Galicia) and numerous country rambles. Although no dinner is available, eating at the Michelin-rated Restaurant Roberto just metres away is a mouthwatering experience – Maica may even join you. A big and bountiful breakfast is served by Lola, the cook/housemaid with a twinkle in her eye. Your stay here will be as friendly and relaxed as she is. *A Rusticae & Pazos de Galicia Hotel.*

rooms	11: 9 doubles, 2 singles.
price	€ 66–€ 100; single € 54.
meals	Breakfast € 6. Excellent restaurant nearby.
closed	Rarely.
directions	From Santiago, N-525 for Orense. At km 336, by petrol station, right for San Xulian de Sales. Here, at end of village, Pazo Cibran signed to right.

Carmen Iglesias Gaceo

tel	+34 981 511515
fax	+34 981 511515
e-mail	cibran@arrakis.es
web	www.arrakis.es/~cibran

map 1   entry 5

Casa Grande de Cornide

Cornide (Calo-Teo), 15886 Santiago de Compostela, La Coruña

This very special B&B just 15 minutes from Santiago is surrounded by exuberant Galician green. Casa Grande may be likened to a good claret: refined, select, worth paying a bit more for. José Ramón and María Jesús are both lecturers (he writes books, including one called *The Way to Compostela*) and a love of culture is evident throughout their home. It houses a large collection of modern Galician paintings, hundreds of ceramic pots, a huge library and decoration that is a spicy cocktail of old and new: exposed granite, designer lamps, wooden ceilings, and, everywhere, art. A place to come to read, to paint in the beautiful mature garden — surprisingly full of palms for so far north — and to cycle: four bikes are provided free for guests. The studied décor of the lounges and library is mirrored in the bedrooms and suites, some of which are in a separate building. They have all mod cons and the same mix of modern and old; there are books, ornaments, paintings and exquisite little details such as handmade tiles in the bathrooms to create a special feel. "A glorious place," enthused one reader. *A Pazos de Galicia hotel.*

rooms	10: 6 doubles, 4 suites.
price	€70–€95; single €55–€60; suite €80–€95.
meals	Breakfast €6.
closed	Rarely.
directions	From Santiago, N-550 for Pontevedra. After 7km, just after Cepsa petrol station, turn left & follow signs for 2km to Cornide.

María Jesús Castro Rivas

tel	+34 981 805599
fax	+34 981 805751
e-mail	info@casagrandedecornide.com
web	www.casagrandedecornide.com

Hotel As Artes

Travesia de Dos Puertas 2, 15707 Santiago de Compostela, La Coruña

Where would anybody, pilgrim or tourist, want to stay when visiting Santiago? As close as possible to the great Cathedral, of course. Look no further than this delightful small hotel 50 yards from the great edifice. It is the creation of two exceptionally friendly Galicians, Esther and Mateos, inspired by a night they once spent in an old Parisian hotel; they were so taken by the experience that they decided to open a similarly intimate hotel in Santiago. Guest bedrooms look to the Seven Arts for their *leitmotiv*: choose between spending a night in the company of Rodin, Dante, Vivaldi, Gaudí, Picasso, Duncan or Chaplin. All are stylishly furnished with parquet floors, repro wrought-iron bedsteads, rugs, French café-style chairs and tables, paintings and prints. And there's a sauna. It is fantastic value but what makes this place doubly special is the care and generosity of your hosts. At breakfast you are treated to fresh orange juice, fruit salads, cold meats, cakes and different breads. For other meals there are dozens of restaurants a short walk away. Brilliant value in a brilliant position.

rooms	7 doubles/twins.
price	€ 52–€ 86.
meals	Breakfast € 7.
closed	23 December–23 January.
directions	In Santiago head for Praza do Obradoiro. Rua de San Francisco just to left of Cathedral. Hotel 50m past cathedral on right.

Esther Mateos & Carlos Elizechea

tel	+34 981 555254
fax	+34 981 577823
e-mail	recepcion@asartes.com
web	www.asartes.com

map 1   entry 7

Pazo Xan Xordo

Xan Xordo 6, Lavacolla, 15820 Santiago de Compostela, La Coruña

The attractive granite façade, square-paned windows, paved yard and flowerbeds are surprisingly reminiscent of Celtic peninsular farmsteads further north – you could almost be looking at a Cornish farmhouse or a little manor house in Brittany. The weather, however, is unmistakeably Spanish (though Santiago does have the highest rainfall in Spain…), as is the imposing column supporting a statue of the Crucifixion. The *pazo* has comfortable bedrooms (including a 'special' one with a four-poster bed), and a big sitting room with a polished wooden floor, chintzy furnishings and a piano. You can hire bicycles to explore the countryside or drive into the city itself – an easy trip compared to the pilgrimages of the Middle Ages. Pilgrims used to follow the 800-kilometre Camino de Santiago from Roncesvalles in the Pyrenees on foot; some even on their knees. Santiago is still busy – a lively mix of local people, friars, students and tourists – and of course, it is packed with remarkable things to see. If you're looking for a civilized place to stay away from the bustle of the city, this would be a very good choice. *A Pazos de Galicia hotel.*

rooms	10 doubles/twins.
price	€40–€60.
meals	Breakfast €4.
closed	Rarely.
directions	From Santiago, N-634 (single-carriageway, not m'way). After 5km, before Lavacolla, left following signs for pazo. 200m from junc.

Alfonso Barca Pérez

tel	+34 981 888259
fax	+34 981 888293
e-mail	xanxordo@pazosdegalicia.com
web	www.pazoxanxordo.com

Pazo de Sedor

Castañeda, 15819 Arzua, La Coruña

One of a number of grand Galician manors (*pazos*) open to guests, Pazo de Sedor is a delectable place to stay if you're on the road to or from Santiago – or anywhere, come to that. It is an imposing, 18th-century country house surrounded by wooded hillsides and fields of maize and grazing cattle. Inside you get a definite sense of its aristocratic past: cavernous rooms and a broad balustraded staircase joining the two floors. The most memorable feature is the open fireplace that spans an entire wall of the dining room, with bread ovens at each side; an airy second dining room has been created from an outbuilding and has sweeping views. The bedrooms are a treat; they are high-ceilinged, decorated with family antiques, have embroidered bedcovers and shining parquet floors. Half have their own balcony. One room has beautiful Deco beds, all are big enough to take an extra bed and the apartment has full facilities for the disabled. Meals are as authentic as the house: all the flavours of Galicia with many of the vegetables home-grown and meats free-range. Maria is charming, and fills the house with flowers. *A Pazos de Galicia hotel.*

rooms	7: 6 doubles/twins, 1 apartment.
price	€ 50–€ 66.
meals	Breakfast € 4; dinner € 12.
closed	February.
directions	From Lugo N–540, then N–547 for Santiago. 400m past km57 marker, right to Pazo.

María Saavedra Pereira

tel	+34 981 193248
fax	+34 981 193248
web	www.pazosdegalicia.com

map 2   entry 9

Pazo da Trave

Galdo, 27850 Viveiro, Lugo

Climbing plants scramble over old stone, the garden creeps right up to the house, the vines hang heavy under the trellis … even the shutters are green. This lovely garden is an integral part of the place, with its big shade-giving trees and beautiful ceramic sculptures dotted about. There is even an *horio* – a slotted wooden storage box where food could be stored and meat hung well away from the animals. Food is taken seriously at Pazo da Trave and the dinners are a delight, with traditional food made from mouth-watering ingredients. The service is as friendly as can be. Beautiful bedrooms have big oak beds, beamed ceilings and art on the walls; children are thoughtfully catered for with the provision of small beds and cots. There is a lovely whitewashed beamy sitting room with an open fire – cosy for winter nights in – and a gallery on the first floor with a *chaise longue* and armchairs where you can sit and look out over the garden, or read one of the many books. A sauna, a gym and a billiard room are further reasons to stay in this friendly, arty and delightfully unstuffy hotel. *A Pazos de Galicia hotel.*

rooms	19 twins/doubles.
price	€ 63–€ 90; single € 48; suite € 114–€ 144.
meals	Breakfast € 7.21; lunch/dinner € 22. Restaurant closed 1–15 November.
closed	Rarely.
directions	From N-642 to Viveiro, take C-640, Lugo road. After 2km, Galdo signed to right. Pazo on right after village.

Josefa Ramallal Bouso

tel	+34 982 598163
fax	+34 982 598040
e-mail	trave@pazosdegalicia.com
web	www.pazodatrave.com

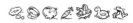

Pazo de Villabad
Villabad, 27122 Castroverde, Lugo

In a delectably quiet corner of Galicia, on one of the old routes to Santiago, Pazo de Villabad is worth a long diversion. This fine old manor house sits beside the village church, and behind its sober façade and fine granite entrance is a charming family home. There are heirlooms at every turn, with stacks of lovely pieces in the big, airy bedrooms – old brass or walnut beds, dressers and tables – and in the corridors, statues, a *chaise longue* and family portraits above the grandest of stairwells. Endearingly, the bedrooms are named after beloved family members: Aunt Leonor, Great-Grandmama. Most seductive of all is the breakfast room with its gallery and enormous *lareira* (inglenook fireplace) where you feast on cheeses, home-made cakes and jams and good coffee. The heart and soul of it all is Señora Teresa Arana, a hugely entertaining and sprightly lady, so determined to get it right that she studied rural tourism in France before opening her house. Meet her and share a wonderful home and gardens. "Totally special, a fascinating place," wrote a reader.

rooms	6 doubles/twins.
price	€72–€99; single €60–€72.
meals	Breakfast €5.11; lunch/dinner on request.
closed	15 December–15 March.
directions	From Madrid towards La Coruña on A6. Exit to Castroverde. There C-630 for Fonsagrada, & after 1km left to Villabad(e). House next to church.

Teresa Arana

tel	+34 982 313000
fax	+34 982 312063
web	www.elpazo.com

map 2   entry 11

Casa Grande da Fervenza

A Fervenza, 27163 O Corgo, Lugo

The River Miño laps at the walls of this ancient mill – girdled round by no fewer than 20 hectares of magnificent ancient woodland (alder, oak, birch), beautiful and precious enough to have been declared a Nature Reserve. Casa Grande da Fervenza is both museum and hotel and pays homage to the rich cultural traditions of Galicia. The dining room is in the oldest part and dates from the 17th century; the hotel is named after the room's amazing rocky waterfall, *fervenza* being the Galician word for the sound of rushing water. The culinary philosophy here is to give you the sort of food which was around when the building was built: hearty Galician hot-pots and rich rabbit stews. Wines are the region's best. Bedrooms, quiet, attractive, comfortable, are across the way, in the house where the miller once lived. Restoration has been meticulous in its respect for local tradition and lore – yet there's no stinting on creature comforts. Antiques have been beautifully restored, rugs woven on local looms, there are linen curtains, chestnut beams and floors and hand-painted sinks. *A Rusticae Hotel.*

rooms	9: 8 doubles, 1 suite.
price	€60; single €42; suite €84.
meals	Breakfast €4.81; lunch/dinner €12 set menu, €15–€30 à la carte. VAT included.
closed	Rarely.
directions	From Lugo, N-VI for Madrid. After 4km in Conturiz, right by Hotel Torre de Núñez for Páramo for 11km, then right at sign for 1km to hotel.

Juan Pérez Orozco

tel	+34 982 150610
fax	+34 982 151610
web	www.fervenza.com

Casa de Labranza Arza

Reigosa-San Cristobo do Real, San Cristobo, 27633 Samos, Lugo

Hard to decide whether it's the smell of newly baked bread, the panoramic views or the farmhouse welcome that makes this place so special. Whichever it is, you'll feel at home the moment you kick the (often copious) mud from your feet at the door. And the views really *are* something special, with mountains of over 6,000 feet strung together like a dowager's diamonds for you to admire; on a clear day you can see as far as Portugal. Casa Arza is on the slopes of Monte Oribio, and a working dairy farm — hence the delicious soft cheese and butter at breakfast. Ramona cooks meat in a wood oven and fresh veg from the farm; the bread is kneaded in an old bread chest and baked daily in the original bread oven. This is back to basics in the best possible sense, and the warmth of the hospitality puts many a grander place in the shade. The slate walls and roof of the house are typical of the area, and the bedrooms have exposed stone walls and simple furniture, including antique beds widened to cope with the generous proportions of modern mattresses. Be sure to visit the Monasterio de Samos nearby, the biggest monastic cloister in Spain.

rooms	9 doubles/twins.
price	€ 35. VAT included.
meals	Breakfast € 4; dinner € 10.
closed	Rarely.
directions	From Lugo, N-VI for Ponferrada, then C-546 to Sarria. Left on LU-633 to Samos. Through San Cristobo do Real, house signed to right. 4km uphill on left, on entering Reigosa.

Jaime Arza Mourelo

tel	+34 982 187036
fax	+34 982 187036

map 2   entry 13

Casa Grande de Rosende

27460 Rosende-Sober, Lugo

Sleep in the Bedroom of the Drunkards — so named because of the Goyaesque fresco whose lurching figures will make you feel tipsy even if you don't already. This monument to medieval life is full of local colour, from the suits of armour standing to attention to the huge stone-walled rooms, the setting for many a feast in former times. The tower is medieval, the rest is 18th century — additions which Galician noblemen felt befitted their station. The vibrant personalities of Pauloba and Manuel add to the sense of fun, and Manuel's knowledge of history and general erudition is worthy of investigation. His grandmother left this, the family home of many decades, to become a celebrated pastry chef in Madrid; she returned to share her knowledge with the locals, and now the area is renowned for its stupendous pastries and cakes. Pauloba serves a delicious fresh almond pudding — worth a long detour. Guests are invited to sample the home-made digestif *aguadiente* in the sitting room, magnificent with its neo-classical painting and a piano crowded with family photos. Not the easiest place to find, but well worth several possible false starts. *A Pazos de Galicia hotel.*

rooms	9: 6 doubles, 3 singles.
price	€ 46–€ 58; single € 29–€ 36.
meals	Breakfast € 5.
closed	Rarely.
directions	From Orense, N-120 for Monforte. At km50, exit for Canaval. Right at 1st T-junc., following signs for house. Pazo 3km down road.

Manuel Vieítez

tel	+34 982 460627
fax	+34 982 455104
e-mail	rosende@pazosdegalicia.com
web	www.casagranderosende.com

Ferrería de Rugando
27329 Quiroga, Lugo

If you consider the long history of human activity in the Cordillera Cantábrica (thought to have been settled by Paleolithic people in the early stages of the last Ice Age), this smithy is a positive newcomer. Built by the monks of Samos in the 16th century at the south-west end of the mountain range, it has been converted into an attractive *casa rural* and stands on a rocky, tree-dotted hillside. In front is a natural pool, with the river Soldón close by. The bedrooms are airy and pleasing, simply furnished, with gleaming wooden floors and ceilings. Bathe, fish, walk or cycle; there's plenty to see here, too. At Las Médulas is an extraordinary landscape of rock pillars and pinnacles, formed by wind and water and by collapsed galleries mined in the Roman quest for gold. At Montefurado, the river Sil flows through underground passages that may also have been part of the gold-workings. A tortuous route across the hills joins the Ponferrada-Lugo road; there, in the Valvarce valley, is the line of Sir John Moore's retreat in 1809, where hundreds of his men perished in the cold after over-indulging in the wine cellars of Ponferrada. Be warned. *A Pazos de Galicia hotel.*

rooms	8: 6 doubles, 2 suites.
price	€ 46–€ 52; suite € 55–€ 64.
meals	Breakfast € 4; lunch/dinner € 12.
closed	10 January–10 February.
directions	From Orense, N-120 to Quiroga. 4km after Quiroga, left for Paradaseca & Paradapiñor. Hotel 11km from junction

Carmen Rodríguez

tel	+34 982 428852
e-mail	rugando@pazosdegalicia.com
web	www.pazosdegalicia.com

map 2   entry 15

Pazo do Castro

O Castro , 32318 O Barco de Valdeorras, Orense

Once this area was exploited by the Romans for alluvial gold. Now it's the dramatic landscapes and exciting water sports which bring the revenue in. The river Sil provides both. Rising high in the Cordillera Cantábrica, it twists down through Ponferrada to Orense, plunging through a series of gorges before joining the Miño on its journey to the Atlantic. Ponferrada was the Roman *Interramnium Flavium*, rebuilt in the 11th century as a refuge for pilgrims. Pazo de Castro, about 40km downriver, is a restored country house, with high wrought-iron gates opening on a wide courtyard. The first impression is of a long façade with serried, balconied windows above a graceful series of rose-coloured arches. The 'parlours' are full of antique furniture and paintings, the bedrooms light and well-equipped. There's a library and a little carriage museum — and lovely views towards the river. As well as the tennis and swimming available on site, the valley offers a whole range of water sports, walks and cycle trails. If you need a culture fix, take the tortuous drive to the monastery of San Esteban de Ribas del Sil. It's worth it. *A Pazos de Galicia hotel.*

rooms	18: 16 doubles, 2 suites.
price	€63–€106; suite €153–€183.
meals	Breakfast €6; lunch/dinner €15.
closed	Rarely.
directions	From Orense, N-120 for Ponferrada. 53km after Monforte, right on N-536 to O Barco. Left over N-120 to O Castro. Pazo on left at village entrance.

Montserrat Rodríguez González

tel	+34 988 347423
fax	+34 988 347482
e-mail	castro@pazosdegalicia.com
web	www.pazosdegalicia.com

Casa Grande de Trives

Calle Marqués de Trives 17, 32780 Poboa de Trives, Orense

Occasionally, grand family homes converted to receive guests cease to be either 'grand' or 'family'. Not so Trives where the balance between caring for you and respecting your intimacy is just right. This noble old village house (it has its own chapel) was one of the first in Galicia to open to guests; like good claret it has got better and better. The rooms are in a separate wing of the main building, big and elegantly uncluttered with lovely wooden floors, the best of mattresses and wonderful cotton sheets. There is a sitting room where you can have a quiet drink, and a truly enchanting garden. Breakfast is taken in an unforgettable dining room, where the richness of the furnishings, the cut flowers and the classical music vie with the grand buffet breakfast – a feast. Home-made cakes, fresh fruit, big pots of coffee, croissants… it all makes its way up from the kitchen via the dumb waiter. Fine bone china adds to the elegance of the meal. A marvellous place and a most gracious welcome from mother and son. *Grand Cru* Galicia!

rooms	9 twins/doubles.
price	€ 48–€ 57; single € 39–€ 57.
meals	None available.
closed	Rarely.
directions	From Madrid, A-6 for La Coruña. Exit 400 for N-120 for Monforte de Lemos. At km468, branch off for A Rua & Trives, then right at lights onto C-536 for Trives. On left in centre of village.

Adelaida Alvarez Martínez

tel	+34 988 332066
fax	+34 988 332066
e-mail	informacion@casagrandetrives.com
web	www.casagrandetrives.com

map 2   entry 17

Pazo Paradela

Carretera Barrio km 2, 32780 Puebla de Trives, Orense

You are at the heart of Galicia's green interior, close to the sleepy village of Trives. Your home for the night is a 17th-century manor house with long views of the surrounding hillsides. Your host, Manuel, is a delightful fellow who speaks superb English; he grew up in the States, dreamed of returning to his native soil, and ended up restoring the imposing old granite stones of the house his father bought some 30 years back. His natural generosity is reflected in the renovation: "you have to be proud of your work," he says. Bedrooms were given only the best: chestnut floors and beds, marble-topped tables, state-of-the-art heating and air conditioning, Portuguese marble in the bathrooms, antique mirrors on rustic stone walls. Views are long and green. The treats continue at table: in the vast granite-hearthed dining room, home-made honey for breakfast and, for dinner, the best of Galician country cooking with many of the vegetables fresh from the kitchen gardens. This is real hospitality: share a Queimada with your hosts, the local hot brew that keeps the evil spirits at bay.

rooms	8: 7 doubles, 1 suite.
price	€53–€68; single €43; suite €65. VAT included.
meals	Breakfast €5.51; dinner €19. VAT included.
closed	22 December–2 January.
directions	From Leon, N-VI to Ponferrada, then N-120 into A Rua Petin; C-536 to Trives. Through centre of town, cross bridge, then 1st right; follow signs.

Manuel Rodríguez Rodríguez

tel	+34 988 330714
fax	+34 988 337001
e-mail	1pa712e1@infonegocio.com

Pazo de Soutullo

Soutullo de Abaixo, 32152 Coles, Orense

Within six kilometres of Orense is a big estate. Within that big estate is a medieval settlement. Within that settlement is an 18th-century house. Within that house are… well, probably no woodcutter's children or lost princesses. Rather, an interior patio and cream-walled rooms with beamed ceilings and period furniture. The impression is of comfortable and stylish country living. Outside there's the garden and an orchard, a large, serene swimming pool and a tennis court. And lots of places to visit close by, including the Cistercian monastery of Santa Maria la Real de Osera. Partly in ruins but very impressive, it became known as the Escorial of Galicia after various baroque additions. Orense, too, is worth a visit. It's a busy commercial town, once famous for its waters, with a delightful old quarter and a 13th-century cathedral. It also has a lovely, seven-arched bridge – one of the finest in Spain – built in 1230 on Roman foundations and restored in 1449. John of Gaunt would have ridden over it when he held court in the town during his brief 'reign' as King of Castile in 1386-87. *A Pazos de Galicia hotel.*

rooms	8 doubles.
price	€ 76; single € 61.
meals	Breakfast € 6.50.
closed	Rarely.
directions	From Orense, N-525 to Gustei. Then right on CP-6. After 50m, 1st right. Pazo 500m further.

Benito Vázquez

tel	+34 988 205611
fax	+34 988 205694
e-mail	soutullo@pazosdegalicia.com
web	www.pazosdegalicia.com

map 2   entry 19

Pazo Bentraces

Bentraces, 32890 Barbadás , Orense

The old granite stones of Bentraces are steeped in history. Built for a bishop, this delectable *palacio* was passed on to a noble Galician family who in turn sold it on, and on… there are no fewer than six different coats of arms on different parts of the building! Angeles will unravel the web of its history and tell of the three long years of restoration which have resulted in one of the most elegant manor-house hostelries in Spain. The plushness within is hinted at by a Florentine-style southern façade and the gorgeous ornate gardens that lap up to the walls. Push aside the heavy doors to discover a world of books, rugs, engravings, parquet floors, marble staircases and warm colours. Anyone with an interest in antiques would love it here and no one could fail to enjoy the choice of sitting rooms, the enormous breakfast room in the palace's vibrant kitchen and the sumptuous guest bedrooms: bathrobes in marble bathrooms, top-of-the-range mattresses and bed linen, suites with room for a cocktail party. Romanesque chapels and monasteries are nearby and Santiago is an hour to the west. *A Rusticae hotel.*

rooms	7: 5 doubles, 2 suites.
price	€94–€105; single €80; suite €130.
meals	Breakfast €9; dinner €40. Restaurant closed Monday & Sunday night.
closed	22 December–2 January.
directions	From Orense for Madrid N-525; just past km7 marker, N-540 for Celanova to Bentraces. Here at 'Bar Bentraces', right; house beside church. Ring bell at main gate.

Angeles Peñamaría Cajoto

tel	+34 988 383381
fax	+34 988 383035
e-mail	info@pazodebentraces.com
web	www.pazodebentraces.com

Pazo de Esposende
Esposende, 32145 Ribadavia, Orense

Enrico bought this 16th-century manor four years ago, right in the heart of the Ribeiro wine district. and has been knee-deep in builders ever since. Nothing if not thorough, he was half-way thorough the restoration process when we visited. Things have moved on! The road outside the house is bordered by kiwi fruit trees and grape vines; beyond are dramatic valley views. There is a lovely entrance, with a quirky piece of exposed rock, and a pretty garden with flower beds. At the heart of the house is a peaceful galleried interior patio with stone floor, plant trough and some curious ceramic figures (for sale). Bedrooms are comfortable if not inspirational, with beautiful dark wood floors, striped and check bed linen and fresh country colours. Most have views over the vines or up to the village church. The food is good value, and the wine... Ribeiro, of course. The countryside of the Rivadavia provides every sort of walk going, and if some want to take the highroad while others take the low, there are wine trails, Romanesque and monastery trails and the Ribeira Sacra, which takes you through the Sil gorges. Something for everyone. *A Pazos de Galicia hotel.*

rooms	10: 7 doubles, 1 single, 2 family.
price	€80–€95; single €57–€71.
meals	Lunch/dinner €20.
closed	Rarely.
directions	From Orense, A-52 for Vigo. Exit 252 for Rivadavia. At 1st r'bout take last exit, over m'way to 2nd r'bout, then last exit for Esposende. Pazo on right at village entrance.

Enrique Galino

tel	+34 988 491891
fax	+34 988 491824
e-mail	info@pazodeesposende.com
web	www.pazodeesposende.com

map 2   entry 21

Pazo Viña Mein

Lugar de Mein-San Clodio, 32420 Leiro, Orense

Here, far off the beaten track, cradled among the steeply banked Ribeiro vineyards, monastic silence and peace. But don't imagine you'll be sleeping in a cell: these rooms are among the finest we have seen, with beds and bathrooms to scale, terracotta floors, antique furniture and wonderful rich fabrics and prints. One has a double door leading to a private terrace where you can sit and absorb the quiet beauty of Viña Mein. In the living and dining rooms wood and granite harmoniously combine, and the enormous lounge has a traditional *lareira*: a fireplace large enough to seat a whole family on its benches during cold winters. Central heating means you won't need to huddle in your inglenook today, but you can expect a fire to be lit. There are lots of books, too – the owner Javier Alen has a bookshop in Madrid. In the warmer months you breakfast on the terrace. Although no dinners are served here you'll find good restaurants in nearby San Clodio. There are mountain bikes for exploring the surrounding countryside, and a pool, too. Be sure to visit Viña Mein's state-of-the-art *bodega*: the wine is superb. *A Rusticae hotel.*

rooms	5: 4 doubles, 1 family.
price	€ 60–€ 90.
meals	Restaurants nearby.
closed	20 December–1 February.
directions	From Orense N-120 for Vigo. At km596 marker, right for Carballiño. Continue for 10km, then right to San Clodio. There follow signs to Viña Mein.

Visitación Simón Vázquez
tel +34 988 488400
fax +34 988 488732
e-mail vinamein@wol.es

Rectoral de Fofe

Covelo, 36873 Fofe, Pontevedra

Hard to believe this was once a rectory; what is now the 'special' bedroom was once the priest's own. He chose well: from the shuttered windows are wonderful views to the Valle de Tilas. A high vaulted ceiling gives the room an airy quality, while the austerity of the stone walls is softened by a wrought-iron bedstead and rugs on the floor. The other bedrooms are decorated simply and pleasingly in yellow and blue. Some have balconies and one has a big wooden platform cantilevered out over the door. Reached by a ladder, it makes an entertaining eyrie that would much appeal to a child. The old kitchen has been turned into an attractive sitting room, with a beamed ceiling and a fireplace where the oven used to be. Paintings and ceramics look well against the natural stone walls. But you'll want to be outside, making the most of those green valleys and hills. You are deep in the countryside here and there are some superb walks, as well as bicycles to hire and rivers to fish. You can't go far along the twisting road towards Pontevedra without being stunned by panoramic views of this part of Galicia's ancient, broom-covered granite massif. *A Pazos de Galicia hotel.*

rooms	6: 5 doubles, 1 single.
price	€48–€72; single €34–€42.
meals	Breakfast €5; lunch/dinner €12.
closed	Rarely.
directions	From Vigo, A-52 for Madrid. Exit 282 to Paraños. Take service road into village & continue on to Covelo, through Maceira to Fofe. Hotel on right at village entrance.

Amador Barcia

tel	+34 986 668750
fax	+34 986 668737
e-mail	fofe@free.recynet.com
web	www.ywz.com/rectoraldefofe

map 1   entry 23

Hostal Restaurante Asensio
Rua do Tollo 2, 36750 Goian, Pontevedra

At first glance you may wonder how this unprepossessing hostelry earns its place in the pages of this guide. But there are two excellent reasons for coming here. One, Dolores ('Loli') and Fernando, who lived for many years in the UK and who love receiving English-speaking guests, and two, the food. Fernando's claim that he can satisfy even the most demanding of palates is no idle boast. With the river Minho a spit away the menu naturally gravitates towards fish: lamprey and elvers are house specials, seafood too – and to accompany it all is a quality-rather-than-quantity wine list; the wine from the village is superb. Excellent meat dishes are also available. Tables are beautifully laid – Loli's artistry with flowers is always a feature – in the small, pine-clad dining room, which leads from the bar area upstairs where you breakfast. With food this good rooms could be just an afterthought but they're as spruce as can be, comfortable rather than memorable – our favourites are the newest ones grafted onto the original building a few years ago. But oh, what food!

rooms	6 doubles.
price	€42; single occ. €36.
meals	Breakfast €2.40; lunch €9; dinner €24 à la carte.
closed	15 September–14 October.
directions	E-1 Vigo to Tuy, then exit at km172 onto N–550 La Guardia & A Guarda. On for 15km. Hostal on left on passing through Goian.

Fernando Asensio

tel	+34 986 620152
fax	+34 986 620152

Finca Río Miño

Carril 6, Las Eiras, 36760 O Rosal, Pontevedra

The green hills and rivers of northern Portugal and Galicia are dear to Tony and Shirley Taylor-Dawes, who know the people, villages, food and wines like few others. Perhaps it was their passion for fine wine that led them to this 350-year-old farm with its terraced vineyards and *bodega* carved in solid rock. And what a position, up on the bank of the Miño with views to Portugal. In the vast garden are two pine-clad lodges built by Tony: simply furnished, each has its own small kitchen (though breakfast can be provided), sitting room and two bedrooms. Terraces have the same wonderful wide view over the river. In the main house there is a guest room with bathroom, a sitting room with pretty Portuguese furniture, a breakfast room and an unforgettable terrace with a rambling passion fruit that provides extra shade. Don't miss dinner if you happen to be here on a Sunday: it makes good use of port, whether in sauces for meat or in puddings such as 'Duero lemon haze'. There's a pool-with-a-view, river beaches at the end of the farm track and the Atlantic close by. *Minimum three-night stay July/August in lodges.*

rooms	1 double. 2 self-catering lodges for 4.
price	€54; lodge €66–€96.
meals	Breakfast €8. Gourmet dinner from €30 inc. port tastings: book ahead (Sundays only).
closed	November-March.
directions	Vigo N-550 to Tuy. La Guardia exit, then C-550 for 15km. Just after km190 marker, left at 'Restaurante Eiras' sign, over next x-roads; signed to left after 1.5km.

Tony & Shirley Taylor-Dawes

tel	+34 986 621107
fax	+34 986 621107
e-mail	finca_dawes@email.com
web	www.fincariomino.com

map 1   entry 25

Pazo da Touza

Rua dos Pazos 119, Camos, 36350 Nigran, Pontevedra

A jagged series of deep coastal inlets make up the Rías Bajas, one of Galicia's most attractive regions. Vigo Ría is the southernmost inlet, running from Hío to Baiona. It's sheltered from the full force of the Atlantic by the Cies Islands, now a *parque natural* and an important marine bird breeding site. Baiona itself is a fishing port (where the ship 'Pinta' returned in 1493 with news of the discovery of the New World) and Pazo de Touza lies a few kilometres inland. An imposing, grey stone building, it looks wholly at ease in its setting of lawns, hedges and wooded slopes. A square, three-storeyed tower occupies one corner, adding a majestic note and dominating the two-storeyed wings on either side. Both tower and balcony are typical of traditional Galician architecture. There are the usual comfortable and elegantly furnished rooms inside and the whole house gives an impression of robust, confident old age. Follow the flat coastal road south and you will pass the baroque façade of a former Cistercian monastery at Oia before reaching La Guardia. There, climb Monte Santa Tecla for views across the river Miño into northern Portugal. *A Pazos de Galicia hotel.*

rooms	9 doubles/twins.
price	€ 72–€ 96.
meals	Breakfast € 4.25.
closed	January.
directions	From Vigo on A7. Exit 11 for Playa América. Then N-550 for Vigo. After 3 sets of lights, right for Vincios. Pazo 3.5km further.

Alejandra & Betty Lepina

tel	+34 986 430533
fax	+34 986 383047
e-mail	touza@pazosdegalicia.com
web	www.pazodatouza.com

Rectoral de Cobres 1729

San Adrian de Cobres, 36142 Vilaboa, Pontevedra

Mussel platforms, fishing boats and the majestic sweep of the Rijo de Vigo come into view as you park outside the gate (there is also a small logging factory in the panorama, but it is wooden and discreet!). The house was built for a priest in the 17th century and has been beautifully renovated by Randi, a Norwegian architect, who, with husband Juan Carlos, has created a really special place to stay. There are two sitting rooms linked by a stone arch with a lovely aged Persian carpet and cast-iron lamps, and a library with books in every conceivable language that opens onto a terrace where you can drink in the view of the Ria. Bedrooms are sensitively designed (one with the disabled or elderly in mind) and show an architect's love of clean lines and uncluttered spaces. A huge double has a massive stone fireplace adapted to become a writing desk, and river views. Gravitate to the bar, where the strong local Galician beer is served, and where Juan Carlos may pick up the guitar or the Gallic pipes and serenade you. Outside, the *horio* — the old food store — has been converted into a sitting area: *the* place to watch the sun go down. *Multi-lingual. A Pazos de Galicia hotel.*

rooms	8 twins/doubles.
price	€ 70–€ 108.
meals	Breakfast € 6.
closed	15 January–15 February.
directions	From Pontevedra, A-9 for Vigo. Exit 146 for Cangas. After toll, left following signs for Vilaboa & Cobres. 2km from junc., at km8 marker, take track on right. Pazo 100m from road.

Juan Carlos Madriñán

tel	+34 986 673810
fax	+34 986 673803
e-mail	info@rectoral.com
web	www.rectoral.com

map 1   entry 27

Pazo Carrasqueira
Carrasqueira 6, 36638 Sisán, Pontevedra

Records from 1742 show that rent for the house was paid in wheat, rye and... a hen. Two and a half centuries later, the prices are in euros. But the *pazo* has endured and now earns its keep as a small hotel. Built of great blocks of mellow stone, with a stone porch raised on sturdy pillars, it looks capable of withstanding all weathers. Outside there's a leafy garden to relax in, and a swimming pool; inside, a library, a pretty sitting room and various well-furnished bedrooms. The wines on offer in the restaurant are from Carrasqueira's own extensive vineyards. Ribadumia (on the banks of the river Umia) is close to Cambados. There, a palace occupies two sides of the splendid Plaza de Fefiñanes, with arcaded houses and a 17th-century church opposite. This whole area is on the Ría Arosa, which runs from the fishing port of Riveira to the pine-tree-covered island of La Toja. It was here that a health-giving spring was discovered after a sick donkey, abandoned by his owner, miraculously recovered; it's a lovely place to visit but don't count on an invigorating draught when you get there: the spring has run dry. *A Pazos de Galicia hotel.*

rooms	9: 2 doubles, 7 twins.
price	€36–€72.
meals	Breakfast €6; lunch €18; dinner €15.
closed	24 December–1 January.
directions	From Vigo, A-9 for Santiago de Compostela. After Pontevedra, exit Vía Rápida 41; then exit for Cambados & O Grove. After 2.5km, cross River Umia, 1st left after bridge for Sisán. Pazo 1km further.

Gonzalo Pintos

tel	+34 986 710032
fax	+34 986 710032
e-mail	p.carrasqueira@eresmas.net
web	www.pazosdegalicia.com

Pazo La Buzaca

Lugar de San Lorenzo 36, 36668 Moraña, Pontevedra

In the hallway is a framed copy of the Varela family tree with, at the bottom, the name of the charming present owner, Enrique: an impressive pedigree fitting for a beautiful place. The house has been in the family since the 16th century, and after a complete overhaul is now operating as one of Galicia's top *pazos*. The food is top notch (try the *salmon en escabeche*) and the service would be hard to better: smiling and friendly faces eager to please but happy to leave you alone to enjoy the hotel and its lovely garden. The sitting room, with its massive medieval fireplace and dark beams, is disarmingly domestic, with antique knick-knacks dotted around and floral sofas. Bedrooms have period furniture and warm colours and are nicely uncluttered. Pretty vine-covered paths lead down through the garden to the pool and on through a gate to the *palmera* (dovecote), without which no self-respecting *pazo* is complete. If you're here during the July fiesta, you'll see the Pontevedrans round up the wild horses from the forests, assemble them in the square, trim their manes, then let them free — hairdressing on a dramatic scale. *A Pazos de Galicia hotel.*

rooms	13: 10 doubles, 2 suites, 1 room suitable for handicapped person.
price	€ 65-€ 100; suite € 135-€ 160.
meals	Breakfast € 7.25; lunch/dinner € 18.
closed	Rarely.
directions	Pontevedra-Santiago A-9. Exit 110a on N-640 for Caldas de Reis & A Estrada for 2km. Right at T-junc. on PO-221, for Campo Lameiro. 4km after Moraña, right at T-junc. & follow rd down. 800m further.

Enrique Varela Ruiz

tel	+34 986 553684
fax	+34 986 552902
e-mail	info@pazolabuzaca.com
web	www.pazolabuzaca.com

map 1   entry 29

Photography by Michael Busselle

ASTURIAS &
CANTABRIA

*"I never become tired of walking round, delighted by the
easy good manners of the market people and their sense
of beauty — of the beauty of common things…"*
H V MORTON

La Corte
33843 Villar de Vildas, Asturias

Cows perambulate down tiny steets: Villar de Vildas is a genuine working village, a delight to visit. Your inn is a 19th-century farmhouse of wood and stone, converted by Adriano to create a small guesthouse-restaurant. You enter via a small courtyard, then up old stone steps to a wooden-floored guest lounge. Here are books and photographs (spot your host as a young boy), a handsome hearth and a galleried balcony that catches the afternoon light. A narrow wooden spiral staircase takes you up to your rooms; ask Adriano to help you with your cases. The five double rooms vary in size; two have dormer windows looking to the stars and peaks, all have good bathrooms, pine furniture, comfy beds. The studio in the raised granary is huge fun and the restaurant is welcoming; low-ceilinged, beamed and with basket lamps. Expect to meet the locals who come for the Asturian cooking – or just a drink. At the western flank of the Somiedo Park – where some of the last bears in Europe roam free – there is no sweeter place from which to discover the walks of the Pigüeña valley.

rooms	5 doubles. 1 self-catering apartment for 4; 1 studio.
price	€ 55; studio € 60; apartment € 90. VAT included.
meals	Breakfast € 3.90; lunch/dinner € 10.
closed	Rarely.
directions	From Oviedo N–634 west. Just before Cornellana, left on AS-15 to Puente de San Martín. Here AS-227 south to Aguasmestas. Here, right to Pigüeña; climb on up via Cores to Villar de Vildas.

Adriano Berdasco Fernández

tel	+34 985 763131
fax	+34 985 763131
e-mail	lacorte@grama.es
web	www.gramacom.org/lacorte

map 3   entry 30

Hotel Villa La Argentina
Villar de Luarca, 33700 Luarca, Asturias

This flamboyant building was built in 1899 by a returning emigrant who made his fortune in South America; it was later abandoned and then rediscovered by the González Fernández family who saw in the crumbling building a brighter future. Thanks to their gargantuan efforts it once again breathes an air of light-hearted elegance and optimism. The reception rooms are parquet-floored and high-ceilinged with pastel-coloured walls, their light and colour enhanced by stained-glass windows and fine net curtaining. Enormous gilt-framed oil paintings, candelabras and tall mirrors add to the lofty, elegant feel. The dimensions and style of the bedrooms are in harmony with the rest of the house; yours will be large with a stuccoed and corniced ceiling, period furniture and a king-sized bed. Really good mattresses and hydro-massage tubs add to the feel-good factor. And La Argentina's low, slate-walled restaurant is the perfect place to end your day; your hosts may recommend the turbot or the steak 'ultramar'. After dinner, slip off for a game of billiards, or wander the Villa's garden where you may chance upon the house's ornate little chapel.

rooms	15: 12 doubles, 3 suites.
price	€51–€81; suite €81–€102.
meals	Breakfast €5.41; lunch/dinner €20.
closed	Rarely.
directions	From Oviedo towards Ribadeo via A-66 then A-8. Exit for Barcia & Almuña. At petrol station just before Luarca right, following signs Luarca por El Faro–Villar. Signed.

Antonio González Fernández

tel	+34 985 640102
fax	+34 985 640973
e-mail	villalaargentina@ctv.es
web	www.villalaargentina.com

Hotel Torre de Villademoros
Villademoros s/n, 33788 Valdés, Asturias

In meadowland high above the Cantabrian coast sits this elegant retreat – a restored 18th-century Asturian house with its own medieval tower. Manolo, the owner's son, is both interior designer and attentive host – and his hotel's old granary exterior gives no clue as to the modernity within. All is stylishly minimalist, from the big lounge with its fireplace, sculpted lighting and sleek sofas to the glazed breakfast room with its slate floor. Carefully-chosen colours and paintings add depth. Manolo has achieved an intimate and relaxed atmosphere here; the bedrooms are finely finished with polished chestnut and pine, the bathrooms have superb modern fittings. Most rooms look over the Sierra de Las Palancas and have their own sitting rooms. Dinner is an inexpensive and convivial affair with traditional food (stuffed tuna is a seasonal delicacy), good wine and fine desserts. But breakfast was our favourite meal: a hearty feast of pastries, cakes, crêpes and home-made jams, with a full cooked breakfast on request and glorious views of the old tower and lush green countryside beyond. *A Rusticae hotel.*

rooms	10 twins/doubles.
price	€ 64–€ 106; single € 48–€ 58.
meals	Breakfast € 5.5; dinner € 13.
closed	7 January–15 February.
directions	From Oviedo, N-632/E-70 for La Coruña. Exit Cadavedo, then left at junc. for Villademoros. Before railway bridge, right & follow signs to hotel.

Manolo Santullano Martínez

tel	+34 985 645264
fax	+34 985 645265
e-mail	correo@torrevillademoros.com
web	www.torrevillademoros.com

map 3   entry 32

La Casona de Pío
Riofrío 3, 33150 Cudillero, Asturias

Cudillero is one of the prettiest fishing villages of the Asturian coast, a huddle of houses around a sheltered cove where you can still watch the catch being landed first thing. As you enter this elegant little hotel (one street back from the main square) it is hard to believe that Pío, a well-known local personality, once had a fish-salting factory here. Fish is still the focus: this is one of the area's very best fish restaurants and it would be hard to fault it – beautifully presented tables and food, an extraordinarily crafted wooden ceiling, and a chef who is making waves. When we visited we were ushered through to the kitchen to see all kinds of good things on the go in boiling pots and sizzling pans. Out of season Pío's charming owners will let you choose your bedroom. We might choose No. 104 because of its private terrace, or one on the top floor which gets more light. Most of the furniture is chestnut; there are crocheted linen curtains, gleaming tiled floors and hydro-massage tubs. All of the rooms are smart, and amazingly good value at any time of the year. Picnics can be prepared for walks and other sorties.

rooms	11: 10 doubles, 1 suite.
price	€45–€69; single €36–€55; suite €65–€85.
meals	Breakfast €5.50; lunch/dinner €19 set menu, €25–€35 à la carte.
closed	7 January–6 February.
directions	From Oviedo, A-66 to Aviles; then on for Luarca. Turn right off road for Cudillero. Hotel in town centre, just off main square.

Manuel Alfredo Valle

tel	+34 985 591512
fax	+34 985 591519
e-mail	casonadepio@arrakis.es
web	www.arrakis.es/~casonadepio/

Casona de la Paca

El Pito, 33150 Cudillero, Asturias

La Casona de la Paca is one of Asturias's many *casonas de Indiano*: flamboyant edifices built by *émigrés* who made their fortune in the Americas, then headed for home and local-boy-makes-good celebrity. Its strawberry-coloured façade and exotic garden with many New World species immediately grab the eye – as was intended. The atmosphere within reflects the building's early years; the elegant interior is softened by a contemporary idea of colour and distribution of space. Uniformed staff serve you in the dining room. The well-upholstered lounge is a lovely place to read and there are lots of books to choose from in the library. Bedrooms are in the main house and a purpose-built annexe; the Tower Suite is worth the extra for the privilege of having the wonderful wrap-around terrace. Colonial-style furniture is 'in sync' with the spirit of the place: mahogany and teak in abundance combined with contemporary fabrics and Deco-ish floor tiles. You are close to the fishing village of Cudillero whose many restaurants, to quote the brochure, "reveal the secrets of Cantabria and the sweetness of its customs". *A Rusticae hotel.*

rooms	19: 17 twins/doubles, 2 suites.
price	€50–€78; single €46–€65; suite €82–€101.
meals	Breakfast €5.75.
closed	10 December–30 January.
directions	From Oviedo A-66, then A-8 for Ribadeo. At Avilés, N-632 west through Soto de Barco, then right at signs Cudillero for El Pito. House on right after approx. 1km.

Montserrat Abad

tel	+34 985 591303
fax	+34 985 591316
e-mail	hotel@casonadelapaca.com
web	www.casonadelapaca.com

map 3   entry 34

Hotel Casa del Busto

Plaza del Rey Don Silo 1, 33120 Pravia, Asturias

Parts of this fine old mansion, which has a South American, hacienda feel, date back to the 16th century. After some lean years it has seen careful and thorough renovation. Ceilings are high, floors are polished parquet, the staircase is marble and – most unusual – some of the walls are original *tabique* (wattle and daub). The owners now run courses in furniture restoration and many of the pieces you'll see at the hotel come straight from their workshop. Tapestries, sculptures and chandeliers embellish the whole yet, in spite of the grandness, a relaxed, soothing atmosphere pervades. The dining area is in an interior courtyard, and guest rooms give onto the gallery one floor up, each with stacks of period furniture, the decoration a harmonious potpourri of the simple and the grand. Pravia is an attractive village, you are seven kilometres from the sea, and the soaring grandeur of the Somiedo Park is an easy drive. This was once was a favourite haunt of the famous liberal politician Jovellanos who said of Busto, "the food and the bed were always to my liking". We think you'll feel the same.

rooms	29 twins/doubles.
price	€ 36–€ 80. VAT included.
meals	Dinner/lunch € 10 set menu, € 18 à la carte. VAT included. Closed Mondays.
closed	Rarely.
directions	From Oviedo, N–634 to Grado. Then AS–237 to Pravia. Hotel in village centre. From airport, head for Soto del Barco, then Pravia.

Alberto Mencos Valdés

tel	+34 985 822771
fax	+34 985 822772

Casa Camila

Fitoria 28, 33194 Oviedo, Asturias

Casa Camila, perched high above busy Oviedo, shares the same magic mountain as the exquisite churches of Santa Maria del Narranco and San Miguel de Lillo; its lofty position makes it special, with views across the surrounding meadows to the distant Picos. Asturias has a tradition of innovative architecture (returning emigrants have always wanted to be noticed!) and the modern lines and rich pomegranate colour of this building strike a bold note of welcome. Within is a light, modern edifice; wood has been beautifully fashioned throughout, especially in the oak parquet of second-storey bedrooms. There's a good library, a small salon, and Antonieta is absolutely lovely. Views from the dining room are magical at night, and Camila's food is a match for the setting: Asturias is its main inspiration but the Mediterranean tradition is also there, salads are interesting and the veggie side of things hasn't been neglected (stuffed onions and aubergines are specialities). This is an amazingly peaceful spot; do walk from the hotel for a couple of kilometres or so and wonder at those early Romanesque churches.

rooms	7: 6 doubles, 1 suite.
price	€ 67–€ 79; € 85–€ 109.
meals	Breakfast € 6; lunch/dinner € 26 à la carte.
closed	Rarely.
directions	In Oviedo, signs for train station & on to new bus station. At r'bout 1st right, then left, signed to hotel. At end of c/Palmira Villa, left to lights, then right. At end of c/Eugenio Tamayo, left under bridge. Signed 1.5km up hill on right.

Antonieta Domínguez Benito

tel	+34 985 114822
fax	+34 985 294198
e-mail	info@casacamila.com
web	www.casacamila.com

map 3   entry 36

Hotel Quinta Duro

Camino de las Quintas 384, 33394 Cabueñes, Asturias

The estate of the Velázquez-Duro family is a haven of greenery and mature trees, girdled by a high stone wall. Just to the east of Gijón you overlook the city; the house, though 800m from the main road, is quiet and secluded. The hospitable Carlos has recently redecorated the 11 guest rooms as well as the rest of the interior and the veranda at the rear; the result is stylish yet homely. Panelled walls, period Portuguese and English furniture show the family's love of quality and detail. The bronze statue in the garden is of Carlos's grandfather who casts a wistful eye on all those who visit – he would surely approve of his grandson giving the house this new lease of life. Only breakfast is served at the Quinta but there are two good restaurants close by – or head for the lively resort itself. The beach is clean but can get busy, so carry on round the town to the harbour where you'll find two Austurian specialities in abundance: fish and cider. The former comes in varieties distinct to the Cantabrian sea, the latter poured from a bottle held above the waiter's head into a glass held at knee height. Enormous fun.

rooms	11 doubles/twins.
price	€72–€10. VAT included.
meals	Restaurants close by.
closed	Mid-January-mid-February.
directions	From Gijón towards Santander on m'way, then N-632. Then right for Santurio & Cefontes. After 500m, left, then 400m further to large entrance gates on right.

Carlos Velázquez-Duro

tel	+34 985 330443
fax	+34 985 371890
e-mail	quintaduro@terra.es
web	www.hotelquintaduro.com

La Quintana de la Foncalada

Argüero, 33314 Villaviciosa, Asturias

You are welcomed with unaffected simplicity at this honeysuckle-clad farmhouse at the heart of the coastal *mariña* area of Asturias. Severino and Daniela are keen that their guests should learn about the people and traditions of the area and they encourage you to try potting (potters worked here in the 18th century) or help with the Asturian ponies or the organic veg patch. Much is home-produced: honey, cheese, juices, jams. The inside of the house is what you might expect from such folk: bedrooms are light, cheerful and uncluttered, with smallish bathrooms; many of the fittings, like the unusual table lamps, were made by Severino himself. The atmosphere is relaxed – make yourself a hot drink in the large kitchen whenever the mood takes you. Upstairs is a guest lounge with wicker furniture and lots of information on walks and visits. Severino will happily guide you towards some delectable beaches, good eateries and the best excursions from La Quintana by bike or pony. Equinophiles should know that Severino has created a museum dedicated to the Asturian pony, the *asturcón*; he also breeds them.

rooms	7 doubles/twins.
price	€ 40–€ 45; single € 35; suite € 60–€ 80. VAT included.
meals	Breakfast € 4; lunch/dinner € 15. VAT included.
closed	Rarely.
directions	From Gijón N-632 for Santander. 23km from Santander turn for Argüero. Here follow signs for Foncalada & La Quintana de la Foncalada.

Severino García & Daniela Schmid

tel	+34 985 876365
fax	+34 985 876365
e-mail	foncalada@asturcon-museo.com
web	www.asturcon-museo.com/inicial.html

map 3   entry 38

Hotel Castiello de Selorio

Castiello de Selorio, 33312 Villaviciosa, Asturias

Hotel, or family home? The Castello de Selorio manages to combine refinement with informality, a balance hard to achieve. Antonio and Marian are often to be found chatting to their guests in the sitting room or on the terrace, adding to the house-party feel, and their love of all things cultural inspires you while you're here. Behind the rather grand exterior (it was quite a place in former days, although abandoned when Antonio and Marian discovered it) you find elegant, even opulent, rooms: a sitting room and library, bedrooms with wonderfully comfortable beds and wall-to-wall carpeting, and old-fashioned bathrooms with huge deep bath tubs and audible plumbing! Dinner is something to look forward to, since Marian likes an element of surprise and generally gives her home cooking a creative twist. The monastery nearby has concerts in summer, there's a 'Jurassic' Park at Colunga, the beaches at Rodiles are golden and uncrowded, and it's hard to believe you are only three kilometres from the motorway — you are as quiet and as secluded here as you could possibly be.

rooms	9 doubles/twins.
price	€75–€126.
meals	Breakfast €6; dinner €27.
closed	15 January–15 February.
directions	From A-8 for Santander, exit for Lastres. Through Venta del Pobre on N-632. 200m past km32 marker, left & follow track up. Hotel entrance on left, at end of stone wall.

Antonio Alvarez Atelaníz

tel	+34 985 996040
fax	+34 985 996013
e-mail	info@castiellodeselorio.com
web	www.castiellodeselorio.com

El Correntiu

Sardalla 42, 33560 Ribadesella, Asturias

What a treat to stay in a grain silo as swish as this! The building, in nine acres, is off to one side of a traditional Asturian farmhouse, and the unusual renovation works wonderfully well. It is elegantly simple and almost Scandinavian in its crisp use of wood, with ochre tones to impart warmth, discreet lighting and lots of space. Each apartment even has its own kitchen garden from which you may pick to your heart's content. One has a sitting room and fireplace, both have books, games, sheets and towels... everything you need. If you're more of a traditionalist there is a also a little cottage in the grounds, equally well-equipped for self-caterers. There is an abundance here of fruit trees (even bananas): the region has a micro-climate and nearly everything thrives. A stream babbles by just behind your dwelling: *escorentia* means 'place that collects rain water'. You are close to the little fishing village of Ribadesella at the mouth of the River Sella, there are magnificent beaches and Maria Luisa (her English is excellent) can supply you with eggs and milk fresh from the farm.

rooms	2 apartments for 2; 1 cottage for 4.
price	Apartment € 46–€ 55; cottage € 65–€ 85.
meals	Self-catering.
closed	Rarely.
directions	From Ribadesella head for Gijón on N-632. After bridge, left for 'Cuevas-Sardalla'. From here, exactly 2km to El Correntiu.

María Luisa Bravo Toraño

tel	+34 985 861436
fax	+34 985 861436
e–mail	elcorrentiu@fade.es
web	www.elcorrentiu.com

map 3   entry 40

Hotel Casona de Bustiello

Ctra. Infiesto - Villaviciosa s/n, 33535 Infiesto, Asturias

Cave paintings and monasteries, beaches and mountains, towns and tranquillity, all within easy reach of this little hotel on the western edges of the Picos de Europa. Its mix of traditional Asturian and modern architecture gives the house an eccentric look, the shallow roof being dominated by a large, obtrusive dormer window, but enter that room in the attic space and you'll find it delightful, with rosy walls, sloping ceilings and an entertaining mass of beams. The hotel has only recently been converted and the owners have done a great job. All the rooms are painted in warm colours and furnished with confidence and restraint, keeping a cosy, rural feel. From the sitting room, with its big bookcases, a door leads to a long, windowed gallery – a wonderful place to sit and take in the views of the Sierra de Ques. If the solitude and wildlife of the mountains appeal, head south-east into the wild magnificence of the Picos de Europa. Covadonga is the site of a battle fought in 722, when a small Spanish force is reputed to have crushed the Moorish invaders – literally, with the aid of a providential avalanche.

rooms	10 doubles/twins.
price	€ 60–€ 95.
meals	Breakfast € 6; lunch/dinner c.€ 13.
closed	Rarely.
directions	From Oviedo, N-634 for Santander. 2km before Infiesto, left on AS-255 for Villaviciosa. Hotel on right after 4km.

Aurora R. Huergo

tel	+34 985 710445
fax	+34 985 710760
e-mail	info.hcb@hotelcasonadebustiello.com
web	www.hotelcasonadebustiello.com

Palacio de Cutre

La Goleta s/n, 33583 Villamayor-Infiesto, Asturias

Javier worked for one of Spain's largest hotel chains but is now a firm convert to the 'small is beautiful' school of hostelry. He and his wife Alejandra have lavished energy and care on this intimate yet luxurious small hotel. Part of the spirit is captured by the leaflet describing the hotel: it's written as if all were seen by the old oak which towers gloriously over Cutre's lovely gardens. It tells that it was born in the same century as the palace – the 16th – and looks in on beautifully decorated guest rooms where no detail is lacking. It sees flounced and beribboned curtains, cushions on beds, Tiffany-style lamps, antique bedsteads, luxurious bathrooms and the best fabrics. It also glimpses the cheerful dining room with its rush-seated chairs and astonishing views. But we give Alejandra herself the final word: she insists that what makes the place so special is Cutre's food, an innovative mix of traditional Asturian dishes with more elaborate fare, such as duck breast with red peppers. We would add that the wonderful old *pueblo* of Villamayor-Infiesto is worth a visit.

rooms	17: 15 doubles, 2 suites.
price	€97–120, single €72, suite €150.
meals	Breakfast €8; lunch/dinner €30.
closed	February-7 March; Christmas.
directions	From Santander N-634 Oviedo. At km356 marker, right for Borines & Colunga. Over r'way line, then river, then right for Cereceda; signs for 2km to Palacio.

Javier Alvarez

tel	+34 985 708072
fax	+34 985 708019
e-mail	hotel@palaciodecutre.com
web	www.palaciodecutre.com

map 3   entry 42

Los Cuetos

Piloña-Infiesto, 33537 Santianes, Asturias

Los Cuetos is a totally rebuilt 16th-century farmhouse in a commanding position with views of the valleys and mountains of Asturias. The driveway, lined with flowers and fruit trees, leads you to the wooden façade – the plain house's most striking feature. Inside, however, furnishings are 'designer smart' with well-matched prints, warm fabrics, tiled and wooden floors and pastel walls. All is warm and friendly and blends serenely with the majestic setting. Seila, a great hostess, is happy in the kitchen cooking breakfast, or creating one of her special fish dishes or meat casseroles for dinner. The sweeping curved staircase takes you up to the first floor where the great galleried window lets the light in; there's a sizeable sitting room and five regal guest rooms. Each one is themed and utterly delightful: perfectly lit and furnished with good-looking wooden beds and rugs. Les Mimoses with its jacuzzi occupies an entire wing. The garden is memorable too, with a vast granary. Under the marquee you sit at a great round table that comes from an old bread oven and spins – watch your glass while watching the view.

rooms	5 doubles/twins.
price	€50–€85. VAT included.
meals	Breakfast €4; dinner €12.
closed	Rarely.
directions	From Santander E-70/N-634 towards Oviedo. Exit at km363 to Infiesto & as you enter village left for Lozana on PI-III. Los Cuetos on right after 1.5km; large black entrance gate just beyond house.

Seila Sánchez Barro

tel	+34 985 710656
fax	+34 985 710874
e-mail	loscuetos@loscuetos.com
web	www.loscuetos.com

La Casa Nueva
33584 Cereceda-Infiesto, Asturias

Tick-tock goes the clock. Time has come to a standstill in this quiet valley in the shadow of the Sueve mountains. The ancient region of Pilona is home to La Casa Nueva, a former village house where cattle were stabled and which had its own cider press. And apples are an important link to the past for José María: he has planted big orchards that are already bearing fruit; although only for personal consumption at present, they will be a source of revenue in the future. The house is coming to fruition, too, after a refit funded by a grant from Brussels. The layout is simple, and the entrance hall is the main guest sitting room, with a high pitched ceiling, wooden staircase and balcony, and big iron candelabra to light it all. We did feel that some of the detail was a touch twee but the bedrooms are simple and clean with only the odd creaking floorboard to break the peace. The Wild Horse Fair in August is an important fiesta, accompanied by the wail of bagpipes and the rowdy consumption of free-flowing cider. Enjoy your stay in old Asturias, remote and magical with mysteries in every glade. *E-mail bookings preferred.*

rooms	5 doubles/twins.
price	€51–€60.
meals	Breakfast €4.50.
closed	Rarely.
directions	From Santander west on E-70 & N-634. Pass Arriondas; at km355, just before Villamayor, right on AS-259 for Borines & Colunga. After 500m right on PI-II into Cereceda; house signed on right.

José María Muñoz Suárez & Purificación Pérez Pérez
tel   +34 985 923737
e-mail   sugope@navegalia.com

map 3   entry 44

Hotel Halcón Palace

Cofiño s/n, Carretera AS260 Arriondas-Colunga, 33548 Cofiño-Arriondas, Asturias

A soul-stirring area of Spain cradled between the mighty Picos mountains to the south and the rugged coast to the north. Hard to believe it but a few years ago the 17th century palace was overrun with vegetation and doomed to ruin... until this Spanish-Swiss couple arrived with the energy and conviction to create their dream hotel. The wonderful thing here is the incomparable view of the Cantabrian mountains and the Picos de Europa. The dining rooms are elegant yet still conducive to long, lazy meals; in all the communal areas, antique and modern furnishings mix well. The bedrooms are smart, sparkling clean and have chestnut furniture, the best of mattresses and stirring views, every one. There is a cosy bar for an aperitif before dinner, and century-old trees in gardens that are a mass of colour – this part of Asturias enjoys a micro-climate. The gentle good manners of your two hosts communicate themselves to the very building. "Leo is a super host," enthused one reader, and many others have said how much they have loved staying here.

rooms	19: 18 doubles, 1 suite.
price	€ 58–€ 91; single € 45–€ 75; suite € 81–€ 114.
meals	Lunch/dinner € 13.
closed	Rarely.
directions	From Arriondas take SA-260 for Colunga. After 5km turn left following signs for hotel.

Leo Benz
tel   +34 985 841312
fax   +34 985 841313

Hotel Posada del Valle

Collia, 33549 Arriondas, Asturias

Nigel and Joann Burch lived in eastern Spain for nearly 20 years but longed for greener pastures. After two years of searching the hills and valleys of Asturias they found the home of their dreams – a century-old farmhouse just inland from the rugged north coast with heart-stopping views to mountain, hill and meadow. And they are nurturing new life from the soil (they are a fully registered organic farm) while running a small guesthouse. The apple orchard has been planted, the flock graze the hillside, the menu celebrates the best of things local, and the guests delight in this sensitive conversion that has created one of the area's most beguiling small hotels. Rooms are seductive affairs with polished wooden floors below, beams above and carefully matched paint and fabric. Most memorable of all is the glass-fronted dining room with glorious views. You are close to the soaring Picos, the little-known beaches of the Cantabrian coast and some of the most exceptional wildlife in Europe. And loads of info on the best local rambles available from Nigel and Joann. *A no-smoking hotel.*

rooms	8 doubles.
price	€49–€62.
meals	Breakfast €6; dinner €15.
closed	15 October-15 April.
directions	N-634 Arriondas, then AS-260 for Mirador del Fito. After 1km, right for Collia. Through village (don't turn to Ribadesella). Hotel 300m on left after village.

Nigel & Joann Burch

tel	+34 985 841157
fax	+34 985 841559
e-mail	hotel@posadadelvalle.com
web	www.posadadelvalle.com

map 3   entry 46

Hotel Aultre Naray

Peruyes, 33547 Cangas de Onis, Asturias

A mid the greenest green, beneath the highest peaks of the Cuera Sierra, this must be one of the loveliest places to stay in Asturias. The town's grand *casonas* date from a time when returning emigrants invested the gains of overseas adventures in fine, deliberately ostentatious homes. The transition from grand home to fine hotel has been a natural progression at Aultre Naray; the name comes from a medieval motto meaning, 'I'll have no other'. The hotel continues to flourish under new ownership and the mood remains warm, relaxed and comfortable. Designer prints, fabric and furniture have been married with the rustic core elements of beam and stone walls. No expense was spared to get things just right – how often do you get the chance to sleep beneath a Dior duvet? We marginally preferred the attic rooms, but all are memorable. It is a treat to breakfast on the terrace in the English-style garden, with a choice of crêpes, home-made cakes – or eggs and bacon! – to accompany the heavenly views. And there are lots of good places to eat nearby. *A Rusticae hotel.*

rooms	10 doubles.
price	€ 62–€ 93.
meals	Breakfast € 3.50–€ 6; lunch/dinner € 22 à la carte.
closed	10 November–3 April, weekends only.
directions	From Oviedo for Santander on m'way, then N-634. After passing Arriondas at km335 marker, right for Peruyes. Climb for 1km; hotel on left just before village.

Maxi Suarez & Teresa Barreiros

tel	+34 985 840808
fax	+34 985 840848
e-mail	aultre@aultrenaray.com
web	www.aultrenaray.com

Casa El Ama de Llaves

Hontoria s/n, 33593 Llanes, Asturias

The senses are in paradise here. The exterior delights the eye (the deepest eaves you'll ever see), you can almost hear the sea, and the smell wafting from the homely kitchen is delectable. Manuel loves his food and takes huge pleasure in cooking for his guests: Asturian food at its best. Generous use of chestnut wood on ceilings and floors lends warmth to the interior and Justine clearly has a great eye for antiques. In her passion for detail, she has studied every corner minutely and her choice of furnishings, fabrics and paintings enhances the exquisite rooms. They are big and the beds sumptuous under their cascades of drapery. Bright ceramic tiles and modern fittings in the bathrooms make for a lively setting to your ablutions – to the sound of music if you so choose. But relaxation is the main theme: aromatic oils pervade the air (and can be purchased here, too) and the cosy, unhurried restaurant is another olfactory indulgence. Just sit here relishing good food and wine in congenial surroundings – not a care in the world can reach you. *A Rusticae hotel.*

rooms	8: 6 twins/doubles, 2 suites.
price	€ 56–€ 85; suite € 78–€ 100.
meals	Dinner € 18.
closed	Rarely.
directions	From Oviedo east on E-70-N-634. Exit at km313 for Villahormes & Hontoria. Through Villahormes, then right for Hontoria. Follow signs for Ama de Llaves.

Manuel Rodriguez

tel	+34 985 407322
fax	+34 985 407697
e-mail	asturias@amadellaves.com
web	www.amadellaves.com

map 4   entry 48

La Montaña Mágica
El Allende, 33508 Llanes, Asturias

The rehabilitated farmstead perches on the hillside; the mighty Picos mountains rise up behind, the valley lies far below. Ecologically-minded Carlos, who has his own tree-planting programme, had already had experience of building and restoration for others when he decided to develop this ruined site. The finish is rustic and cheerful with lots of stonework and old beams. The small reception/information area – replete with maps of the peaks – leads to a log-fired sitting room with library. There are six bedrooms in this part of the house; some are split-level with huge woodburning stoves, all have stunning mountain views. Another more recently completed section has good, well-insulated, pine-finished rooms with large bathrooms. The dining room stands on its own beside the old *horreo* (granary), now converted into a children's playroom. Good value lunches and dinners tend to be traditional Asturian with Riojan wine and there's a small bar where you can enjoy a digestif. This is superb walking and riding country, and staff will help organise a trek on one of the many ponies stabled nearby.

rooms	16: 12 doubles, 4 suites.
price	€ 46–€ 64; suite € 65–€ 85.
meals	Breakfast € 4.50; lunch/dinner € 12.
closed	Rarely.
directions	From Santander west on E-70/N-634. Past Llanes & at km307 right for Celorio, then AS-263 to Posada. Here left on AS-115 for Cabrales to La Herreria. Here right, cross Roman bridge & on past Allende.

Carlos Bueno Sánchez

tel	+34 985 925176
fax	+34 985 925780
e-mail	magica@llanes.as
web	www.lamontanamagica.com

Hotel El Habana

El Pedroso s/n (La Pereda), 33509 Llanes, Asturias

Lush meadows, grazing cows, dry-stone walls – you might be forgiven for supposing we were describing the Cotswolds. Such is the rural beauty of Asturia, where gently rolling farmland gives way to the Guera Mountains. The hotel is modern, a clever contemporary version of the traditional Asturian house, its white-framed windows set against washed yellow-ochre walls. Inside: plants, warm terracotta floors, subtle lighting. Much of the furniture comes from owner Maria Eugenia's home in New Dehli and an air of colonial elegance prevails. The friendly atmosphere, noticeable the moment you arrive, goes up a gear in the dining room – the hub of the hotel. Here, regulars and visitors congregate to sample Sirio's excellent cooking with its strong Asturian flavours. Bedrooms are big and light, the two with patios leading to the garden being our favourites. Your hosts will advise you on the many walks, dinosaur trails and caves to visit in this neck of the woods; if, however, such pursuits do not appeal, head for nearby Llanes with its handsome galleried buildings. *Multi-lingual. A Rusticae hotel.*

rooms	10:9 doubles, 1 suite.
price	€72-€85; single €63-€75; suite €110-€125.
meals	Breakfast €5.70; lunch/dinner €21, à la carte €27. VAT included.
closed	5 October-29 February.
directions	From N-634, at km301 marker, Llanes exit, do a U-turn & cross over N-634 for La Pereda, following signs on right for Prau Riu Hotel. 1500m further, hotel signed. Follow path.

Sirio Sáinz

tel	+34 985 402526
fax	+34 985 402075
e-mail	hotel@elhabana.net
web	www.elhabana.net

map 4　entry 50

Casa de Aldea La Valleja

Rieña, 33576 Ruenes, Asturias

If you fancy turning your hand to preserve-making, cheese-culturing or mountain honey-gathering, then head for La Valleja. Tending the livestock and pottering in the garden are also a must: Paula, your hostess, is passionate about rural tourism and loves her guests to lend a hand. You'll probably pick up a few tips too. The house was built in 1927 and the original materials – bricks, tiles, stones and chestnut beams – maintain the rustic charm. Each bedroom has been named after one of the fruits used in the jam-making, and if your room seems a little sombre, throw open the windows and drink in the view. This is rugged terrain, well off the beaten track, and the walking in the Peñamellera Alta is superb. The best-known walk takes you along the spectacular Cares gorge. You will be well fortified before any mountain trip: meals here are enjoyed with fellow, mainly Spanish, guests around a groaning table and the food is all organic and lovingly prepared. So whether you want to sit and enjoy the scenery or go off yodelling on the slopes, this is the place. Be sure to buy some of the home-made produce to take back.

rooms	5 doubles/twins.
price	€39-€48.
meals	Breakfast €4; lunch €15, dinner €11.
closed	Rarely.
directions	N-634 Santander-Oviedo for 67km; left to Panes. Here, right onto AS-114, left after bridge for Lagos de Covadonga; through Pastorias. After 0.8km, right up steep road to Rieña. Park at top; up on right.

Paula Valero Sáez

tel	+34 985 925236
e-mail	valleycas@yahoo.es

Hotel Torrecerredo

Barrio Vega s/n, 33554 Arenas de Cabrales, Asturias

Torrecerredo is just outside the busy town of Arenas de Cabrales, a hub for walkers and sightseers visiting the Picos. The views are stunning, more so even than the photograph suggests – "a double glory for hearts and eyes". The hotel itself is a rectangular, modern building on a hillside just outside the town with a somewhat garish frontage. Bedrooms are simple, spartan affairs with no great charm; the best are those on the first floor at the front. But what lifts the hotel into the 'special' league for us is its pine-clad dining/sitting room in which guests are treated to simple home cooking, just the thing for when you return from a day in the mountains. Walking is the main activity here; Jim is a mountain guide and when not leading group walks can take you out. Few know the area as intimately as he and Pilar; they are generous with time and advice on routes and can help plan excursions including nights in mountain refuges, canoeing, riding, climbing or caving. A good value place to stay but absolutely without frills – and be prepared for the bumpy track! Ask about special offers in the low season.

rooms	19: 15 doubles, 4 singles.
price	€29–€61; single €17–€33.
meals	Breakfast €3; lunch/dinner €8.50.
closed	January–February.
directions	From Santander N-634 for Oviedo then left on N-612 for Potes. In Panes C-6312 (A-S114) to Arenas de Cabrales. Through town & right after Hotel Naranjo de Bulnes. Signed.

Pilar Saíz Lobeto & Jim Thomson
tel +34 985 846640
fax +34 985 846640
e-mail torretours@fade.es
web www.picosadventure.com

map 4   entry 52

La Tahona de Besnes

33578 Alles, Asturias

In a valley of the Picos de Europa, surrounded by oak and hazelnut trees, and a crystalline brook babbling by, the Tahona de Besnes consists of a number of old village houses that have been carefully converted into a country hotel. The main building was a bakery, another a corn mill, a third a stable. At the new heart of it all, the bakery-cum-restaurant, prettily decorated with dried flowers, gentian-blue tablecloths and old farm implements. Choosing from the menu is hard, but do try the sirloin steak with *salsa* of Cabrales cheese, and the dishes cooked in cider. There is also a terrace beside the brook, a restful place for a cool glass of cider before dinner. Rooms and apartments are decorated to match their rustic setting: comfy beds, good bathrooms, nothing too fancy. The hotel has plenty of literature on the area and can arrange for you to ride, walk, canoe, fish or take trips out by jeep. And by the time you finally drag yourself away, make sure you take a local cheese and a bottle of honey liqueur with you, or goodies from the bakery. A beautiful, welcoming place to stay.

rooms	13 doubles/twins.
price	€53–€66.
meals	Breakfast €5; lunch/dinner €12 set menu, €27 à la carte.
closed	10–30 January.
directions	From Santander N-634 for Oviedo; after 67km, left to Panes at Unquera. In Panes, right after bridge towards Arenas de Cabrales & Lagos de Covadonga to Niserias. Here towards Alles; then follow signs.

Sarah & Lorenzo Nilsson

tel	+34 985 415749
fax	+34 985 415749
e-mail	latahona@ctv.es
web	www.latahonadebesnes.com

Hotel La Casona de Villanueva

33590 Villanueva de Colombres, Asturias

Nuria left a city career in search of a quieter life and fell in love with the old stones of this solid, 18th-century village farmhouse. Thanks to careful restoration and imaginative decoration she has created a truly exceptional place to stay in the tiniest of hamlets close to the Cantabrian coast. Rooms vary in size, as you'd expect in an old house, and have smallish bathrooms, but this place is special: warm pastel colours on walls, rugs and cushions from Morocco, lots of paintings and etchings and heaps of antiques. Then there are the smaller details, the home-made jams and flowers at breakfast, the classical music which accompanies every meal. The food is good – there are often home-made soups and fish fresh from the slate – and the wine list places the emphasis on quality. Nuria's biggest passion is her walled garden, the most peaceful of retreats – wander among fish ponds, flowerbeds and the vegetable garden which supplies your table. She speaks good English and will help plan your sorties: visit Romanesque churches and sleepy fishing villages, or walk the rocky coastline and the Picos de Europa Natural Park.

rooms	8: 6 doubles, 2 suites.
price	€55–€120; single €45–€50; suite €80–€100.
meals	Breakfast €7; dinner €22.
closed	January & February.
directions	From Santander N-634 for Oviedo. At km283 marker, left for Colombres. Through village, then 2km to Villanueva. Signed in village.

Nuria Juez

tel	+34 985 412590
fax	+34 985 412514
e-mail	casonavillanueva@hotmail.com

map 4   entry 54

Hotel Don Pablo

El Cruce s/n, 39594 Pechón, Cantabria

Don Pablo enjoys a beguiling spot between two estuaries on the outskirts of the hamlet of Pechón. The sea is just a few hundred yards away and a track snakes towards it through green fields from the hotel. This is all the creation of an exceptionally cheery and kindly ex-banker Pablo and his wife Magdalena who never faltered in their conviction that 'it could be done'. Don Pablo is a well-dressed hotel: stone, antiques and oak beams decorate the inside, greenery adorns the outside, and there's a terrace for sitting out when it's warm. There is a large sitting room with a television of enormous proportions, and downstairs, a spick-and-span little dining room where breakfasts include fresh fruit juices and Cantabrian cakes. The bedrooms are medium sized with good wooden beds, chests, handsome oak ceilings and well-equipped bathrooms. We especially liked the attic rooms looking out to the Cantabrian Sea. This is a modern hotel with looks – and a heart.

rooms	34: 30 doubles/twins, 4 suites.
price	€48–€54; singles €42–€48; suite €70–€73.
meals	Restaurant next door.
closed	Rarely.
directions	From Santander on newly built dual-carriageway A-67/N-634 for Oviedo. Exit for Unquera, Panes & Potes. Ask hotel for directions from here.

José Pablo & Magdalena Gómez Parra
tel +34 942 719500
fax +34 942 719523

La Posada de Tollo

Calle Mayor 13, 39575 Tollo (Vega de Liebana), Cantabria

Imagine having the full majesty of the Picos de Europa at the bottom of your garden. Visit the Posada de Tollo and experience that very thing: Nature at her boldest looms at the door of this 400-year-old house. Alfonso and Pepa live in the house, and the guest quarters are in the former granary. High gates open on to a very Spanish garden with a fountain, a palm tree and stepping stones in the lawn while the full-length front window gives a hint of the rather cosmopolitan interior – and there is the most antiquated wooden balcony above. The living room is modern and light with its polished oak floor and log fire; beyond is the towering heart of the house. Here you find a super great mural of an American bar scene on one wall and black and white photographs of flamenco singers in the dining area. Pepa is chef, and there is a good chance your hosts will sit and join you for a glass of wine. A central stairwell leads to the guest rooms which are light, airy and modern: no rustic furniture but some interesting ornaments on shelves set into the walls. It is relaxed and friendly and the view from the back garden carries the day.

rooms	8: 7 doubles, 1 suite.
price	€42–€62; single €30–€36; suite €75–€90.
meals	Breakfast €5; dinner €12.
closed	February.
directions	From Santander, A-67/N-634 for Oviedo. Left at Unquera onto N621 to Potes. Then San Glorio & Vega de Liébana road for 3.5km, left for Tomo & Tudes for 3.5km, then right. House signed 200m from junc.

Pepa Estevez Ortega

tel	+34 942 736284
e-mail	posadadetollo@hotmail.com

map 4   entry 56

Casa Gustavo Guesthouse

Cillorigo de Liébana, 39584 Aliezo, Cantabria

In the beautiful Liébana valley lies the tiny hamlet of Aliezo and the old farmhouse of Casa Gustavo. Lisa and Mike are not typical ex-pats; they love their adopted land, have learned its language, know its history and its footpaths. Within the thick stone walls of their house are low timbered ceilings and wood-burning stoves and good smells wafting out from the kitchen. For home it is; don't expect hotelly trimmings. Rather, the house is organic and shambolic; some rooms are small, some large, some have balconies. But walkers will be more than happy with the country cooking, hot showers and decent beds. Redstarts nest beneath the eaves and there are dogs and cats, a cosy lounge, magazines and books. The main protagonist is Nature and her Picos mountains; Mike and Lisa know the best walks, will advise according to what the weather is doing and should be able to provide you with the best maps of the area. Casa Gustavo is a superb place for ornithology and botany — and there are ski-mountaineering courses in winter. Your hosts offer free transport to the beginning of walks.

rooms	5: 1 double, 2 twins, 1 single, 1 family.
price	€60–€70; single €24.
meals	Packed lunch €5, dinner €15. VAT included.
closed	Rarely.
directions	From Santander A-67/N-634 for Oviedo. Left at Unquera onto N-621 for Potes. Shortly before Potes, through Tama; after 200m, left to hamlet of Aliezo. Follow tight bend up to top of village.

Lisa & Michael Stuart

tel	01629 813 346
fax	01629 813 346
e-mail	istuart727@aol.com

Casona de Naveda

Plaza del Medio Lugar 37, Hermandad de Campóo de Suso, 38211 Naveda, Cantabria

Walk out of the front door and follow the river along to the village, or pick your way through pastures full of cows and wild flowers. The area is studded with Romanesque churches too, and the nearby town of Reisona, with its galleried houses and fine central square, is quite a find. The *casonas* of Cantabria are cousins, as it were, of the *pazos* of Galicia, and if this one is anything to go by they are every bit as wonderful. It was built 300 years ago by one of those enterprising *indianos* who returned from Cuba after making a fortune and wanted a dwelling grand enough to proclaim his newfound wealth and status. Rich oaks and walnut, on floors, ceilings and fireplaces, have the kind of sheen which only centuries of polishing can achieve; the ancient stone pillars in the sitting room would look quite at home in one of the local churches. Bedrooms 6 and 7, with their wooden galleried sitting areas, have a *Romeo and Juliet* charm; the others are distinctive in different ways. The menu is a celebration of simple food superbly cooked, with a line-up of the best of Spain's wines to go with it. Rural bliss, foodie heaven. *A Rusticae hotel.*

rooms	9 doubles/singles/suites.
price	€75–€90; single €60; suite €105–€111.
meals	Breakfast €6; dinner €17.
closed	Rarely.
directions	From Santader, N–611 to Reinosa. Then C-625 to Espinilla, & onto C-628. Left turn to Naveda, signed.

Paloma López Sarasa

tel	+34 942 779515
fax	+34 942 779681
e-mail	info@casonadenaveda.com
web	www.casonadenaveda.com

map 4   entry 58

Posada La Casona de Cos

Cos Mazcuerras, 39509 Mazcuerras, Cantabria

In a quiet village of Cantabria, just a short drive from Santillana, this could be a super place to stay before or after you take the ferry. It is small, family-run, unpretentious – a place where locals still far outnumber foreign visitors; Spanish to the core. Bright-eyed, ever-smiling Natalia has built the reputation of the place over the past 30-odd years and what is so refreshing is not only her pride in her four-hundred-year-old home but also the relish with which she greets you as hostess. Enter by way of a busy bar (where would the Spanish be without them?); beyond is the dining room, the hub of the place. Low, beamy, with marble-topped tables and a fire in the hearth it has the feel of a French bistro. The reader who discovered this place for us enthused about Natalia's home cooking and waxed more lyrically still about the delicious fruit juices at breakfast (a mix of apple, pear, grapefruit and lemon). Upstairs you'll find simple, spotless guest bedrooms. There's also a quiet lounge along the corridor from your room. A great little place.

rooms	12 doubles.
price	€ 48. VAT included.
meals	Lunch/dinner € 12.
closed	Rarely.
directions	From Santander for Oviedo, on A-67, then E-70. Exit Cabezón de la Sal. Then CA-180 for Reinosa; over bridge at Santa Lucía; left on CA-812 to Cos. Casona on right in village.

Natalia San Martín & Elias Puente San Martín
tel   +34 942 701550
fax   +34 942 802091

Casona Torre de Quijas

Barrio Vinueva 76, 39590 Quijas, Cantabria

This is a grand yet intimate little hotel within striking distance of Santander and only minutes from the beach. Along with a sizeable farm, it once belonged to a rich lawyer who lost everything at cards – except the house. It fell into ruin; Pilar and her husband bought it as a family home, then transformed it into a hotel. It's splendidly furnished with fine antiques; fresh fruit and dried flowers set the mood and the modern art reflects your hosts' taste and flair. A log fire and deep, comfortable chairs covered in pale cotton make for a stylish and attractive sitting room. Polished chestnut floors run throughout, and the bedrooms are mostly white with a fresh cotton theme. Our favourite is the Lemon Room, in the former chapel, carefully renovated so that the original arches still stand. Rooms are more intimate in the upper part of the house with its old oak beams. We also liked the small bar with its cane furniture and bright lace-covered lamps, and the quiet covered patio full of greenery. No dinners, but there are two good restaurants nearby. Perfect for a first or last night in Spain – and the staff are charming, too.

rooms	19: 15 doubles, 2 singles, 2 suites.
price	€ 59–€ 102; single € 37–€ 47; suite € 77–€ 108.
meals	Breakfast € 6.
closed	15 December–15 January.
directions	From Santander A-67/E-70 for Oviedo. Exit at km238 for Quijas. In village hotel on left, next to tower.

Pilar García Lozano

tel	+34 942 820645
fax	+34 942 838255
e-mail	informacion@casonatorredequijas.com
web	www.casonatorredequijas.com

map 4   entry 60

Hostal Mexicana

Juan de Herrera 3, 39002 Santander, Cantabria

The photograph says it all: at the Mexicana you enter another era. This modest little *hostal* first opened its doors in 1955 (when the picture was taken) and has been run by the family of María Eufemia ever since. Do consider the Mexicana if you are looking for something not too grand; a kinder and more gentle family you could not hope to meet. You would probably not write home about the rooms but you will have a comfortable night here. Bedrooms are net-curtained, furniture is unmistakably Spanish, bathrooms are spick and span, and, considering that you are right in the town centre, the place is excellent value. But what we like most about the Mexicana is its tiny restaurant: with its cornices, deliciously dated 50s furniture and sense of timelessness, it's like an English seaside B&B. The food, as you might expect, is simple home cooking. Santander has the charm of a slightly down-at-heel port; watch boats on the quay, admire the peaks of Cantabrian Cordillera on a clear day, eat fish of the day in authentic sailors' restaurants.

rooms	31 doubles/twins.
price	€31–€63; single €20–€34.
meals	Breakfast €3; lunch/dinner €11.
closed	Rarely.
directions	In town centre, close to Plaza del Ayuntamiento, next to Banco Zaragoza. Underground parking in square offers reduction for Mexicana guests.

María Eufemia Rodríguez & Caridad Gómez Rodrígu

tel +34 942 222350
fax +34 942 222350

Palacio de Soñanes

Barrio del Quintanal 1, 39640 Villacarriedo, Cantabria

You can only stand and gaze in awe. This architectural gem, with its astonishingly well-preserved stone façade, deserves a mention in any Cantabrian guide. It was decaying gracefully when the owners found it empty, years of neglect having saved its innards from being torn out by developers. Thanks to the vision of the owners, you can now enjoy its magnificence not as an earnest sightseer, guidebook in hand, but as a guest. And the baroque style of the exterior is mirrored on the inside: wherever you look, beautifully carved, honey-soft stone. The central tower has fluted stone columns that appear to stand upon each other's shoulders to span dome to floor, and the décor is luxurious, one might almost say regal (are those *fleurs de lys* on the carpets?). No-one need worry about stepping out of bed onto a cold stone floor. Pedro Jerez presides over the kitchens and is a master of nouvelle cuisine; the mouthwatering puff pastry starters disappear off the plate with alarming speed. The dining room may be a touch formal for some, but is likely to be redeemed by the Spanish habit of never whispering in restaurants. *A Rusticae hotel.*

rooms	30: 28 doubles, 2 suites.
price	€ 100-€ 180; single € 90-€ 142; suite € 212-€ 405.
meals	Breakfast € 8; lunch/dinner € 24-€ 38 à la carte.
closed	Rarely.
directions	From Santander, A-67 to Torrelavega. Then N-634 for Bilbao. At km223, N-623 for Burgos. Through Puerto Viesgo to El Soto; left on CA-270 to Villacarriedo. Hotel 500m on left, signed.

Elena Ortega

tel	+34 942 590600
fax	+34 942 590614
e-mail	informacion@palaciodevillacarriedo.com
web	www.palaciodevillacarriedo.com

map 4   entry 62

Hotel Torre de Ruesga
39810 Valle de Ruesga, Cantabria

Sitting on the banks of the river Asón, the historic building matches elegance with sobriety: a perfectly renovated 17th-century palace surrounded by idyllic gardens. You enter through one of three glazed arches into a stone-finished hall with a cosy little bar to your right: this is a charming hotel, and the feel is informal and peaceful. The interior has been lovingly embellished with frescoes by the 19th-century Catalan painter, Leon Criach – our favourite is in the pink-coloured banqueting hall on the first floor. On either side are recreational rooms for board games or a quiet read. Guest bedrooms are palatially finished in stone and wood, with the fittings of a modern hotel. In the restaurant – equally ornate – dinner is a mixture of Cantabrian and international cooking accompanied by fine wines from the well-stocked *bodega*. For the best view of Torre de Ruesga, take tea on the terrace or sit in the garden; the delightful grounds also house a large swimming pool with its own gymnasium and sauna, and five new suites with hydro-massage. This is a marvellous place to relax and unwind. *A Rusticae hotel.*

rooms	15: 6 twins/doubles, 9 suites.
price	€78-€102; suite €96-€132.
meals	Lunch/dinner €18 set menu; €25-27 à la carte.
closed	2 weeks in January.
directions	From Santander, A-8 for Bilbao. Exit Colindres, then south on N-629 to Ramales de Victoria. Right on C-261 to Arredondo to Valle, then right at sign for hotel.

Carmen Caprile Stucchi

tel	+34 942 641060
fax	+34 942 641172
e-mail	reservas@t-ruesga.com
web	www.t-ruesga.com

BASQUE COUNTRY, NAVARRA & LA RIOJA

"I speak Spanish to God, Italian to women, French to men and German to my horse."

EMPEROR CHARLES V (ATTRIB.)

Atalaya Hotel

Passeo de Txorrokopunta 2, 48360 Mundaka, Vizcaya

Atalaya is one of the friendliest and most 'family' of Vizcaya's small hotels and owner Maria Carmen is a bundle of positive energy. You couldn't better the hotel's position, a stone's throw from the lively fish market and yards from beach and fishing boats on the edge of a deep inlet carved by the Cantabrian sea. The house was built circa 1911, protected by the Basque authorities as a building of national importance; an open, galleried frontage lets in the ever-changing light and allows you to contemplate sand, sea and the church tower of Santa María. The owners – kind, straightforward folk – proudly maintain their hotel, and will find time to help you plan your visits. The best rooms have sea views but they're all worth a night: quiet and comfortable with modern oak furniture, king-size beds and more gadgets than you need. A smart new bar is for the exclusive use of guests; sandwiches and Spanish ham are on the menu. This would be the perfect place to spend a last night before the ferry (and car and belongings are safe in the free car park). One of our favourites, with the wonderful Guggenheim at Bilbao so close by.

rooms	11 doubles/twins.
price	€ 80–€ 88; single € 64–€ 71.
meals	Breakfast € 7.50; dinner c. € 20.
closed	Rarely.
directions	From Bilbao, A-8/E-70 m'way exit 18. Then BI-635 via Gernika to Mundaka; left to village centre. Hotel near Santa María church, 50m from ferry.

María Carmen Alonso Elizaga

tel	+34 946 177000
fax	+34 946 876899
e-mail	hotelatalaya@hotel-atalaya-mundaka.com
web	www.hotel-atalaya-mundaka.com

Agroturismo Txopebenta

Barrio Basetxetas, 48314 Gautegiz-Arteaga, Vizcaya

Between Gernika and the rugged north coast, in an area of great natural beauty, Txopebenta is one of the most remarkable of a number of first-class B&Bs in the Basque country. The house bears witness to the boundless energy and optimism of its owner Juan 'Txope' Bizkarra. He decided that in order to create a guesthouse at his 19th-century farmhouse he would have to add another floor, and did so by careful use of old railway sleepers which he fashioned in every possible way – as lintels, stairs, roof supports, even benches and tables. The sitting/breakfast room is ideal for a convivial breakfast with delicious local cheese and fruit juice; a fire is lit in the hearth during the colder months. The rooms at the top are small and low-ceilinged but cosy; light sleepers should know that insulation between rooms is minimal. There is a terrace where you can sit out in summer. Your hosts love their native land and are keen that you should visit its every corner. Don't miss the 'painted forest' in the Oma valley and the Biosphere Reserve of Urdabai with its spectacular birdlife. And there are beaches just a walk away.

rooms	6 twins/doubles.
price	€38–€44.
meals	Breakfast €4.
closed	Rarely.
directions	From Gernika, Lekeitio road. After 6km left for Elanchobe. House on right after 0.8km.

Juan Angel Bizkarra

tel	+34 946 254923
fax	+34 946 254923
e-mail	txopebenta@terra.es

map 5   entry 65

Urresti

Barrio Zendokiz, 12, 48314 Gautegiz Arteaga, Vizcaya

One of the very latest Basque B&Bs to open, this is a dream come true for María and José María, Urresti's two friendly young owners, who have completely transformed the ruins of the old farmhouse they chanced upon in the deeply green countryside. From the outside it still looks like a 17th-century farmhouse; inside has a more modern feel. Breakfast is served in the large sitting/dining room, and good value it is too, with cheese, home-made jam, fruit from the farm and plenty of coffee. For other meals guests have free rein in a fully-equipped kitchen. Smart, impeccably clean bedrooms have parquet floors and new, country-style furniture; some have their own balcony and no. 6 is particularly roomy with a sofabed. The house stands in beautiful rolling countryside with the sea not far away – and Gernika, too. There are old forests of oak and chestnut to be explored on foot, or on the bikes which are available for guests. The whole area is a Natural Park and many come here just for the birdlife.

rooms	6 doubles. 1 self-catering apartment for 2; 1 apartment for 4.
price	€38–€44; apartments €58–€84.
meals	Good restaurants 3km; self-catering available.
closed	Rarely.
directions	From Gernika, Lekeitio road. At fork continue on lower road for Lekeitio. After 6km, left for Elanchobe. House on right after 1.2km at sign 'Nekazal Turismoa' (don't follow earlier sign for a different B&B).

María Goitia

tel	+34 946 251843
fax	+34 946 251843
e-mail	urresti@wanadoo.es

Ziortxa-Beitia

Goiherria 13, 48279 Bolibar, Vizcaya

Our inspector arrived with a bag of pears and green peppers and asked the owner – known as 'Paco' to all and sundry – if they could be incorporated into his evening meal. Without batting an eyelid, Paco whisked the ingredients off to the kitchen. The peppers later appeared with some freshly cooked pork and the pears poached in wine. This is not so much an example of Basque hospitality, rather an illustration of your practical host's no-fuss-no-frills attitude. His old farmhouse sits in remote countryside below a Cistercian monastery on the famous pilgrim route to Santiago de Compostela. The rooms are basic modern-rustic but comfortable and very clean. Food is of the home-cooked variety and although the bar can get quite lively in the evenings, the nights are blissfully quiet – just the hoot of the odd owl to serenade you. Nearby Bolibar is the birthplace of Simon Bolivar, the liberator of South America. The museum is well worth a visit, as is a walk round the grounds of the monastery.

rooms	6 doubles/twins.
price	€38–€44; single €35.
meals	Breakfast €4; lunch/dinner €12.
closed	Rarely.
directions	From Bilbao A-8 for San Sebastián; exit 17 to Durango; here BI-633 for Markina. In village of Iruzubieta, left to Bolibar. Here left for Ziortxa & Colegiata. House on right after 2.5km.

Francisco Rios

tel	+34 946 165259
e-mail	zdiber@teleline.es

map 5   entry 67

Mendi Goikoa

Barrio San Juan 33, 48291 Axpe-Atxondo, Vizcaya

Peaceful it is, and utterly beautiful. *Donde el silencio se oye*: a place of silence, as the owners describe their hotel. Mendi Goikoa is one of a new breed of chic country hotels which provide *Cordon Bleu* cooking and a bed to match. The hotel is made up of two 19th-century farms — big, handsome buildings in a huge meadow with wide views from every room. The main restaurant, once the old barn, is vast and high-ceilinged and packed with antiques; the emphasis is on traditional Basque dishes with a few of the chef's own creations. There is a smaller breakfast room and a gem of a bar in the other building. It is a popular venue for the suit-and-tie brigade though you shouldn't feel uncomfortable if you are not one of them; it is, however, a wedding-feast place and does get lively at times. The bedrooms are as good-looking as the dining room with beams, exposed stones, some lovely old pieces of furniture, lots of carpet and seductive views. And there are great walks up to (or towards!) the surrounding peaks to work up an appetite for dinner; do check that it will be available when you make your booking.

rooms	11 doubles/twins.
price	€87; single €59.
meals	Breakfast €8; lunch/dinner €26 set menu, €50 à la carte.
closed	15 December–15 January.
directions	From A-8, exit 17 for Durango. Then BI-632 for Elorrio. In Atxondo, right to Axpe. House up above village, signed.

Agurtzane Telleria & Iñaki Ibarra

tel	+34 946 820833
fax	+34 946 821136
e-mail	mendigoikoa@interbook.net
web	www.mendigoikoa.com

Hostal Alemana

Calle San Martín 53 - 1°, 20007 San Sebastián, Guipúzcoa

When visiting northern Spain do spend at least one night in San Sebastián, the country's culinary capital. La Concha, a marvellous sweep of golden sand, is the centre of life here and, just one street back from the promenade, Hostal Alemana: an ideal place to stay if the grander hotels are not your thing. The *hostal* occupies the upper floors of an elegant turn-of-the century townhouse, and the Garagorri family has run an inn here for more than 30 years. Bedrooms have been designed with business folk in mind, replete with safes, credit card keys, trouser presses, minibars and internet access; they are wonderfully roomy with good beds and large bathrooms. The breakfast room is a lovely place to start your day with a big buffet, good coffee and freshly squeezed orange juice; the light pouring in from the three windows in its curved wall should distract you from the taped music pouring in from elsewhere. It would be tempting to use this as a last stop before the ferry and have dinner at one of the seafood restaurants like La Nicolasa. Or bar hop and feast on any number of the delicious *pinchos* in this town where going out to eat is an adventure.

rooms	21 doubles/twins.
price	€ 57–€ 78; single € 45–€ 48 (low season only).
meals	Breakfast € 4.50.
closed	Rarely.
directions	From town centre head for beach (Playa de la Concha). Hostal short walk from here, behind 1st two rows of buildings, half-way around crescent shape of La Concha.

Luis & Roberto Garagorri Esnoz

tel	+34 943 462544
fax	+34 943 461771
e-mail	halemana@adegi.es
web	www.hostalalemana.com

map 5   entry 69

Iketxe

Apartado 343, 20280 Hondarribia, Guipúzcoa

Another enchanting B&B in the rolling green Basque. Very near the lovely town of Hondarribia yet entirely rural, Iketxe is a house that matches its owners: quiet and unpretentious. You can only wonder at the energy of the engaging owner, Patxi, who built his home virtually single-handed and made much of the furniture too. He finished it all just a few years ago but you would hardly know Iketxe is new, so faithfully have local building traditions been respected. The rooms are wonderful, both for their views and their decoration – wooden floors, bright kilims, handsome bathrooms; no two are alike, and there's no television to break the spell. Floors are terracotta and two of the upstairs rooms have their own balcony. It would be hard to choose a favourite but ours would probably be no. 1. Fátima will happily help at breakfast time when it comes to planning your visits or recommending one of the many restaurants in Hondarribia. Hats off to Patxi for realising his dream and sharing it with us: several readers have written to say how much they approve of the place and children love it here, too.

rooms	6 doubles/twins/singles.
price	€45–€50; single €36–€40.
meals	Breakfast €4.
closed	Rarely.
directions	From Irún towards Hondarribia. Before airport, left for Arkoll, then follow signs to house.

Patxi Arroyo & Fátima Iruretagoiena

tel	+34 943 644391
fax	+34 943 644391
e-mail	iketxe5@terra.es

Antigua Bodega de Don Cosme Palacio

Ctra. Elciego s/n, 01300 Laguardia , Álava

Don Cosme Palacio is one of Rioja's most reputed *bodegas*: the tempranillo grape has been working its magic here, in casks of French oak, for more than a century. Visitors have been coming from all over the world to taste and buy so it seemed right and proper that they should be offered food as good as the wine itself. Thus was born the restaurant – large rather than homely – where Jean-Pierre is Don Cosmé's French-Basque cook. Before or after dinner head down to the cellars where there is a bar for tastings and the main wine stores which have been decorated with a remarkable series of frescos depicting all things oenological: Dionysius, Noah (an early wine buff), harvest time and so on. Bedrooms are named after a different grape variety and are beautifully decorated. The emphasis here is more *bodega* than hotel, so this would be an entirely suitable stopover if you are on the Rioja wine trail.

rooms	13: 12 doubles, 1 suite.
price	€ 71, single € 62, suite € 91.
meals	Breakfast € 6.50; lunch/dinner € 20-€ 28.
closed	24 December-24 January.
directions	A-68, exit 10 for Lenicero. Through village, left to Elciego, on to Laguardia. Hotel on right on entering village.

Begoña Viñegra Uzquiano

tel	+34 945 621195
fax	+34 945 600210
e-mail	antiguabodega@cosmepalacio.com
web	www.habarcelo.es

map 5   entry 71

Sancho de Estrada

Castillo de Villaviciosa, 05130 Solosancho, Ávila

Dreaming of castles in Spain? Here, then, is a real 12th-century one which lets down its drawbridge to paying guests. It took Avelino Mayoral 22 years of careful renovation and reconstruction before he felt ready to receive guests; he is a man who likes to get things right. Decoration is deliberately 'historical' with lances, suits of armour and heavy, Castillian-style furniture; at the building's centre is a galleried dining room where medieval-style banquets are occasionally held. But most of the time the menu features the time-tried recipes of the Meseta: the roasted meats are memorable and the mark-up on the wines is surprisingly little. To reach some of the bedrooms you wind up the original spiral staircases pushing aside heavy crimson curtains – all very cloak-and-dagger. Following the dictates of the original building some rooms are large, others small, some have arrow-slit windows and a couple of them are in what was once the castle's prison. The last time we stayed some of the furnishings were beginning to look a little tired but a night at Sancho de Estrada remains a memorable and entertaining experience. *Reopens early 2003.*

rooms	12: 10 twins/doubles, 2 suites.
price	€62–€65; single occ. €43–€46; suite €84–€90.
meals	Breakfast €6; lunch/dinner €18 set menu, €27 à la carte. Restaurant closed Tuesdays.
closed	7 January–7 February.
directions	From Ávila, N-110 for Plasencia. After 5km, left on N-502 for Arenas de San Pedro. In outskirts of Solosancho, hotel signed to left.

Avelino Mayoral Hernández

tel	+34 920 291082
fax	+34 920 291082
e-mail	hotelesmayoral@hotelesmayoral.com
web	www.hotelesmayoral.com

Venta de Donamaría

Barrio Ventas 4, 31750 Donamaría, Navarra

A mouth-watering address! Donamaría is hidden away off to one side of a pass through the mountains between France and Spain, within striking distance of Pamplona; there's been a restaurant here for 150 years. The place has a long tradition of receiving travellers and your present-day hosts are sophisticated, amusing folk whose love of the finer things in life is given ample expression. These two old village houses (guest rooms in one, restaurant in the other) are packed full of antiques, old toys, dried flowers and a few surprises to boot; it all creates an intimate, relaxed atmosphere, some of it tongue-in-cheek. This is most certainly a place to linger over lunch or dinner; connoisseurs rave about the traditional Navarre dishes which have "a French touch and modern elements", and the *foie gras* is superb. The rooms are all that you'd hope for: big, with antique furniture, timbered ceilings, lots of dried flowers and richly-coloured fabrics. Mother, father and daughter welcome you most graciously into their home, set among old oak forests to make the heart soar.

rooms	5 twins/doubles.
price	€ 60.
meals	Lunch/dinner € 12 set menu, € 27–€ 30 à la carte. No meals Sunday evenings or Mondays.
closed	Rarely.
directions	From San Sebastián, N-121A for Pamplona. Then right into San Esteban & Doneztebe for Saldías. Donamaría 2km from San Esteban.

Elixabet Badiola & Imanol Luzuriaga

tel	+34 948 450708
fax	+34 948 450708
e-mail	donamariako@jet.es

map 6   entry 73

Hotel Peruskenea

Beruete, 31866 Basaburua Mayor, Navarra

The journey up to Peruskenea is by way of Navarre's deep forests; you are headed for a place of great natural beauty. The old ruin of this country manor was rescued by José María Astíz and has undergone a complete metamorphosis to become one of the Basque country's most charming small hotels. The building stands alone with its whitewashed façade and bright wooden galleries looking out across a glorious valley. Breakfasts here are unforgettable: not just for the great spread laid before you but for those amazing vistas – you may feel inspired to don walking boots and head off along one of the many pathways which criss-cross the countryside. The beamy bedrooms on the first and attic floors have handsome oak parquet floors, plumped pillows, large double beds and warm duvets. They feel light and airy and the bathrooms are excellent. There are two lounges, one on the first floor and the other up in the attic, with a fireplace. The hotel's food is trad-regional: hearty soups, stews and roast meats. You are at the heart of the Navarrese vineyards where the tempranillo grape rules supreme: do choose a local wine. *A Rusticae hotel.*

rooms	9 twins/doubles.
price	€ 68–€ 103; single € 54–€ 60.
meals	Lunch/dinner € 18.
closed	Rarely.
directions	From Pamplona, A-15 for San Sebastián. Exit km118, following signs to Udabe. Through Jauntsarats, then left at sign for hotel.

José María Astíz & María Cruz Barberena

tel	+34 948 503370
fax	+34 948 503284
e-mail	peruskenea@peruskenea.com
web	www.peruskenea.com

Venta Udabe

Valle de Basaburua, 31869 Udabe, Navarra

On the edge of a tiny Navarrese village, a small country inn where the food is out of the ordinary and the owners delightful: Juan José and Estela are young, friendly and keen for guests to discover this beautiful area. The cosy timbered dining room has ochre walls, a fireplace and stacks of antique pieces. There are two sitting rooms, one downstairs with a fireplace, one upstairs with peace and quiet. There are dried flowers and masses of old farm implements. The bedrooms have been decorated with the same affection, books and flowers echoing the warmth of the wooden furniture and floors. Rooms at the front are slightly smaller and give onto a (quiet) road. Udabe's food has already won it laurels and is highly rated by all the guides: Juan José formerly managed one of Vitoria's best restaurants. Specialities are *arroz con almejas y borraja*: rice with clams and borage, and *chuletón*, a superb beef steak served on a sizzling iron. The reputation is spreading and the meals are generously priced. Breakfast is a feast of fruits, yogurt and home-made jams... after which you may set off on bike – or horse – into the deep green of the Navarre hills.

rooms	8: 5 doubles, 3 twins.
price	€ 75–€ 120.
meals	Lunch/dinner € 18 set menu, € 45 à la carte. Closed Mondays.
closed	24 December-24 January.
directions	From Pamplona, N-240A, then N-130 for San Sebastián. In Latasa Uriza, at km117, 2nd right for Udabe. Inn on left as you pass through village.

Juan José Mate López & Estela Gordo Juarez

tel	+34 948 503105
fax	+34 948 503400
e-mail	udabe@jet.es
web	www.hotelventaudabe.com

map 6   entry 75

Hospedería Señorío de Briñas

Travesía de la Calle Real 3, 26290 Briñas-Haro, La Rioja

Briñas is one of the prettiest villages of La Rioja. Its stately houses and ornate churches pay witness to its golden age, the 16th century, when the region reached its economic zenith and many noble families set up home. The façade of this *casona* (mansion house) gives no clue as to the artistic treats that lie within. Most special are the *trompe l'oeil* frescoes which will have you groping for a walking stick, looking out of a window or pulling back a curtain… the fantastic creations of a Polish artist. Such decorative flair; it is hardly surprising to learn that Angela and Pedro are interior designers. They embarked on this project when the building was little more than a ruin (previous owners had ransacked the place in search of a mythical hidden treasure trove!). Treasures galore await you now: a vast, individually decorated, parquet-floored and blissfully quiet bedroom, a breakfast with freshly squeezed juices and a cosy bar where you can get to grips with Rioja's most famous export, its superb oaky red wine. *A Rusticae hotel.*

rooms	14: 11 doubles, 3 suites.
price	€ 108; single € 71; suite € 131–€ 143.
meals	Evening snacks available.
closed	Rarely.
directions	From A-68, exit 8 for Miranda & Zambrana. Then N-232 for Logroño. Through tunnel, then up hill & after 8km, left for Laguardia, Labastida & Ábalos. 300m to hotel.

Angela Gómez

tel	+34 941 304224
fax	+34 941 304345
e-mail	reservas@hotelesconencanto.org
web	www.hotelesconencanto.org

Hospedería Señorío de Casalarreina

Pza. Santo Domingo de Guzmán 6, 26230 Casalarreina, La Rioja

The bathrooms are a medieval extravaganza, with brick hydro-massage corner baths, heraldic scenes on walls, and windows that look across to the great portico of the monastery of St Dominic. The large, impressive edifice stands in the village square, delightfully with bandstand and weekend market; part of the building is still lived in by monks. The rest of the Hospedería has been transformed by Pedro, who won his hospitality spurs by effecting a similar transformation on an equivalent building in nearby Brinas. The building is grand, the furnishings lavish, yet the place somehow manages to avoid being impersonal, with local knowledge and expertise having been brought to bear at every stage. The frescoes are by a local friend of Pedro, the curtains and covers are made by his sister, the floorboards, of American oak, were once rioja wine casks. Just around the corner is the justly renowned restaurant, La Vieja Bodega (owned by another of Pedro's friends), which is said to offer some of the best food and wine in the region – and that's saying something. *A Rusticae hotel.*

rooms	15 doubles/twins.
price	€ 135–€ 145; single € 100.
meals	Excellent restaurant 5-minute walk.
closed	Rarely.
directions	From Bilbao, A-68 for Logroño. Exit 9 for Haro, then N-126 to Casalarreina. Hostal part of monastic building in main square.

Pedro Ortega

tel	+34 941 324730
fax	+34 941 324731
web	www.hotelesconencanto.org

map 5   entry 77

La Venta del Alma

Camino Alante 2, 24893 Robledo de la Guzpeña, León

Rural Spain at its most epic: wild mountains, forests, caves, waterfalls... and in a corner of this spectacular province, the weary traveller spots a light shining through the trees. You will be warmly welcomed at the Venta del Alma, where winter log fires and big comfortable sofas beckon. The house, rebuilt stone by stone by the enterprising José and his friend Guzmán, has been in the family for years, and combines traditional materials with modern comfort. The four bedrooms in the main house have lovely unrendered stone walls and beamed ceilings, their own bathrooms, beds and bedding way above average, and some well-restored pieces of furniture. Both house and apartment have excellent kitchens with solid wood tables from where day trips can be planned and meals eaten. Guests staying in the house will be given an epic breakfast (to match the scenery) and there are plenty of places to dine in Puente Almuhey. The combination of warm stone and mellow wood, log fires and rug-strewn floors makes this place as desirable in winter as in summer. Imagine those snow-clad mountains...

rooms	1 house for 8; 1 apartment for 2.
price	House € 168 per day; apartment € 57 per day.
meals	Self-catering.
closed	Rarely.
directions	From Leon, N-601 for Valladolid. At Mansilla de las Mulas, left on N-625 to Cistierna, then right for Guardo. At Prado de la Guzpeña, left for Robledo, over level crossing & up hill into village. House on left.

Guzmán Gutierrez Rodríguez

tel	+34 687 872137 / 630 700254
fax	+34 94 423 9578
e-mail	laventadelalma@terra.es
web	www.laventadelalma.com

Photography by Michael Busselle

ARAGON &
CATALONIA

*"I distrust camels, and anyone else who can go a week
without a drink."*

JOE E LEWIS

Hotel San Marsial

Avenida de Francia 75, 22440 Benasque, Huesca

Benasque is a pretty place in the Aragonese Pyrenees, a centre for winter sports – and, once the snows melt, walking. The San Marsial is an immensely warm, friendly little hotel with a smile at reception and rooms of human proportions, lovingly created by the family. A sensitive commingling of slate floors, beamed wooden ceilings and rustic furniture makes this feel like a home from home, a place to linger over breakfast... or a good book. Wood is the basic material: many of the pieces were made or installed by the carpenter owner. The bedrooms are very smart, with wooden floors and ceilings and matching curtains and bedcovers; many have hand-painted bedheads. Nine rooms have their own small terrace, all of them are light, medium-sized and have good bathrooms. In corridors, sitting and dining rooms there is a collection of old farm implements, skis, chests... and, in the middle, a hearth diffusing yet more warmth. The nearest ski stations are only five kilometres away and the hotel has special offers which include lift passes and/or skiing courses: ring for details.

rooms	25: 23 twins/doubles, 2 suites.
price	€60–€87; €132–€150. VAT included.
meals	None available.
closed	Rarely.
directions	From Lleida (Lérida) N240 to Barbastro then N123 to Graus. From here C139 to Benasque. Through village & hotel on left.

Marisa Garuz

tel	+34 974 551616
fax	+34 974 551623
e-mail	sanmarsial@pirineo.com

Casa de San Martín

22372 San Martín de la Solana, Huesca

It's quite an approach: once you've left the main road, prepare to stay in second gear – a long, rough five-kilometre track leads to the hotel. The house stands on a little green summit, surrounded by the foothills of the Pyrenees – it has glorious views. A dwelling is said to have stood here since 1200 but the present building is 18th century, with a tall, galleried front; you'll probably see a young Saint Bernard sunning himself on the patio. A copy of a painting by Goya dominates the hall, the portrait of an earlier owner who gave Goya shelter in the War of Independence. In the sitting room – formerly a chapel – bare stone walls, comfortable tartan-covered sofas, soft lights and a big fire: rustic chic. The bedrooms, too, are decorated with style and individuality, each named after a flower. Fresh ingredients for the *casa's* menu come from the garden; Mario describes his cooking as a mix of regional Spanish, Brazilian and seasonal. It's certainly good – as are the Somontano wines – and Mario and David make excellent hosts. *A no-smoking house.*

rooms	10 twins/doubles.
price	€90–€150. Single €90.
meals	Dinner €25.
closed	Rarely.
directions	From Barcelona, A-2/E-90 for Lleida. Junc. 6, N-240 for Huesca. Before Barbastro, right on N-123, then onto A-138 to Ainsa. Left to Boltana. 10km further to San Martín de la S. 5km track to hotel.

David Robinson & Mario Reis

tel	+34 974 503105
fax	+34 974 341147
e-mail	info@casadesanmartin.com
web	www.casadesanmartin.com

map 7   entry 80

La Abadía

Calle La Iglesia s/n, 22349 Sieste, Huesca

Birdwatchers will love La Abadía in the high village of Sieste. Train your binoculars on the skyline and follow majestic birds of prey – or, perhaps, the odd witch chortling by! Fear not, the hotel is armed with an *espantabruja* (a pointed, witch-scaring chimney) to stop them landing. This old manor has lintels dated 1571 and heraldic insignia from the Knights Templar. Solid stone walls support a stone roof with the amazing chimney – go into the sitting room, sit by the open plinth-like fireplace and look up: this astounding towering construction epitomises the quirkiness of the place. Rooms vary in size and numbers of beds; all have large bathrooms, some have air conditioning (check when booking). The restaurant is in the basement of the old stables: it is perfectly lit and serves hearty stews, roasts and steaks. Breakfast is continental or cooked. The hotel looks over forests filled with wildlife and clear, fish-teeming rivers, all set against the backdrop of the mighty Pyrenees – it is awe-inspiring. And there's masses to do, including rafting or floating down river canyons in a life jacket.

rooms	14 doubles/twins.
price	€36–€60; single €30; suite €60. VAT included.
meals	Breakfast €3.30; dinner €9. VAT included.
closed	20 December-15 February.
directions	From Lleida (Lérida) N-240 Barbastro then C-138 Ainsá. There HU-640 Ainsá then N-260 Boltaña. Just before village, left, cross bridge, signs to Sieste. To left of church.

Fernando Rodríguez Bielsa

tel	+34 974 502044
e-mail	info@laabadia.com
web	www.laabadia.com

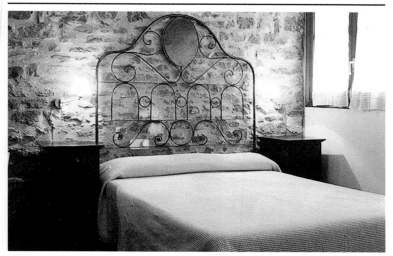

La Choca

Plaza Mayor 1, 22148 Lecina de Bárcabo, Huesca

Lecina de Bárcabo is for lovers of high places: a tiny hamlet in a rugged, wild part of Huesca perched at the edge of a limestone outcrop. Miguel Angel and Ana left teaching to restore this several-hundred-year-old fortified farmhouse and… to farm rabbits. But La Choca cried out to be shared so they opened the house: first as a farm school, later as a guesthouse. You will be captivated by the indescribable beauty of the views and the utter tranquillity of the hamlet. We fell asleep to the hooting of an owl and woke to the sound of a woodpecker. The public rooms have stone walls and ancient timbers; the bedrooms too are rustically simple, and TV-free. Three of them are big enough for a family and one has its own terrace. You'll eat well here (perhaps to background classical music): home-made jams at breakfast, regional dishes with a French influence at main meals, and Ana's own recipes, too. Cave paintings nearby, bikes to be rented in the hamlet and gorgeous walks straight from the door into the Sierra de Guara National Park. A favourite address, with two exceptionally kind hosts. Two self-catering apartments have recently been added.

rooms	9 doubles. 2 self-catering apartments, for 4 & 6.
price	€ 40; singles € 29; apartment € 36–€ 58. VAT included.
meals	Breakfast € 4; lunch € 22 (weekends only); dinner € 12.
closed	November & Christmas.
directions	From Huesca, N-240 for Barbastro, then A-1229 for 4km. After Angües, left to Colungo; after 15km, left for Lecina de Bárcabo. House 1st on left in village.

Ana Zamora & Miguel Angel Blasco

tel	+34 974 343070
fax	+34 974 343070
e-mail	chocala@wanadoo.es

map 7   entry 82

Hostería Sierra de Guara

Oriente 2, 22144 Bierge, Huesca

Rosa and her sisters run this new *hosteria* with advice from their parents, who set up the old and well-established joint across the road. A new building, which was still a little *al dente* when we visited, nonetheless has lots of potential, thanks to its position in a Parque National, and to the unaffected charm of its owners. Rosa's husband works at the celebrated Vinos del Vero and will arrange a free guided tour of the palace and *bodegas*. You can go rafting, horse-riding and climbing nearby, or take a guided birdwatching tour and see eagles and vultures feeding. Birds are a bit of a theme here: note the painted wooden panels on the reception desk. Bedrooms are uncluttered, with cool modern tiled floors, beds with slender metal bedheads and muslin or cotton drapes, and an armchair or two. The large terrace has views of the village and its hilltop church, floodlit at night. The dining room is huge, with frescoes of medieval viticulture adorning the walls – a sort of latter-day *Book of Hours*. At the back of the house is an almond orchard, which comes into its own in February when the blossom begins. *A Rusticae hotel.*

rooms	14: 11 doubles, 3 suites.
price	€ 60 (half-board € 86); single occ. € 44 (half-board € 57); suite € 74–€ 89 (half-board € 110).
meals	Lunch/dinner € 13 set menu, € 24 à la carte.
closed	January; 24 & 25 December.
directions	From Huesca, N-240 for Lleida. 5km after Angües, left to Abiego, then left to Bierge. Hostería on left at village entrance.

Rosa Viñuales Ferrando

tel	+34 974 318107
fax	+34 974 318107
e-mail	info@hosteriadeguara.com
web	www.hosteriadeguara.com

Hospedería de Loarre
Plaza Miguel Moya 7, 22809 Loarre, Huesca

This fine 16th-century 'palace' graces the prettiest of main squares in the little village of Loarre; breakfasting on the terrace is a treat. The building was recently restored, thanks to local government initiative, and no corners were cut in its complete facelift (the hotel retains full facilities for the disabled). You'll probably mention the food before the rooms on the postcard home: Aragonese and French Basque cooking and the best cuts of meat. Stay in autumn when wild mushrooms and game are on the menu. And do try one of the local Somantano reds (let yourself be guided by your waiter): they are all reasonably priced and honest, robust wines. Loarre's bedrooms are comfortable, clean and furnished with pine beds and tables and the occasional antique; the best have balconies giving onto the square while those at the rear have a view over the rooftops to the almond groves beyond. Do visit the medieval castle (see photo) and the fabulous rock formations – and griffon vultures – of the nearby Mallos de Riglos range. Jorge and wife Anna are young and friendly and make a great team; this is a place very much at ease with itself.

rooms	12: 10 doubles, 2 singles.
price	€37–€51; single €25–€32. Half-board €58–€72; single €35–€43.
meals	Lunch/dinner €11 set menu, €24 à la carte.
closed	Approx. 30 days in November/December.
directions	From Huesca, A-132 to Ayerbe. Here, right onto HU-311 Loarre. Hotel in main square; garage space for 3 cars.

Jorge Valdés Santonja

tel	+34 974 382706
fax	+34 974 382713
e-mail	hospederialoarre@yahoo.es
web	www.hospederiadeloarre.com

map 6   entry 84

Posada Magoría
Milagro 32, 22728 Ansó, Huesca

This 1920s family home has a genuine mood and has been caringly restored by the much-travelled Enrique. It's a well-insulated house with good winter heating and a pale-coloured interior finely finished with period furniture. Louvred shutters let in the natural light, the austere bedrooms are uncluttered and finely attired, good quality mattresses lie on 1920s beds and bathrooms have glass-brick walls to let the daylight in. But the real heart of the place is the communal dining area where a huge rock juts into the room beside the long table and the full-length wall tapestry lends the space weight. Here you will be served the most delicious vegetarian food – salads, soups, cheeses and home-made bread with lashings of organic cider. Breakfast is a purifying selection of muesli, cereals and mountain honey with good tea and organic milk. Enrique, with his intimate knowledge of the region and stories of foreign travel, will deepen your understanding of this undiscovered peak. "There's bears in them there hills!" You may not see one but it's worth making a trip to this wonderfully remote place. *Vegetarian food only.*

rooms	7 doubles/twins.
price	€43–€62; single €30. VAT included.
meals	Breakfast €6; dinner €12. VAT included.
closed	Rarely.
directions	From Pamplona N-240 for Jaca. Left at Berdun on HU-202 to Ansó. Here, 2nd left into village past wood mill, then bear left along narrow street up to church. Posada last house on right.

Enrique Ipas
tel +34 974 370049

La Pastora

Calle Roncesvalles 1, 50678 Uncastillo, Zaragoza

Uncastillo, as the name implies, is an attractive castle-topped town just to the north of Zaragoza in the Sierra de Santo Domingo. Just behind the town's beautiful Romanesque church of Santa Marta is this grand, 18th-century house – by far the nicest place to stay. The house's traditional elements of old flags, wrought-iron window grilles, terracotta tiles and wooden beams have been preserved and restored. Massively thick outer walls mean that even at the height of the Spanish summer it remains cool inside; in winter a woodburner keeps the little lounge as warm as toast. Guest rooms have no delusions of grandeur but with the same heavy stone walls, simple rustic furniture and antique washbasins they feel wonderfully snug. Inma is as charming and as unassuming as the delightful hostelry which she has created. Uncastillo is all too often passed by; visitors to the area prefer to make for Sos del Rey Católico, another medieval town whose claim to fame is that the local-boy-made-good was no other than Fernando II, whose marriage to Isabela would so radically change the course of Spanish history. *A Rusticae hotel.*

rooms	8 doubles/twins.
price	€45–€74; single €32–€38.
meals	Breakfast €5.
closed	Rarely
directions	From Pamplona N-121 south t hen N-240 Huesca; NA-127 to Sangüesa. There, A-127 to Sos del Rey Católico & Uncastillo. Here go round the church of Santa María & park in small cobbled square. 20m to house.

Inma Navarro Labat

tel	+34 976 679499
fax	+34 976 679211
e-mail	lapastora@lapastora.net
web	www.lapastora.net

map 6   entry 86

Hotel Monasterio de Piedra

Afueras Nuévalos, 50210 Nuévalos, Zaragoza

Prepare to enter a secret world of natural beauty. This 800-year-old monastery, a tranquil retreat in the hills above Nuévalos, is one of those gems of Spanish culture that ravish the senses and remind you why exploring Iberia is such a joy. Your room is a converted monk's cell in an imposing vaulted building overlooking the quiet monastery gardens. Impressive corridors invite contemplation but there's not a horsehair mattress or cold shower in sight: rooms are smart and the restaurant is air conditioned. So relax and take a guided tour of the cloisters, altars and tombs... and the first European kitchen where chocolate was made. In one of the former cellars, the Wine Museum gives another glimpse of life in days gone by. Or there is the Life of the River Centre with its three-dimensional audio-visual presentation of the life cycle of the trout. But the dense natural ecosystem of the park is the true jewel in this Aragonese crown. A 174-foot waterfall, a mirror lake, a sunken grotto: spellbindingly beautiful, it all awaits you – just go and lose yourself in the secret gardens and walkways.

rooms	61: 60 doubles, 1 suite.
price	€ 86; single € 53; suite € 106.
meals	Breakfast € 4; lunch/dinner € 20 set menu, € 30 à la carte.
closed	Rarely.
directions	From Madrid N-II E90 for Barcelona. Exit at km204 marker for Nuévalos & Monasterio de Piedra. In Nuévalos, signs for Monasterio de Piedra. Hotel 2.5km outside village in grounds of monastery.

Sr. Rabasó

tel	+34 976 849011
fax	+34 976 849054
e-mail	hotel@monasteriopiedra.com
web	www.monasteriopiedra.com

Las Tres Voces

Desaparecidos s/n, Espejismo, 50163 Farlete, Zaragoza

Don't be mistaken; Las Tres Voces is not for everyone. But if what you are after is a stay in the middle of one of the most forbidding environments in Spain, this may be the place for you. "They'll have the experience of a lifetime – if they can find us", says Esteban. This elusive explosion of greenery in the otherwise monotonous Monegros mountains is not unlike a mirage in the African desert... worth seeking out. Esteban confesses that the *Mozárabe* building he inherited from his grandfather is built on an underground canal, unknown to the outside world, that dates back to the Arab invasion. The Arab legacy is also evident in the beautifully carved door. A maze of rivulets fed by the canal criss-crosses the lush surroundings; an ingenious gravity system brings canal water – somewhat stagnant, but oh-so-natural – to each of the three bedrooms, where authentic horsehair mattresses reward the determined traveller. These rooms on the attic floor have open views of the Monegros to the south, while charmingly dilapidated balconies provide a refreshing spot to read... Who could resist?

rooms	3: 2 doubles, 1 twin.
price	€ 10–€ 15. Singles from € 10.
meals	Best avoided.
closed	January-December.
directions	From Zaragoza, Z-28 for Farlete. After approx. 73km road splits; take right fork; zig-zag up Sierra de Alcubierre hills & down to Monegros plains. Pass Espejismo, then left onto track by water tank. After 5km Las Tres Voces is visible; 20km further.

Esteban Perdidos

tel	+34 (0)999 123456
fax	+34 (0)999 234567
e-mail	info@lastresvoces.zg
web	www.lastresvoces.zg

map 0   entry 88

La Casona del Ajímez

Calle San Juan 2, 44100 Albarracín, Teruel

Hidden in the heart of the old religious quarter of Albarracín, this 200-year-old house sits on ancient foundations. Javier has transformed it to remind one of the Muslim, Jewish and Christian communities who once lived here in harmony. Rooms fuse style with simplicity, each with its religious theme. El Canónigo, once a library, has a studious feel; El Menora, with its plush four-poster bed, has a Jewish candelabra as its headboard; the two Muslim rooms are split-level. Detail is fine: wrought-iron beds, hand-painted wall designs, wood impregnated with scented oils, warmly-lit, exquisitely finished bathrooms. In the library-like dining room, writing desks become tables, the walk-through kitchen lends an air of informality and delicious meals are served with good regional wines. You will need the fortifying breakfast of toast, honey, cakes and fruit if you are planning a mountain walk, but if relaxation is all you're after, sit and admire the old walled town from the terraced garden: the tiled cathedral roof is almost within reach. Excellent barbecues are prepared here and Javier also runs Restaurant Gallo, a short walk away.

rooms	6 doubles/twins.
price	€ 72–€ 90.
meals	Meals available.
closed	Rarely.
directions	From Teruel, N–324 for Calatayud, then left on TE901 to Albarracín. Here, just before tunnel, left up hill to car park by Cathedral then up narrow cobbled street past museum towards church spire. House on left after 300m.

Javier Fernández Martínez

tel	+34 978 710321
fax	+34 978 700326
e-mail	c.ajimez@arrakis.es
web	www.casonadelajimez.arrakis.es

Hostal Los Palacios

Calle Palacios 21, 44100 Albarracín, Teruel

Albarracín is one of Teruel's most attractive walled towns; its narrow streets tumble down the hillside beneath the castle and eventually lead you to a lovely main square and the medieval cathedral. Los Palacios is a tall, balconied building just outside the city walls whose earthy colours seem to fix it to the hillside on which it stands. The 50-year-old building was recently thoroughly refurbished and thus was born this small *hostal*. The bedrooms, on the small side, are furnished with workaday wooden furniture; floors are decked in modern tiles. The fabrics are a shade satiny but forgive this little lapse; these are utterly Spanish rooms, impeccably clean and the views from their small balconies are second to none. It is good to escape from telephone and television; the owners are keen not to disturb their guests' silent nights. The little breakfast room/bar area has views, too. While busy preparing your breakfast the owners will happily chat about trips from the *hostal*. This little inn has few pretensions, is amazingly cheap and we recommend it wholeheartedly if you are happy with more simple accommodation.

rooms	16 doubles/twins.
price	€ 30; single € 18. VAT included.
meals	Breakfast € 1.8; lunch/dinner € 8.
closed	Rarely.
directions	From Teruel N-234 north for Zaragoza. After 8km, left on TE-901 to Albarracín. Here through tunnel, right after 150m. Hostal 2nd house on right.

Valeriano Saez Lorenzo

tel	+34 978 700327
fax	+34 978 700358

map 14   entry 90

El Tozal
Rincón 5, 44001 Teruel, Teruel

Utterly, delightfully Spanish, though not for the fainthearted. Nor for those who like to take breakfast in quiet corners. But the *fonda* philosophy is all about celebrating and preserving the traditions of the region and its people, and this El Tozal does to the letter. Come in the middle of the *feria* and you will find the oldest inn in Spain heaving with people, some of them sleeping off the excesses of the night before. A vibrant meeting place, in the heart of town, and with live jazz most weekends: this is where it all happens. The façade is deep pink, dotted with wrought-iron balconies jammed with geraniums, and you enter via a huge bar, a meeting place for young and old alike. The bedrooms, with their antique furniture and tiled floors, have an appropriately 'period' feel, which is just as Rafael, your ebullient host, intended. You will notice also his vast collection of traveller's memorabilia on display in the bar: trunks, bedwarmers, time-pieces – and more in the attic! – giving a sense of a long and reverent, if slightly quirky, tradition of hospitality. A proud institution, rooted firmly in the past.

rooms	19 twins/doubles.
price	€30–€45; single €21–€27. VAT included.
meals	Restaurants nearby.
closed	Rarely.
directions	Located in old quarter of Teruel. Ask for market ('el mercado') & arches ('los arcos').

Rafael Tolosa Montón
tel +34 978 601022

Hotel Esther

44431 Virgen de la Vega, Teruel

The high mountains and hilltop villages of the Maestrazgo have only recently begun to awaken the curiosity of those in search of new pastures to walk and ski. At the heart of this wild and beautiful area the modern little Esther is one of our favourite places. It is a purely family business – father, mother and son look after bar, reception and restaurant. The focus is the dining room. It is modern, but a timbered roof, mounted ceramic plates and a lovely tiled picture of Jaca help to create intimacy. You can expect a memorable meal here: specialities are roast lamb and kid as well as jugged meats like turkey and rabbit. Try the junket with honey for dessert. There is a good choice of wines and you can trust Miguel's recommendations. Decoration is the same upstairs and down: tiled floors, simple wooden furniture. The bedrooms have small bathrooms and are irreproachably clean. Hotel Esther is another of the small places included here which prove that modern hotels can have a heart, too. Honest prices for rooms and food; you may well be the only foreigner staying here and if you're not, we bet the others are travelling with this guide!

rooms	23: 5 singles, 13 doubles, 2 family, 3 suites.
price	€54–€74; single €27; family €84; suite €90–€108.
meals	Breakfast €4.50; lunch/dinner €15 set menu, €27 à la carte.
closed	8-25 September.
directions	From Valencia for Barcelona; at Sagunto, left on N-234 for Teruel. TE-201 to Mora de Rubielos, then TE-201 for Alcalá de la Selva. 2km before Alcalá on right.

Miguel Andrés Rajadel García

tel	+34 978 801040
fax	+34 978 808030
e-mail	hotelesther@gudar.com

map 14   entry 92

Hostal Guimera
Agustín Pastor 28, 44141 Mirambel, Teruel

You are in the heart of the old quarter of Mirambel, one of the most beautiful of the hilltop villages of the Maestrazgo – a place so well preserved that when Ken Loach came to film his 1930s drama *Land and Freedom* it was enough to move a few cars and the cameras were up and rolling. A lovely arch leads you through the town walls and straight into the village's main street; on your left is Hostal Guimera. The inn is just ten years old but you would never guess: it is a lovely stone building that is utterly faithful to local tradition and fits perfectly between much older houses on both sides. On the ground floor are the bar and the restaurant, which serves simple home cooking. Upstairs the rooms are as unpretentious as your hosts but they lack nothing and are impeccably clean with simple wooden furniture and shutters. Bathrooms are smallish but have good quality towels. The rooms at the back look over terracotta roofs to the mountains beyond; a few have their own terrace. When leaving you may be tempted to question your bill; can it really be so little?

rooms	17 doubles/twins.
price	€24–€30; single €15. VAT included.
meals	Breakfast €3; lunch/dinner €8. VAT included.
closed	Rarely.
directions	From Valencia A-7 for Barcelona; exit for Vinarós. Here N-232 to Morella; just before Morella, CS-840 to Forcall. Here road to La Mata de Morella, then Mirambel. Under arch, Guimera along on left.

Pedro Guimera
tel	+34 964 178269
fax	+34 964 178293
e-mail	guimera@turismomaestrazgo.com

Masía del Aragonés
44586 Peñarroya de Tastavins, Teruel

Rising majestically above open pastures this lovingly restored, 16th-century Aragonese farm has a three-storey stone tower with six guest rooms. It was once a weekend retreat for wealthy locals; today it is more simply furnished. Its airy, sitting/dining room has stone walls hung with old farm implements, contemporary tiles, pine furniture and a fine wood-burning stove. This is where you enjoy Pilar's cooking with nearly all ingredients home-grown or reared: she prepares wholesome soups and stews and simple puddings accompanied by her home-brewed wine and liqueurs. Bedrooms are somewhat spartan but a good size and have iron bedsteads, homespun curtains and modern bathrooms. With arched windows and an open layout, we liked those on the top floor best, where it would be wonderful to sit and decide which of the many possible excursions to make into the historic and remote hinterland. The scenery is epic, the mountains are home to ibex and eagles, there are crystalline rock pools above Beceite, and Valderrobres is worth a visit. The Andreu family go out of their way to make sure your stay is memorable.

rooms	6 doubles/twins.
price	€28–€42.
meals	Lunch €9,50–€12; dinner €9–€12.
closed	Rarely.
directions	Barcelona A-7, exit junc. 38 for L'Hospitalet de L'Infant y Móra. On to Valderrobres. There, left to Fuentespalda, on for Monroyo, left for Peñarroyo de T. After 500m right to Herbes; signed after 1.6km; 3km of track.

Pilar & Manuel Andreu
tel   +34 978 769048

map 15   entry 94

La Torre del Visco
Apartado 15, 44580 Valderrobres, Teruel

Bajo Aragón is one of Spain's best-kept secrets: beautiful, wild, unspoilt, stacked with natural and man-made treasures. Stay with Piers and Jemma and renew body and spirit in their superbly renovated medieval farmhouse. Standards of comfort, decoration and food are high yet the atmosphere at Visco is deeply relaxing. Their farmland and forests protect the house from modern noise and nuisance; peace is total inside and out, with neither phone nor TV to disturb you in your room. After a day of discovery settle with one of their 7,000 books in front of a great log fire, delight in their eclectic taste – each piece of furniture, be it antique, modern or rustic, Art Deco or Nouveau, fits exquisitely with old tiles, beams and exposed brick. Food is their passion and you will eat superbly round the big polished table: a feast of own-farm produce accompanied by a fine selection of wines. Breakfast in the great farmhouse kitchen is also renowned. A night at Visco is a treat never to be forgotten and it is refreshing to come across ex-pats who have mastered the language of their adopted country and who are so knowledgeable about its culture.

rooms	14: 11 doubles, 3 suites.
price	Half-board €200–€240; suite €300.
meals	Breakfast and dinner included.
closed	Rarely.
directions	From Barcelona A-7 south for Valencia. Exit junc. 38 for L'Hospitalet de L'Infant y Móra. Signs to Móra la Nova, then Gandesa. There for Alcañiz, but left in Calaceite to Valderrobres. There left for Fuentespalda; after 6km, right. Follow track to house.

Piers Dutton & Jemma Markham

tel	+34 978 769015
fax	+34 978 769016
e-mail	info@torredelvisco.com
web	www.torredelvisco.com

Hotel El Convent

El Convent 1, 44596 La Fresneda, Teruel

El Convent's massive front door is set in a creamy stone archway, flanked by a pair of cypress trees. One quarter of the door – a door within a door – swings open to admit visitors. It's an intriguing place; the site was acquired in about 1900 by a forebear of today's owners, and with the land came the ruins of a church built in 1613, part of the Convent of the Order of St Francis of Paula. By the time the forebear arrived on the scene, little more remained than the church's outer walls – the shell for his grand new house. A century on, the house, in turn, has been converted into an unusual hotel with a tranquil garden. The structure imposed by the original building makes for lofty, unexpected rooms, and there is an arresting mix of ancient and modern: beamed, vaulted ceilings and glass floors, exposed stone walls and high tech fittings, conventual austerity and secular comfort. Particularly striking are the central patio and restaurant in what were once the choir and nave, with former side chapels providing intimate dining areas. The food, as you might expect, is traditional Mediterranean with a contemporary slant.

rooms	10: 6 doubles, 2 twins, 2 suites.
price	€ 79; suite € 109.
meals	Lunch € 30–€ 40.
closed	2 weeks in January; 2 weeks in June.
directions	From Barcelona, A-7 to Reus, then N-420 for Falset, Calaceite & La Fresneda. From Madrid, A-2, N-II to Zaragoza, then N-232 for Alcaniz, then N-231 for La Fresneda.

Mariano Romeo Arbiol

tel	+34 978 854850
fax	+34 978 854851
e-mail	hotel@hotelelconvent.com
web	www.hotelelconvent.com

map 15 · entry 96

Hotel La Parada del Compte

Antigua Estación del Ferrocarril, 44597 Torre del Compte, Teruel

The old railway station of Torre del Compte, hidden away in the valley below the village, has recently been given a new lease of life, thanks to the dynamism of owners who believed that rural tourism and modern design could be happy bedfellows. At the end of the road cutting down from the village a highly original ochre-and-Bordeaux-coloured hotel awaits. Here to be discovered: designer furniture, bold use of glass and metal, state-of-the-art bathrooms and beds – it works wonderfully well. Each bedroom's colour and decoration is inspired by a different town in Spain; thus Madrid is about classical elegance, Mérida is inspired by Roman motifs, and the whites and blues of Valencia evoke the Mediterranean. It's hard to choose a favourite but we would go for França because it gets the sun first thing. All fittings and furnishings are top of the range, from taps to beds to sofas. Relax in a light, airy reading room, dine on innovative and beautifully presented, contemporary Mediterranean food, then head out (perhaps along the old railway track, by bike) to discover the wilderness and wonder of this part of Spain. *A Rusticae hotel.*

rooms	11: 8 doubles/twins, 3 suites.
price	€ 100–€ 145; single € 90; suite € 160.
meals	Breakfast € 10; lunch/dinner € 30 set menu, € 40–€ 50 à la carte.
closed	10-31 January.
directions	A-7 exit for Hospitalet Del Infante & Mora de Ebru. From Mora, N-420 Alcañiz. Just after Calaceite, left to Torre del Compte.

José María Naranjo & Pilar Vilés

tel	+34 978 769072
fax	+34 978 769074
web	www.hotelparadadelcompte.com

Mas del Pi

44580 Valderrobres, Teruel

This is the stuff of which back-to-nature dreams are made. High on a hilltop, Mas del Pi is literally at the end of the road – a road to remember. Ramón and Carmen have worked their 70-hectare farm for nearly 20 years; there are vines, olives and almonds, ducks and chickens and a big vegetable garden. What better way for them to meet new people and share their love of the place than by setting up a small B&B? Thus an old tradition has been rediscovered: 200 years ago this was a coaching inn. Things here are definitely rustic, hosts and house utterly unaffected. The Salvans are proud of their simple guest rooms with their tiled floors, old furniture and views across the farm; a new suite has its own garden; two doubles have living rooms. At breakfast there are home-made jams and cakes and newly-laid eggs. We have fond memories of roast duck and easy conversation; nearly everything from meat to veg to wine to liqueur is home-produced. Outside there is the farm to explore and glorious walks, with the Pyrenean sheepdog to accompany you if you want. "We would readily stay here again," enthused one reader; children love it because of the little pool.

rooms	7: 6 doubles, 1 suite.
price	€ 72; single € 36; suite € 125. Half-board only. VAT included.
meals	Lunch € 10.20; dinner included. VAT included.
closed	Rarely.
directions	Barcelona A-7; exit 40 L'Aldea & Tortosa. C-235 to Tortosa, then C-230 Mora la Nova. After 16km, left to Valderrobres. Just before village, right for 'Ermita de los Santos'. 4km, then track for 3km.

Carmen & Ramón Salvans

tel   +34 978 769033

map 15   entry 98

El Cresol de Calaceite

Santa Bárbara 16, 44610 Calaceite, Teruel

Then, an olive mill turned gentleman's residence; now, a small, sophisticated hotel with bags of charm. The historic little town, too, is a gem, with two or three really fine churches and a lovely network of 18th-century houses. This one takes its name from the old dialect word for the hand-lanterns which were fuelled by olive oil. There are reminders of the building's former function everywhere – the huge stone pillars, the olive press, the thick stone walls – but the transformation into modern hotel has been unusually subtle and stylish. Bedrooms have elegance and beauty, one with a lovely writing desk, another with an old Singer sewing machine, another with an antique Chinese costume on the wall, all with subtle lighting. Cinta is a thoughtful hostess, placing a jug of water and a bite-size paperback beside each bed, and there is pot-pourri at the window and artisan lavender soaps and oils in the perfect bathrooms. Breakfast is served at a huge farmhouse table and you can sample the local black olive paté before going out to explore this richly historic place.

rooms	4: 2 doubles, 2 suites.
price	€80–€90; suite €122–€150.
meals	Meals available at fonda down on main road.
closed	Rarely.
directions	Barcelona-Tarragona A-7. Exit for Hospitalet de l'Infant, then C-233 Mora la Nova. 3km before Mora, left on N-420 for Alcañiz/Calaceite. Hotel up in old quarter.

José Vicente Enguídanos

tel	+34 978 851174/ 609 908190
web	www.elcresol.net

Venta de San Juan
43786 Batea, Tarragona

Wonderful, the sort of place that some of us dream of finding in this apparently empty – and vast – Spanish countryside. If you begin your search for the *venta* in Batea you will be in benign mood, for it is a beautiful little town. There is a long drive up to the solid old house, deserted-looking among the fields and woods. Jorge and Clotilde are filling it with life, having inherited it from a grandfather who made his fortune in Cuba but decided to cut his losses and return after Independence... if you love dilapidated old houses you'll love it here. The entrance is full of country clutter, flagstone-floored with doors leading into ancient rooms still dressed in flock wallpaper and exactly as they were when conversation first sparked them into life. Some might focus on the (minor) inconveniences; others will appreciate the sheer authenticity of the house and thank us for bringing them here. The food alone makes the trip worthwhile and much of what you eat will have been grown on the farm. Jorge and Clotilde are young, modern, Catalan and charming – addicted to this mad, unkempt old house. *Minimum stay two nights.*

rooms	3 twins/doubles.
price	€ 36–€ 54; single € 18. VAT inc.
meals	Breakfast € 4; dinner € 11. VAT inc.
closed	December-February
directions	Barcelona A-7 Valencia. Exit junc. 38 L'Hospitalet de L'Infant y Móra & Gadesa. There to Alcañiz, right to Batea; P-723 for Nonaspe. At km7.3 before boundary sign for Zaragoza left on dirt track. At any fork keep left; house 2km.

Clotilde de Pascual

tel	+34 649 644724
fax	+34 93 4143854

map 15   entry 100

Cal Mateu

Calle Mayor 27, 43372 La Bisbal de Falset (Priorat), Tarragona

Every so often you meet someone who has taken on the role of 'mine host' for no other reason than the desire to share their home with others. To stay at Cal Mateu is rather like rediscovering a lost relative; guests have been known to shed a tear when they take their leave! Carmen has created a warm, authentic, comfortable home in a quiet cul-de-sac in the medieval town of La Bisbal – known for its ceramics and its old mansion houses built by a once-thriving Jewish community. Cal Mateu is of more recent construction but has the spirit of an older building. Its lounge, dining room and kitchen are low-beamed and interlinked, separated by stone arches; two further sitting rooms on each of the upper floors offer splendid views of the Sierra Montsant. The six guest rooms take their decorative cue from the rest of the house: they are smallish, beamed, and have simple red-chequered fabric for bedspreads, lampshades and curtains. The whole house breathes an air of unaffected warmth while meals are, as you would imagine, simple and wholesome and prepared by the most *simpática* of hostesses. Extraordinarily good value, too.

rooms	6: 2 doubles, 2 twins, 2 family.
price	€27–€45; single occ. €21. VAT included.
meals	Breakfast €5; lunch/dinner €11.
closed	Rarely.
directions	From Reus N-420 to Falset & there right on T-710 to Gratallops then to La Vilella Baixa. On via Cabassers (Cabacès) to La Bisbal de Falset. House in centre on main street leading to church.

Carmen Perelló Masip
tel   +34 977 819112
fax   +34 977 819285
e-mail   casapagesmateu@terra.es

Can Cuadros

Major 3, 25211 Palouet-Massoteres, Lérida

Arriving in the dreamy silence of siesta time, you'd never imagine the hamlet of Palouet could possibly contain a place like Can Cuadros. To describe this thousand-year-old castle as a mere hotel is to do it an injustice: each room is a step back in time, free of intrusions from the electronic age. Josep and Àngels are seeking not only to revive but to relive the traditions and culture of this corner of Catalonia. Bedrooms are full of fascinating artefacts and tapestries and nothing escapes the hand of history – not even the bathrooms, wittily named Can Felip after the infamous oppressor of the Catalans. Each has antique fittings which blend in perfectly with the centuries-old atmosphere. The dining room is magical, like a medieval fairy grotto, with an old wine press for a fireplace. You dine on ancient recipes, expertly cooked by Àngels using organic produce: Segarran pancakes, nettle soup, medieval Jewish puddings... all washed down with organic wines and home-made laurel brandy. Josep's vast knowledge of Catalan folklore, local artisanal activity and walks add to the whole, wondrous experience.

rooms	8 twins/doubles.
price	€ 50.
meals	Breakfast € 4.50; lunch/dinner € 12.
closed	Rarely.
directions	From Barcelona N-II to Cervera. Here, right to Guissona, then right to Massoteres, then follow signs to Palouet.

Josep Arasa & Àngels Miró

tel	+34 973 294106
e-mail	can_cuadros@airtel.net
web	www.cancuadros.com

map 8   entry 102

Casa Mauri

Santa Engracia, 25636 Tremp, Lérida

Few villages in Spain can match spectacular Santa Engracia for setting; from its rocky ledge you look across to hill, lake and mountain. The heady magic of the place soon worked its spell on Anne and Mike who have gradually restored and renovated a clutch of 200-year-old houses. Guests can choose between three-bedroom Casa Mauri and the two-bedroomed cottage, El Pajar. A new sitting room/terrace is being added to Casa Mauri as we go to press; expect a glorious backdrop when you come to open that first bottle. Rooms come with radiators and woodburners – concessions to modern creature comforts – and attractive wooden furniture; stone walls, beams, rugs and bamboo lamps lend character. Should you tire of that grandest of views you could follow dinosaur footprints from the door, visit Romanesque churches, birdwatch or choose between any number of fabulous walks in the area – you may see wild horses and boar. Ask Anne and Mike for advice: they've written a book on walks in the area. Rooms and dinner are both excellent value; from May to October weekly lets are preferred, and Anne and Mike will cook for you on request.

rooms	2 self-catering houses.
price	€ 60; singles € 30. Houses € 210–€ 645 & € 240–€ 745 per week. VAT included.
meals	Breakfast € 5; dinner € 15. VAT inc.
closed	Rarely.
directions	From Tremp, north for La Pobla de Segur on C-13. After garage on right, pass left turn to Talarn; after bends, left for Santa Engracia. Under r'way, on for 10km to village. Park & walk 300m up to house.

Anne & Mike Harrison

tel	+34 973 252076
fax	+34 973 252076

Casa Guilla

Santa Engracia, Apartado 83, 25620 Tremp, Lérida

This is a matchless position, a veritable eagle's nest. As you soar higher and higher to the hamlet perched high on a rocky crag you can only wonder at the courage of Santa Engracia's earliest inhabitants. Richard and Sandra Loder have a head for heights and after returning from Africa quietly set about restoring the buildings that make up Casa Guilla. A fortified Catalan farmhouse, parts of which are 1,000 years old, the house is a labyrinth, twisting and turning on different levels. There is a large sitting room with an open hearth and a library on the mezzanine floor. The bedrooms are simply but cosily furnished, with own bathrooms and terracotta tiles, heavy old beams, low ceilings... all deliciously organic. Tuck into big breakfasts with home-baked bread, generous dinners with lots of game – accompanied by that incomparable view from dining room and terrace. Caring and informative hosts in a fascinating part of Catalonia: many readers have written to say just how much they have enjoyed their stays with the Loders. Geologists, lepidopterists, ornithologists and botanists especially will be in their element.

rooms	4: 2 doubles, 1 twin, 1 family.
price	€ 92 half-board, € 46.50 single. VAT included.
meals	Packed lunch € 4.50; dinner inc.
closed	1 November-30 February.
directions	After 1.5 km on C-13 from Tremp to Pobla de Egur, left on road signed 'Santa Engracia 10 km'. House next to church, reached by own road; parking at house.

Richard & Sandra Loder

tel	+34 973 252080
fax	+34 973 252080
e-mail	info@casaguilla.com
web	www.casaguilla.com

map 7   entry 104

Besiberri

Calle Deth Fort 4, 25599 Arties-Valle de Aran, Lérida

If you're headed for the Val d'Aran, stay at the Besiberri: it is small, intimate and managed by the friendliest of families. The pretty, flower-clad building looks to the Alps for its inspiration and may remind you of sojourns in Austria. You enter through a small sitting room, with the dining area to one side: be greeted by an open hearth, a beamed ceiling, Carmen's flowers, a collection of pewter. It is wonderful to warm yourself in front of the fire after a long day on the slopes, and enjoy the light that streams in first thing. The 16 smallish bedrooms are cheerfully done, clad throughout in wood, with deeply comfortable beds and window boxes brimming with geraniums. Each floor has a balcony which looks out across the river; it runs fast – and deep – past the hotel. Splurge out and take the suite at the top of the building – it has windows to both sides, its own balcony *and* a small lounge. No meals are served apart from breakfast but you are just yards from one of the best restaurants in the Pyrenees. You'll long remember Carmen's natural ebullience; visit her before the village falls prey to further development.

rooms	17: 16 twins/doubles, 1 suite.
price	€ 67–€ 87; single € 53–€ 69; suite € 120–€ 150.
meals	Good restaurant nearby.
closed	May & November.
directions	From Lleida (Lérida) N-230 to Viella then C-142 to Arties. Signed to right as you enter village.

Carmen Lara Aguilar

tel	+34 973 640829
fax	+34 973 640829
e-mail	info@hotelbesiberri.com
web	www.hotelbesiberri.com

Fonda Bíayna
Sant Roc 11, 25720 Bellver de Cerdanya, Lerida

The meeting place and heart of the village for many generations, this *fonda* proudly upholds its tradition of hospitality. It is bang in the heart of hunting, shooting and fishing country and the busy proprietor, Jordi, can organise a pass for the trout fishing nearby, or point you in the direction of the Camino de Buenos Hombres (named in reference to those who passed along it while fleeing the Spanish Inquisitors). On your return, head for the restaurant where hearty and delicious regional food, and an impressive array of Spanish wines, are enjoyed by a fast turnover of visitors and locals alike. Bedrooms have polished wooden floors and are solidly furnished with beds and looming wardrobes reminiscent of a great aunt's, perhaps; some on the upper floor open onto a wooden balcony edged with geraniums. The bathrooms are unremarkable but have decent-sized baths. A place for those who love the great outdoors – the Cerdanya mountains are there to be explored – and who like to return to the comforting, communal warmth of a village inn.

rooms	17: 10 doubles, 7 twins.
price	€ 53; single € 35. Half board € 43–€ 86. VAT included.
meals	Lunch € 12.60; dinner € 14. VAT included.
closed	25 December.
directions	From Barcelona, C-1411. After Cadi tunnel, follow signs for El Seu de Urgell & Bellver. In Bellver, park in Sant Roc square. c/Sant Roc leads to Fonda from the square.

Jordi Solé

tel	+34 973 510475
fax	+34 973 510853
e-mail	fondabiayna@civ.es
web	www.fondabiayna.com

map 8   entry 106

Can Boix de Peramola

Can Boix s/n, 25790 Peramola, Lleida

Ten generations of the Pallarés family have lived and worked at Can Boix; three of them have turned this seductively located inn into something of an institution. But this is not a family to sit back on its laurels. Two years ago the main building was completely demolished and replaced with a pristine new structure which makes up in modern comfort what it lacks in venerability. All rooms are big and awash with mod cons: air conditioning, minibar, piped music, satellite TV, mirrored wardrobes, jacuzzi; those in the main building have a small balcony or terrace, those in the annexe a big terrace overlooking gardens or valley (and free and direct access to the hotel sauna and solarium). The food is a celebration of what is locally grown or raised; you can go full- or half-board. Presentation is superb, the wine list long, and even if the dining room is big enough for a banquet the accompanying views are as scrumptious as the meal and it still feels welcoming. The great ridge lowering above the hotel is a constant reminder of the sublime scenery of the Pyrenees. An immensely friendly hotel which caters for business people and travellers alike. *A Rusticae hotel.*

rooms	41 doubles/twins.
price	€79–€107; single €63–€86.
meals	Breakfast €8.50; lunch/dinner €18 set menu, €35–€45 à la carte.
closed	2 weeks November; 4 weeks January/February.
directions	Barcelona-Lleida (Lérida) on N-II. Exit Cervera & La Seu d'Urgell, Andorra. Through Cervera to Ponts; there, right on C-14 to Oliana. 3km after Oliana, after bridge, left to Peramola. 4km to hotel.

Joan Pallares

tel	+34 973 470266
fax	+34 973 470281
e-mail	hotel@canboix.com
web	www.canboix.com

Can Borrell

Retorn 3, 17539 Meranges-La Cerdanya, Gerona

Can Borrell was once the shelter of mountain shepherds who brought their flocks up to the high slopes of La Cerdanya for the rich summer grazing. High up on one side of a valley, this 200-year-old Pyrenean farmhouse of granite and slate is in the tiniest of villages with meadows in front and conifer-clad mountains behind. Wood is all about in beam, shutter and chair, while slate floors mirror the building's exterior. Its conversion from home to hotel has been sensitively accomplished; it is not over-prettified but has the warmth and intimacy of a little Cotswolds pub. The rooms welcome you with fabulous views and excellent beds. They vary in size because they follow the idiosyncrasies of an old house – and are uncluttered by hotelly gadgetry. Expect something out of the ordinary, though, at your (small) dinner table, where the cooking is, in the owner's words, "traditional Catalan – with a special touch". Uniformed waiting staff add a surprising note for such a rustic place. There are waymarked walks to neighbouring hamlets and cycle trails, too.

rooms	9: 8 doubles, 1 suite.
price	€ 73-€ 103; single € 61-€ 67; suite € 121-€ 145.
meals	Lunch/dinner € 24 set menu, € 33 à la carte.
closed	Rarely.
directions	From Barcelona, A-18 via Terrassa & Manresa, then C-1411 to Berga. Through Tunel del Cadí, then towards Andorra. After 5km, right for Puigcerdá on N-260; left at Ger to Meranges. Signed in village.

Laura Forn

tel	+34 972 880033
fax	+34 972 880144
e-mail	info@canborrell.com
web	www.canborrell.com

map 8   entry 108

Cal Pastor

Calle Palos 1, 17536 Fornells de la Muntanya-Toses, Gerona

Ramón and Josefina are quiet, gentle folk whose families have farmed this tranquil valley for generations. Originally two rooms next to their house were opened to guests; more recently Ramón's parents' former home was converted to create six new guest rooms. These are spotlessly clean and simply furnished, with tiled floors, a very Spanish choice of fabric and good beds. Our favourites were those in the attic where wooden ceilings create a cosier feel. The dining room is slightly soulless but don't be put off; you will be served eggs and bacon at breakfast if you ask, and Josefina's dinners are hearty and wholesome. She is happy to cook veggie dinners, too. Be sure to visit the Museo del Pastor (Shepherd's Museum) – a testimony to the work of four generations of Ramón's family on the surrounding mountainsides. The trans-Pyrenean, Mediterranean-to-Atlantic footpath runs right by the house and you may feel inspired to do part of it. In the evening, choose between Josefina's cooking and the quiet little restaurant next door. An unpretentious, authentic and peaceful B&B in a delightful and friendly hamlet – a perfect antidote to city life.

rooms	6: 3 doubles/twins, 3 triples.
price	€ 45–€ 56.
meals	Breakfast € 6; dinner € 12.
closed	Rarely.
directions	From Barcelona, N-152 for Puigcerdà via Vic & Ripoll. Just past Ribes de Freser, left at km133.5 marker, then 2km to village. House by restaurant.

Josefina Soy Sala

tel	+34 972 736163
fax	+34 972 736008
e-mail	ramongasso@logiccontrol.es

Hotel Calitxó

Passatge el Serrat s/n, 17868 Molló, Gerona

Molló is a pretty mountain village, over 3,000 feet up in the Pyrenees, on the edge of the French border. Hotel Calitxó has more than a hint of the Tyrolean chalet; strange to say, this building was once was a warehouse for the potatoes for which the village is famous. The hotel is set back from the road with an attractive balconied façade brightened by the pots of geraniums on the balconies. You enter through the rather barn-like restaurant; on the day we visited there was a merry atmosphere and nearly all the diners were local – a very good sign. The menu is a mix of Catalan and traditional Spanish with ingredients coming fresh from the market. Prices are more than reasonable. The bedrooms are all you need, generous-sized with local wooden furniture, each with a view of the surrounding mountains. Some have their own balconies – when booking ask for one *con balcón*. There are walks through orchid-strewn fields, skiing in the winter and beautiful Romanesque churches close by. An attractive conservatory has recently been added and we were won over by the Fajula family's easy cheeriness.

rooms	26: 23 doubles, 3 suites.
price	€85; single €64; suite €164. VAT included.
meals	Lunch €17–€21; dinner €14–€21. VAT included.
closed	Rarely.
directions	From Ripoll C-151 to Camprodón, & continue on C-151 to Molló. Hotel in village on left.

Josep Sole Fajula

tel	+34 972 740386
fax	+34 972 740746

map 8   entry 110

Hotel Grèvol

Carretera Camprodón a Setcases s/n, Vall de Camprodón, 17869 Llanars, Gerona

Close to ski slopes, mountain trails and a swag of Romanesque churches. Your first glimpse of El Grèvol may remind you of the Swiss Alps: carved pine balconies, exposed stone, slate and wooden floors and furniture provide the perfect backdrop for après-ski. But no cuckoo clocks reside here – rather, high ceilings, a free-standing central hearth in the sitting room and big windows to pull in the light. *Grèvol* means 'holly' in Catalan (a protected species here) and the décor uses the leaf for its *leitmotif*. Guest bedrooms, each named after an alpine flower, are four-star comfortable; those on the first floor give onto a balcony that runs round the building while attic rooms have pine ceilings, dormers and smaller stand-up balconies. The hotel has a warm, enveloping feel and the food is a mix of regional, international and *haute cuisine*. "It tastes good and looks good," says Antonio. There is also a vast choice of wines. The hotel, which in season fills with skiers heading off for the slopes in Vallter, has an indoor swimming pool and a bowling alley. Most seductive of all... the mountains all around you.

rooms	36: 30 doubles, 6 suites.
price	€ 112-135; junior suite € 134-€ 162.
meals	Lunch/dinner € 27.
closed	2 weeks in May; 2 weeks in November. Phone for dates.
directions	From Barcelona A7 for France then C-17 (former N-152) via Vic to Ripoll. There C-151 to Camprodón. Hotel 1500m from Camprodón on road to Setcases.

Antonio Solé Fajula

tel	+34 972 741013
fax	+34 972 741087
e-mail	info@hotelgrevol.com
web	www.hotelgrevol.com

Mas el Guitart

Santa Margarida de Bianya, 17813 La Vall de Bianya, Gerona

El Guitart is a good example of a new, more dynamic approach to rural tourism that has emerged in Spain in the last couple of years. Lali and Toni are young, friendly hosts; he left television, she left design, to launch themselves with gusto into the restoration of this old dairy farm. Thanks to their hard work – and stacks of good taste – they have succeeded in creating one of Catalonia's very best *casas rurales*. We loved the rooms: each is decorated in a different colour with Lali's stencilling to match; there are wooden floors and beams, old beds and washstands, rugs, decent bathrooms and good views. The sitting rooms are decorated in similar vein. Although no meals are available there are two fully-equipped kitchens as well as a washing machine at your disposal: this would be an excellent choice for a longer stay. Drink in the views from a hammock, laze by the safely fenced pool, set off on foot to explore the surrounding mountains: Toni has researched and marked new walking routes in the valley. Exceptional hosts, home and countryside and a wonderful place for families. *Minimum stay two nights.*

rooms	4 doubles. 2 apartments for 4.
price	€ 40; apartment € 80. VAT included.
meals	Self-catering.
closed	Rarely.
directions	From Gerona, C-66 to Besalú. On to Castellfollit de la Roca. Here follow signs for Camprodón on C-26. House signed in Vall de Bianya.

Lali Nogareda Burch

tel	+34 972 292140
fax	+34 972 292140
e-mail	guitart@agtat.es
web	www.turismerural.com/guitart

map 8   entry 112

Rectoria de la Miana

17854 Sant Jaume de Llierca , Gerona

Incomparable La Miana is not for those who are looking for standardised hotelly trimmings, but poets, artists and romantics will love it. In the middle of a vast stand of beech and oak, at the end of six kilometres of rough and winding track sits the old rectory in a fabulous setting. History is ever present: in the eigth century there was a fortified manor, in the 1300s a rectory was built – with vaulted ceilings, escape tunnel and chapel. It took courage and vision for Frans to embark on the old building's restoration and from the ruins has emerged a beautiful and simple – some might say spartan – hostelry. Much has been left as it was: the original flagged walls and the undressed walls. The old black and white photographs are touching in their directness, such as one of a group of people marvelling at the first radio to arrive at La Miana. Bedrooms vary in size, some with pastel walls, some with open stonework; all are furnished with rustic furniture and bright kilims and each old handmade floor tile is a delight. In the vaulted dining room downstairs, sitting on century-old pews, you will be treated to a genuine Catalan breakfast and regional dishes for dinner.

rooms	9 doubles/twins.
price	Half-board € 70; children under 7 half price.
meals	Breakfast and dinner included.
closed	Rarely.
directions	Figueres N-260 Besalú & Sant Jaume de Llierca. Left into village, 2nd left into c/Industria. 6km track to house following signs to Rectoria de la Miana (marked at all junctions). Just past Can Jou farmhouse.

Frans Engelhard & Janine Westerlaken
tel   +34 972 190190

Can Jou

La Miana, 17854 Sant Jaume de Llierca, Gerona

You won't forget your arrival at Can Jou: as you negotiate the six-kilometre-long dirt track you really do feel you are leaving the rest of the world behind. Round a final bend and you catch sight of the farm: high on a hill, overlooking miles of forest of oak and beech — wonderful. No wonder Mick and Rosa were inspired to revive this old Catalan farmstead in search of the good life: by working the land, by giving the house a family (they have four children), and by restoring the old barn to share the beauty of it all with guests. Bedrooms are simply furnished with a mix of old and new and lively colour schemes. Six have their own balconies. This would be a great place for a family holiday, with the farm to explore and horses to ride (a perfect place for beginners, and with marked forest bridleways for more adventurous riders). Rosa's cooking is excellent and many of the ingredients come straight from the farm; dinners are friendly affairs around one huge table. Close to the house is a beautiful spring-filled rock pool. If you're looking for Nature without the hotelly extras, head here.

rooms	14 doubles/twins.
price	€ 110 half-board; € 124 full-board. VAT included.
meals	Lunch and/or dinner included.
closed	Rarely.
directions	From Figueres, N-260 to Besalú & Sant Jaume de Llierca. Left into village, then 2nd left into c/Industria. On for 6km along track to house, marked at all junctions.

Rosa Linares & Mick Peters

tel	+34 972 190263
fax	+34 972 190444
web	www.canjou.com

map 9   entry 114

Mas Salvanera
17850 Beuda, Gerona

In a blissfully quiet part of the wooded Pyrenean foothills this solid 17th-century Catalan farmhouse has been transformed into the smartest of country hotels – your hosts still glow with enthusiasm for the project that changed their lives. The guest bedrooms, in an old olive mill next to the main house, are named after signs of the zodiac; one contains the old bread oven which once fed the village. Rocío's decorative flair is on show throughout: beneath old, darkening beams colourful fabrics have been mixed with antiques, many of which she has restored herself. Bedrooms are large and elegant and have generous bathrooms. The main building has an old well, vaulted ceilings, open hearths and exposed stone; the dining room is up one level and its centrepiece is an 18-place dining table. Everyone eats together here. Many of Rocío's recipes at dinner are Basque (paella and rabbit are two of her specialities) and rioja is *de rigeur*. Breakfasts are big and buffet, taken at any time you like. There is also a library – and a quiet walled garden with a pool sculpted in beneath the olive trees.

rooms	9 doubles/twins.
price	€ 113.
meals	Lunch/dinner € 27.
closed	1–10 January; 1–10 July; 11–19 September.
directions	Barcelona A-7 Gerona. Exit 6, signed Gerona Norte. Then C-150 to Banyoles & Besalú. Here right on N-260 Figueres, then left for Maià de Montcal & then follow signs to Beuda; 1.6km to hotel.

Rocío Niño Ojeda & Ramón Ruscalleda

tel	+34 972 590975
fax	+34 972 590863
e-mail	salvanera@salvanera.com
web	www.salvanera.com

Mas Falgarona
17742 Avinyonet de Puigventós, Gerona

Severino and Brigitta spent a decade searching for Mas Falgorana and what a find it is. Built from pale, almost golden stone, the farm is said to be the oldest in the region, dating from 1098. Their restoration is a deft blend of ancient and modern: light, mood-enhancing colours lift the spirits as does their passion for old things and old ways. The result is a vivid, Mediterranean look, enhanced by the surrounding cypress, olive and palm trees. An aquamarine pool and stunning views over the Pla d'Estany almost gild the lily; the interior is a stylist's dream. Dominated by beautiful arched ceilings, lounge and dining room have cool, neutral tones and their fabrics blend with the old flags and terracotta tiles. In contrast, a feast of colours runs riot in the bedrooms and bathrooms. A small, chic and cosy room has been set aside for aperitifs – a delightful spot for a pre-prandial cocktail. Cooking is innovative and Mediterranean, based on aromatic herbs and olive oil, and includes many vegetarian dishes. After more than 30 years in the hotel business Severino has achieved his dream, summarised by a favourite quote: "One eye sees, the other feels".

rooms	12: 10 doubles, 2 suites.
price	€ 145–€ 185; suite € 207–€ 249.
meals	Dinner € 29–€ 45. Restaurant closed Monday & Thursday.
closed	First 3 weeks of January.
directions	From Figueres N-260 for Besalú & Olot. After 5km turn right to Avinyonet & follow signs to Mas Falgarona.

Severino Jallas Gándara & Brigitta Schmidt

tel	+34 972 546628
fax	+34 972 547071
e-mail	email@masfalgarona.com
web	www.masfalgarona.com

map 9   entry 116

Finca Paraíso Darníus

Cami del Club Nautic, 17722 Darníus, Gerona

You are a stone's throw from the water's edge – 200 metres to be exact – in an area of astonishing natural beauty. There is enough walking, riding, tennis or sailing to satisfy the most hardened fitness fanatic. Finca Paraíso is decorated in rustic style, with comfortable, reasonably priced rooms and apartments. There is a large grassed garden, full of colour, with chairs and sunloungers dotted about in the shade of the cork trees. Beyond the sitting room is a lovely terrace – very much a highlight – with a huge pine table and pretty lamps. Christiane is French, and will give you a good continental breakfast in the garden or on the terrace. For other meals, you can nip across to the Club Nautic on the edge of the reservoir, or to Darníus with its bars and one good restaurant. The bedrooms are unremarkable but adequately furnished – some with nice bamboo and reed furniture – and are generally uncluttered. Not for Sybarites, perhaps, but a sound base for lovers of the great outdoors.

rooms	6: 3 doubles, 3 twins. 2 self-catering apartments.
price	€48, single occ. €40. Apartment €400–€550. VAT included.
meals	Restaurants nearby.
closed	10 December–1 January.
directions	From Figueres, N-II for La Jonquera. After 9km left to Darníus. At lights left to Club Nautic, signed. Finca Paraiso further on, on left.

Christiane Vernet
tel   +34 972 535662
fax   +34 972 535662

Can Xiquet
Afores s/n, 17708 Cantallops, Gerona

Stylish modernity on ancient foundations. With the lovely white and blue fishing village of Cadaques – the favoured haunt of Salvador Dali – up the road, one might expect nothing less. Indeed, this whole region is steeped in the art of the early 20th century, with Matisse and les Fauves having spent time up the coast at Collioure; and works by local artists hang here, a reminder that the artistic tradition is alive and kicking. The hotel is designed to make full use of its position, with huge windows keeping the sea and the surrounding hills permanently in view. Natural light and neutral colours are the keynote of the bedrooms, some opening onto their own terraces, and all beautifully furnished to emphasise the light and airy feel of the place. Dine under the cork oaks by candlelight, loll by the pool, make the most of the gleaming new gymnasium. An unusual addition to the ménage is the riding centre with its 20 horses and organised excursions as far afield as the Eastern Pyrenees. Young and enthusiastic staff complete the picture: Can Xiquet deserves the impressive reputation it is rapidly earning for itself. *Multi-lingual. A Rusticae hotel.*

rooms	11: 5 doubles, 2 singles, 4 suites.
price	€ 115–€ 180; single € 60–€ 70; suite € 145–€ 260.
meals	Breakfast € 8; € 21 dinner, € 35 à la carte.
closed	8-30 January.
directions	From Figueres, N-II for La Jonquera. Before La Jonquera, right to Cantallops. Hotel signed on left after 5km. Follow track.

Ingrid Teixidor

tel	+34 972 554455
fax	+34 972 554485
e-mail	info@canxiquet.com
web	www.canxiquet.com

map 9　entry 118

El Molí
Mas Molí, 17469 Siurana d'Emporda, Gerona

Unusually for this guide, El Molí is a modern building, but it more than earns a place in the 'special' category alongside its older Catalan neighbours. Although a relative newcomer it has already been awarded a Diploma for B&B excellence. Its position couldn't be better; you are seven kilometres from wonderful Figueres and the Dalí museum, while a 10-minute drive will get you to the beach at San Pere Pescador. The house is modelled on the traditional Girona *mas*. It has tiled floors, wooden furniture and big rooms with views across the garden to the fields and woods beyond. Maria's food is exceptionally good value. Vegetables, chicken and beef come straight from the farm and are accompanied by a good local red wine as well as an infusion of *hierbas* to finish. At breakfast, try the home-made yogurt and jams. This would be a good place to break the journey travelling north or south and Maria, who speaks excellent English, will help you plan your trips out, perhaps to the Roman ruins at Empuries or to the pretty fishing village of Cadaqués.

rooms	6: 5 doubles, 1 suite.
price	€51; suite €65. VAT included.
meals	Dinner €11. VAT included.
closed	Rarely
directions	A7 exit 4; for Figueres on N-II. After 3 km, right on C-31 for La Escala & Bisbal. After 4 km, right for Siurana. Signed in village.

Maria Sanchís Pages

tel	+34 972 525139
fax	+34 972 525139
e-mail	casaelmoli@teleline.es
web	www.girsoft.com/elmoli

Can Navata

Baseia, 17469 Siurana d'Empordà, Gerona

The village of Siurana is home to a small farming community, close to Figueres and the Costa Brava. Amparo has lived here all her life and renamed this 19th-century farmhouse after her father's native village. You enter through an invitingly shady porch into the living areas; decorated in the colourful regional style they have low, arched ceilings and traditional Spanish furniture. All the bedrooms are furnished with family heirlooms and four have a seasonal theme – we loved the 'summer' room, light and airy with an antique embroidered sheet for a curtain and lovely old mirrors. Another room and its bathroom have been converted for wheelchair access. This is an excellent place for children: there is a playroom on the ground floor, a big garden and farm animals to meet. Amparo has also provided an elegant library (pcitured below) as a refuge for parents. Ever obliging, she will send you details of places to visit, make bookings and prepare cycling and walking routes. Can Navata is almost a home from home: indeed, among the 'facilities' offered, you'll find *amistat*, the Catalan for friendship.

rooms	6 doubles/twins. 1 self-catering apartment.
price	€ 60–€ 70. Apartment € 125 per day (minimum 3 nights).
meals	Dinner (winter only) € 12.
closed	Rarely.
directions	From Figueres N-II then GI-31 (C-252) for L'Escala. After 4km right for Siurana. Can Navata on left as you enter Bascia.

Amparo Pagés

tel	+34 972 525174
fax	+34 972 525756
e-mail	apages@teleline.es
web	www.cannavata.com

map 9   entry 120

Can Fabrica

17845 Santa Llogaia del Terri, Gerona

On top of a gentle hill sits this 17th-century *masía* surrounded by fields, woods and Pyrenean views. Ramón is an engineer, Marta a designer, and their carefully restored farmhouse is now a characterful holiday home – the perfect place for a family reunion. Bedrooms are smallish, nicely furnished with old pieces and soft materials that set off the bare stone walls. The kitchen/dining room is beautifully equipped, the sitting room cosy with woodburning stove (there's central heating, too), and there's a swimming pool in the garden. Your hosts have environmentalist leanings, and by planting trees and farming their 17 acres of land have created a blissful corner of peace from which to explore the villages and Romanesque churches of the region. They'll tell you all you need to know about the many walks and cycling routes in the area. A lovely place with an exceptionally kind, vivacious hostess; without question, one of our very favourite places to stay in Spain. Be sure to try Marta's delicious sauces and jams. And if you are here in summer, do visit the Dalí museum – by night! *Minimum stay two nights.*

rooms	4: 3 doubles, 1 single.
price	€ 210 per day; € 1,200 per week.
meals	Self-catering.
closed	4 weeks January-February.
directions	Leave A-7 at exit 6 onto C-66 for Banyoles. After 8km bear right for Cornellà del Terri then at r'bout towards Medinya. After 2.5km left to Santa Llogaia; through village, 400m of track to house on left.

Marta Casanovas

tel	+34 972 594629
fax	+34 972 594629
e-mail	canfabrica@terra.es

Hotel Aigua Blava

Platja de Fornells , 17255 Begur, Gerona

It's something of an institution in Catalonia, this large hotel, but thanks to careful, friendly management and clever design it manages to remain welcoming and intimate. The bedrooms are individually decorated and ranged on several terraced wings that look out across gardens to a delicious hidden cove; so rugged a coastline is hard to spoil. Run by the same family (the manager has been here since he was 15), nourished by the same chef, tended by the same gardener for almost a half century, the hotel has a strong tradition of personal attention. Señor Gispert genuinely cares for each and every one of his guests, you are made to feel that you are special, and customer loyalty is strong. Breathe in deeply the sweet-smelling pinewoods, bask beside the huge pool, tuck into fresh lobster in the dining room as you look out across the sparkling waters of the small fishing port. Or linger over a cool drink at the snack bar on the uncrowded beach just below. The village, too, is one of the prettiest on the Costa Brava. You are close to the medieval town of Pals, and Palafrugell with its lively market.

rooms	88: 82 twins/doubles, 6 suites.
price	€121–€276; single €90–€136; suite €168–€300.
meals	Lunch/dinner €30 set menu, €39 à la carte. VAT included.
closed	3 November–21 February.
directions	From Gerona C-255 to Palafrugell. From here, GE-650 to Begur. Signed on entry to village.

Joan Gispert–Lapedra

tel	+34 972 622058
fax	+34 972 622112
e-mail	hotelaiguablava@aiguablava.com
web	www.aiguablava.com

map 9   entry 122

Hotel Sant Roc

Plaça Atlàntic 2, 17200 Calella de Palafrugell, Gerona

The Costa Brava remains a stunning stretch of coastline and this quiet little hotel could restore your faith – should you have lost it – in seaside holidays in Spain. It is very much a family affair – not just family-owned and run but a place where guests are valued like old friends. Many return. The setting is marvellous: a perch at the edge of a cliff, surrounded by pine, olive and cypress trees. The sea is ever with you at Sant Roc, its colours changing with every hour, and from terrace and dining room are views across the bay with its bright little boats to the pretty village beyond. The best rooms have seaward terraces but we like them all. Very striking are the hand-painted beds and many original oil paintings. With Franco-Catalan owners you would expect something special from the kitchen and you won't be disappointed: the fish is excellent and the range of fairly-priced wines good. A path from the hotel leads down to the beach and longer walks around the bay. Bertrand and Teresa remain humorous and charming hosts even in high season; their generosity permeates this exceptional (wonderfully child-friendly) small hotel.

rooms	48: 44 doubles, 4 suites.
price	€63–€113; single €51–€90; suite €166–€230.
meals	Breakfast €9; lunch/dinner €20–€30.
closed	Early-November-mid-March.
directions	From Barcelona A-7 north to exit 6 (Girona Norte) then follow signs for La Bisbal via Palamos then on to Palafrugell; from here to Calella; hotel signed.

Teresa Boix & Bertrand Hallé

tel	+34 972 614250
fax	+34 972 614068
e-mail	santroc@grn.es
web	www.santroc.com

Hotel Llevant

Francesc de Blanes 5, 17211 Llafranc, Gerona

On the car-free sea front in the lively village of Llafranc, Hotel Llevant is one of the Costa's most popular independent hotels. The building is 60 years old but you would never know; everything sparkles, from bathroom to crockery to the turquoise sea that (almost) laps its way to the door. The Farrarons family are proud of their creation, constantly improving and refurbishing. The bedrooms are all-white, straightforward affairs, large and airy, with every mod con. But what makes the hotel special is the restaurant/terrace on the promenade – ever animated, especially come evening *paseo* (stroll) time. Beyond this, the sea. What better place to watch the world go by than from this lovely terrace, with the hotel's prize-winning cooking an accompaniment? The beach at Llafranc is sandy, clean and safe. The Llevant is good value at any time of the year and has redecorated only recently. Note that in high season you are required to eat at least one meal apart from breakfast in the hotel.

rooms	24 doubles/twins.
price	€ 61–€ 83; single € 46–€ 61; € 102–€ 185 (half-board); single € 57–€ 145. VAT included.
meals	Breakfast € 8; lunch/dinner € 22 set menu, € 36 à carte. VAT included.
closed	10-30 November.
directions	Barcelona A-7 to exit 9 (San Feliu); past Palamos to Palafrugell. Signs to Llafranc; hotel in centre on sea front. Park in street.

Familia Farrarons-Turró

tel	+34 972 300366
fax	+34 972 300345
e-mail	hllevant@arrakis.es

map 9   entry 124

Xalet La Coromina

Carretera de Vic 4, 17406 Viladraú, Gerona

Viladrau is an elegant little town close to the stunning Montseny Natural Park. Its woodlands are grandiose, water flows and falls, indigenous trees and rare plants flourish. It is a wonderful place for walking. The building dates from the turn of the century when wealthy Catalans (they still come to Viladrau) built themselves summer retreats away from sticky Barcelona. The building, which looks more French than Spanish, has kept its elegant exterior but has been thoroughly modernised inside. The ancient/modern mix is visible in the decoration: the little sitting room has an old fireplace, and each bedroom has its own personality with antiques, English and French fabrics, good bathrooms and stupendous views. And the car rally memorabilia? Gloria's husband, Antonio Zanini, was one of Spain's most successful drivers. The Coromina prides itself on its food too, and on using local produce in season. Expect delicious mushroom dishes made with local *setas* when they spring up after the rain. A gentle small hotel which won its Michelin star for good food in its first year: "The food was equal to that of a five-star hotel," writes one reader. *A Rusticae hotel.*

rooms	9 doubles/twins.
price	€84–€88; single €68–€72.
meals	Breakfast €7.50; lunch/dinner €18.
closed	26 January–20 February
directions	From Girona C-25. Exit km202, then follow GI-543 to Viladraú. In village towards Vic: hotel on right after 50 yds.

Gloria Rabat Blancafort

tel	+34 93 884 9264
fax	+34 93 884 8160
e-mail	xaletcoromina@xaletcoromina.com
web	www.xaletcoromina.com

La Tria
08589 Perafita, Barcelona

This area of the Pyrenean foothills remains puzzlingly undiscovered; wandering through Perafita's delightful backstreets you meet few visitors. But it is lovely. Snug in the lushest countryside and just a short walk from the village, this monumental old Catalan *mas* could not have been more sensitively or beautifully renovated. Gentle-mannered Maite is a painter and her creativity is reflected in the restoration and country-style antiques; rooms are fresh, light, uncluttered. The place is really geared to self-catering lets – there are two kitchens – but Maite will happily prepare you a Catalan (or continental) breakfast and there are two cheap-and-cheerful restaurants in Perafita. In the main farmhouse are an enormous wooden-floored dining room and two sitting rooms, one very cosy with an open hearth. The whole place is blissfully quiet and, with the enormous garden and the dairy farm to explore, is perfect for families. The newly added pool, with its glorious views, will also appeal. Central heating means you'll be comfortable at La Tria in the cooler months, too. A delicious place, run by kind, unobtrusive hosts.

rooms	8 doubles.	
price	€ 60 (rooms let individually, weekdays only); weekends from € 280 for 3-bedroom house.	
meals	Self-catering. Breakfast € 6 (when rooms rented individually).	
closed	Rarely.	
directions	From Barcelona N-152 to Vic. Bypass town to west, then turn for Sant Bartolomeu del Grau. Towards Perafita; La Tria signed left before village.	

Maite Tor Pujol-Galcerán
tel   +34 938 530240
e-mail country@latria.com
web   www.latria.com

map 8   entry 126

El Jufré

08511 Tavertet-Osona, Barcelona

The medieval hilltop villages of this part of Catalonia rival those of Provence. Driving up to Tavertet past craggy limestone outcrops and stands of forest is an adventure in itself; once you arrive and look out over the plain below you'll be captivated. Stay with Josep and Lourdes and their two young children in this very old house: rebuilt in the 1600s, parts of it date back to 1100; Lourde's family have been in residence for 800 years! Rooms are simple and attractive, and they happily marry old (beams, exposed stone) and new (beds, lighting, bathrooms). Choose one that looks out over the craggy ledge on which El Jufré is perched. Linger later on the terrace over an aperitif to the sound of distant cowbells. Good, simple food at dinner includes veg straight from Josep's vegetable garden, and at breakfast there's milk from the family's cows. El Jufré is for lovers of high places, of utter tranquillity – full-time residents here number 40 – and for those delighted to trade car for foot.

rooms	8 doubles/twins.
price	€ 90. VAT included.
meals	Dinner € 15 on request only.
closed	24 December-7 January; 1-15 September.
directions	From Vic C-153 for Olot & Roda de Ter to L'Esquirol & Santa María Corco. Here, right to Tavertet. House on left as you enter village.

Josep Roquer & Lourdes Rovira

tel	+34 938 565167
fax	+34 938 565167

Can Rosich

Apartado de Correos 275, 08398 Santa Susanna , Barcelona

You are very close to the beach, Barcelona and Figueras are an easy drive and yet you're hidden away up a thickly wooded valley in 20 hectares of bucolic loveliness. This old *masía* is more than two centuries old yet has been completely rebuilt in recent years. To one side of the large hallway is a beamed dining room with six tables decked in bright chequered cloths. Cooking is wholesome, delicious and amazing value when you consider that the price includes good Catalan wine. Among Montserrat's specialities are rabbit, pork from the farm and *asado de payés* (order in advance!), a thick stew with three different meats, plums and pine nuts. Breakfast, too, is a hearty meal: cheese and cold meats, fruit and orange juice. Can Rosich's bedrooms, named after birds and animals of the region, are large and comfy and big enough to take a third bed. Beds are antique but mattresses new and you'll find a be-ribboned, neatly-ironed bundle of towels on your duvet, a nice touch from a gracious hostess. Five minutes away are trains that can whizz you to and from Barcelona in just one hour. A great favourite with our readers. *Multi-lingual hosts.*

rooms	6: 5 doubles, 1 twin.
price	€ 42–€ 52.
meals	Breakfast € 6, dinner € 13.
closed	20-27 December.
directions	From A-7, exit 9 Maçanet; N-II for Barcelona to Santa Susanna; here, right at 1st r'bout for 'nucleo urbano'; signs for 2km to Can Rosich. From Barcelona, C-32 Mataró & Girona; exit 22 Pineda & S. Susanna, then as above.

Montserrat Boter Fors

tel	+34 937 678473
fax	+34 937 678473
e-mail	canrosich@canrosich.com
web	www.canrosich.com

map 9   entry 128

La Morera

08553 El Brull, Barcelona

If you've ever dreamt of escaping the rat race and heading for the hills, head here. This is precisely what the quartet who run La Morera did some years ago: a gentler existence beckoned, and they set to restoring this 17th-century *masía* in the Montseny massif. The relaxed atmosphere is palpable the minute you enter the walled courtyard and meet the dogs dozing in the sun. The cosy, shambolic dining room is dominated by a magnificent Catalan fireplace and a communal dining table; this takes pride of place in winter when the aromas of home-reared meats mix with good conversation and robust Priorat wine. The sitting room is beguilingly unpretentious, furnished with a miscellany of old furniture, sofas and ancient chandeliers. Restoration is still ongoing so unvarnished floors and exposed plasterwork may be expected. Bedrooms are mezzanine with old, carved beds and antique mirrors and steepish stairs which lead down to the sleeping area. Bathrooms are newish with showers. Hearty dinners are eaten to the beat of Catalan rock while breakfast is simple but delicious: home-made cheeses, jams, cold meats.

rooms	8 doubles/twins.
price	Half-board €71–€116; full-board €86–€146. VAT included.
meals	Lunch and/or dinner included.
closed	Rarely.
directions	From French border, A7 to Girona, then west on Eix Transversal. Exit Viladrau; continue to Seva, then signs for El Brull. Just past village at km30.5 marker, house signed on right (easily missed); then 2km track.

Ramón Casamitjana, Sergi Peytibi, Juan Carlos Ca
tel   +34 93 8840477

El Folló

08593 Tagamanent, Barcelona

It's hard to believe that El Folló, with its dramatic views of pine-clad mountains and wild flowers, is just an hour from Barcelona. A traditional Catalan *casa pairal* (father's house), it has been masterfully restored by Mercè and Jaume: their B&B is a triumphant mix of old and new. The bedrooms are exceptional with their original natural stone invigorated by bold colours and a fruit and flower motif throughout. Hues range from the vibrant red of the Strawberry Room to the gentler mauvish tones of Mallow. Lighting is subdued and complements the beamed ceilings, simple white curtains and fine bed linen. Bathrooms have free-standing tubs, natural wood surrounds and breathtaking views. Reminders of a rural past are never far away: the dining room, once a stable, has a long wooden table as its focal point. A feeling of abundance and well-being abounds: the original trough groans under piles of fruit and traditional kitchen tools. Mercè is proud of her cooking; although a vegetarian she caters for meat-eaters too. Be sure to try her courgette bread and her locally produced traditional *cava* (Catalan bubbly).

rooms	8 doubles/twins.
price	€ 60. VAT included.
meals	Breakfast € 6; lunch/dinner € 24. VAT included.
closed	Rarely.
directions	From north A-7 towards Barcelona, then exit 14; C-17 for Vic. At km36 (opposite petrol station) right then ahead at r'bout. Follow signs for 2km to El Folló.

Merce Brunés & Jaume Villanueva
tel +34 938 429116
web www.elfollo.com

map 8   entry 130

El Trapiche

Can Vidal, Els Casots, 08739 Subirats, Barcelona

A dream: imagine waking from a deep slumber to see the crags of Montserrat silhouetted against a blushing dawn and vineyards all around... *cava* vineyards at that. It is easy to see what drew this couple to this 400-year-old *masía*. Michael is front of house and will probably be cook. Dinner is served by request only and you may meet the whole family at drinks beforehand. The focus here is very relaxed and your hosts are generous with the wine, too. Bedrooms are large: two are twin-bedded with showers and two are huge; the Pink Room has its own sitting area and terrace overlooking the lovely Penedes Valley and Montserrat. All have simple pine furniture, warm colours, darkened beams and wooden floors, and central heating for the colder months. If you are interested in wine, visit the Codorniu cellars which are just down the road, or Bodegas Torres a few kilometres on past Vilafranca, where there is also an interesting wine museum. There are a number of pleasant but non-strenuous walks nearby which you can enjoy in the company of the Johnstons' two dogs. Another big plus: you are 40 minutes by train from Barcelona.

rooms	4 doubles/twins.
price	€85.
meals	Lunch/dinner €24.
closed	Christmas & New Year.
directions	From A-7 exit 27 Sant Sadurni. As leave m'way, signs to Barcelona & Ordal N-340. Continue for 3km to Els Casots; 600m beyond hamlet, 1st track on left.

Marcela & Michael Johnston

tel	+34 93 7431469
fax	+34 93 7431469
e-mail	michael.johnston@bmlisp.com

Hotel La Santa María

Passeig de la Ribera 52, 08870 Sitges, Barcelona

Sitges has been a fashionable resort town with wealthier Catalans for many years. The crowd is more international now but the town has kept its intimacy and life still centres on the promenade and beach. At the heart of it all is the Santa María. It is a cheery building: the pale peach façade is set off by a rambling bougainvillaea; a bright apricot and orange awning covers the lively terrace. The atmosphere here is somehow redolent of a smart British seaside hotel, only the food is possibly better; there's a lot of seafood and fish on the menu, and the sea laps almost up to the table. It all ticks over beautifully, thanks to Señora Ute, the hotel's indefatigable owner, who effortlessly switches between half a dozen languages. Some bedrooms have balconies and a view across the palm trees to the bay beyond, all are well furnished with functional wooden beds, tables and desks, and one or two have their original tiled floors and older furniture. All, too, have prints of Sitges, and there may well be fresh flowers. You'll need to book ahead here, especially in season.

rooms	80 doubles/twins.
price	€ 75-€ 92; single € 65-€ 72; suite € 96-€ 115.
meals	Lunch/dinner € 10 set menu, € 23 à la carte.
closed	20 December-10 February.
directions	From Barcelona, A-16 through Tuneles de Garaf. Take 2nd exit for Sitges centre, follow signs to Hotel Calipolis. Hotel on sea front; residents car park.

Antonio Arcas Sánchez

tel	+34 938 940999
fax	+34 938 947871
e-mail	info@lasantamaria.com
web	www.lasantamaria.com

 map 8   entry 132

Photography by Michael Busselle

CASTILLA-LEON
CASTILLA-LA MANCHE
MADRID

"Scenery is fine - but human nature is finer."
JOHN KEATS

Guts Muths

Calle Matanza s/n, Barrio de Abajo, 24732 Santiago Millas, León

Santiago Millas and other villages in the area drew their wealth from the transport of merchandise by horse and cart throughout Spain. The coming of the railways put an end to all that; what remains of this past glory are some grand old village houses of which Guts Muths is a fine example. It is a big, solid house with a rather colonial feel – hats off to owners Sjoerd and Mari Paz for the easy-going and intimate atmosphere they have created within. Enter under an imposing arch to find yourself in a flower- and palm-filled courtyard. Decorative flair-and-care is evident throughout – beds are of new pine but interesting murals and paintings add an individual touch. Downstairs are dried and fresh flowers, exposed stonework and a dining room with well-stocked *bodega*, ceramic tiles, dark roof beams and old bread oven. A proper backdrop for honest regional cooking. Sjoerd is a no-nonsense sort: he loves to talk and will regale you with local history and folklore. He might even take you out to explore the nearby gorges on foot or mountain bike... or attached to the end of a rope. *A Rusticae hotel.*

rooms	8 doubles/twins.
price	€ 99; single € 47.
meals	Breakfast € 6.25; dinner € 12.50.
closed	Rarely.
directions	From Astorga, LE-133 for Destriana. After approx. 10km, left for Santiago Millas & Barrio de Abajo, signed.

Sjoerd Hers & Mari Paz Martínez

tel	+34 987 691123
fax	+34 987 691123
web	www.gutsmuths.com

map 3   entry 133

La Posada del Marqués

Plaza Mayor 4, 24270 Carrizo de la Ribera, León

There are few places to stay in Spain as special as this old pilgrim's hospital, originally part of the Santa María Monastery next door. Pass through the fine portal to a pebbled cloister and mature garden with a gurgling brook, a big old yew and walnut trees: with its high walls and rambling roses it reminds one of an English rectory garden. Carlos Velázquez (his family have owned the *posada* for generations) and his wife graciously greet their guests before showing them to their rooms. These are set round a gallery on the first floor and are filled with family heirlooms: Portuguese canopied beds, oil paintings, old lamps and dressers. One has a terrace over the cloisters; all are enchanting. The sitting and games rooms downstairs are similarly furnished with heavy old wooden doors, carved chests and tables and comfy armchairs and sofa in front of the hearth. At dinner there's good regional food and wine with a choice of two or three starters, main courses and puddings; afterwards, a post-prandial game of snooker. Kind and erudite hosts in the most beguiling of settings. Be sure to visit the monastery for the plainsong.

rooms	11 twins/doubles.
price	€ 69–€ 80. VAT included.
meals	Dinner € 14. Book ahead.
closed	10 January-end-February.
directions	From León, N-120 for Astorga. After 18km, right on LE-442 to Villanueva de Carrizo. Cross river into Carrizo de la Ribera. Ask for Plaza Mayor.

Carlos Velázquez-Duro

tel	+34 987 357171
fax	+34 987 358101
e-mail	marques@aletur.es
web	www.aletur.es/marques

La Posada Regia
Calle Regidores 9-11, 24003 León, León

The stained-glass windows of Leon's Gothic cathedral are reason enough to come to this lively provincial capital − and there is much more to do besides. By far the best place to stay here is the Posada Regia, plumb in the centre of the old town: it can be noisy at night, but this is a bright star in the firmament of newly-opened hotels in Spain. The building first saw the light in 1370 and the dining room incorporates part of an old Roman wall. The warm ochre and beamed reception strikes a welcoming note as you arrive and the staff could not be more friendly. A fine old staircase leads up to the bedrooms which are some of the cosiest and most coquettish that you'll come across. Soothing pastels, bright kilims, shining planked floors, old writing desks, brightly painted radiators, and snazzy bathrooms with all the extras: bathrobes, embroidered towels, hairdryers. Avoid the attic rooms in summer. The hotel's restaurant, La Bodega Regia, which predates the hotel by 50 years and was founded by Marcos's grandfather, is one of Léon's most renowned. *Pets by arrangement.*

rooms	20: 14 doubles, 6 singles.
price	€ 84–€ 120; single € 51.
meals	Lunch € 15 set menu, € 30 à la carte.
closed	Rarely.
directions	Hotel in town centre 150m from Cathedral. Park in Parking San Marcelo on Plaza de Santo Domingo, then 100m walk to hotel.

Verónica Martínez Díez

tel	+34 987 213173
fax	+34 987 213031
e-mail	marquitos@regialeon.com
web	www.regialeon.com

map 3   entry 135

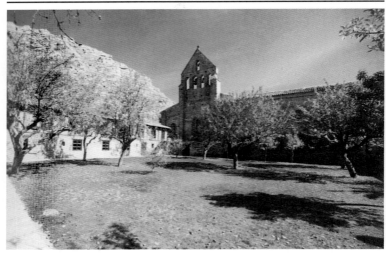

Posada de Santa María la Real

Avenida de Cervera s/n, 34800 Aguilar de Campoo, Palencia

In a wing of the Cistercian monastery of Santa María la Real, 18 guestrooms have been created by the local *escuela taller* – a scheme that teaches traditional skills to the young unemployed. While they have been utterly faithful to local building and restoration techniques, they have let 1990s design play a part too and the result is a hotel full of surprises. A pebbled patio leads up to the entrance; the façade of timbers, stone, wafer-bricking and eaves is a beguiling sight. Inside, the mix of old and new works well: every last corner has been carefully considered and restored. There are pebbled and parquet floors, designer chairs, and lamps snug beside hearth and beam. The design of the attractively decorated guest rooms follows the dictates of a tall building: they are small and 'mezzanined'. We feel they work well although one of our readers found the singles cramped, and too warm in summer. If you are sensitive to cigarette smoke then the low-ceilinged dining room could be an ordeal. But you will be struck by the peacefulness of the place: which is, we presume, why the cowelled-ones came here in the first place.

rooms	22 doubles/singles.
price	€ 48–€ 74; single € 35–€ 43. VAT included.
meals	Lunch/dinner € 12 set menu, € 30 à la carte.
closed	Christmas & 15-30 January.
directions	From Santander A-67 for Oviedo, then N-611 south to Aguilar de Campoo. Posada on left of road from Aguilar to Cervera de Pisuerga.

Elena Martín Millán
tel	+34 979 122000
fax	+34 979 125680
e-mail	posada@jazzviajeros.com

Hostería 'El Convento'

Monasterio de Santa María de Mave s/n, 34492 Santa María de Mave, Palencia

Leave traffic, city and pollution far behind when you come and stay at El Convento. The Moral family laboured long and hard to nurse this vine-clad 18th-century Benedictine monastery back to good health and it is now classified as a national monument. On weekdays the cloister, gardens and old stone walls remain as conducive to meditation as in the days when the Brothers were here; at weekends the place's popularity means there are many more visitors. Some bedrooms are in what were once the monks' cells; they are medium-sized, simply furnished in the dark-wooded Castillian style and most give onto the cloister. The two suites have curtained four-poster beds and swish corner tubs. You dine in the old chapter house where heavy antique furniture, low beams and terracotta tiling are in keeping with the building's past. Food is traditional Castilian and very good: thick chick pea or bean soups and plenty of lamb. Roasts from a wood-fired oven are the house speciality, as are freshly-picked strawberries when in season. Don't miss the chapel; it dates from 1208 and is considered one of the finest of Palencia's many Romanesque buildings.

rooms	25: 23 doubles, 2 suites.
price	€ 47–€ 53; single € 34–€ 40; suite € 75–€ 81.
meals	Breakfast € 4.50; lunch/dinner € 13 set menu, € 25 à la carte.
closed	Christmas.
directions	From Aguilar de Campo south for Palencia on N-611. After 5km, in Olleros de Pisuerga, left at sign for Santa María de Mave.

Ignacio Antonio Moral
tel +34 979 123611
fax +34 979 125492

map 4   entry 137

Posada de la Casa del Abad de Ampudía

Pza. Francisco Martín Gromaz 12, 34160 Ampudía, Palencia

The impressive church of San Miguel beckons you into Ampudía, a village steeped in history. Angel García has blended authentic detail with modern technology to create a wonderful, hedonistic hideaway out of this 17th-century abbot's house on the main square. Beyond the stately porch is the six-metre vaulted orange hallway – beams are original, décor is contemporary. Bright pinks, blues, greens and yellows mix with columns, arches, cornices and adobe walls to create an informal and hospitable atmosphere. The central patio, another riot of colour, is the place to enjoy an aperitif before settling into the distinctive wood-beamed restaurant where you will eat well and imbibe some of the rarer, more robust Iberian wines. There's an intimate little bar, too, with its own entrance and garden. The bedrooms are individual masterpieces, a blend of antique wood and furnishings, sumptuous beds and superb bathrooms. All this and a salt-purified, solar-heated swimming pool, a sauna, a gym, a tennis court, friendly staff – and a village whose wooden colonnaded streets date from the 1600s. *A Rusticae hotel.*

rooms	17: 12 doubles, 5 suites.
price	€ 108–€ 124; single € 90–€ 102; suite € 160–€ 500.
meals	Breakfast € 11; lunch/dinner € 35 set menu, € 40 à la carte.
closed	Rarely.
directions	Burgos N-620 Valladolid. 12km s. of Palencia, right at km92 to Dueñas. Here, right for Ampudía; bear left at petrol station & follow wooden columns to square with willow. Posada on left.

Angel García

tel	+34 979 768008
fax	+34 979 768300
e-mail	hotel@casadelabad.com
web	www.casadelabad.com

Casa Zalama

09569 San Pelayo de Montija, Burgos

Not to be missed! In this little known area of northern Spain, the Casa Zalama is a place in which to linger. Maria and Graeme uprooted from Brighton in search of a guesthouse in Spain, and found this quiet farming village purely by chance. They converted the house with great care, and Maria's interior design skill is matched by Graeme's green fingers in the garden – he is an ex-landscape gardner. The beamed bedrooms have sumptuous double beds and lovely earth colours; those with balconies have stunning views of the Merindad hills. Dinners, served in the little dining room (formerly the stables), are home-made and excellent: the local sausage is a treat, the pear tart legendary. Breakfast can be full English if that's what you like. And the garden… wander at your leisure, and into the countryside beyond. Next to the house is a studio where Graeme and Maria run workshops; join them if you're feeling creative, or use the workspace to do something independently. Your hosts will give you lots of advice about what to see and do here. A great place, and only an hour from Bilbao and Santander.

rooms	5 doubles.
price	€ 45.
meals	Breakfast € 4; dinner € 10.
closed	Rarely.
directions	From E-70 for Bilbao, exit km173 for Colindres. Follow N-629 up over Alto de los Tornos. At Aguera, left for San Pelayo. House past church, on left.

Maria Cruz Totorika

tel	+34 947 565961
fax	+34 947 565961
e-mail	info@casazalama.com
web	www.casazalama.com

map 5   entry 139

El Prado Mayor

Quintanilla del Rebollar 53, 09568 Merindad de Sotoscueva, Burgos

After several years' restoration work on this 16th-century village mansion, the owners' dream of living and working in the Las Merindades region has come true. The impressive façade of the Prado Mayor hides behind a solid arched gateway. Via a small garden with a columned terrace − lovely for summer breakfasts − you enter what feels like a warm family home. The cream-coloured stone gives the house a sheltered and peaceful air and the unfussy, stylish décor stands in perfect harmony with the architecture. Here are period antiques, colourful blankets and dried flowers, wonderful wooden cabinets under basins, marble tops and ornate framed mirrors. Breakfast is a must: home-made cakes, biscuits, local bread from a wood oven and fresh organic milk. Lunch and dinner are stout affairs with home-grown vegetables and good local meats; the rabbit is rather special. Your hosts are delightful people, and the lush landscape of the area is one of Spain's best-kept secrets, breathing culture and history. The Ojo Guareña cave system, from where you can trace humanity's religious expression from Paleolithic times, is one of the biggest in the world.

rooms	5 doubles/twins.
price	€ 48-€ 54; single € 36-€ 42. VAT included.
meals	Breakfast € 5; packed lunches; dinner € 12. VAT included.
closed	Rarely.
directions	Burgos N-623 Santander & Puerto del Escudo. At Cilleruelo de Bezana C-6318 Bilbao. Village 7km before Espinosa de los Monteros; right at house no.52 to reach no.53.

Fernando Valenciano Velasco & Olga Fernández A
tel   +34 947 138689
fax   +34 947 138689
e-mail   pradomayor@arrakis.es
web   www.arrakis.es/~pradomayor

Posada Molino del Canto

Molino del Canto s/n, 09146 Barrio La Cuesta, Burgos

This jewel of a place is remote and heavenly in an Eden-like valley, lapped by the river Ebro. It is a 13th-century mill, restored by the young owner Javier, and is both authentic and exquisite. The stonework blends perfectly with its surroundings and the style of the simple façade is continued inside. The dark little entrance hall, cool in summer and warm in the colder months, takes you through a curtain to a cosy, low-beamed wood and stone sitting room with a log fire and handmade furniture. This is the only communal area but go up the old, wooden staircase to discover the bedrooms, a splendid surprise: each has a homely sitting room down and a bedroom up, with generous bed, large classic wardrobe, stylish bathroom. Deep sleep is guaranteed. Breakfast here is a great start to the day and the home-cooked regional food is good, too. Go on a birdwatching walk with Javier and get him to show you the old mill house. It sits on a promontory down by the river and is, amazingly, 1,000 years old; it still contains the old flint wheels which spin into action when the sluice gate is opened.

rooms	6 doubles/twins.
price	€ 74; single € 52. VAT included.
meals	Lunch € 20; dinner € 18. VAT included.
closed	Rarely.
directions	From Burgos N-623 towards Santander. North of Quintanilla de Escalada, at km 66, exit for Gallejones. On for Villanueva Rampally. There left for Arreba. Posada signed to right after 2.6km.

Javier Morala Muñoz

tel	+34 947 571368
fax	+34 947 571368

map 4   entry 141

Balneario de Valdelateja

Ctra Burgos-Santander N-623 km 137, 09145 Valdelateja, Burgos

The original spa hotel at Valdelateja first opened its doors in 1872, when the well-heeled would ride up from Burgos or down from Santander to take the waters. But spas ceased to be fashionable, then came the war and, by the beginning of the decade, the site lay abandoned. After the Dark Ages, the Renaissance! Total restoration of the two original buildings has produced a most interesting small hotel. The setting is wonderful: you look out to woods of holm and evergreen oak that cling to the sides of the canyon cut by the River Rudrón. The building is rather Swiss-chalet, with wooden balconies, galleries and ornately carved eaves; wood is the primary element inside too, whether in darkened beam or polished parquet. The lantern-ceiling of the lounge – the former ballroom – is a real beauty. No two guest rooms are the same; some have antique bedsteads of wrought iron, other beds are of padded fabric; they have wonderful walnut floors and all have big bathrooms with full-length baths. The dining room looks out to the river, and the views are a wonderful accompaniment to the home cooking. A convenient and friendly stopover before the Santander ferry.

rooms	34: 30 doubles, 4 suites.
price	€61-€145; single €49-€90; suite €73-€108.
meals	Breakfast €6; lunch/dinner €15 set menu, €25 à la carte.
closed	10 December-1 March.
directions	From Burgos N-623 for Santander. Through San Felices, & just before Valdelateja right to Balneario; signed.

Elena Cagigas

tel	+34 947 150220
fax	+34 947 150220
e-mail	grupocastelar@mundivia.es
web	www.grupocastelar.com

Hotel Arlanza

Calle Mayor 11, 09346 Covarrubias, Burgos

Mercedes and Juan José, two of the friendliest hoteliers you could hope to meet, have created a hotel which matches the charm and intimacy of the town. Covarrubias is well off the tourist-beaten track and a must if you love places where tradition still counts; the heart of the town is a wonderful colonnaded square, with the Arlanza to one side. You enter under the colonnade through an arched doorway. Inside: lovely terracotta floors, ceramic wall tiles from Talavera, old chandeliers, original beams and lintels. Downstairs it is all a little dark because of the small, old windows. All of the bedrooms are reached by an impressive staircase – they are large, with tiled floors, old lamps and rustic furniture, and those that give onto the square are the lightest. There is good regional food in the restaurant and period costume banquets – fun but boisterous! – every Saturday night out of season. Do find a chance to chat to the owners; they visit the UK every year, know its farthest corners and speak the language, too.

rooms	40: 38 doubles, 2 suites.
price	€ 62; single € 36; suite € 65. VAT included.
meals	Lunch/dinner € 12 menu; € 20 à la carte.
closed	15 December-February.
directions	From Burgos N-1 for Madrid. In Lerma, left on C-110 for Salas de los Infantes. Hotel in Covarrubias on Plaza Mayor.

Mercedes de Miguel Briones

tel	+34 947 406441
fax	+34 947 400502
e-mail	reservas@hotelarlanza.com
web	www.hotelarlanza.com

map 5   entry 143

Hotel Santo Domingo de Silos

Calle Santo Domingo 14, 09610 Santo Domingo de Silos, Burgos

The highlight of a stay in Santo Domingo de Silos is the Gregorian chant in the monastery chapel. You can hear it every day of the year and it is well worth a detour on your journey north or south. Consider overnighting at this simple family hotel which has recently doubled in size thanks to a large extension. Its real *raison d'être* is its vast dining room: at weekends visitors come from far and near to eat roast lunch or dinner prepared by Eleuterio in a wood-fired oven. On weekdays you'd feel a bit lonesome in this large space so ask Nati to serve you dinner in a second, smaller dining area – or in the cosy bar next door. The cuts of lamb, kid and suckling pig are worthy of a medieval banquet – and the prices are astonishingly low. As far as the bedrooms go we'd recommend asking for one in the newly-built extension: they have hydro-massage showers and tubs (ask for *una habitación en la parte nueva*) and are much bigger than the older rooms, which are fairly unremarkable. A friendly, unpretentious place where you come for the food, the value... and the Gregorian chant.

rooms	50 twins/doubles.
price	€45–€55; single €35.
meals	Breakfast €3–€5; lunch/dinner €10.
closed	Rarely.
directions	From Burgos, N-I for Madrid, then N-234 for Soria. Left in Hacinas on BU-903 to Santo Domingo de Silos. Hotel on right as you pass through village.

Eleuterio del Alamo Castrillo

tel	+34 947 390053
fax	+34 947 390052
e-mail	hotelsilos@verial.es
web	www.verial.es/hotelsilos

Casón de la Pinilla

La Rinconada s/n, 40592 Cerezo de Arriba, Segovia

Those *Madrileños* in on the secret flee the noise and pollution of the capital and drive over the mountains to be guests of Luis and Rocío — who have recently left successful city careers to start a new life as hoteliers in the peaceful outskirts of Cereza de Arriba. Their aim was to create more than simply a convenient stopover for the skiers who head for the lifts at nearby Pinilla, where it often snows from the end of December to March... this is more an informal 'home-from-home'. The actual building is functional rather than beautiful but books, comfy chairs and a dining room of human proportions provide timeless warmth. Bedrooms are large and somewhat plain. At dinner expect something really special from Rocío and her co-chef Pilor: pigs trotters stuffed with wild mushrooms, home-made pâté, fresh local veg, fruit and home-made puddings — strong country flavours prevail. When dining on the terrace, as the mountains turn purple, you'll be glad you stopped an hour short of Madrid. *Cookery courses also on offer — write or call for details.*

rooms	12: 5 doubles, 7 twins.
price	€62–€71.
meals	Breakfast €5.50; lunch/dinner €13 set menu, €27 à la carte.
closed	Rarely.
directions	From Madrid, N-I for Burgos. Exit 104 onto N-110 for San Esteban. After 1.5km, right for Cerezo de Arriba. Hotel on right before village entrance.

Luis y Rocío García de Oteyza
tel	+34 921 557201
fax	+34 921 557209
e-mail	casonpinilla@retemail.es

map 12   entry 145

Posada del Acebo

Calle de la Iglesia 7, 40165 Prádena, Segovia

Prádena sits snug in the lee of the Guadarrama Sierra, the high chain of mountains that lie just north of Madrid. Its older houses are surprisingly grand: from an age when the villagers were granted royal privileges for the magnificence of their livestock whose meat and wool were famous throughout the land. You enter the house through the small, truly snug dining/sitting room, with its bench seating and smell of seasoned timber, fire in the wood stove and photos of shepherds and their flocks. Ramón will show you upstairs by way of a fine old bannistered staircase to the bedrooms, which are real gems, a charming mix of the old (washstands, wrought-iron bedsteads, lamps, prints) and the new (central heating, properly firm mattresses, double-glazing to keep the fearsome Meseta winters at bay). There are mountain walks on your doorstep, the mighty Duratón river gorges to explore (on foot or by canoe), a feast of Romanesque churches and then dinner back in that cosy dining room. Both rooms and food are excellent value — if you're missing them, don't be afraid to ask for eggs and bacon for breakfast!

rooms	8: 5 doubles, 1 single, 2 family.
price	€43-€68; single €40. VAT included.
meals	Breakfast €4; dinner €14.
closed	Rarely.
directions	From Madrid, N-1 for Burgos. At km99 marker, exit Santo Tomé del Puerto; N-110 for Segovia. After 12km, right into Prádena. House off main square.

Ramón Martín Rozas

tel	+34 921 507260
fax	+34 921 507260
e-mail	acebo@tursegovia.com
web	www.el-acebo.com

La Tejera de Fausto

Carretera la Salceda a Sepúlveda km 7, 40173 Requijada , Segovia

The stone buildings of the Tejera del Fausto stand in glorious isolation, a mile from the nearest village, close to the banks of the Cega river. It is no coincidence that the roofs are terracotta: tiles (*tejas*) were made here, hence the building's name. Decoration is warm, simple and appealing: bedrooms have simple wooden furniture, and there's no telephone or TV to distract you from the views. This is a gorgeous part of Castille: a fertile valley in the lee of the Guadarrama mountains which cut a jagged scimitar between Madrid and the Meseta. The restaurant here is wonderful, a series of interconnecting rooms where fires blaze in colder months, as snug as an Irish pub; specialities are roast lamb, suckling pig and boar. Jaime is a gregarious host and regales you with nuggets of information about the area. He would have you visit the Romanesque chapel next door whose foundation stones were pillaged from a Roman villa. Walk out from La Tejera along the old transhumance routes that criss-cross the region: Castillian to the core. There are often wedding parties at the weekend during the summer so visit on a weekday. "Very, very good," wrote a reader.

rooms	9: 7 doubles, 2 suites.
price	€ 70; suite € 100–€ 140.
meals	Breakfast € 5.40; lunch/dinner € 25 à la carte.
closed	Rarely.
directions	From Segovia, N-110 for Soria to La Salceda. Then left for Pedraza. Hotel on left, after Torre Val de San Pedro.

Jaime Armero

tel	+34 921 127087
fax	+34 915 641520
e-mail	armero@nauta.es
web	www.nauta.es/fausto

map 12   entry 147

El Zaguán

Plaza de España 16, 40370 Turégano, Segovia

Turégano gets forgotten as people flock by en route for nearby Pedraza. But this village is every bit as attractive. It has a porticoed main square and an enormous castle dominating the skyline: King Ferdinand rested here between crusades to oust the infidel. On the main square, El Zaguán is every inch the grand Castilian house: casement windows, dressed stone and its own stables, grain store and *bodega*. A warm, quiet and cosy hostelry awaits you. Downstairs is a lively bar and dining room: pine beams, wafer bricks and terracotta floors, with beautifully dressed tables and soft lighting. There's a wood-fired oven where roasts are prepared: beef and lamb as well as the ubiquitous suckling pig. In the lovely upstairs sitting room and in the bedrooms you could be stepping into the pages of an interior design magazine – and the underfloor heating is a real boon during the Castillian winter. The sitting room has squashy sofas, a woodburner and a view of the castle and you sleep in style and comfort in the bedrooms; no two are the same and they are among the most handsome we've seen. A special hotel with hardworking, cheery and likeable Mario at the helm.

rooms	15: 12 doubles, 3 suites.
price	€60; single €42; suite €90.
meals	Breakfast €4.80; lunch/dinner €10–€18 set menu, €20–€25 à la carte.
closed	22 December–8 January.
directions	From Segovia, N-601 Valladolid. After 7km, right for Turégano & Cantalejo. Hotel in main village square.

Mario García

tel	+34 921 501165
fax	+34 921 500776
e-mail	zaguan@el-zaguan.com
web	www.el-zaguan.com

La Abubilla

Calle Escuelas 4 posterior, 40181 Carrascal de la Cuesta, Segovia

The Oneto family have lavished love, care and decorative *savoir-faire* on their latest project: the complete restoration of an old farmhouse in a hamlet whose daytime population numbered two at the last count! La Abubilla (the name means 'hoopoe') is a typical Segovian farm with main house and outbuildings wrapped around a sheltered courtyard where you breakfast in fine weather; a line of shimmering poplars provides welcome shade during the Meseta's long, hot summer. Every detail of the guest bedroom's decoration has been fussed over by Alfredo Oneto: even the light switches were individually crafted. Suites are in the old hay barn, the prettiest rooms imaginable; tiles are hand-painted, beds are four-poster, paint and fabric schemes praised in designer magazines. A split-level lounge and diner where a log fire glows in winter is equally special. You may even indulge in a spot of hydro-massage in the grounds – new this year. Segovia is close by and you could easily visit Madrid, Ávila and Salamanca should you decide – wisely – to stay for several nights. *A Rusticae hotel.*

rooms	5: 1 double, 4 suites.
price	€80–€93; single €68–€79; suite €91–€121. VAT included.
meals	Dinner €16. VAT included.
closed	24 December.
directions	From Segovia towards Soria on N-110. In Sotosalbo turn left for Turégano to Carrascal de la Cuesta.

Hermanos Oneto

tel	+34 921 120236
fax	+34 916 617278
e-mail	oneto@oneto.com
web	www.laabubilla.com

map 12 entry 149

Hostal de Buen Amor

Eras 7, 40170 Sotosalbos, Segovia

When Madrid folk tire of the capital they often head over the mountains to the green and fertile valleys of Segovia; tradition demands that a roast meal completes the excursion. Dora and Victor's restaurant has long been famous, while their delightful small hotel, yards away, opened its heavy old doors more recently. Their niece, a designer, took on the job of nursing the hamlet's finest old house back to good health; the result is a warm and intimate blend of comfort and authenticity. The house is memorably silent: when sipping your aperitif you hear just the grandfather clock or perhaps distant church bells; the blaze from the central, suspended chimney warms all sides. Dora, a self-confessed antique shop addict, has waved a magic wand over the bedrooms: you'll find old writing tables, cheery fabrics and superb mattresses (*not* antique!). She and Victor have lived in England and speak English brilliantly. You are pampered in every way: underfloor heating to keep you warm when temperatures plummet in the wintertime and a breakfast that will send you contentedly on your way. The Romanesque church in the hamlet draws visitors from miles around.

rooms	12: 11 doubles, 1 suite.
price	€ 65–€ 95; single € 49; suite € 132.
meals	Breakfast € 4.50; lunch/dinner € 30 à la carte (weekends only).
closed	Rarely.
directions	From Madrid N-VI for La Coruña. After tunnel, right for Segovia. Here, N-110 for Soria; on left after 18km.

Victor L. Soste & Dora P. Villamide

tel	+34 921 403020
fax	+34 921 403022
e-mail	hosbamor@infonegocio.com
web	www.infonegocio.com/hostaldebuenamor

Hotel Los Linajes

Dr. Velasco 9, 40003 Segovia, Segovia

A stone's throw from Segovia's Plaza Mayor and wondrous cathedral, Los Linajes stands cheek-to-jowl with the old city wall; the land drops away steeply here so the building is 'stepped' to give the maximum number of rooms a view across the green valley of the River Eresma. Miguel Borrequero officiates in reception: this amiable gent has been in charge at Los Linajes for years and he constantly strives to improve the hotel. Parts, it's true, feel a little dated but a thorough revamp is under way. The oldest section of the building is 17th century: its portal of dressed sandstone leads to a beamed reception area furnished with heavy Castilian-style furniture and oil paintings. What makes the rooms special are their views across the river valley, and the best have terraces too, where you can breakfast if the weather's right. You're only really aware this is a 53-room hotel when you enter the cavernous dining room and bar. The food is classically Castillian-Spanish. If you prefer a cosier venue for dinner there are plenty of restaurants very close. A huge plus is the hotel's large underground car park.

rooms	53: 39 doubles, 5 singles, 9 suites.
price	€92; single €66; suite €119.
meals	Breakfast €8.50; lunch/dinner from €18 à la carte.
closed	Rarely.
directions	As you arrive in Segovia from Madrid, follow signs 'Zona Oriental & Acueducto'. By Roman aqueduct, signs for El Alcázar, then signs for hotel.

Miguel Borrequero Rubio

tel	+34 921 460475
fax	+34 921 460479
e-mail	hotelloslinajes@terra.es

map 12   entry 151

Posada de Esquiladores

Los Esquiladores 1, 05412 San Esteban del Valle, Ávila

The granite exterior and rush blinds at the windows give no clue as to what lies within; nor is there any sign to trumpet the building's status as a hotel. So it's a delightful surprise to discover, on entering, a big sitting room with huge hearth, comfortable armchairs and a great atmosphere. In the exquisite mountain village of San Esteban, the *posada* was a village shop until 1989: some of the original goods are still on display in the dining room. Today's interior is a harmonious mix of stone, terracotta and carefully chosen fabrics; bedrooms are delightful, bathrooms excellent. All this has been achieved by Almudena, a former journalist who worked for *TV Espana*. She is also a talented cook and if you're lucky you'll sample treats at dinner like pork filled with cheese and raspberries. This is a good base from which to explore the wild villages of the region. There is a twice-yearly festival in honour of St Peter Baptist, the Franciscan missionary martyred at Nagasaki (whose skull rests in the church), and an annual horse-race, El Vitor, in which riders race bareback from the square to the cemetery.

rooms	12 doubles/twins.
price	€ 60–€ 100. VAT included.
meals	Breakfast € 6–€ 9; lunch/dinner € 9 set menu, € 21 à la carte.
closed	22-27 December.
directions	From Madrid, N-V/E90 for Talavera de la Reina. At km123, right on N-502 for Arenas de San Pedro, then right for Santa Cruz & on to San Esteban. Posada opp. Town Hall (Ayuntamiento).

Almudena García Drake

tel	+34 920 383498
fax	+34 920 383456
e-mail	posada@esquiladores.com
web	www.esquiladores.com

El Canchal

Calle de La Fuente 1, 05400 Arenas de San Pedro, Ávila

Arenas de San Pedro is an attractive little town, topped by a medieval castle and sculpted into the southern flank of the Sierra de Gredos. Walkers come for some of the most memorable paths in central Spain. The town is a hop away from the main trailheads, and El Canchal is bang in the middle. This once nobleman's residence dates from the Middle Ages; fortunately other parts are more recent. Isabel is the perfect innkeeper: relaxed, flexible and eager to tell you about the history of the village and El Canchal. Each of her bedrooms is named after a variety of mushroom – the area is popular with mycologists. Rooms are smallish but homely thanks to antique beds and dressers, lace-edged curtains, old washstands, parquet floors and low ceilings. The lounge and dining room feel similarly cosy. Try Isabel's home-made cake at breakfast and have dinner with her at least once: meals are simple and wholesome and the house red is good. Be sure to visit the labyrinthine wine cellars deep beneath the building; one of Isabel's many projects is to fill them with her own selection of bottles.

rooms	6 twins/doubles.
price	€ 46–€ 55.
meals	Breakfast € 3; lunch/dinner € 15.
closed	Rarely.
directions	Madrid N-V for Badajoz. Exit Casar de Talavera, then N-502 Arenas de San Pedro. Here, over r'bout for 'Centro Urbano'. Before castle, right into c/Isabel La Católica. Round church; park in Plaza del Ayuntamiento. Walk up c/Cejudo, right; house on left.

Isabel Rodríguez

tel	+34 920 370958
fax	+34 920 370914
e-mail	reservas@elcanchal.com
web	www.elcanchal.com

map 11   entry 153

El Milano Real

Calle Toleo s/n, 05634 Hoyos del Espino, Ávila

If, like the Good Samaritan, you see this unassuming modern hotel and pass by on the other side, you will miss a rare treat. Surrounded by the Gredos mountain range, it is rather like a Swiss chalet – a feeling heightened by the carved wood of the balconies and the warm atmosphere within. The beautiful ornamental garden at the front, however, owes more to the Italians than the Swiss. Inside are some superb new 'themed' suites; one is Japanese, stunning with futon and low furniture – not for the stiff-jointed! One is New York penthouse-style, another English, with four-poster. There are two lovely sitting rooms, one up under the eaves... but it is the dining room that draws people like a magnet, and the food justly wins a mention in all the famous guide books. Francisco ('Paco') has a selection of over 100 of his favourite wines to choose from and alongside each he lists year, *bodega*, D.O. – and then his own personal score out of ten. Food and rooms are incredible value, worth a very long detour, and the Gredos are one of Spain's better-kept secrets. and there is nowhere better for star-gazers than the observatory. *A Rusticae hotel.*

rooms	21: 13 doubles, 8 suites.
price	€ 70–€ 95; single € 62–€ 84; suite € 125.
meals	Breakfast € 7.27–€ 12; lunch/dinner € 28–€ 40 à la carte.
closed	Rarely.
directions	From Avila N-110 for Bejar & Plasencia. After 6km, N-502 left for Arenas de San Pedro; after 40km, right on C-500 to Hoyos del Espino. Hotel to right.

Francisco Sánchez & Teresa Dorn

tel	+34 920 349108
fax	+34 920 349156
e-mail	info@elmilanoreal.com
web	www.elmilanoreal.com

La Casa Inglesa
37700 Béjar, Salamanca

When we stayed with Anna every other house guest was Spanish: they come for fine food, good company and to escape the snarled-up roads and frenetic pace of life in the capital. La Casa Inglesa is both home and retreat, hidden away in a magnificent forest of chestnut trees (from which the nearest village of El Castañar takes its name). Decoration has a distinct feel of Kensington: drop-leaf tables, crystal decanters, books, candelabras and oriental vases. Anna likes the good things of life so expect candles at dinner, classical music at most times and very good food: she had three restaurants in London during the Sixties when she fed everyone from Nureyev to the Rolling Stones. Anna is no typical ex-pat: since setting up home in Spain she has never been one to search out fellow compatriots, and her cooking looks both west and east. Dinners have a Lebanese slant and she will happily prepare you a cooked breakfast. A charming hostess and home; stay a couple of nights and visit the beautiful village of Candelario, minutes away.

rooms	3 doubles/twins, 1 triple.
price	€ 60–€ 80. VAT included.
meals	Lunch € 25, dinner € 20.
closed	Rarely.
directions	From Salamanca for Cáceres; exit Sorihuela & Béjar. In Béjar pass two petrol stations, then left for El Castañar. Immed. opp. Hotel Los Duques, sharp left down steep cobbled track. At 3rd loop sharp left again to black entrance gate of house. Ring bell.

Anna Antonios
tel +34 923 404499 or 636 363476
e-mail casa.inglesa@teleline.es

map 11   entry 155

Hostelería Don Fadrique

Ctra. Salamanca-Alba de Tormes , 37800 Alba de Tormes, Salamanca

Don Fadrique is just outside town on the road to Salamanca. When we visited the hotel had just opened and its hillside perch looked rather stark but gardens were being planted and once you get inside you'll be surprised at just what a handsome hotel and restaurant the Sánchez Monje family have created. The heart of the place is the large wafer-bricked and chestnut-beamed dining room; the family had already made a name for themselves at the bar they own in the town, but now, with a prize-winning chef in the kitchen, a wine list of more than 200 bottles and a policy of buying only the best meat and season-fresh vegetables, the Michelin-man will surely soon be on his way. There is even an eight-course *degustación* menu if you are up to it. A beautifully carved walnut staircase leads to your bedroom. Those on the attic floor have very low ceilings; all are unbelievably good value. A brilliant choice if you can't find lodgings in nearby Salamanca, or if religious relics are your thing – the heart and arm of Santa Teresa are on view in Alba de Tormes's Carmelite monastery.

rooms	21 twins/doubles.
price	€72–€97; single €48.
meals	Breakfast €4.20; lunch/dinner €33.
closed	Rarely.
directions	From Salamanca follow signs for Madrid & almost immediately right on C-510 for Alba de Tormes. Don Fadrique to left of road 1km before you arrive in village.

Familia Sánchez Monje

tel	+34 923 370076
fax	+34 923 370487
web	www.donfadrique.com

Hotel Rector

Paseo Rector Esperabé 10, Apartado 399, 37008 Salamanca, Salamanca

A two-minute walk from the cathedral and close to the Roman bridge this *palacete*, or town mansion, is one of western Spain's most perfect small hotels – a joy to come across in a city of such interest and ineffable loveliness. Señor Ferrán is a man who like things to be 'just so' and his meticulous care is reflected in every corner. Wood is used to good effect throughout; there are sparkling parquet floors in the public areas, and inlaid bedside tables, writing desks and hand-crafted bedheads in mahogany and olive in the bedrooms. You have all the fittings of a five-star hotel: you might not need the phone in the bathroom, or the fax point, but you'll appreciate the double glazing, the air conditioning, and the deeply comfortable armchairs. Bathrooms hold the same luxurious note: marble, double basins, thick towels. High standards at breakfast too – service and ingredients are excellent. You can leave your car safe in the hotel car park and head out on foot to explore the city: right next door is the wonderful Casa Lis, a museum dedicated to Spanish Art Nouveau and Art Deco, and the incomparable Plaza Mayor is just minutes away.

rooms	13 doubles/twins.
price	€ 108–€ 139; single € 86; suite € 139.
meals	Breakfast € 10.
closed	Rarely.
directions	From Madrid on N-501, 1st right at signs 'Centro Ciudad'. At r'bout, left into Paseo Rector Esperabé. After 300m, hotel in front of two walls, by Casa Lis museum. Drop bags at reception; they will direct you to car park.

Eduardo Ferrán Riba

tel	+34 923 218482
fax	+34 923 214008
e-mail	hotelrector@telefonica.net
web	www.hotelrector.com

map 11   entry 157

La Posada del Pinar

Pozal de Gallinas s/n, 47450 Pozal de Gallinas, Valladolid

Exuding quality and charm, La Posada del Pinar captures the very essence of Castilla-León. It is a plush hideaway, idyllically sheltered from any hubbub by 300 acres of pine forest. Dating back to the early 17th century, the low vaulted brickwork in the centre of the building is the oldest part, but the new brickwork is the colour of the earth in the fields and works well with the light tones used inside. The sitting room with enclosed log fire is relaxed and intimate and leads through to an elegant arched dining room with woodburning oven, frequently used: mouthwatering roasts are on the menu. Behind the hotel is the old chapel, whose airy grandeur is perfectly suited to wedding and communion receptions and banquets. The guest bedrooms, each named after a local town famous for its *mudéjar* monuments, are large and well furnished. We did feel the coloured mosaic tiles in some of the bathrooms were a bit garish but the overall impression is classy. The area is full of places and things of interest, the nearby town of Olmedo is well worth visiting and there are plenty of natural marvels to see. *A Rusticae hotel.*

rooms	19 twins.
price	€ 66–€ 96; single € 56; suite € 93.
meals	Breakfast € 5.10; lunch/dinner € 15.60.
closed	7-27 January.
directions	From Valladolid, N–620 for Tordesillas, then N–VI for Madrid. Exit km157 for Olmedo to Pozal de Gallinas. Posada signed to right on entering village; 3.2km further.

Ignacio Escribano

tel	+34 983 481004
fax	+34 915 646191
e–mail	info@laposadadelpinar.com
web	www.laposadadelpinar.com

Hotel Albamanjon

Laguna de San Pedro 16, 02611 Ossa de Montiel, Albacete

Like Tennyson's eagle, who clasps the crag with crooked hand, this hotel seems to cling to the very rock, or even grow out of it. The upper rooms are embedded in some of the strange rock formations which characterise the vast plains of Quixote's la Mancha, and their terraces have lovely views down to the turquoise lake which gleams like an unexpected oasis in this rocky terrain. The hotel has a distinctive windmill frontage and was built in the 1970s in traditional style. The nine bedrooms, in which the rock will sometimes appear unannounced, are large and comfortable, each with a woodburning fire lit every evening in winter. You can sample Raul's cooking on a large terrace in fine weather, romantically lit up at night with circular lamps and fairy lights. The food is described by Raul as "traditional Manchegan", with such diverse and pungent flavours as green beans and partridge, and *atascaburras* (puréed cod with nuts, potatoes and peppers). This is the Ruidera National Park, so expect some good walking and birdwatching. You can also hire rowing boats, kayaks or mountain bikes from the hotel and explore, pioneer-style.

rooms	9: 5 doubles, 4 suites.
price	€ 77-€ 96; suite € 111-€ 141. VAT included.
meals	Lunch/dinner € 15 set menu, € 18-€ 28 à la carte. VAT included. Closed Tuesdays.
closed	Rarely.
directions	From N-IV, exit Manzanares & head east on N-430 for Albacete. At Ruidera follow signs to lakes. Hotel signed from lakes.

Raúl Arés Espílez

tel	+34 926 699048
fax	+34 926 699120
e-mail	hotel@albamanjon.net
web	www.albamanjon.net

map 19 entry 159

Palacio de la Serna

Calle Cervantes 18, 13432 Ballesteros de Calatrava, Ciudad Real

In the wide landscapes of Castilla-La Mancha the divide between vision and reality seems to blur — not just for hapless Quixotes lancing windmills. In a forgotten village this neo-classical palace may have you wondering whether the sun hasn't got to you: its unexpected opulence is a throwback to the time when mining made many a local fortune. It was all abandoned to the Meseta, until designer Eugenio Bermejo saw in Serna a perfect outlet for his creative impulse. Nearly every corner of the Palace is embellished with his sculptures, paintings and the flourishes of his own particular brand of interior design. No two bedrooms are alike; all are huge fun. In one, you enter an amazing world of cow-hide print bedspreads, rich burgundy fabrics and cast-iron chandeliers: post-modern to the core. There are red roses in the gardens, music plays — from Nyman to Bach — and dinners are by torchlight; you half expect a Knight of the Calatrava Order to wander in, or Quixote himself. Well worth a detour if you have a taste for the Gothic. *A Rusticae hotel.*

rooms	19: 7 double/twins, 12 suites.
price	€ 100; suite € 130–€ 160.
meals	Breakfast € 9; lunch/dinner € 25.
closed	Rarely.
directions	From Ciudad Real round town for Puertollano, then left on CR-512 for Aldea del Rey, then right to Ballesteros de Calatrava. Palace to left, signed.

Eugenio S. Bermejo

tel	+34 926 842208
fax	+34 926 842224
e-mail	palacioserna@paralelo40.org
web	www.palaciodelaserna.com

Los Baños de Villanarejo

13193 Navalpino, Ciudad Real

It feels more like a home than a hotel: sofas drawn up around the open hearth and the family coat of arms on the chimney breast. You are surrounded by 2,000 hectares of magnificent woodlands, and olive, cork and evergreen oak are home to foxes, wild boar, mongoose, muflon and deer. Although the Marquis and Marchioness of La Felguera have long received private hunting parties they only recently opened their home to paying guests too. There are rugs and oils and – predictably – any number of hunting trophies. Twelve guest rooms have period furniture, some with period tiles on the floors. Breakfast is a hearty spread of eggs and bacon, croissants, cakes and cold meats and at dinner you might be served pumpkin soup followed by game from the estate; the dessert will be home-made, the wine is *à volonté*. As well as hunting, other activities on offer include archery, clay-pigeon shooting, horse-riding, cycling and ballooning. Mineral water springs rise here and people have come to take the waters since Roman times. *Address for correspondence: Calle San Bernardo 97-99, 28015 Madrid.*

rooms	12: 9 twins/doubles, 3 suites.
price	Twin € 70; suite € 140; single € 100. VAT included.
meals	Breakfast € 6; lunch/dinner € 21, including wine. VAT included.
closed	Rarely.
directions	From Madrid N-IV. Then N-430 to Cuidad Real. On to Piedrabuena then CR-721 via Arroba de los Montes & Navalpino for Horcajo de los Montes; at top of pass, left at green gate; track to house.

Alvaro Colomina Velázquez-Duro

tel	+34 914 488910
fax	+34 915 933061
e-mail	acolomina@hotmail.com
web	www.fincarural.com

map 18   entry 161

La Casa del Rector

Pedro Oviedo 8, 13270 Almagro, Ciudad Real

One of the jewels in the crown of La Mancha, Almagro was once tipped to become home to the next great Spanish university. It never happened, and the Casa del Rector and a couple of other grand 17th-century edifices – built as part of this noble but unrealised dream – passed into private hands. Three years ago, restaurateur Juan Garcia bought the dilapidated building and with the help of local craftsmen transformed its ashen pallor into a rosy, healthy glow. Behind the sandstone façade are 11 lavishly furnished rooms and suites, all opening onto a glorious galleried central patio, where water bubbles and cascades into carved stone troughs. Most of the bedrooms have their own sitting space, plus woodburning stoves and luxurious modern bathrooms. There is an idiosyncratic touch to each: an Indian four-poster here, a sauna/shower there, a mosaic hot tub straight out of a James Bond film. The young, friendly staff serve an excellent breakfast with Manchegan cheese and meats; for supper look no further than the owners' own acclaimed restaurant, El Corregidor, just around the corner. *A Rusticae hotel.*

rooms	11: 8 doubles, 1 single, 2 suites.
price	€85–€132; single €75; suite €180.
meals	Breakfast €7; lunch/dinner €22–€30 at El Corregidor (see above).
closed	Rarely.
directions	From Ciudad Real, CM-412 to Almagro. At 1st r'bout follow hotel signs; right, then 2nd on right.

Luis R. Horcajada

tel	+34 926 261259
fax	+34 926 261260
e-mail	recepcion@lacasadelrector.com
web	www.lacasadelrector.com

Casa Bermeja

Plaza del Piloncillo s/n, 45572 Valdeverdeja, Toledo

Angela González happened upon this old house in a village that the 20th century seemed to have passed by. Here, far from the noise and pollution of Madrid, she realised a long-nurtured dream, to share this place with friends. Luckily for us she later decided to stretch a point and share her home with paying guests too. Architect brother Luis took renovation in hand and Angela, an interior designer, took care of furnishings and fittings. (Note that you are only likely to meet her at weekends.) Beyond the exuberant terracotta and cream façade with its stately entrance is a truly coquettish home, where the sun and red earth of Castille inspired the warm colours of paint and fabric. Antiques mingle with contemporary pieces, the sitting room and dining room have beamed ceilings and terracotta floors, and a scattering of magazines and books in several languages. Bedrooms are attractive, comfortable and blissfully quiet. This corner of the Meseta is an ornithological dreamland – and children bored by birdwatching can seek out the one-eyed turtle said to live in the garden. *A Rusticae hotel.*

rooms	16: 7 doubles, 9 suites.
price	€72–€91; singles €57–€73; suite €102–€168.
meals	Lunch/dinner €18.05–€21.05.
closed	Rarely
directions	From Madrid, N-V/E-90 for Badajoz. Exit at km148 marker for Oropesa. From here, signs to Puente del Arzobispo; then right to Valdeverdeja. In main square, opposite Town Hall (Ayuntamiento), left to house.

Angela González

tel	+34 925 454586
fax	+34 925 454595
e-mail	zabzab@arrakis.es

map 11   entry 163

Casa Los Arcos

Finca El Egido de Oritranca, Ctra. de Extremadura Km. 142, 45687 Alcañizo, Toledo

Conchita works on the best take-us-as-you-find-us principle of hospitality, and you will find the slightly shambolic charm of the place appealing. With its many outbuildings (some in use and some not), paddocks and stables, Los Arcos seems strung together like a charm bracelet of agrarian elements. Inside, the sitting room is peppered with Conchita's oil paintings, and mellow 200-year-old tiles adorn the floor. Bedrooms are comfortable, some with bright Mexican fabrics, and the twin rooms with their alcoved sitting areas and windows onto the garden are charming. Before you eat dinner – around a large table in the family dining room – you can have a drink on the open porch where tables and chairs jostle with assorted bits and pieces of a vaguely agricultural nature. Ask Conchita for a taste of the local *chorizo* as an accompaniment to your rioja. There are sunburnt fields all around, some geese, a friendly dog, and Conchita's beautiful horse in the paddock – reminders that you are miles from the noise and traffic of the city. Toledo is a 45-minute drive.

rooms	3: 2 twins, 1 suite.
price	€ 60; suite € 72.
meals	Breakfast € 5; lunch/dinner € 20.
closed	Rarely.
directions	From Madrid, N-V/E-90 to Talavera de la Reina. After Talavera, exit 142 for Alcañizo. Follow road to Finca El Egido; straight on, ignore 1st T-junc. on left. Finca entrance on left. House 800m along track.

Conchita Granda Lanzarot

tel	+34 625 609758
e-mail	casalosarcos@terra.es
web	www.terra.es/personal9/casalosarcos

Hotel Pintor El Greco

Calle Alamillos del Tránsito 13, 45002 Toledo

At the heart of Toledo's old Jewish quarter, just yards from the El Greco house and the synagogue museum, this small hotel, once a bakery, has had much praise heaped upon it. Its restoration has been a success, and both façade and patio have been handsomely returned to their former glory. Although the main building is 17th century, parts were standing when Toledo was the capital of the Moorish kingdom; there is even an escape tunnel, built when the Inquisition was at work. The interior is cool, quiet and plush, most of the furniture is modern, there are terracotta floors, lots of paintings and ceramics by local artists, and plenty of greenery. Guest rooms are on three floors, wrapped around the inner patio; some have balconies. There are armchairs, thick Zamora blankets and more paintings; the colours are warm, beds have excellent mattresses and there is plenty of space to add extra beds if you are more than two. At breakfast expect fresh fruit juice, cheese and cold sausage as well as fresh bread (alas, no longer baked in situ). *Residents-only parking opposite, for € 12 per day.*

rooms	40 twins/singles.
price	€ 104–€ 178; single € 80–€ 101.
meals	Restaurants nearby.
closed	Rarely.
directions	From Madrid N-401 to Toledo, then follow signs to old town. At town walls right; continue with wall on left until r'bout. Left here, along to end of tree-lined avenue. Left through wall; along this street to Tránsito & hotel.

Mariano Sánchez Torregrosa

tel	+34 925 285191
fax	+34 925 215819
e-mail	info@hotelpintorelgreco.com
web	www.hotelpintorelgreco.com

map 12   entry 165

Hostal Descalzos

Calle de los Descalzos 30, 45002 Toledo

Make sure you get a room with a view. Hostal Descalzos sits high up by the old city wall, just yards from El Greco's house. It is very different from some of this book's grander hotels but having spent two happy nights here we feel that it, too, is special enough to be included. Fittings are modern, furniture is pine, floors are white-tiled, bedspreads are spotless, and the new outdoor pool and terrace-jacuzzi are a big success: a first for Toledo. But it is the view – especially at night when the old bridge across the Tagus is illuminated – that you will remember: when you book, choose room 11, 12, 21 or 22. The family who run the *hostal* are quiet, unassuming folk, and serve you breakfast in a tiny downstairs room. A cheap but adequate lunch and dinner are available in the recently opened cafeteria/restaurant. At the foot of the hostal is a pretty walled garden with a fountain and flowers, a good place to sit out and watch the sun set over the Meseta after a day exploring the city. *Hotel garage € 10 per day.*

rooms	12 doubles/twins.
price	€ 40–€ 50.
meals	Lunch/dinner.
closed	Rarely.
directions	In Toledo, signs to old town. At town walls (Puerta de la Bisagra), right; cont. with wall on left until signs for hostel to left; hostal signed to right in front of Hotel Pintor El Greco.

Julio Luis García

tel	+34 925 222888
fax	+34 925 222888
e-mail	h-descalzos@jet.es
web	www.hostaldescalzos.com

Hostal del Cardenal

Paseo de Recaredo 24, 45004 Toledo

Toledo remains a quintessentially Spanish place – it has absorbed the richest elements of Moorish and Christian Spain – and it is tempting to stay at the Cardenal, built as a mansion house by the Archbishop of Toledo, Cardenal Lorenzana, in the 13th century. The gardens are lovely: fountains and ponds and geraniums and climbing plants set against the rich ochres of the brick. Go through the elegant main entrance to discover patios, screens, arches and columns. There are lounges with oil paintings and *mudéjar* brickwork. A peaceful mantle lies softly over it all, to the background tock-tock of the grandfather clock. Wide *estera*-matted corridors and a domed staircase lead up to the bedrooms; they have latticed cupboards, tiled floors, sensitive lighting and heavy wooden furniture. You can choose between several small and delightful dining rooms where you feast on roast lamb, suckling pig or stewed partridge. And the El Greco museum is a short stroll through the fascinating streets of old city.

rooms	27: 25 doubles/twins, 2 suites.
price	€76–€96; single €47–€60; suite €103–€132.
meals	Lunch/dinner €30 set menu, €33 à la carte. Closed Christmas Eve.
closed	Rarely.
directions	From Madrid N-401 to Toledo. As you arrive at old town walls & Puerta de la Bisagra, right; hotel 50m on left beside ramparts.

Luis González

tel	+34 925 224900
fax	+34 925 222991
e-mail	cardenal@asernet.es
web	www.cardenal.asernet.es

map 12   entry 167

La Almazara
Carretera Toledo-Argés y Polan km 3.4, Apartado 6, 45004 Toledo

One of Toledo's most illustrious cardenals had this delectable house built as a summer palace in the 16th century; high on a hillside overlooking Toledo, it catches the breezes that sweep in across the Meseta. He milled oil here: there are still huge vats of the stuff deep in the gunnels of the building. You arrive by way of a grand old portal and long drive to be greeted by Paulino: he is incredibly helpful and takes obvious pleasure in welcoming you. Downstairs is a large sitting room with a fire in winter but in summer you may prefer to linger in the vaulted dining room which looks over the fruit orchards to Toledo. Take a closer look at those oil paintings – all painted by Paulino's teenage daughter. Bedrooms are clean and comfortable and bathrooms have repro taps and gallons of hot water. Rooms 1-9 are our favourites, with double windows opening onto large terraces where you can gaze down at the old gardens below and the extraordinary city beyond. A private car park is a real plus: leave the car and wander down to the town, about a 20-minute stroll. Brilliantly priced so book ahead.

rooms	28: 26 doubles/twins, 2 singles.
price	€39–€55; single €28–€35.
meals	Breakfast €3.
closed	10 December–20 February.
directions	From Madrid, right in front of town wall for Navahermosa. Over bridge (Puente de San Martín), turn left; hotel on left after 2km ('Quinta de Mirabel' over entrance).

Paulino Villamor
tel	+34 925 223866
fax	+34 925 250562
e-mail	hotelalmazara@ribernet.es

Casa Palacio Conde de Garcinarro

Calle Juan Carlos I, 19, 16500 Huete, Cuenca

The owner spent his childhood just along the street from this imposing baroque mansion house and has given back the building its lost dignity by a complete restoration. He has been helped in this formidable task by his wife Encarna, an artist and antique restorer by profession; every last corner of the palace shows an eye for detail and a feel for what's right. This is every inch a noble Castillian residence: a fine portal of dressed sandstone with coat of arms above, grilled windows and, beyond, an enormous studded door leading to a colonnaded courtyard. Climb a wide walnut staircase to the first floor; off to one side the old chapel is home to a vast lounge decked out in rich burgundy colours. If it feels too imposing there is a second, less formal lounge. Bedrooms are vast, high-ceilinged and painted in wonderful pastel colours. Old prints, window seats, cushions, easy chairs and hand-painted furniture: it's surprisingly sumptuous given Garcinarro's more than modest prices. Breakfast in the old kitchen on bright chequered tablecloths, then head off to discover the delights of this wild and untouristy part of Castille. *A Rusticae hotel.*

rooms	14: 10 doubles, 3 suites, 1 quadruple.
price	€49-€58; suite €64-€73; quadruple €85. VAT included.
meals	Breakfast €4.50. El Duque restaurant nearby.
closed	Rarely.
directions	Madrid-Valencia on N-III. Exit Tarancón, follow signs for Cuenca & Carascosa, then CM-310 to Huete. Palace in village centre next to Santo Domingo church.

Conchi & Ramiro Fernández

tel	+34 969 372150
fax	+34 91 5327378
e-mail	garcinar@teleline.es

map 13   entry 169

Posada de San José

Julián Romero 4, 16001 Cuenca

Cuenca is unique, a town that astonishes and engraves itself on the memory. Sitting on the rim of its unforgettable gorge, this is an inn to match. A sculpted portal beckons you to enter but you would never guess at what lies beyond. This is a labyrinthine house and only from inside do you realise that it is multi-levelled. Staircases lead up and down, twisting and turning... the perfect antidote to mass-produced hotels and made-to-measure rooms. Every room is different, some small, some large, some with balconies, some without; most have bathrooms, a few share. Nearly all have old furniture, perhaps a canopied bed or a little terrace. We would ask for one that looks out across Cuenca's spectacular gorge but all of them, view or no view, are worth a night and are witness to Antonio and Jennifer's decorative flair; they, like us, value a vase of fresh flowers more than a satellite channels or a trouser-press. In the welcoming little restaurant with that heart-stopping view and a good meal to come, you'll be glad you cut across the Meseta to Cuenca. Do visit the town's wonderful museum of contemporary art. *A Rusticae hotel.*

rooms	22 doubles/twins.
price	€56–€84; single €37–€41.
meals	Snacks (good tapas!) available in evening, except Mondays.
closed	Rarely.
directions	From Tarancón, N-400 to Cuenca. Follow signs to Casco Antiguo. Posada 50m from cathedral main entrance. Parking 150m up near castle wall (avoid Plaza Mayor where cars are often clamped).

Antonio & Jennifer Cortinas

tel	+34 969 211300
fax	+34 969 230365
e-mail	psanjose@arrakis.es
web	www.posadasanjose.com

Las Nubes

Camino de Cabanillas , 19117 Albalate de Zorita, Guadalajara

Clinging to a hilltop with breathtaking views of the Marques valley and river Tagus, 'The Clouds' is well named. Carlos has taken the lofty position, added a dash of Hollywood and created a conservatory sitting room from which you can follow the sun from its rising to its setting – MGM could hardly improve on this. Space and light and subtle neutral colours are the hallmarks of this splendid, peaceful hotel. Down from reception is a huge open-plan sitting area with a suspended canopy log fire in the middle and glorious vista beyond; the dining room too is on this floor, where Valentin the chef serves lovingly prepared regional dishes using vegetables from the garden. Bedrooms scented with lavender oil have sliding windows opening onto a communal balcony and again, that glorious panorama. Each bedroom has contemporary furnishings, perfect lighting and an original headboard made from a large black and white photograph in a wooden frame. The suite has a four-poster bed as its centrepiece in a soft setting of cascading cream drapes and wheat-coloured walls. Stay at Las Nubes, enjoy a bird's-eye view of the world, drink in the peace. *A Rusticae hotel.*

rooms	6 doubles.
price	€72–€93; single €60; suite €108.
meals	Breakfast €6; lunch/dinner €24.
closed	Rarely.
directions	Madrid N-II Guadalajara; exit 23 Alcalá de H. Round town on M-300; M-204 through Villabilla to Yebra. Then left for Pastrana, right for Almonacid de Z. to Albalate de Z. Here for Ermita & Ruinas Históricas; house signed (village 8km, last 3.7km on track).

Carlos Sánchez

tel	+34 949 214500
fax	+34 949 826897
e-mail	lasnubes@csh.e.telefonica.net
web	www.casarurallasnubes.com

map 13   entry 171

El Nido de Valverde

Calle Escuelas 1, 19224 Valverde de los Arroyos, Guadalajara

El Nido de Valverde is hidden away in one of Guadalajara's furthest-flung corners. The village house which Concha and Mario have restored is a wonderful example of Guadalajara's *arquitectura negra* which uses the region's dark slate for walls and roofing: "the slates glint like fish-scales after the rain," says Mario. Your hosts are sympathetic, sensitive and care deeply for their guests – in the same way that they cared for the children in the workshops they used to organise. They are also passionate defenders of the fragile ecosystem and much of their food is organic. The house wraps you in its warm embrace the moment you enter and catch a first delicious waft of linseed oil or baking bread. There is the cosiest of dining rooms and above, two underfloor-heated, split-level suites whose decoration is as heart-warming as the rest of the house. Nearly everything you eat at breakfast and dinner is home-made. Stay at least a couple of nights; the nearest petrol station may be 50km off but you'll surely agree there can be few nicer places to stay in Spain. *A Rusticae hotel.*

rooms	2 suites.
price	€ 156.
meals	Breakfast € 11; lunch € 36; dinner € 28.
closed	Rarely.
directions	Burgos-Madrid on N-I. Exit for Riaza. Here to Santibañez de Ayallón, then follow signs for Atienza. Turn right for Cogulludo then right again to Valverde. Hotel in village square.

Concha Sanz Hipólito & Mario Alvarez

tel	+34 949 854221/971 307448
fax	+34 949 854221/949 307448
e-mail	contxa@nidodevalverde.com
web	www.nidodevalverde.com

Hospedería Rural Salinas de Imón

Calle Real 49, 19269 Imón, Guadalajara

Salt is still produced at Imón: you'll see the crystallising beds as you arrive. Just beyond is a tiny square and the salmon-pink Hospedería. This elegant house began life as a convent in the 17th century, then became a lowly salt warehouse. The heavy old studded door now opens onto another radical conversion, a mosaic of different styles and atmospheres. A sitting room vibrates with bright sofas, antiques and ornaments, old dolls and books, framed prints and huge repro paintings by Luis Gamo Alcalde, whose art is a thrill throughout the house, and a colourful stairway leads to the guest rooms, each differently themed. One is decorated with musical scores and signed photos of famous musicians, another has a Louis XVI-style cradle; Carlos III has Empire beds and family photos. Right at the top, a cosy log-fired library leads to a patio and a peaceful garden where the two towers of the original building rise and a secluded swimming pool blends in with its surroundings. Furniture restoration and painting courses are held here, in Spanish, Franch or English. A highly likeable place, professionally run but with a personal touch.

rooms	12: 11 doubles, 1 suite.
price	€ 57–€ 72; suite € 99.
meals	2 restaurants in village.
closed	Rarely.
directions	From Madrid N-II/E-90 towards Zaragoza. Turn left to Sigüenza; here take C-110 for Atienza to Imón. Hotel on main square of village.

Jaime Mesalles de Zunzunegui

tel	+34 949 397311
fax	+34 949 397311
e–mail	sadeimon@teleline.es
web	www.salinasdeimon.com

map 13   entry 173

Hotel Valdeoma

19266 Carabias, Guadalajara

Gregorio left a busy life in Europe and West Africa to restore a ruined house in the hamlet of Carabias, overlooking the mountains of Guadalajara. Now a small hotel, it is unmistakeably modern with large glass windows, stainless steel structures and minimalist interior – fine features that blend beautifully with the older elements of wood and granite. The entrance, with its metal staircase, low reception desk and parquet floor made by Gregorio himself gives Valdeoma a lovely informal feel. Bedrooms – five on the raised entrance level, the rest at ground level – have been finished in warm colours and have bathrooms of earth-coloured marble. Both dining room and sitting room glow with period furniture, with fireplaces for the winter and big glass balcony doors for the summer. From here, Valdeoma's most precious jewel: the view. Whether you're having breakfast or dinner or just lounging in one of the hotel's deeply comfortable armchairs, those huge views will be pulling you outside. And don't miss the medieval magic of the fine city of Sigüenza, a short drive away. *A Rusticae hotel.*

rooms	10 doubles/twins.
price	€90.
meals	Lunch/dinner €24.
closed	Rarely.
directions	From Madrid N-II/E-90 for Zaragoza then left for Sigüenza; there CM-110 for Atienza. After 7km left for Carabias & Palazuelos. In Carabias left past church, up hill; Valdeoma is at end of a narrow street on right.

Gregorio Marañón

tel	+34 600 464309
fax	+34 600 466921
e-mail	valdeoma@airtel.net
web	www.valdeoma.com

El Molino de Alcuneza

Carretera de Alboreca km 0.5, 19264 Alcuneza, Guadalajara

The quintessence of rural charm and fine taste: El Molino is proof of just what can be achieved when love and energy are present in great measure. Little remained of the 400-year-old mill buildings when Juan and Toñi fell for this swathe of delicious greenery whose rushing millrace promised soothing respite from the baking summers of Spain's vast Meseta. Originally it was to be a weekend bolt-hole for the family but then the idea of a hotel was mooted and Juan was hooked. Every last detail of the interior decoration has been carefully mused upon: pine floors, dark beams, rich fabrics, a glass floor under which flows a rivulet of crayfish and trout, framed pressed flowers (by an aunt), fine table linen, beautifully lit tables. Our favourite rooms are 3 and 4 but all are special. Guests are given separate tables, and dinner is a feast of locally grown produce: partridge with chickpeas, trout baked in Albariño wine, *cèpe*. Breakfasts are hearty and picnic hampers can be arranged. Sigüenza and Atienza, two great medieval villages, are a must-see. Arrive as a guest, leave as a friend – the Morenos are a delightful family. *A Rusticae hotel.*

rooms	11 doubles/twins.
price	€ 108; single € 72; suite € 180.
meals	Breakfast € 7.25; dinner € 27.05. Closed Sunday.
closed	Rarely.
directions	From Sigüenza, signs for Medinacelli. Molino well signed before you reach Alboreca, on right.

Juan & Toñi Moreno

tel	+34 949 391501
fax	+34 949 347004
e-mail	molinoal@teleline.es
web	www.molinodealcuneza.com

map 13   entry 175

Hotel Santo Domingo

Plaza Santo Domingo 13, 28013 Madrid

Hotel Santo Domingo is larger than the other hotels in this book but we include it because, in spite of its size, it manages to retain an intimate and friendly atmosphere. It is right at the hub of old Madrid, close to the Opera, the Plaza Mayor and a stone's throw from the shops of the Gran Vía. Step in off the street to find reception and lounge newly-decorated, paintings on the walls, a sparkling marble floor and comfy sofas to flop into. Masses of art is on display throughout the hotel and – take it on good authority – the décor in each of the 120 bedrooms is different. They contain all the extras you might expect given the four-star status: mini-bars and TVs, bathrobes and stacks of toiletries, safety boxes, writing sets, and, in the 'superior' rooms, hydro-massage baths. The desire to be as people-friendly as possible in the bedrooms holds true in the restaurant, too. Surprisingly for such a large hotel there is "good home cooking" on the menu, to quote Ana Hernández, the hotel's ever-friendly manageress. Santo Domingo won its laurels long ago, but still aspires to be first past the post.

rooms	120: 60 doubles, 60 singles.
price	€ 153–€ 208; single € 90–€ 158. Breakfast included at weekends.
meals	Breakfast € 11; lunch/dinner € 29 set menu, € 40 à la carte.
closed	Rarely.
directions	Along Gran Vía away from Cibeles; pass Plaza de Callao, left into c/San Bernardo to Plaza de Santo Domingo. Hotel on right. Porter will park car.

Antonio Núñez Tirado

tel	+34 91 5479800
fax	+34 91 5475995
e-mail	reserva@hotelsantodomingo.com
web	www.hotelsantodomingo.com

La Residencia de El Viso

Calle Nervión 8, 28002 Madrid

El Viso is one of Madrid's most chic areas, a quiet and leafy suburb surprisingly close to the centre. Only five years ago La Residencia was another smart, private domicile; now, thanks to the efforts of its young and engaging owner, this interesting Thirties-style edifice has become a reliable port of call for those visitors wishing to escape the noise and fumes of the city centre. Beyond the cheery façade and swing-glass doors is a marbled reception area where you are greeted by piped music and friendly staff. The long glass French windows bring in the light (no high-rise buildings in this area to rob you of the sun) and draw your attention to a walled patio garden — eat here in summer under the shade of the magnolia. The rooms are slightly faded around the edges but comfortable: some have carpet, others parquet, and colours and fabrics have been well matched. All but two of the rooms look out across the garden, and the air conditioning is, of course, a plus at the height of summer. In colder weather dine in the conservatory-style restaurant on good traditional Spanish food and wines.

rooms	12: 9 doubles, 3 singles.
price	€ 127; single € 76–€ 101.
meals	Breakfast € 9; lunch/dinner € 21, € 35 à la carte.
closed	Rarely.
directions	From Puerta de Alcalá, down c/Serrano towards Plaza de la Republica Argentina; just before reach square, left into c/Nervión; hotel has yellow awning.

Miryam Escudero

tel	+34 91 5640370
fax	+34 91 5641965
e-mail	reservas@residenciadelviso.com
web	residenciadelviso.com

map 12   entry 177

La Casa del Puente Colgante

Carretera a Uceda km 3, 28189 Torremocha de Jarama, Madrid

In this beautiful wooded spot on the banks of the Jarama River it's hard to believe that Madrid is less than an hour away. The name means 'the house of the suspension bridge': walk across it to discover a waterfall, a river pool for bathing and a grassy knoll from where to observe the exceptional bird life — you'll see kingfishers and herons if you're patient. The peace and beauty of the setting are reflected in the house: no TV but classical music, the sound of the river, even the song of a nightingale in spring. Silvia loves the spot dearly, knows its every tree and shrub and hopes that her guests leave with something of the tranquillity of her home deep within them. Bedrooms vary in size, are fairly plain but sparkling clean and have the best mattresses for comfort and eiderdowns for warmth. Silvia prepares simple lunches and dinners using organic fruit and veg, local cheeses and cuts of meat; try her delicious apple cake. You can bus in and out of Madrid from here to avoid yet more driving. *No-smoking.*

rooms	5 doubles/twins.
price	€60. VAT included.
meals	Lunch/supper €15. VAT included.
closed	23-25 December.
directions	From Madrid, N-1 Burgos; exit km50 marker for Torrelaguna. Towards Patones de Arriba, then right to Torremocha. Through village & signs 'farmacia & turismo rural'; after 3km, 'casa rural' sign on left by white columns.

Silvia Leal

tel	+34 91 8430595
fax	+34 91 8430595
e-mail	silvialeal@wanadoo.es

Sara de Ur

Corcho 26, 28751 La Cabrera, Madrid

Where else (except on *The Antiques Roadshow*) will you find such an assortment of finds? Such is the irrepressible enthusiasm of Alejandro for the antiques trade that the hotel is an Aladdin's Cave of Nepalese rugs, French furniture, Art Deco, African sculpture. There is nothing cave-like about the building however, which is sprucely modern and lacks the gentle patina of age. But though a purist might raise an eyebrow at the sudden jumps from old to new, as a guest you can enjoy. Colour-washed bedrooms are a good size, bathrooms are luxurious, split-level suites come with kitchenettes. Gardens are new but maturing well, and tennis and swimming are round the corner, thanks to an agreement with the campsite 200m away for guests to use their facilities for free. This is vibrantly fun place, with a hugely likeable host, at the foot of the dramatic craggy outline of Honey mountain. Do visit Patones, a completely intact 17th-century village untouched by modern times. And, in case you are wondering, Sarah of Ur was Abraham's wife, from that oldest of inhabited towns in Mesopotamia. *A Rusticae hotel.*

rooms	12: 6 doubles, 6 suites.
price	€85–€100; single €65–€70; suite €105–€130. VAT included.
meals	Lunch/dinner €28.
closed	Christmas & New Year.
directions	From Madrid, N-I for Aranda de Duero. Exit 57 to La Cabrera. Left by petrol station for Valdemanco. Right to hotel after approx. 20m.

Alejandro & Cecilia Burgos

tel	+34 91 8689509
fax	+34 91 8689514
e-mail	info@saradeur.com
web	www.saradeur.com

map 12   entry 179

Photography by Michael Busselle

LEVANTE

*"Two men look out through the same bars: one sees
the mud, and one the stars."*

FREDERICK LANGBRIDGE

El Molino del Río Argos

Camino Viejo de Archivel s/n, 30400 Caravaca de la Cruz, Murcia

The fruit and walnut farm is secreted away beside a rocky canyon cut by the Río Argos; its abundant waters explain why grain was milled here for nearly four centuries. Carmen and her Swedish husband Jan restored mill and outbuildings to create this small hostelry; it could be an 'eco' hotel. The earthy colour of the building was mixed to make the least impact on its physical setting, natural dyes were used for doors and beams, floor tiles were handmade following a 16th-century technique, and an organic orchard was planted on the terraces. A lost tradition has been revived, for in former times the mill was a kind of market-cum-inn when peasants came to barter their goods for flour. Nowadays you exchange your coins for a beautifully decorated apartment or room, and excellent Mediterranean and international dishes (including local venison and wild boar) served in a low-beamed dining room. An enjoyable alternative to dinner is the occasional crayfish and schnapps buffet supper: this tradition is slightly less local, being a variant on the Swedish midsummer *shindig*. An enchanting and blissfully quiet place and the kindest of hosts.

rooms	1 double. 6 self-catering apartments.
price	€42; apartment €59-€91. VAT included.
meals	Breakfast €4; lunch/dinner €22.
closed	Rarely.
directions	From Andalucia, A-7; after Lorca, direction Caravaca de la Cruz & Barranda. Farm signed from Benablón (before Barranda), 4km.

Carmen Alvárez

tel	+34 968 433381
fax	+34 968 433381
e-mail	elmolino@molinodelrio.com
web	www.molinodelrio.com

map 20   entry 180

Hacienda Los Sibileys

Nogalte 84, 30800 Lorca, Murcia

There are a number of ex-pats who have made their homes in the remotest of places; the Lanchburys are among them. They built their hacienda-style country hotel around an old farmhouse, lost in a sea of olive and almond trees in the border territory between Andalucía and Murcia. They saved all they could of the original edifice: a timber-lintelled fireplace, old roof beams, some original doors. The rough render of the newer parts makes it feel older: the house is a tribute both to times past and to the skill of local craftsmen, who completed the project in seven months... Bedrooms are large, light and beautifully upholstered, their Mexican beds, wardrobes, chests and bedside tables well-suited to their rural, southern-Spanish context. The large lounge/diner also shows a will to get local craftsmen in on the act: the long eat-together dining table is a copy of an English original, crafted by a local cabinet maker. (There are separate tables if you prefer.) *Tapas* lunches are full of local flavour, while dinners are inspired both regionally and further afield, and puds are home-made.

rooms	4 doubles/twins.
price	€70.
meals	Tapas-style lunch €6; dinner €21.
closed	Rarely.
directions	Murcia E-15/N-340 Puerto Lumbreras, then N-342 Granada. Exit 93 Henares. At small r'bout 2nd exit, signed 'servicios'. Pass petrol station, after 1.5km left over m'way to r'bout. Last exit, after 100m right on dirt road, signs for 3km.

Karl & Judith Lanchbury

tel	+34 968 439024
fax	+34 968 439024

El Fraile Gordo

Apartado 21, 03650 Pinoso, Alicante

Multi-talented David Bexon – singer, interior designer, upholsterer, actor – moved on to a new career as innkeeper and chef-in-residence of El Fraile Gordo. Why is it named 'The Fat Friar'? The fine *masia* stands where the Brothers of the Franciscan order once lived. Old farm buildings have been beautifully, even eccentrically renovated; you'd think David had been here for years, he introduced so many antiques, photos and mementos when he nursed the building back to life. And this is no simple farmhouse: stained-glass windows, grand piano, statues and original sculptures add sophistication to lowly origins. Guest bedrooms are fresh and welcoming, with beds for big sleeps and glorious wraparound views. There's a delightful walled garden with a small pool, a terrace that captures the morning sun, inspired cooking (do buy David's cookery book!) and a host whose hospitality and kindness run beyond the call of duty. "Bliss," said one of our readers. A self-catering cottage has recently been added which sleeps up to five, with full wheelchair access. *Children over 12 welcome.*

rooms	4: 3 doubles, 1 twin. 1 self-catering cottage.
price	€ 50–€ 60. Cottage € 110.
meals	Lunch/dinner € 21 à la carte. VAT inc. No meals Monday or Saturday evening.
closed	Last week January.
directions	Through Monovar to Pinoso & El Pino. Here, C-3223 for Fortuna. After 8km, right towards Cañada del Trigo; house in hamlet after 700m.

David Bexon

tel	+34 968 432211
fax	+34 968 432211
e-mail	david@fraile-gordo.com
web	www.fraile-gordo.com

map 20 entry 182

Ryder

Toledo 19, Casco Antiguo, 03002 Alicante, Alicante

This beautifully restored townhouse of colour and character in the slightly ramshackle old Casco is all yours. Its narrow face hides three floors, two terraces and a little patio. Straight in from the street is the high, darkly atmospheric kitchen/dining room where you find ancient stones (the house was built 200 years ago on Moorish foundations), a modern kitchen and the door to the cool beferned patio where a spring rises in an ancient smugglers' cave. Up to the wonderful pale green sitting room (which is also the twin bedroom) with red and green beams, good armchairs and an olive-picker's ladder to hang your clothes on – a brilliant touch of Marianna's, the creative owner of this unusual place. Up again to the blue and white double bedroom – colours get cooler as you get higher – with its shower room and little terrace for private views of old rooftops and the Moorish castle. Then up the precipitous spiral to the roof, through the pretty single room which perches here like a hat on a head, and out onto the larger terrace with its table, chairs and big parasol. A five-minute walk from the sea. *Not suitable for toddlers.*

rooms	3: 1 double, 1 twin, 1 single.
price	€ 500–€ 600 p.w., incl. linen & cleaner.
meals	Self-catering.
closed	October–May.
directions	In centre of Alicante. Owner will provide details on booking.

Marianna Ryder

tel	+34 965 204976
fax	+34 965 204976
e-mail	ornithogalum19@yahoo.es

Casa del Maco

Pou Roig, 03720 Lleus/Benissa, Alicante

It's described as a rustic farmhouse but the reality is grander. An imposing paved terrace, statuesque trees and Lloyd Loom furniture around the pool give Casa del Maco a gracious air. Inside, 18th-century rooms are similarly luxurious. The décor and furnishings show flair and restraint and only the beamed ceilings and the small, deeply recessed windows betray their farmhouse origins. The restaurant, too, is sophisticated rather than rustic, providing French haute cuisine and special wines. Behind the hotel, a bare shoulder of rock juts through the pine-covered hills of the Lleus valley. The grounds cover 4,000 square metres of terraced land, with vineyards, olive groves and almond orchards... there are excellent walks straight from the door. If you can face the crowds, and long for the sea, the Costa Blanca is only a short drive. From Calpe, you can walk up to the flat top of the Peñón de Ifach (or, if you're an experienced crag rat, do one of the desperate rock climbs on its south face). Either way, you'll get great views of the saltpans, the mountains and the precipitous coastline to Cape La Nao.

rooms	6 doubles.
price	€66-€99. VAT included.
meals	Breakfast €9; lunch €19; dinner €30-€52. VAT included.
closed	January.
directions	From Alicante, A-7 for Valencia. Exit for Calpe & Altea, then N-332 for Benissa. 900m after sign for Calpe, by BP petrol station, left for Casa del Maco, signed.

Bert de Vooght

tel	+34 965 732842
fax	+34 965 730103
e-mail	macomarcus@hotmail.com
web	www.casadelmaco.com

map 21   entry 184

El Sequer

Traviesa 17, Partida Frontó, 03769 Benimelí, Alicante

It's impossible to imagine it raining here, yet the lush fertility of the valley suggests that it must do sometimes. This beautifully restored *riu-rau* (a farm building used for drying grapes) and its gardens are full of light and colour. Orange trees beside a dazzlingly blue pool, corn-yellow walls and blue-painted shutters create a Mediterranean, sunlit mood. You are nicely tucked away here too, at the tail end of the village and with panoramic views to the smattering of villages ringed in a horseshoe around the valley. The garden is a delight, with an unusually well-integrated pool, lots of lush citrus trees, and lovely tile-clad tables and chairs for leisurely meals. Your living space is open-plan and airy, thoughtfully furnished and with a well-equipped kitchen. The double has a great antique bed; the bathroom a whirlpool bath. The bamboo-slotted ceilings, intersected with stout blue beams, are a hallmark of this type of building. Hospitable Jennifer will greet you warmly, and provides a little welcome pack for her guests, with tea, coffee, milk, juice, fresh fruit, bread… just the thing after a long drive.

rooms	2: 1 double, 1 twin.
price	Week € 600–€ 750; weekend € 260–€ 330. Minimum stay 2 nights; July/August 7 nights.
meals	Self-catering.
closed	Rarely.
directions	From Alicante, A-7 for Valencia. Exit 62 for Ondara, follow signs Ondara & Valencia. Then CV-731 & CV-732 to Beniarbeig. At bridge, left to Benimeli. 1st road up to right, signed.

Jennifer Pilliner

tel	+34 966 424056
fax	+34 966 424056
e-mail	jpilliner@telefonica.net
web	www.mediterraneorural.com

Casa Pilar

Calle San José 2, 03793 Castell de Castells, Alicante

This is *turismo rural* at its best: a proudly kept and genuinely friendly hotel of great charm, full of family furniture, books and paintings. From here you can explore the mountains of the Sierra de Aitana and return each evening to a 13-course dinner of unbelievable value: no wonder it is a favourite with hikers. The house has been in the Vaquer family for generations – both Pilar and her mother were born here – and is one of the largest in this quiet village; it was built originally for the priest. The dining room was once the stables, and still has its stone walls and hay manger – now filled with home-made jams and marmalades. This is where Pilar dishes out her gargantuan feasts, eaten around the great communal table. Bedrooms are light and bright and – best of all – deliciously cool in summer. Pilar is a warm and benign presence, ready to help with maps, picnics or tips on places to visit. Those who prefer a more sedentary existence can choose a book from the shelves in the sitting room upstairs and retreat to an armchair with one of Pilar's newly picked herbal infusions. Either way, you'll be well looked after. *No smoking.*

rooms	6 doubles/twins.
price	€48–€78; single €30. VAT included.
meals	Packed lunch €6; dinner €15. VAT included.
closed	Rarely.
directions	A-7 exit Ondara. Right at junc. to Parcent. Left at 1st junc., right at 2nd junc. opp. Pizzeria Tramontini to Benichembla & Castell de Castells. In Castells, left at lamp post junc. for town centre.

Pilar Vaquer

tel	+34 965 518157
fax	+34 965 518334
e-mail	casapilar@grupobbva.net
web	www.casapilar.com

map 21   entry 186

Hotel Els Frares

Avenida del País Valencià 20, 03811 Quatretondeta, Alicante

Brian and Pat left the UK to head for the Spanish hills. Herculean efforts have borne fruit at their village inn and restaurant – a 100-year-old ruin when they first set eyes on it. Now its attractive pastel frontage and a constant flow of visitors are adding life and colour to the village. Just behind, jagged peaks rise to almost 5,000 feet – the hotel takes its name from them. Rooms with private terraces look out across surrounding almond groves to those lofty crags. Good mattresses ensure deep sleeps, fabrics are bright, there are framed photos of the Sierra Serella, and some rooms have their original floor tiles. The cosy dining and sitting rooms are just right for the hotel; you'd look forward to returning here after a walk (though not in the height of summer!), perhaps with Brian as your guide. At supper choose from a menu that celebrates local dishes and *tapas* yet still finds a place for imaginative veggie alternatives; many ingredients – from olive oil, to fruit, to herbs – are home-grown. Your immensely likeable hosts have made many Spanish friends. *No smoking.*

rooms	9 doubles.
price	€48–€55; single €32.
meals	Breakfast €5, lunch/dinner €16–€22.
closed	8-25 January
directions	From Alicante A-7, junc. 70, onto A-36 Alcoi; CV-70 Benilloba, left to Gorga; sharp right through village & 5km to hamlet of Quatretondeta.

Patricia & Brian Fagg

tel	+34 965 511234
fax	+34 965 511200
e-mail	elsfrares@terra.es
web	www.mountainwalks.com

El Chato Chico

Plaza de la Iglesia 6, 03788 Beniaya - Vall d'Alcalá, Alicante

Don't expect much street life in Biniaya: at the last count there were just 14 inhabitants! Yet in the Middle Ages it was important enough for the Imam of the Moorish King Al-Azraq (the 'Blue-eyed one' – Jakki will tell you more about him) to have built himself a fine residence next to the mosque. It is this very building that the Walmsleys have nursed back to life and you can see one of the original Moorish arches in the beamed sitting room. The guesthouse has a snug, enveloping feel; bedrooms and public rooms (including a reading room) are smallish but your well-being is guaranteed thanks to good beds, central heating and the most peaceful of settings. At dinner don't expect purely Spanish food but do expect the lamb to be delicious: an enthusiastic reader wrote that "the quality of the food was outstanding for the price". If you prefer holidays with a theme, make a note that your hosts arrange courses in cookery, Spanish conversation and painting. Easy to see why they gave up their work in Benidorm to open this small inn, surrounded on all sides by glorious walking country.

rooms	5 doubles/twins.
price	€ 44–€ 60; single € 28. VAT included.
meals	Dinner € 18, incl. wine. VAT included.
closed	Rarely.
directions	From Alicante, direction San Vicente, then A-36 Alcoy, then N-340. 3km before Alcoy, right to Benilloba & Gorga. At Gorga junc. take Facheca road. Just before Tollos, sign to Beniaya (4km).

Paul Walmsley & Jakki Spencer

tel	+34 96 551 4451
fax	+34 96 551 4161
e-mail	elchatochico@wanadoo.es
web	www.elchatochico.com

map 21   entry 188

Casa Rural Almasera - Guesthouse

Abadía 20, 03828 Margarida-Planes, Alicante

Painted a bright and happy red, Casa Almasera is a *casa rural* high in the mountains of Alicante province; its proud aim is to make you feel good in body and spirit. Masses of relaxation therapies are on offer here: sauna, massage, yoga, meditation, respiration techniques, anti-stress courses, magneto-therapy, acupuncture, TaiChiChuan. As far as more energetic pursuits go, the walking round here is glorious as the area is full of natural limestone gorges; you can swim in secret lakes formed millions of years ago, explore caves and fascinating medieval villages, even visit a herb centre. The Almasera's rooms are light and airy, with beamed ceilings and simple, comfortable furnishings, and outside is a tiled terrace with sunloungers and views. Food is good and wholesome, most organically grown. The mountain air and the silence will soon heal body and soul. For culture, visit Cocentaina: once capital of a vast earldom, it has a 15th-century palace, a Clare convent and a Renaissance church.

rooms	5: 4 twins/doubles, 1 family. 3 self-catering apartments.
price	€ 50; single € 40; apartment for 4, € 80; apartment for 2, € 60.
meals	Lunch/dinner € 15.
closed	15-20 July.
directions	From Valencia, N-332 to Oliva. Exit Pego. Into Pego, right at 1st lights, following signs Cocentaina & Adsubia. Approx. 8km after Alpatró, left for Margarida.

Michael Vietze & Julian Mittelmann

tel	+34 965 514232
fax	+34 965 514314
e-mail	almasera@wanadoo.es

Casa el Pinet

Masía el Pinet s/n, 03459 Alfafara, Alicante

Deep in the dramatic Sierra Mariola nature reserve, a 200-year-old castellated beauty. The former residence of Dona Maria Luisa Gil-Dotz del Castellar y Catalina, grandmother of the present owner, it is a home that has been cared for by generations of Ortegas. Sergio and warm-hearted Dolores offer you B&B or self-catering. Ground-floor El Pinet is perfect for a large party; on the first floor in the coachman's quarters a smaller group will be as happy as Larry. Beams, terracotta floors, original features... rooms are cosy, shower rooms sparkle, furniture is a delightful mix of rustic antique and not so new. Rugs, quilts and rocking chairs give the *masia* a relaxed feel. Each apartment has its own lovely terrace (one huge and canopied), and you have a barbecue and an exquisite pool, with chairs and changing rooms, floodlit at night. Birdsong, cicadas and perhaps the distant hum of a tractor are all you hear in these 60 hectares of olive groves, pines, fields and hills. The area is known for its aromatic plants and herbs, you can visit nearby caves and ice-wells and the hiking and riding are magnificent. *Minimum stay two nights.*

rooms	El Pinet: 3 doubles, 1 triple. Pinet II: 3 doubles.
price	El Pinet: B&B €57–€63; self-catering €216 per day; Pinet II: €132 per day.
meals	Breakfast or self-catering
closed	Rarely.
directions	From N-330, exit at Villena & head east for Ontinyet. After Bocairent, right to Alfafara. House signed on left, 1.5km before village.

Sergio Castelló

tel	+34 965 529039
e-mail	info@elpinet.com
web	www.elpinet.com

map 21   entry 190

Masía la Safranera

Partida Serratella 13, 46650 Alcoy, Valencia

You may have heard of Alcoy because of its annual Fiesta de Moros y Cristianos when the whole town engages in mock battle until Saint George (Santiago) intervenes and puts the infidels to rout. You are less likely to have heard of La Safranera, a century-old farm and *bodega*. It is just five miles from the scene of the mock-medieval madness, protected by wooded hillsides and at the centre of a recently created Natural Park. The ever-courteous Rafael Llace Vila and his extended family have vested much love and labour in nursing these old buildings back to good health. Simple guest rooms strike a balance between traditional and functional, with old beams, modern tiles and decent beds and bathrooms. More striking is the dining room which has enormous old wine barrels and other oenological instruments on display as well as a mounted boar's head above the inglenook – a hunting trophy. The plastic chairs feel incongruous but food is from the regional recipe book and there is excellent bottled cider. Come for the tranquillity and be sure to walk from the house up to the old Sanctuary of Font Roja.

rooms	14 doubles/twins.
price	€ 48; single € 30.
meals	Breakfast € 6. Lunch/dinner € 6.
closed	Rarely.
directions	From Alcoy CV-795 towards Bañeres. 200m beyond signpost 'Bañeres 12km' turn left following signs to 'Alojamiento Turístico La Safranera'. Hotel 3km from junc.

Rafael Llace Vila

tel	+34 609 617280
fax	+34 962 245383
e-mail	lasafranera@teleline.es

La Casa Vieja

Calle Horno 4, 46842 Rugat, Valencia

This most peaceful of houses combines 450 years of old stones with a contemporary feel for volumes and shapes. There are original arches, columns and capitals (it was a nobleman's house), twisty beams, ancient floor tiles and a well in the lounge. In a more recent vein the swimming pool occupies part of the courtyard, and there are views to the orange-clad hillsides. A double-height sitting area faces an immense inglenook where deep sofas hug you as you sip your welcome sherry before dining, indoors or out. Many of the antiques have been in Maris's family for as long as she can remember – a 16th-century grandfather clock, Persian rugs, carved mahogany table, oil paintings. Bedrooms are full of character, the beds firm; kettles, tea and coffee remind you of home. Cooking follows the seasons; expect market-fresh produce with interesting veggie alternatives but if there's some dish you'd particularly like to try, just ask. The new restaurant is just the place for your feast: we really enjoyed the grilled goat's cheese with fig and orange confit and trust Maisie's recommendations when you choose your wine.

rooms	7: 6 doubles, 1 suite.
price	€ 80; single € 60; suite € 110.
meals	Dinner € 24.
closed	Christmas & New Year.
directions	From Valencia A-7 south, then exit 60. From Alicante exit 61 on A-7 northbound. N-332 for Gandia; exit onto CV-60 for Albaida. Exit for Terrateig, Montechelvo, Ayelo de Rugat & Rugat. Through Montechelvo; Rugat 2nd village to left, signed.

Maris & Maisie Andres Watson

tel	+34 962 814013
fax	+34 962 814013
e-mail	info@lacasavieja.com
web	www.lacasavieja.com

 map 21   entry 192

Hostería Mont Sant

Subida al Castillo s/n, 46800 Xátiva (Játiva), Valencia

The Arab Castle towers above, and the views over the red-roofed city and countryside below are stunning. Terraced gardens glistening with orange trees and 1,000 newly planted palm trees soften the habitat of fascinating archaeology... Iberian and Roman shards, Moorish fortifications, Cistercian monastery walls. A Moorish irrigation system has guaranteed water in all seasons since the 12th century and the mountain streams are channelled, refreshing the air as they go, into a vast cistern under the garden. Javier Andrés Cifre is proud of his old family house and delights in showing guests some of the relics he has uncovered during excavations – and the idyllic nooks and corners he has created in the natural gardens. Cool, beamed living areas have intimate alcoves; rooms above are furnished with antiques, different in feel to the new, timber-framed and highly sophisticated bedrooms under the pines. Overlooking the gardens they are air conditioned during summer, centrally heated in cooler months. Enjoy exotic food produced in state-of-the-art kitchens; should you over-indulge, turn to gym, sauna and jacuzzi. *A Rusticae hotel.*

rooms	12: 11 doubles/twins, 1 suite.
price	€90–€96; suite €270.
meals	Half-board €33; full-board €58.
closed	7-13 January.
directions	From Valencia N-340 for Albacete. Xátiva (Játiva) exit; follow signs for 'Castillo'. Signed.

Javier Andrés Cifre

tel	+34 962 275081
fax	+34 962 281905
e-mail	montsant@servidex.com
web	www.servidex.com/montsant

Casa del Pinar

Ctra. Caudete Km.3, 46354 Los Cojos de Requena, Valencia

Ping-pong in the shade of the pines — what more could you wish for on a summer's evening? There is plenty here to delight all the senses. Ana Maria and Phillipe took over the old *finca* 14 years ago. Ana speaks fluent English and used to write *tapas* programmes for the BBC; Phillipe, whose awards as a chef line the dining room, knows a thing or two about food — you'll eat well here. He has been known to share his culinary expertise by running the odd cookery course, and uses local produce such as the delicious Requena sausage, to which an entire festival is devoted every February. You can stay in the hotel, with its elegant, galleried sitting room, or in one of the self-catering houses, beautifully furnished in traditional style. All the buildings open onto the courtyard and enjoy an unusually close relationship with the outdoors. Flowers are everywhere, romping across the courtyard or amassed in great urns in the garden; beyond, almond orchards and olive groves. Oh, and a pool of Olympic proportions, from which to admire the view.

rooms	6 doubles. 2 self-catering houses.
price	€ 72; single € 60; suite € 90. House for 8, € 725 p.w.; house for 7, € 525 p.w.
meals	Lunch/dinner € 18.
closed	December-January.
directions	From Valencia, A-3 to Requena. Then N-322 for Albacete. After Los Isidros, right to Los Cojos. Pass turning for village. Hotel 1km further, on left.

Ana María Castillo
tel +34 962 139008
e-mail diment@wanadoo.es

map 14 entry 194

Hotel Cardenal Ram

Cuesta Suñer 1, 12300 Morella, Castellón

The whole of Morella is a national heritage site: you'll see why when you first catch sight of this fortress town girt about with its medieval walls. In one of its grandest mansions is a hotel as remarkable as the town. Just to one side of the colonnaded main street, the proportions and arched windows of the Cardenal Ram give it a slightly Venetian air; when it was built there was a cross-cultural exchange between the Genoese and the eastern Spaniards. Enter through the 15th-century arched doorway beneath the coat of arms of the Ram family and you may well be greeted by genial Jaime Peñarroya. A vaulted stairwell sweeps up to the bedrooms — and what rooms! They are big, with polished parquet floors, and bedheads, writing desks and chairs are all of carved wood. Bright bedcovers and rugs add a welcome splash of colour and the bathrooms are as good as they come. Truffles are a speciality here, and the puddings are home-made. Book several nights and discover the wild beauty of the Maestrazgo: there's a long distance pathway (GR route) linking these remote hilltop villages.

rooms	19: 17 doubles, 2 suites.
price	€55–€70; single €35; suite €65.
meals	Lunch/dinner €12 set menu, €30 à la carte. Restaurant closed Monday and Sunday out-of-season.
closed	Rarely.
directions	From Valencia A-7 for Barcelona; exit for Vinarós. Here N-232 to Morella. Up into old town (if lost ask for Puerta de San Miguel); hotel in main street 200m from cathedral.

Jaime Peñarroya Carbo

tel	+34 964 173085
fax	+34 964 173218
e-mail	hotelcardenalram@ctv.es

Photography by Michael Busselle

EXTREMADURA

"There is a good deal of Spain that has not been perambulated. I would have you go thither"
DR JOHNSON

Rocamador

Ctra. Nacional Badajoz-Huelva km. 41, 06171 Almendral, Badajoz

The monastery of Rocamador, long forgotten amid the wide, wild spaces of Estremadura, has had new life breathed into its old stones by remarkable owners, Carlos and Lucía. It is home and hostelry and so much more, and its food has earned a Michelin star. Inner patios are filled with lush greenery and fountains, labyrinthine buildings fan out around the cloister and chapel – a magical setting for dinners where music and candlelight accompany you into the early hours. You may recognise some of your fellow guests here: it's that kind of place. Bedrooms may not be the best lit but are among the most extraordinary we've seen; most are vast. So are the bathrooms, some with shower heads four metres up, some with a *chaise longue* next to the bath where you can recline like Madame Récamier. There are hand-painted tiles, enormous beds, three-piece suites, rich fabrics, wafer-bricking, vaulted ceilings, open hearths, incredible views. Never mind the hum from the main road as you linger by the pool... the Rocamador stands in a class of its own: sumptuous, daring, escapist, unique. *A Rusticae hotel.*

rooms	31: 26 doubles, 5 suites.
price	€ 120–€ 200; single € 130; suite € 250.
meals	Breakfast € 10–€ 15. Lunch/dinner € 30 set menu, € 40 à la carte, special set menu € 40–€ 48.
closed	Rarely.
directions	From Madrid N-V; exit La Albuera (km382 marker). Into village, then for Jerez de los Caballeros. At km41, right, over bridge, follow drive to Rocamador.

Carlos Dominguez Tristancho

tel	+34 924 489000
fax	+34 924 489001
e-mail	mail@rocamador.com
web	www.rocamador.com

Hospederia Convento de La Parra

Santa María 16, 06176 La Parra, Badajoz

Once here, you will become a devotee — like a former inhabitant of the convent who checked in when she was 13 and didn't leave until she was 84. This tranquil place, formerly home to the nuns of the Order of St Clare, has been subtly and beautifully transformed into a hotel of understated elegance: cool white walls, muted colours, mellow tiled floors. Rooms open off the central cloister, with orange trees and fountain, on two levels; twin woodburning stoves grace the high-beamed sitting room. Bedrooms have the simplicity of their former cell status but none of the austerity: the furniture is handmade, the tiling is impeccable, and old and new have been brilliantly married to provide comfort while preserving serenity. Some of the bathrooms have partly sunken baths and basins of beautiful earthenware or galvanised tin; others have double-arched ceilings. From the stork's nest on the bell tower to the cloister with its quietly bubbling fountain to the exquisite turquoise pool this is a special place — and there are no televisions or children to disturb the peace. A treasure.

rooms	21: 14 doubles, 5 singles, 2 suites.
price	€ 100–€ 120; single € 45; suite € 155. VAT included.
meals	Lunch/dinner € 25–€ 30.
closed	Christmas.
directions	From Sevilla, N-630 for Mérida. Then N-432 for Badajoz. Left for Feria & on to La Parra. Pass petrol station, left & up into village. Hospederia signed.

Javier Muñoz & María Ulecia

tel	+34 924 682692
fax	+34 924 682619
e-mail	laparra@wanadoo.es
web	www.laparra.net

map 17　entry 197

Hotel Huerta Honda
Avenida López Asne 30, 06300 Zafra, Badajoz

Travelling through western Spain do visit Zafra. There is a castle, a beautiful arcaded main square and any number of churches to visit, and Huerta Honda is the best place to stay. It is an unmistakably southern-Spanish hotel: geraniums, bougainvillaea, fountains in abundance and décor positively kitsch in places. In the guest sitting room are roaring log fires in winter and an extraordinary miscellany of decorative styles – wicker furniture, balsa parrots, geometric tiles, statue-lamps, a deer's head on the wall. The dining rooms feel snug with their ochre walls, heavy beams and beautifully laid tables, but other parts of the hotel feel less intimate; wedding parties come here and the hotel bar is always busy. The food is excellent, the cook is Basque and you may be tempted to splurge, but there is a cheaper menu if you prefer less elaborate food. Most bedrooms have balconies overlooking the plant-filled patio and are decorated with a whimsical mix of paintings, hand-painted furniture, rugs and wickerwork. Three much grander suites have recently been added which take Moorish, Christian and Jewish Spain as their touchstone.

rooms	48: 39 doubles, 9 suites.
price	€72–€90; single €57; suite €150.
meals	Breakfast €6; lunch/dinner €21 set menu, €24 à la carte. Closed Sunday evenings.
closed	Rarely.
directions	From Mérida south to Zafra. Hotel in city centre, near Palacio de los Duques de Feria.

Antonio Martínez Buzo

tel	+34 924 554100
fax	+34 924 552504
e-mail	reservas@hotelhuertahonda.com
web	www.hotelhuertahonda.com

Finca Santa Marta

Pago de San Clemente, 10200 Trujillo, Cáceres

Santa Marta is a fine example of an Extremadura manor house where the farmer lived on the top floor and the olive oil was made below. It has been totally transformed by interior designer Marta Rodríguez-Gimeno and husband Henri into a wonderful country retreat. Some of Santa Marta's bedrooms are tiny but each has a character of its own, with antiques in some, hand-painted Portuguese furniture in others. Those in the next-door building, the Finca Santa Teresa, are more rustic with locally-crafted furniture, but the effect is just as appealing. In the vaulted old olive-pressing area is an enormous, cool and elegant sitting room-cum-library with *estera* matting, neo-*mudéjar* ceiling, antique furniture and subtle lighting. Why so many South American bits and pieces? Henri was Dutch ambassador to Peru and it was the Latin readiness to share that inspired him to open his home to guests. He and his wife are not always in residence but when they are away a charming housekeeper steps in. There is fabulous birdlife in this part of Spain — and fabulous wine too, by all accounts: they now produce their own from Cabernet Sauvignon grapes. *A Rusticae hotel.*

rooms	14 doubles/twins.
price	€ 85.
meals	Lunch/dinner € 26.
closed	Rarely.
directions	From Trujillo, ex-208 for Guadalupe. After 14km, on right where you see eucalyptus trees with storks' nests (km89 marker).

Marta Rodríguez-Gimeno & Henri Elink

tel	+34 927 319203
fax	+34 927 334115
e-mail	henri@facilnet.es
web	www.fincasantamarta.com

map 17   entry 199

Hotel Rural Viña Las Torres

Ctra. Ex-208, Km. 87,6, 10200 Trujillo, Cáceres

A spectacular setting, and heaven for birdwatchers. Perched on the side of a hill, this undoubtedly curious building – a former private house that belonged to a Belgian entrepreneur – has views of epic proportions, particularly if you are lucky enough to get one of the tower rooms with their 180° panoramas. These also have most to offer in the way of comfort – a sofa to lounge on and a chair or two – for those who want to keep to their tower like Rapunzel. Bedrooms are on the whole simply furnished with modern furniture; bathrooms have more than a whiff of the 1970s. But the white marbled floors of the main sitting area, the working fireplaces and the kindness of the young owners more than make up for it. Those with small children will not feel the usual pang of anxiety when entering the dining room: meals are served on unpretentious oil-cloth-covered tables. You can sit outside in the shade of the colonnaded patio or wander around the unmanicured garden to the pool or tennis court, floodlit at night.

rooms	8: 5 doubles, 3 suites.
price	€ 68–€ 110; single € 56; suite € 93.
meals	Lunch/dinner € 16.
closed	Rarely.
directions	From Trujillo, ex-208 for Guadalupe. After 10km, take track on right, signed to hotel, for 800m.

Juan Pedro Gonzalez

tel	+34 927 319350
fax	+34 927 319355
e-mail	info@vinalastorres.com
web	www.vinalastorres.com

Casa Salto de Caballo

La Fontañera s/n, 10516 Valencia de Alcántara, Cáceres

An amazing place where it is hard to say which is the more edifying: the journey there, or the arrival. Follow a narrow road across glorious, rolling hills to this, the furthest reach of the province of Cáceres — and, indeed, of Spain: you are slap bang on the Portuguese border. This is where the smugglers plied their trade, saddlebags brimming with bread, coffee and garlic. These days you walk, or ride, straight out into Portugal's glorious São Mamede Natural Park along those same secret pathways with not a thought for border patrols. Eva was so taken with it all she left Germany to restore this elegant village house. The old floor tiles are still there, and the shutters, along with good solid comfort and a lack of gadgets and gimmickry. And it is all beautifully clean. Eva prepares innovative vegetarian meals (she is a nutritionist and dietician) and simple, *tapas*-style suppers — or you might prefer to walk into Portugal for dinner! Generous hostess, generous prices and as far from the madding crowd as you could wish to get.

rooms	5 doubles.
price	€ 40. VAT included.
meals	Lunch/dinner € 12.
closed	Occasionally in winter.
directions	From Cáceres N-521 for Portugal; through Valencia de Alcántara, then right for San Pedro. After 2km, right for La Fontañera; last house on left in village, signed.

Eva Speth

tel	+34 927 580865
fax	+34 927 580865
e-mail	saltocaballo@gmx.net

map 16 entry 201

El Vaqueril
Ctra. Ex 207, 10930 Navas del Madroño, Cáceres

The big skies and cork-oaked hillsides of Estremadura make the area one of Spain's grandest visual feasts. Reached by an immensely long track, and in the middle of 320 hectares of cattle ranch, this old farmhouse stands amid carob, olive and palm trees. Its ochre and white frontage gives it a southern face and the house is classic *cortijo*: things gravitate towards a large central patio, the South's most effective technique for ensuring shade at any time of the day. No two bedrooms are the same; they are big, decorated with bright fabrics and family antiques. There are pretty hand-painted tiles in bathrooms, framed etchings and prints, open hearths. There is a vaulted lounge with a riotous ceramic hearth and a cavernous, beamed dining room; pork comes from the farm, of course. This is a hotel that specializes in catering for large numbers at local events: weddings, bullfighting spectacles etc, so it may be lively. There's a big pool with good views. Breakfast is as generous as the evening meal – there may be home-made cake – and you may, once replete, cycle or walk out into the estate. Cáceres and Mérida are an easy drive.

rooms	14: 13 doubles, 1 suite.
price	€ 66; suite € 84.
meals	Breakast € 2.40; dinner € 22 set menu, € 30 à la carte.
closed	Rarely.
directions	From Cáceres, N-521 for Valencia de Alcántara. Then EX-207 for Navas del Madroño. Just before village, left at sign for house; follow long track (have faith!) to farmhouse.

Beatriz Vernhes de Ruanu

tel	+34 927 191001
fax	+34 927 191001
e-mail	elvaqueril@elvaqueril.com
web	www.elvaqueril.com

Finca El Cabezo

Ctra. Hoyos - Valverde del Fresno Km. 22.8, 10892 San Martín de Trevejo, Cáceres

It is an awe-inspiring journey across the western reaches of the province of Cáceres to the farm: rolling hills, cork oak forests, kites and eagles overhead... and the road virtually to yourself. You are headed for a working farm of more than 1,000 olive trees and a hundred head of cattle but don't expect to cross a muddy farmyard. Pass through the gates of this imposing granite-built farm and you enter a magical inner courtyard, softened by a rambling virginia creeper and a mass of potted plants. The guest rooms are in the house's eastern wing and their size and elegance come as a surprise: the decoration mixes old granite and antiques with parquet, warm paint schemes and modern art. The sitting room, too, would have the designer-mag people purring: slate floors and granite walls juxtapose warm paintings and fabrics. Feast on eggs fried in olive oil, goat's cheese, home-made cakes at breakfast, and at dinner, choose between cheerful restaurants in San Martín or a Michelin-listed eatery just down the road. And find time to go for a walk. Finca El Cabezo may be in one of Spain's furthest flung corners but it is worth the detour.

rooms	6 doubles/twins.
price	€ 76; suite € 92.
meals	Good restaurants nearby.
closed	Rarely.
directions	From Salamanca for Ciudad Rodrigo. Here, towards Cáceres; once over pass of 'Puerto de los Perales', right for Valverde del Fresno on EX-205. House on left at km22.8 marker. Signed.

Miguel Muriel García & María Moreno

tel	+34 927 193106
fax	+34 927 193106
e-mail	correo@elcabezo.com
web	www.elcabezo.com

map 10   entry 203

Casa Manadero

Calle Manadero 2, 10867 Robledillo de Gata, Cáceres

This is a really welcoming hostelry where you can self-cater, with a warm and rustic style. All-but-unknown Robledillo lies at the heart of the Sierra de Gata (yet still within easy reach of Salamanca and Portugal): what's so thrilling about Spain are these vast, untamed parts of its interior. The village's buildings make good use of the local slate; it may be christened 'black architecture' by the locals but it is not in the least bit gloomy. This is one of the region's prettiest villages, surrounded by forests of oaks, olive groves and vineyards. No less a man than Cervantes was fond of the local wines. The tiny restaurant has heavy old beams, delicate lighting and excellent regional food – "100% natural products," says Caridad, who has pillaged the family recipe books for your benefit. And there's plenty for vegetarians to get excited about, too. Apartments vary in size and layout following the dictates of the original building; they all are centrally heated, with fully-equipped kitchens and good views. A place which is actively helping to preserve regional differences.

rooms	4 self-catering apartments for 2/4; 1 apartment for 4/6.
price	Apartment for 2, €39–€51; apartment for 4, €60–€66.
meals	Breakfast €5; lunch/dinner €10.50 set menu, €13 à la carte. VAT included. Weekdays only.
closed	Rarely.
directions	Navalmoral de la Mata to Plasencia C-551. Here, C-204 Pozuelo de Zarzón; 100m after village, turn for Robledillo. 30km to village.

Caridad Hernández

tel	+34 927 671118
fax	+34 927 671173
e-mail	info@casamanadero.com
web	www.casamanadero.com

La Posada de Amonaría

Calle de la Luz 7, 10680 Malpartida de Plasencia, Cáceres

Juan Tomé's feelings for Estremadura and its people run deep; he has named his house after his grandmother. The house is at the top of Malpartida: its meticulously restored chocolate-and-coffee coloured frontage is easy to recognise. Its walls bear the gentle finish which only countless layers of limewash can give, while beams have been treated with beeswax and floors with linseed oil in an effort to use only natural finishes. The dining room is staggered on different levels with a handsome slate floor and an enormous hearth; it gives onto the house's original *bodega* where wine was once pressed: the huge amphorae are still in place and you could have a glass of wine and a *tapa* before dinner. Return to light, airy, antique-filled bedrooms which retain the original geometric floor tiles from the last century. The patio with palm tree is divine. Your charming hosts have endeavoured to recreate the spirit of the age when the house was built; perhaps it is affection for that era which explains their love of ballroom dancing. Don't miss the spectacular Tuesday market in Plasencia – or Cáceres, Trujillo, the Jerté valley and the Monfragüe Park. *No smoking. A Rusticae hotel.*

rooms	6: 3 doubles, 3 suites.
price	€60–€70; suite €80–€90. VAT included.
meals	Breakfast €5.
closed	1 July–8 August.
directions	N-630 south to Plasencia, then EX-108 to Malpartida de Plasencia. Take final turning to village; signs to Town Hall (Ayuntamiento). Posada at top of village, next to church.

Juan Tomé & Cruz Ibarra

tel	+34 927 459449
fax	+34 927 459446
e-mail	posada@amonaria.com
web	www.amonaria.com

 map 11   entry 205

Hotel Rural La Casa de Pasarón

La Magdalena 18, 10411 Pasarón de la Vera, Cáceres

Susana Ayala's great-grandparents would surely have approved of the careful restoration that has given the 19th-century house in which they once lived a new lease of life. An elegant portal of carefully dressed sandstone in the building's unusual, russet-coloured façade leads you into the entrance hall with its original vaulted ceiling. The lounge mixes old and new furnishings piecemeal; the photographic portraits are touching, the standard Impressionist prints less so. But the dining room has a really nice feel to it with just five attractively laid tables and the original marble-topped dressers — a lovely spot to begin your day with a breakfast of oven-warm bread, local cheese and fruit compote made by the family. Things from-the-home rather than the supermarket are *de rigeur* at dinner, too: thick cream of vegetable soup, home-made meatballs, a kid stew. Bedrooms are reached via a heavy granite staircase; eight are on the first floor, four in the attic. They are simple, spotless and quiet; those at the top have just skylight windows. Do visit the nearby monastery of Yuste where Charles V spent his final months.

rooms	12 doubles/twins.
price	€ 56–€ 70. VAT included.
meals	Lunch € 18; dinner € 10. VAT inc.
closed	10 January–10 February & 2nd fortnight in June.
directions	From Plasencia towards Jaraiz to Tejeda del Tietar. Here, left to Pasarón. Enter village, 1st turning to left. Signed.

Susana Ayala
tel	+34 927 469407
e-mail	pasaron@pasaron.com
web	www.pasaron.com

Antigua Casa del Heno

Finca Valdepimienta, 10460 Losar de la Vera, Cáceres

Casa del Heno stands superbly isolated on the southern side of the Gredos mountains, hidden away at the end of a four-kilometre track that follows the river out from Losar. The 150-year-old farm has been sympathetically restored by its owners, with granite, beams and cork the recurring decorative *leitmotifs*. Guest bedrooms get the balance just right: good beds, no television and views across the farm. A crystalline river meanders by and beyond are the mountains, criss-crossed with ancient footpaths. The whole of the valley is at its best in spring when the many thousands of cherry trees come into blossom — you'll need to book well ahead if you want a room during this annual spectacle. Ornithologists come to the area from all over Europe to focus their binoculars on azure-winged magpies, kites, vultures, even great bustards. Javier and Graciela are quiet and caring hosts. They offer their guests time-tried home cooking in Heno's slightly oversized dining room, and use only the very best cuts of meat. A reading room, with views down towards the river, has recently been added. You can go horse-riding here, too.

rooms	7 doubles/twins.
price	€ 46–€ 53.
meals	Packed lunches available; dinner € 15.
closed	Christmas & the month after Epiphany.
directions	From Madrid, N-V to Navalmoral de la Mata. Right onto ex-119 for Jarandilla to Losar de la Vera. Behind Town Hall (Ayuntamiento) to 'piscina de Vadilla'; mountain track for 3.5km to hotel, signed.

Graciela Rosso & Javier Tejero Vivo

tel	+34 927 198077
fax	+34 927 198077

map 11   entry 207

Camino Real

Calle Monje 27, 10459 Guijo de Santa Bárbara, Cáceres

Guijo de Santa Barbara is one of the Gredos's highest, prettiest villages, famous for the springs which rise 1,000 feet above. It is also a stopover for walkers heading for the higher peaks, and for shepherds and cowherds leading their livestock up to summer pastures. Camino Real is at the heart of the village, named after the Royal Way, the route that the ailing Emperor Charles V followed as he made his way to the monastery at Yuste. It is a tall building with a new annexe below, and the six bedrooms, each named after a species of tree, are in the older part. They have a snug feel and have been prettily decorated with antiques, old prints and attractive fabrics which complement the dressed stone walls and tiled or planked floors. More antiques in the dining and sitting rooms, next to the terrace with views across oak and chestnut forests to the Gredos. There's also a small library: the generosity of your hosts is captured in a small sign which tells you that if you haven't finished a book by the end of your stay, you send it back when you have. The food is good, the staff friendly and the beautiful monastery of Yuste is well worth a visit.

rooms	6 doubles/twins.
price	Half-board €96; single €60.
meals	Lunch €13; dinner included. VAT included.
closed	Rarely.
directions	From Madrid south-west on N-V, then exit 178 for Navalmoral de la Mata Este. Right on EX-119 to Jarandilla de la Vera. Here right to Guijo de Santa Bárbara. House signed just to right of main street into village.

Carmela Pérez Fontán

tel	+34 927 561119
fax	+34 927 561119
e-mail	caminoreal@casaruralcaminoreal.com
web	www.casaruralcaminoreal.com

Finca El Carpintero

Ctra. N-110 km 360.5, 10611 Tornavacas, Cáceres

The Jerte valley is best seen in spring when the blossom of a thousand cherry trees turns the green sides of the valley a stunning pink. Ana and Javier, a young couple from Madrid, have turned these old farm buildings into a country B&B with a difference: a happy union of rusticity and up-to-the-minute comfort. Enter via a large terracotta-tiled dining room – a bar in one corner, Bigotines (the dog) in another – then climb the stair to an enormous guest lounge. It is most striking: a wall of solid rock, a huge granite hearth, a high-beamed ceiling and an enormous window that lets the light come streaming in. Here – and in the bedrooms, too – are cut flowers, paintings and carefully matched prints. Ana's artistic flair is on show throughout the house and the hand-painted furniture, the bows on the sash windows, the drapes behind the beds are all her work. The older rooms are the most charming. A first-class breakfast is included and you should give lunch or dinner a go: Ana and Javier's food (no menu) follows the seasons and they buy local produce whenever possible. Both speak excellent English.

rooms	9: 7 doubles, 2 suites.
price	€54–€60; suite €72. VAT included.
meals	Lunch/dinner €21.
closed	24 December-8 January.
directions	From Madrid N-VI then N-110 to Ávila; then on for Plasencia. Pass village of Tornavacas; house signed on right after 1.5km.

Ana Zapata de la Salud & Javier González Navarro

tel	+34 927 177089
fax	+34 927 177384

map 11   entry 209

ANDALUCIA

"One never grows tired of the beauty of Spanish light and scenery"

GERALD BRENAN

Casas Rurales Los Gallos

Almonaster la Real, 21350 Estación de Almonaster, Huelva

It sounds unlikely: an old Anis factory and outbuildings perched above the Huelva-Zafra railway line. But wait: you don't have to be a trainspotter or a *Brief Encounter* fan in search of romance to enjoy Los Gallos. Its immaculate whitewashed buildings rest in a labyrinth of different levels, one building out on its own looking towards the rest and a huge wild garden with stunning new pool and overgrown paths, a delight to explore. Equally wild are the surrounding hills with their cork oaks and tortuous paths where you can ride, walk — or get lost. Trains pass twice a day and there's a surprisingly good restaurant on the platform, but if you've had enough of station life you can eat out on your own private patio. Though the buildings are old the interiors are modern, a delicious mix of antique and new, cosy and chic; the smallest is the most rustic in feel. Each apartment has a big living/dining area and beautifully equipped kitchen. Bathrooms are small but space is generous on the patios, where it's most needed, with some good furniture for dining out or enjoying a drink in the shade. Ana lives in the main house and will make you welcome.

rooms	6 self-catering apartments.
price	Apartments for 4 & 6, €84–€120 per day; apartment for 2, €60.
meals	Breakfast €6; packed lunch €6. Good station restaurant.
closed	Rarely.
directions	From Sevilla, N-630 for Mérida. Then N-433 to Aracena. Past Aracena, left at El Repilado, for Estación de Almonaster. Narrow road to station, then uphill. Apartments on left.

Ana Rico Castelló

tel	+34 959 501167
fax	+34 959 501167
e-mail	aracenapark@eresmas.com

map 16   entry 210

Finca la Silladilla

21290 Los Romeros, Huelva

Just to the west of the market town of Aracena lies the Natural Park of the same name – a huge 90% of it is forested yet it embraces some of Andalucía's prettiest villages. Finca La Silladilla stands in glorious isolation at the very western end in the midst of a forest of century-old oaks: you couldn't wish for a more pastoral setting. Choose between two rooms in the old house (a former textile mill) or one of the four nearby farmhouses, more isolated still. The decoration of the rooms could be described as 'smart-rustic': old brass bedsteads, perhaps a Deco table, parquet floors; each is different, and each has a stylish bathroom. The views to the forest are gorgeous. Unusually there is no dining room in the main house, but breakfast is delivered to your room. In the farmhouses the same arrangement applies and there are also kitchens for self-catering; there's a small farm shop where you can buy the makings of a simple meal. (This also doubles as a tiny bar for *tapas*.) A wonderful place to stay for those in search of perfect peace. Call for details of reception opening hours. *A Rusticae hotel.*

rooms	2: 1double, 1 suite. 4 self-catering houses.
price	€ 64–€ 96. 2-bedroom house € 128–€ 154; 3-bedroom house € 192–€ 231. VAT included.
meals	Light snacks € 16. VAT included.
closed	Rarely.
directions	From Sevilla, N–630 for Mérida, then N–433 through Aracena for Portugal. After El Repilado, left for Los Romeros. La Silladilla signed to left, just past cemetery.

Beatrie Iglesias Hernandez

tel	+34 959 501350
fax	+34 959 501351
e-mail	silladi@teleline.es

Finca Buen Vino

Los Marines, 21293 Aracena, Huelva

After many years in the Scottish Highlands, Sam and Jeannie knew that to settle happily in Spain they would need to find a place of wild natural beauty. They chose this divinely isolated spot amid the thick oak and chestnut woods of the Aracena mountains. You would never guess Buen Vino was less than 30 years old: many of the materials they used were old, shipped in from far corners of Spain — the panelled dining room, the arched doors and the wooden staircase leading to the guest rooms have that seductive patina that only time can give. The house's decoration is unaffected yet elegant. Jeannie is a *Cordon Bleu* cook and our candlelit dinner with quail and Iberian pork with woodland *setas* was unforgettable. Meals are star-lit on the terrace in summer. The guestrooms are all different: one has a bathtub with a view, another a sitting-cum-dressing room; the Bird Room has its own hearth. In each you find books, cheery oil paintings, family memorabilia. There are also three independent cottages to rent, hidden away on the edges of the estate, each with its own pool.

rooms	4 doubles. 3 self-catering cottages.
price	€ 130-€ 150. Cottages: contact for details.
meals	Lunch on request (summer only) € 15; dinner € 30.
closed	July & August; Xmas & New Year.
directions	From Sevilla N-630 north 37km, then N-433 for Portugal & Aracena. Los Marines 6km west of Aracena. Finca is 1.5km west of Los Marines, to right at km95 marker.

Sam & Jeannie Chesterton

tel	+34 959 124034
fax	+34 959 501029
e-mail	buenvino@facilnet.es
web	www.buenvino.com

map 17   entry 212

Molino Rio Alájar

Finca Cabezo del Molino s/n, 21340 Alájar, Huelva

Rustling leaves and birdsong. Come for the peace, or for the famously delicious ham or, in November, for the mushrooms. This gentle complex of self-catering stone cottages seems as much part of the natural scenery of this secret valley as the cork trees which surround it. Each has its own terrace, and each is finished to a high standard by the Dutch owners, Peter and Monica. Peter, who once walked from Amsterdam to Santiago de Campostella, is working on a guide to local walks, so you will not be left to wander aimlessly. The larger houses have underfloor heating and log fires, and steep stairs to the upper sleeping area. The smaller house is open-plan and has no kitchen but you can cook in the well-equipped reception building. Each dwelling is beautifully presented, with ceramic tiles from Sevilla and Madrid, mellow terracotta floors and woven rugs. There is a beautiful, shared pool, and plenty of places to eat in Alájar. This is frontier Spain and Portugal is a stone's throw away, but you may not wish to venture very far. You drift off to sleep with a mantle of stars above, and wake to birdsong in the morning. Why leave? *Multi-lingual hosts.*

rooms	5 houses for up to 6.
price	€ 420–€ 700 per week.
meals	Self-catering.
closed	Rarely.
directions	From Sevilla, N-630 for Mérida. Then N-433 to Aracena. Left on A-470 to Alájar. After Alájar, at km13/14, left & follow signs.

Peter Jan Mulder

tel	+34 959 501282
fax	+34 959 125766
e-mail	rioalajar@wanadoo.es
web	www.molinorioalajar.com

Las Navezuelas

A-432 km 43.5, Apartado 14, 41370 Cazalla de la Sierra, Sevilla

A place of peace and great natural beauty, Las Navezuelas is a 16th-century olive mill on a farm set in 136 hectares of green meadows, oak forest and olive groves. Water streams down from the Sierra, often along Moorish-built channels. Boar and deer roam the Aracena range to the north and pretty Cazalla is two miles away. The house is pure Andalucía with beams and tiles; the garden is a southern feast of palms and orange trees, rambling wisteria and jasmine. The rooms are fresh, light and simple with old bits of furniture: nothing in excess yet nothing missing. There are two sitting rooms and a welcoming dining room with log fires in winter. The menu includes delicious local dishes made almost exclusively with ingredients from the farm — vegetables, chicken, lamb, ham. And there's home-made jam for breakfast. The friendly young owners go out of their way to help and give advice on expeditions on foot, horse or bicycle and where best to watch birds: the whole area is an ornithologist's dream. Many of our readers have written to say how much they like it here and hope to return.

rooms	6: 4 doubles, 2 suites. 4 self-catering studios; 1 apartment.
price	€ 51–€ 55; single € 34.50–€ 41. Studio for 2, € 79–€ 82; apartment for 4, € 90–€ 95.
meals	Lunch/dinner € 15. VAT included.
closed	7 January-25 February.
directions	From Sevilla A-431 to Cantillana. Here take A-432 for El Pedroso & Cazalla. Pass km43 marker; after 500m, right at sign for Las Navezuelas.

Luca Cicorella & Miló Tena Martín

tel	+34 95 4884764
fax	+34 95 4884594
e-mail	navezuela@arrakis.es
web	www.arrakis.es/~navezuela

map 17   entry 214

Palacio de San Benito

San Benito s/n, 41370 Cazalla de la Sierra, Sevilla

Four-star treatment with an informal feel... the sandy brick façade, nuzzling up to the 15th-century church with quirky triangular tower, gives no clue as to what lies within. The raised swimming pool with its spouting fountain, the baroque façade of the church-turned-banqueting-hall, the curved, ornately-tiled stair: a splendid theatricality pervades this *palacio*. The delightful Don Manuel, whose noble lineage is attested to in the stately interiors, was a set designer for the opera and he inherited the palace from his grandmother. By a curious feat of stage management he had the building moved, brick by brick, to its present location. Manuel has let his design flare run riot throughout, using bold juxtapositions of colour and style: one bedroom is dominated by a vast 18th-century tapestry, a present from the royal family, while loudly floral fabrics clamber over the four-poster bed and adorn the windows of another. Bathrooms are sumptuous and the central sunny patio with glazed cloisters is a gem. With a top-class chef and a memorable dining room to boot, this is a place where — like a trip to the opera — one should just sit back and let it happen.

rooms	9 doubles/twins.
price	€ 150–€ 210; single € 120.
meals	Lunch/dinner € 30–€ 45.
closed	Rarely.
directions	From Sevilla, N-630 for Mérida, right on A-431 to Cantillana, then A-432 to El Pedroso & onto Cazalla. Palacio on right, up hill, at village entrance.

Don Manuel Morales de Jódar

tel	+34 954 883336
fax	+34 954 883162
e-mail	info@palaciodesanbenito.com
web	www.palaciodesanbenito.com

La Cartuja de Cazalla

Ctra A455 Cazalla - Constantina km 2.5, 41370 Cazalla de la Sierra, Sevilla

An exceptional place, an exceptional owner. The 15th-century Carthusian monastery, one of only four in Andalucía, lay empty for 150 years until Carmen Ladrón, visiting in the 1970s, realised her vision. She founded here a Centre for Contemporary Culture, which now includes an art gallery and a ceramics workshop where the crockery once used by the Brothers is reproduced. Rooms are decorated with works by artist guests; painters, sculptors and musicians have, on occasion, given their art in exchange for their stay. The guest bedrooms, which finance the centre, are in the old monastery gatehouse and have been well restored; light streams through a huge skylight. They have modern furniture and bathrooms, and, in keeping with the gentle spirit of the place, no telephones or TV. Other rooms are in what were once monks' cells. Dine with Carmen in her home next door, unwind in the healing centre, ride horses from the Cartuja stables, roam the surrounding 100 acres. We have happy memories of wandering through the monastery's utterly peaceful grounds in the early morning light. A remarkable place. *A Rusticae hotel.*

rooms	12: 8 doubles, 4 suites.
price	€ 60–€ 90; single € 40–€ 50; suite € 90–€ 120.
meals	Lunch € 15; dinner € 20, wine included.
closed	24 & 25 December.
directions	From Sevilla C-431 to Cantillana then A-432 to El Pedroso & Cazalla. There, right onto A-455 for Constantina. La Cartuja is at km2.5 marker.

Carmen Ladrón de Guevara Bracho

tel	+34 954 884516
fax	+34 954 884707
e-mail	cartujsv@teleline.es
web	www.skill.es/cartuja

map 17   entry 216

Casa Grande

Ctra. Constantina-Cazalla Km 1, 41450 Constantina, Sevilla

In classic hunting country Casa Grande is fast making a reputation for itself. (The King of Spain is said to have been a recent guest.) The house is long and low, standing on its own little hillock well back from the road; all around are oak-covered hills. The mature garden is English in style – apart from its Chirinquito bar – with fine lawns, trees and an organic vegetable garden. There's an English-country-house feel indoors too, and not just because afternoon tea is served... The sitting room is decorated in shades of cream and white, furnished with large sofas, antiques, stately bookcases and some beautiful old paintings and prints. Deep colour-washes on the bedroom walls create a gracious background for simple, stylish furnishings. Luis and Margarita have created a delightful place to stay in this remote area, and are attentive hosts; Margarita is also a very good cook and Luis's wine list is superb. They have a friendly spaniel, and are happy to provide a kennel if you bring your own best friend. Riding – horses or quad bikes – and hunting can be arranged.

rooms	6: 5 doubles, 1 suite.
price	€ 96; suite € 150.
meals	Lunch/dinner € 33.
closed	Rarely.
directions	From Sevilla, N-630 for Mérida. Shortly after leaving city, right on SE-182 for Palma del Rio. At Lora del Rio, left on A-455 to Constantina. House 1km outside village on Cazalla road.

Margarita Molina Arenas

tel	+34 955 881608
fax	+34 955 881608
e-mail	lplaza@viautil.com

Hotel Cortijo Aguila Real

Ctra Guillena-Burguillos, km 4, 41210 Guillena, Sevilla

Aguila Real is every inch the classic *cortijo*: an elegant whitewashed building, surrounded by fields of cotton, sunflowers and wheat, only a dozen miles from the narcotic charms of Sevilla (you can see the Giralda tower from the gardens). Passing under the main gate you enter the huge inner courtyard where there is bougainvillaea in profusion; an old dovecote and water trough remind you this was a working farm. The public rooms are decorated in pastel colours with heavy old tables, paintings, hunting trophies, lots of books, and they have beautiful barrel-vaulted ceilings. In the dining room: silver cutlery, classical music and regional food, with most vegetables home-grown. The wine list is long and *tapas* and *raciones* are available at lunchtime. Bedrooms are set around an inner courtyard and have hand-painted furniture, huge double beds and double-sinked bathrooms; some have their own terrace. The palm-filled garden, carefully lit at night, is enchanting. *Minimum stay two nights.*

rooms	14: 10 doubles, 4 suites.
price	€ 100–€ 120; single € 74–€ 96; suite € 106–€ 170.
meals	Breakfast € 10; lunch/dinner € 24 à la carte.
closed	Rarely.
directions	From Sevilla N-630 for Mérida. After 9km, right on SE-180 Guillena. Through village; at 2nd lights, right on SE-181 Burguillos. Straight across at r'bout: hotel signed after 4km on right.

Isabel Martínez

tel	+34 955 785006
fax	+34 955 784330
e-mail	hotel@aguilareal.com
web	www.aguilareal.com

map 23   entry 218

El Esparragal

Carretera de Mérida Km 795, 41860 Gerena, Sevilla

One of the most beguiling buildings of southern Spain, in a setting of isolated, rare beauty. Medieval monks built a monastery here; later, a *cortijo* was grafted onto the edifice when Disestablishment sent the Brothers packing; at the end of the 19th century came reform and embellishment. The main façade will raise a sigh with its ceramic tiled tower, Roman arched windows and bougainvillaea: beyond it are two main patios (one of them the original cloister) and the guest rooms and suites; you will travel far to find any that quite match them. Approach them past fountains and arches. Spain's best-known designers have created a southern miracle in salons, dining room and guest suites with his and her sinks: the whole hotel is a *Who's Who* of fabric, tile, and furniture 'names'. There are oil paintings, *mudéjar* doors, gilt mirrors, tapestries – elegance permeates every corner. Ride out into Esparragal's 3,000 hectares on Andalucían thoroughbreds, dine on game or estate-raised beef, treat yourself to an Arabian night that you'll never forget. A sumptuous place, with charming staff. (Note: simpler rooms are without air conditioning.)

rooms	18 twins/doubles.
price	€ 106–€ 195; single € 84–€ 130.
meals	Breakfast € 7.21; lunch/dinner € 27.
closed	Rarely.
directions	From Sevilla, N-630 for Mérida. After 21km, left for Gerena (2nd turn for Gerena). Signed on left after 1.5km.

Familia Oriol Ybarra

tel	+34 955 782702
fax	+34 955 782783
e-mail	elesparragal@elesparragal.com
web	www.elesparragal.com

Casa el Marqués

c/ En medio 40-42, 41950 Castilleja de la Cuesta, Sevilla

The Dukes of Sevilla came to this area to escape the oppressive heat of the city. You might be tempted to do likewise, and still be only a 15-minute bus ride from the historic centre. There is a strong sense of being hidden away here: your holiday house is tucked behind the high wall of the Casa de Cultura, in the grounds of a former olive mill. It belongs to Juan and Macarena, whose knowledge of the history and culture of the city will set you on the right sightseeing track. Via a small courtyard (your hosts live opposite) you enter a simply furnished house, with cool tiled floors and some period furniture. The two bedrooms, one with a balcony that overlooks the patio, are clean and uncluttered. Downstairs are the bathroom and living room, with some patio furniture outside should you wish to spill into the sun. There are flashes of bright local colour in the tiling on the stairs and in the pots outside, and those who like to escape the noise and dust of the city will relish the prospect of taking a dip in Juan and Macarena's pool – an added bonus.

rooms	2 twins/doubles.
price	€ 104–€ 125.
meals	Self-catering.
closed	Rarely
directions	Sevilla–Huelva A-49. At km3, exit for Castilleja. Over 1st r'bout, then left. Next r'bout, left onto main street. Right at *Telepizza*, following signs for Casa de Cultura. House next to Casa de Cultura, behind high wall.

Macarena Fernandez-Palacio Gonzalo & Juan Castro

tel	+34 629 791188
fax	+34 954 160419
e-mail	casaelmarquessevilla@yahoo.es
web	casaelmarques.galeon.com

map 23   entry 220

Hotel Simón

Calle García de Vinuesa 19, 4100, Sevilla

A stone's throw from the Cathedral is the Simón, a friendly, unpretentious little hotel – perfect for those travelling on a tighter budget. Gentle-mannered Francisco ('Frank') Aguayo García enjoys receiving guests and practising his excellent English. The hotel is utterly Sevillian; you pass through the main portal, then a second wrought-iron door, and on into a cool inner patio. Tables are laid out among aspidistras and ferns: the perfect retreat from the throbbing heat (in Sevilla temperatures can creep into the 40s in summer). The dining room has old mirrors and ceramic-tiled walls, period tables and chandeliers – reminders that this was a grand, bourgeois residence. The bedrooms are set around the patio and reached via a marble staircase. They are clean, simply decorated and air conditioned: a bonus in the summer. Many of the rooms have been redecorated: Frank is for ever striving to make the Simón a better place to stay. There are plenty of restaurants and bars nearby and friendly staff will advise on where to find the best *tapas*. Light sleepers should note that at weekends local bars stay open until late.

rooms	29 twins/doubles.
price	€ 82–€ 66; single € 50–€ 44; suite € 107–€ 94.
meals	Breakfast € 3.85.
closed	Rarely.
directions	From Plaza Nueva in centre of Sevilla take Avenida de la Constitución (if closed to traffic, tell police you are going to hotel) then right onto c/Vinuesa (one way).

Francisco Aguayo

tel	+34 954 226660
fax	+34 954 214527
e-mail	hotel-simon@jet.es
web	www.hotelsimonsevilla.com

Casa Nº 7

Calle Virgenes 7, 41004 Sevilla

The owner, an exceptionally kind aristocrat from Jerez, has a great fondness for Britain and the British. And perhaps it was memories of England's country houses which inspired the conversion of his home into a hostelry. It was no rush job: he preferred to spend "an extra year or two" ensuring that every last inch would evoke a mood of privileged intimacy in keeping with Sevilla's Moorish architecture. Bedrooms are regal affairs, fabrics, furniture, lighting and bathrooms are top-notch while the photos of famous forebears, books (*Who'sWho!*) and magazines help create the home-from-home mood. Three first-floor reception rooms give onto the patio bedrooms. The cool and elegant drawing room is a distinguished spot for a glass of sherry – from the family's Jerez *bodega*, of course. In a quiet dining room there are scrambled eggs for breakfast served by one of the hotel's two butlers – and perfect marmalade. You are in a quiet Santa Cruz street (you can see the Giralda from the roof terrace), Gonzalo knows all the best places to eat and drink, and nearby is a great flamenco bar. An exceptional small hotel.

rooms	6 twins/doubles.
price	€ 170.
meals	Restaurants nearby.
closed	Rarely.
directions	At heart of Santa Cruz quarter. Park in Aparcamento 'Cano y Cueto' at junc. of c/Cano y Cueto & Menendez Pelayo (next to Jardines de Murillo). Tell attendant you are staying at Casa No. 7. From here 5 minutes' walk to hotel (or take taxi).

Gonzalo del Río y González-Gordon

tel	+34 954 221581
fax	+34 954 214527
e-mail	info@casanumero7.com
web	www.casanumero7.com

map 23   entry 222

Casa de Carmona
Plaza de Lasso 1, 41410 Carmona, Sevilla

The elegant brochure urges you to "enjoy for a few days the lifestyle of a Spanish aristocrat"... it would be easy to wander about this splendid Renaissance palace doing just that. The style is on a decidedly grand scale and the 'state' rooms are especially elegant – though not without those occasional spots of peeling paint which mark many a nobleman's residence. However, the addition of some essentially modern luxuries (a swimming pool, sauna, even a hairdresser) brings us firmly into the 21st-century. It is the beauty of the building and its setting within the walls of the ancient town of Carmona that puts it into the 'special' catergory. The sandstone façade is first seen across the tree-lined square where you park; inside, the warm apricot walls of the two interior patios, with their mass of dark green foliage marshalled into serried ranks of terracotta pots, set the tone. In effecting the transition from 16th-century palace to modern luxury hotel, the owners have managed to preserve something of the indefinable air of an aristocratic residence while catering for the desire in most of us to be well and truly pampered.

rooms	32: 24 doubles, 8 suites.
price	€140–€270; single €135–€205; suite €210–€310. VAT included.
meals	Lunch/dinner €30 à la carte.
closed	Rarely.
directions	From Sevilla, N-IV for Córdoba. After 25km, exit for Carmona. Head for city centre, following signs to Centro Histórico & hotel.

Arancha López-Pazo Terrades

tel	+34 954 191000
fax	+34 954 190189
e-mail	reserve@casadecarmona.com
web	www.casadecarmona.com

Hotel Palacio Marqués de la Gomera

San Pedro 20, 41640 Osuna, Sevilla

Calle San Pedro was *the* address to have in Osuna in the 18th century. Many of the local aristocrats had their townhouses here, and could afford to do themselves proud. (The Duke of Osuna himself owned so much land that he could ride from Sevilla to Málaga without leaving his estate.) The result is a remarkably pretty street in a lovely town dating back to Roman times. Even in this competitive setting, the Marqués de la Gomera is quite something. Above its long, white frontage, the gilded edge of the roof flows in crested waves. The baroque entrance, topped by a marble balcony and coat of arms, is flanked by ornate columns. Exquisite, too, is the galleried central patio inside, with a 17th-century chapel leading off it. Cavernous, luxurious rooms are furnished with 18th-century pieces, as well as more modern, and very comfortable, sofas. The most spectacular of the bedrooms is the tower suite, built on two levels: step onto its balcony for a 360° view of Osuna and the countryside. The very reasonably priced restaurant is another treat: in spite of its star rating, it is relaxed and unstuffy, and provides succulent food and excellent wines.

rooms	20: 18 doubles, 2 suites.
price	Double €72–€150; single €45–€72; suite €120–€210.
meals	Breakfast €9; lunch/dinner €24.
closed	Rarely.
directions	Sevilla-Malaga A-92. Exit km82 Osuna. Over level crossing to r'bout, 1st right, following signs for 'Centro Urbano' on c/Sevilla. Left at church Carmen into c/Cristo, 2nd right into c/San Pedro. Hotel halfway up on left.

Paco Mulero

tel	+34 954 812223
fax	+34 954 810200
e–mail	palaciogomera@telefonica.net
web	www.hotelpalaciodelmarques.com

map 23   entry 224

Hacienda de San Rafael

Apartado 28, Carretera Nacional IV (km 594), 41730 Las Cabezas de San Juan, Sevilla

As southern Spanish as can be, handsome San Rafael lies contentedly amid the gently undulating farmlands of Sevilla's hinterland. Half a mile or so of olive-lined drive leads to its cheery main façade, doors and windows picked out against the white with a simple band of ochre. Andalucía! Olives were once milled here; Kuky remembers it all from her childhood – she could scarcely have imagined that one day she and an English gentleman husband would be at the helm. Bedrooms give onto a cobbled central patio, the inner sanctuary of any true *cortijo*, where glorious bougainvillaea runs riot. There are now 11 split-level 'deluxe' rooms and three self-catering *casitas* (cottages), sharing a private pool. Each room, beautifully furnished in the country style, has a shady veranda with cane furniture; you can eat in the recently enlarged garden dining area if you prefer. There are two lounges where oriental furnishings and prints collected on trips to the East go well with more local pieces, and the vastness of the views from the house are truly wonderful. We like Tim and Kuky's enthusiasm for their home and their role as hosts.

rooms	11 doubles. 3 self-catering cottages.
price	€ 200; single € 150. Cottage € 480 per day.
meals	Lunch € 25 à la carte; dinner, 3 courses with wine, € 50.
closed	16 November-9 March.
directions	Leave Sevilla for Cádiz. Before m'way, branch off onto N-IV. Just past km594, over brow of hill (keep to right); right into main entrance.

Kuky & Tim Reid

tel	+34 955 872193
fax	+34 955 872201
e-mail	trihotelmktg@dial.pipex.com

Cortijo Alguaciles Bajos

Ctra. SE-445 km 22.6, 41710 Utrera, Sevilla

A deeply rural B&B, lost in the rolling wheatlands of the Sevillian hinterland. You arrive by roads along which you are more likely to pass a tractor or a herd of goats than a car. Head up the palm-lined drive, round the corner and into the cobbled courtyard where whitewashed walls are offset by ferns, geraniums and jasmine. Encarna, the housekeeper, greets you and shows you to one of four guest rooms which are sprucely furnished with beds, tables and dressers that form part of the collective memory of the Mencos family (who live in Madrid for most of the year). Our favourite is the massive Naranjo whose bathroom alone would house a bijou studio in London or Paris. No meals are served at the *cortijo* apart from breakfast but there are two utterly authentic roadside restaurants a short drive away. The silence at night is all-enveloping and after staying here you are somehow closer to understanding the elusive Andalucían character. If you are looking for the complete antithesis to chain hotels, you have it here.

rooms	8 doubles/singles.
price	€ 48–€ 84; single € 36.
meals	None available.
closed	Rarely.
directions	From Sevilla N-IV for Cádiz to Cabezas de San Juan. There, at x-roads left on A-371 for Villamartín; after 6.5km left again on SE-445 for Montellano. Farm on left after km22.6 marker.

Maribel Gómez

tel	+34 630 561529
fax	+34 91 5641071
e-mail	alguaciles@inicia.es
web	www.alguaciles.com

map 23   entry 226

Posada de Palacio

Calle Caballeros 11, 11540 Sanlúcar de Barrameda, Cádiz

Wonderful Sanlucar... this sleepy place, at the mouth of the Guadalquivir estuary, gets surprisingly few visitors yet it is one of Andalucía's most appealing towns, famous for its manzanilla wine, a fino-type sherry, and its fish restaurants. A sleepy town whose streets are there to be wandered with no destination in mind – happening upon *tapas* bars and shops reminiscent of another age. La Posada is an inn to match the town – a place plucked from another era; indeed, the Palacio was once used for the filming of a 19th-century period drama. Two large and elegant mansion houses have been joined to create this hotel, and the latest owner has restored and renovated what was already a delectable place. Some of the rooms are tiny, but beds and linen are top of the range, the whole place has been repainted from top to toe, and antiques have been brought in from all over Spain. A new restaurant is planned in the old *bodega* as we go to press, and breakfast is to be lingered over. Be sure to pay a visit to the covered market just beneath the Posada, and immerse yourself in the brouhaha of *Andaluz* life.

rooms	25: 9 doubles, 10 twins, 6 suites.
price	€60–€84; single €47–€59; suite €90–€108.
meals	Restaurant opening early 2003.
closed	Rarely.
directions	At entrance of town, right after r'bout into Camino de la Vía. Then 2nd on left (Avda. Dr. Fleming), pass San Diego Castle & Palacio Ducal. Posada opp. Town Hall (Ayuntamiento).

Carmen Díez

tel	+34 956 365060
fax	+34 956 364840
e-mail	posadadepalacio@terra.es

La Fuente del Madroño

Fuente del Madroño 6, Los Caños de Meca, 11159 (Vejer de la Frontera), Cádiz

Recline among the broom and mimosa in your Mexican hammock on one of the last wild coastlines of southern Spain. Karen worked in the music business before seeing in this group of old farm buildings an outlet for her desire to create something new and unusual. Her guest accommodation, between pinewoods and beach, has grown organically over the years: *Casa Karen 1* and *Casa Karen 2* are the most independent; other rooms and apartments are better if you want to be sociable. Decoration takes its inspiration from the local surroundings and local here means Andalucían and Moroccan – the high mountains of the Magreb are visible on clear days from the garden. The place attracts people with a creative impulse and the atmosphere is totally laid back – like Caños itself, so popular with young travellers. There is walking, riding and biking in the Natural Park and Karen will tell you where best to eat. If self-catering seems daunting, a friend of Karen's can come and cook for you (veggie, local) and a massage with aromatic oils is always available as well as reiki, tai chi and yoga sessions. You can also, if you wish, receive a free session with life coach Alcinoo.

rooms	5 houses; 2 studios; 1 apartment; 2 traditional-style thatched houses.
price	House €52–€159; studio €47–€76; apartment €78–€114; thatched house €42–€76.
meals	Self-catering.
closed	Rarely.
directions	Cádiz-Tarifa N-340. At km35, right for Vejer de la F.; 1st r'bout right for Los Caños. 500m after Faro Trafalgar, left onto track, 'Apts. y Bungalows Trafalgar' right, 500m.

Karen Abrahams

tel	+34 956 437067
fax	+34 956 437233
e–mail	casas@casaskaren.com
web	www.casaskaren.com

map 23   entry 228

Hotel Madreselva

Avenida Trafalgar 102, 11159 Caños de Meca, Cádiz

The beach-loving Sevillanos recognised a good thing when they saw it. So, later, did the hippies. Most have moved on but the seaside village of Caños de Meca retains an 'alternative', relaxed, slightly shabby feel. Its charms grow on you, as do those of this off-beat hotel. Looking at first sight like a large private villa, it has simple uncluttered rooms which are given a strikingly individual flavour by the addition of modern, paintings and Moroccan appliqué lamps (owner James Whaley lived for many years in North Africa). Although a main road wraps round two sides, good insulation means that traffic noise is no bother in bedrooms or lounge. Each room has its own small area of terrace and opens onto a glorious central courtyard; take breakfast out here amongst the mimosa and pomegranates. The beaches in the area are magnificent – some of the most unspoiled on the Atlantic coast – but if surfing, swimming and sunbathing don't appeal, you can wander among the dunes and umbrella pines of the National Park, follow the watchtowers along the coast and look down at the sea from Cape Trafalgar, the scene of Nelson's last, great battle.

rooms	18: 3 doubles, 14 twins, 1 apartment.
price	€ 55–€ 67; apartment € 110–€ 134.
meals	Restaurants nearby.
closed	Mid-September-Easter.
directions	From Cadíz, N-340 for Tarifa. At km35, right for Vejer de la Frontera. 1st r'bout, right for Caños de Meca. Pass turning to Cabo Trafalgar. Hotel on left after approx. 1km.

James Whaley

tel	+34 956 437255
fax	+34 956 437066
e-mail	canos@madreselva.com

Hotel Madreselva
Real 1, 11160 Barbate, Cádiz

James Whaley has the alchemist's touch: a gift for turning that which at first seems uninteresting into something of a wholly different nature. He managed it brilliantly at the Hurricane Hotel (also in this book) and at Madreselva he has again turned a modest *hostal* into a place where you'd want to stay. Barbate isn't known as a destination yet you are close to one of the coast's most beautiful stretches of beach and there are a couple of brilliant fish restaurants where the locals go. Although one of the main roads through town wraps round two sides of the building, good insulation means that lounge and bedrooms are quiet. Decoration is fresh, clean and simple with one of James's favourite old surfboards adding a more exotic note, along with Moroccan lamps and attractive painted furniture. The bar serves breakfasts (with freshly-squeezed orange juice), drinks and *raciones* throughout the day. The hotel can organise tuition in wind or kite-surfing with their 'itinerant van' which takes you straight to the waves. Madreselva, like Barbate, has an off-beat personality all of its own.

rooms	9 twins/doubles.
price	€49–€67; single €40–€55. VAT included.
meals	Tapas and snacks in hotel bar.
closed	Rarely.
directions	From Cádiz south on N-340 for Algeciras. Just past Véjer de la Frontera right to Barbate. As you arrive in Barbate straight across at r'bout & on up hill to hotel.

James Whaley

tel	+34 956 454033
fax	+34 956 433770
e-mail	barbate@madreselvahotel.com
web	www.madreselvahotel.com

map 23   entry 230

Hotel Restaurante Antonio

Atlanterra km 1, Atlanterra km 1, 11393 Zahara de los Atunes, Cádiz

A short drive from the workaday little fishing village of Zahara de los Atunes, and with gardens that lead straight out to one of the best beaches on the Atlantic coast, Antonio Mota's two hotels share a very special position. We prefer his first: small, family-run and popular with the Spanish. The newer venture is huge and four-star. Both are utterly southern in spirit, with repro prints on the walls of some rather kitsch subjects (swans etc) and other rather grisly ones (bullfights), but rooms and restaurants are light, clean and functional, and fish and white wines very good indeed. Choose dinner in the 'old' restaurant from the fish tank… Breakfasts are feasts of eggs, fruit, cheeses and hams. Rooms in the new hotel are of an excellent size but we prefer Antonio's older rooms, some of which have small terraces overlooking the palm-filled gardens to the sea. (Some rooms have a lounge-cum-second bedroom, perfect for families.) There's a lovely pool, a beach bar, too, and horses for hire; stay longer and ride along the beach to Bolonia, where there are Roman ruins and more good restaurants. Faithful guests return time and time again — it's that sort of place.

rooms	68: 20 doubles, 42 twins, 6 suites.
price	€56–€120; single €32–€76; suite €68–€150.
meals	Breakfast €7; lunch/dinner €18 set menu, €25–€35 à la carte.
closed	19 November–4 February.
directions	From Algeciras E-5/N-340 to Cádiz. 25km after Tarifa take left turning to Barbate; Zahara on left after 10km. Hotel signed in village.

Antonio Mota

tel	+34 956 439141
fax	+34 956 439135
e-mail	info@antoniohoteles.com
web	www.antoniohoteles.com

Hurricane Hotel

Carretera de Málaga a Cádiz, 11380 Tarifa, Cádiz

The best waves in Europe pound down just yards from the restaurant and there is a definite whiff of California (fully-equipped gym, two pools, windsurfing school, horses and mountain bikes). You could be on a film set as you look through the Hurricane's high arches to the palm trees, the glinting ocean and the Rif rising on the African shore… But despite echoes of old Spain, this place is anchored in surf culture. The feel of the East is strongest in the guest rooms: uncluttered, decorated with geometric designs and whirling fans, perhaps a keyhole arch over the bath or a couch with cotton bolsters – reminiscent of palace hotels in Rajasthan. Sea-facing rooms are preferable: the busy N-340 might disturb Arabian-night dreams on the other side. The food is an interesting mix of America, Spain and the East. Ingredients are fresh (fish of the day, home-made pasta, herbs from the garden), there are Louisiana prawns with basmati rice, spicy chicken with Peruvian sauce and good vegetarian dishes. The quality, the views and the furnishings make it worth the price and it would be wonderful to ride out from the Hurricane along the beach and up into the mountains.

rooms	35 doubles/twins.
price	€ 74–€ 125; single € 56; suite € 132–€ 228.
meals	Lunch/dinner € 25 à la carte.
closed	Rarely.
directions	From Cádiz, N-340 south. Hotel 7km before Tarifa on right.

James Whaley

tel	+34 956 684919
fax	+34 956 680329
e-mail	info@hotelhurricane.com
web	www.hotelhurricane.com

map 23   entry 232

100% Fun

Carretera Cádiz - Málaga km 76, 11380 Tarifa, Cádiz

With a name like this you expect something out of the ordinary – and this young, funky hotel should catch your imagination. The busy N-340 lies between it and that oh-so-desirable surf but, in the exuberant greenery of the garden with thatched roofs overhead, we felt we were in deepest Mexico... or an Amazonian lodge... or was it Polynesia? The decoration is like the nearby Hurricane's, only simpler with a pleasing combination of chunky floor tiles, warm ochres and fans to beat the sizzling summers. The rooms are vibrant, fresh, with big comfortable beds and terraces that open to the garden. There are gurgling fountains, a gorgeous swimming pool and an airy restaurant with an enormous thatch serving spicy Tex-Mex dishes as well as some interesting vegetarian alternatives. It also has the best-equipped surf shop on the Tarifa coast, selling the owners' hand-crafted windsurfing boards; there's bike hire too. You are eight kilometres west of Tarifa. Especially good value out of (surf) season, this is a young, fun, lively hotel – a splash of Mexico in southern Spain.

rooms	22 doubles/twins.
price	€51-€117; single €48-€72. VAT included.
meals	Lunch/dinner €15 à la carte.
closed	January & February.
directions	From Cádiz, N-340 Algeciras. At beginning of Tarifa Beach, hotel flagged on left, next to La Enseñada, close to km76 marker.

Ursula Walter & Barry Pussell

tel	+34 956 680330
fax	+34 956 680013
e-mail	100x100@tnet.es

Valdevaqueros

Ctra. Cádiz-Málaga km 74, 11380 Tarifa, Cádiz

Valdevaqueros stands just yards back from a mighty sweep of surf and sand, right next to the Mistral surf school; if you fancy trying wind, kite or fly-surfing this is the place. It is more *hostal* than hotel and would appeal to younger travellers rather than those who like things to be 'just so'; the atmosphere is informal and laid-back, reminiscent of places you may have stayed at in south-east Asia. From the outside the building has a not-quite-finished look but the bedrooms feel just fine. They are high-ceilinged with Moroccan lamps, antique bedsteads and have bead curtains separating bathrooms from main living space. If you can put up with a cracked tile or two for the pleasure of hearing the waves thumping down just yards away then you would like Valdevaqueros. Just outside is a bamboo-covered terrace, a great place for a sundowner, and the restaurant/bar area also has a good feel with its driftwood sculpture, bench tables and good music. Vegetarians will appreciate the high salad quotient. Let José Ramón know if you'd like a full meal; this quietly-mannered, *simpático* Spaniard will get something good together.

rooms	8 doubles. 1 self-catering apartment for 4.
price	€ 60–€ 78. Apartment € 84–€ 102.
meals	Lunch/dinner € 10.
closed	January-February.
directions	From Algeciras N-340 for Cádiz. Left for Valdevaqueros shortly after passing Hurricane hotel, opposite Restaurante Copacabana.

José Ramón Vázquez Fernández

tel	+34 956 236705
fax	+34 956 680329

map 23   entry 234

Cortijo La Hoya

Apdo. de Correos 577, 11280 Algeciras, Cádiz

If it's a room with a view you're after, La Hoya could be the place – providing you're happy with deep seclusion. Three long kilometres of track lead to the farm and Fabiola's two *casitas*, hidden away among the eucalyptus and cork oaks in an exquisite corner of the Alcornocales Park. Two lovely self-catering apartments (soon to be three) have been created in buildings whose lowly origins – they were once chicken sheds – are hard to credit. The wonderful garden leads to an 'infinity' pool where the water of the pool merges with that of the straits, above which rises the Moroccan Rif, its colours changing as subtly as the iridescent coastal light. Fabiola has great decorative nous, her colour schemes inspired by the earthy washes of the Mahgreb; she has cut no corners. Although she is mindful of her guests' privacy, do try to speak to this interesting woman, and heed her recommendations about where to eat in nearby Tarifa (a must on a Friday/Saturday night for those who like lively street life). And then there are the dogs… at least half a dozen mutts of all shapes and sizes who will drop by to say hello.

rooms	3 apartments.
price	€85–€103. Check minimum stay requirements for summer months.
meals	Self-catering. Hamper on request.
closed	Rarely.
directions	From Algeciras, N-340 for Cádiz. Through Pelayo; by International Youth Hostel U-turn & head back towards Pelayo. 100m past km96 marker, sharp right. Follow signs to Cortijo for 3km.

Fabiola Dominguez Larios

tel	+34 956 236070
fax	+34 956 236070
e-mail	cortijohoya@hotmail.com
web	www.cortijolahoya.com

Monte de la Torre

Apartado de Correos 66, 11370 Los Barrios, Cádiz

Quentin Agnew's family has farmed this estate for generations. It is puzzling to come across this utterly Edwardian building in the very south of Spain; it was built by the British when they were pushing the railway through the mountains to Ronda. This commingling of northern architecture and southern vegetation and climate is as seductive as it is unexpected. The house stands alone on a hill, surrounded by resplendent gardens; bask in the shade of the trees, gaze onto the Bay of Gibraltar. The drawing room is panelled, the dining room elegant, there are masses of books, family portraits, a grandfather clock and dogs... this is a home, not a hotel, and the living is easy. The bedrooms (reached by a grand staircase) are high-ceilinged, decorated with family heirlooms and have period bathrooms – a festival of tubs and taps. Each is different, all lovely in an old-fashioned way. The apartments are in the former servants' quarters – they'd hardly recognise them now! Sue and Quentin are charming hosts; only breakfast is on offer but there are many good restaurants within easy reach.

rooms	3 doubles. 2 self-catering apartments for 9.
price	€ 105–€ 120; apartment € 530–€ 725. VAT inc.
meals	Restaurants nearby.
closed	15 December-15 January; July/August.
directions	Málaga-Algeciras N-340. 8km after San Roque, A-381 into Los Barrios. At r'bout with fountains, left onto CA-231 Algeciras; after 4km, signed right, up trail.

Sue & Quentin Agnew–Larios

tel	+34 956 660000
fax	+34 956 634863
e-mail	mdlt@mercuryin.es
web	www.montedelatorre.com

map 23   entry 236

Hotel Casa Señorial La Solana

Carretera Cádiz-Málaga, N340 km116.5 North Side, 11360 San Roque, Cádiz

An unmistakably Spanish house, La Solana was built for a noble family in the 18th century. It stands grandly in 14 hectares of lush gardens and parkland; brilliant southern blooms climb the façade. The glazed door beckons you in: the house was restored over a decade ago by the owner – an artist and sculptor – with great sensitivity and its overhanging eaves and the covered patio inside give it a distinctly colonial air. The interior is graced with 16th- and 17th-century antiques from Spain's 'golden' age, a profusion of carved wood, rich rugs, velvets and brocades, crystal chandeliers and heavy wardrobes. Bedrooms are furnished with a mixture of old and less old pieces; bathrooms are modern. The bright 'white' villages of the Grazalema Sierra and the lesser-known beaches of the Atlantic coast are within reach: after a day of of discovery it is a pleasure to return to the secluded comfort of this country mansion. Although central heating has recently been added some readers have felt that a slight air of neglect is creeping in: please let us know.

rooms	24: 18 twins/doubles, 6 suites.
price	€75–€100; single €70; suite €100. VAT included.
meals	None available.
closed	Rarely.
directions	From Málaga, N-340 for Algeciras. Leave road at km116.5 marker; follow signs to hotel for 0.8km. (From Cádiz, exit 117, then U-turn).

José Antonio Ceballos

tel	+34 956 780236
fax	+34 956 780236
e-mail	sanroquehotellasolana@telefonica.net
web	www.sanroquehotel-lasolana.com

La Casa Grande

Maldonado 10, 11630 Arcos de la Frontera, Cádiz

La Casa Grande nudges right up to the very edge of whitewashed Arcos — you couldn't wish for a more spectacular site. At night, from its terrace-of-terraces, you look out to two floodlit churches and mile after mile of surrounding plain. The house is almost 300 years old and many of the original features have survived to tell the tale. In true *Andaluz* style, a central, colonnaded, plant-filled patio is the axis around which the house turns; vaulted reception rooms lead off to all sides. A cosy lounge doubles up as a library: here are thousands of books, some of them written by Elena; she is a journalist who has also worked in theatre, radio and TV. The decoration of the house reflects her and her husband's cosmopolitan taste: Moroccan lamps, prints by Hockney and Bacon, a woven rug, a Deco writing table topped by a designer lamp, a Habitat chair. It is both stylish and homely. Guest bedrooms are gorgeous too, full of antiquey bits and pieces. And how wonderful to breakfast — or take a light *tapas* supper — on that unforgettable roof terrace! *A Rusticae hotel.*

rooms	6: 4 doubles, 2 suites for 4.
price	€70; single €57; suite €82–€131.
meals	Breakfast €6.5; lunch/dinner €15–€18.
closed	13 January–13 February.
directions	In Arcos follow signs to Parador. Park in square in front of Parador & walk to end of c/Escribano (just to left of Parador). Right, past Hotel El Convento, then left. House on right.

Elena Posa Farrás

tel	+34 956 703930
fax	+34 956 717095
e-mail	info@lacasagrande.net
web	www.lacasagrande.net

map 23   entry 238

Hotel Los Olivos del Convento

Paseo Boliches 30, 11630 Arcos de la Frontera, Cádiz

Off a street leading to the old quarter of Arcos, Los Olivos is an unmistakably Andalucían townhouse. A huge oak door leads you into the hall and cool, wicker-furnished lounge; beyond is an arched inner courtyard with geraniums, aspidistra and palms, colonial in feel. The bedrooms give onto this light, airy courtyard and some have views across gentle hills and olive groves, down towards the Atlantic. If you're a light sleeper choose a room at the back; they are extremely quiet. All the bedrooms have high ceilings and a pleasant mix of old and modern furniture. You can breakfast on the patio until the hotter summer days chase you indoors to the air conditioned lounge. The staff seem to genuinely enjoy their work and their eagerness to help you is reflected in the hotel's participation in a scheme which offers visitors free guided tours of Arcos (twice daily in season). The old town with its *arcos* (arches) and narrow winding streets is just a short walk from Los Olivos and so too is the restaurant El Convento which is also managed by the hotel's owners: the food is excellent and has won many prizes.

rooms	19 doubles/twins.
price	€55–€79; single €35–€41. VAT included.
meals	Breakfast €6; lunch/dinner €24 set menu, €30 à la carte.
closed	Rarely.
directions	In Arcos, signs for 'Conjunto Monumenta' & Parador. Follow one-way system up into town; hotel on left of road parallel to main street, with own car park.

María Moreno Moreno & José Antonio Roldán Ca

tel	+34 956 700811
fax	+34 956 702018
e-mail	losolivosdelc@terra.es
web	losolivos.profesionales.org

El Convento

Maldonado 2, 11630 Arcos de la Frontera, Cádiz

Arcos is spread like icing along the top of a craggy limestone outcrop; it was a great stronghold when Moors and Christians fought over the ever-shifting *frontera*. The Convento, a former cloister, is perched right at the edge of the cliff in the centre of the old town. Behind the plain white façade is a deliciously labyrinthine hotel – some rooms have terraces over the cliff where watching the sun set will make your heart soar. José Roldán Caro is proud of his home town and he and his wife have filled their hotel with works by local artists. Decoration varies in the original part of the hotel; in the annexe just across the rooftop terrace furnishings are much smarter. Breakfast is served in an attractive beamed dining room with bar and there's a large terrace above, a perfect spot for a sundowner – and for watching the aerobatics of the kestrels which nest in the cliffs below. José Antonio and María own a restaurant in the covered colonnaded patio of a 16th-century palace just up the road where you can taste some of the best food in the Province of Cadiz.

rooms	11: 5 doubles, 5 twins, 1 single.
price	€43–€73; single €31–€48.
meals	Breakfast €5; lunch/dinner €24 set menu, €30 à la carte.
closed	7-22 January.
directions	In Arcos, signs to Parador & Plaza del Cabildo. Park in front of Santa María church, then walk along c/Escribanos; at end, right into c/Maldonado.

María Moreno Moreno & José Antonio Roldán Caro

tel	+34 956 702333
fax	+34 956 704128
e-mail	elconvento@viautil.com
web	http://webdearcos.com/elconvento

map 23   entry 240

La Casa del Curandero

Lista de Correos, 11630 Arcos de la Frontera, Cádiz

La Casa del Curandero, reached via a bumpy track, lies in the last reaches of the rolling Jérez country, whose landscape is gentler than the jagged limestone and dolomite of the Grazalema Park just beyond. David and Anne ran a language school in Arcos for many years: he is one of the few official non-Spanish park guides in Spain – no mean achievement. Rustic furniture and Moroccan lamps make the farmhouse kitchen of the main house feel snug and authentic, and large picture windows lead to a terrace with views up to Arcos. Guest rooms have been set among the surrounding pines and orange orchard and look towards the pool; their decoration mixes things Spanish and North African. Life at La Casa del Curandero is lived *en famille* in a relaxed and easy manner with the Lanfears and their young children; they are excellent hosts who will find time to help you plan your forays (either guided by David or with walking notes provided). The house takes its name from the natural healer who once lived here: these alternative doctors are still a part of life in the sierras of the south.

rooms	2 twins/doubles. 1 self-catering apartment.
price	€ 50; single € 40; apartment € 60. VAT included.
meals	None available.
closed	21 December–6 January.
directions	A-382 Arcos-Antequera; A-372 km5.5 El Bosque; pass lake & petrol station; right for Girasol onto old road; 300m 2nd Girasol sign; right; 5th on left.

Anne Lacy & David Lanfear

tel	+34 956 231204
fax	+34 956 231204
e-mail	arcosexp@viautil.com
web	www.whitevillagewalks.com

Cortijo Barranco

Ctra. Arcos-El Bosque Km. 5,700, 11630 Arcos de la Frontera, Cádiz

Barranco stands alone, high on a hillside, across from the lovely 'white' town of Arcos de la Frontera. Getting here is quite an adventure: once you leave the main road and follow the winding track up through the olive groves you feel you have left the real world far behind. This is every inch the classic *cortijo*: private living quarters and (former) stables wrapped around a sheltered courtyard. The farm's guest rooms and apartment are soberly decorated with terracotta floors, wrought-iron bedsteads, heavy linen curtains and hand-crocheted and knitted bedspreads. The whole place is uncannily quiet: pin back your ears to hear the owls hoot or the birds hymn the dawn. The sitting room is enormous with space for a billiard table but best of all is the lofty dining room with a gallery, communal tables and an open hearth at one end. It is wonderful to stroll out from the farm at sunset and abandon yourself to the beauty of the surrounding hills. A lovely big pool overlooking the hills of Sierra de Grazalema completes the picture. *The above address is for correspondence and is not that of the farm.*

rooms	8 doubles. 1 self-catering apartment for 4.	
price	€ 73–€ 80; single € 63–€ 70; apartment € 121–€ 130. VAT included.	
meals	€ 18–€ 21, by arrangement only (not Sunday).	
closed	20 December–7 February.	
directions	From Arcos de la Frontera, A-372 El Bosque. After 5.7km marker, at end of long straight section, left at sign onto track – 2km to farm.	

María José Gil Amián

tel	+34 956 231402
fax	+34 956 231209
web	www.cortijobarranco.com

map 23   entry 242

Hacienda El Santiscal

Avenida El Santiscal 129 , (Lago de Arcos), 11630 Arcos de la Frontera, Cádiz

After many years of working with tourists, Paqui Gallardo, the dynamic owner of El Santiscal, had a very clear idea of what a small hotel should be. And it happens to be much the sort of thing that we look for, too. This grand old *cortijo* is a short drive from Arcos, in a place of perfect quiet, and has been sensitively converted from a forgotten family home into an elegant but simple hotel. The building is Andalucían to the core: an austere whitewashed façade, a grand portal and the blissful peace and cool of the inner sanctum, the central courtyard. All of the rooms lead off the patio (nearly all with views across the estate, too). All have a slightly different feel, but scrupulous attention to detail is a *leitmotiv* here: matching fabrics, lovely old beds, terracotta floors, good bathrooms. The suite is really special, and probably worth the extra if you are feeling flush. Either dine in on classical Andalucían dishes or head up to wonderful old Arcos where there are loads of interesting *tapas* bars and a couple of good restaurants. *A Rusticae hotel.*

rooms	12: 10 twins, 2 suites.
price	€64-€99; suite €97-€136.
meals	Lunch/dinner €23.
closed	10-20 January.
directions	From Arcos C-334 for El Bosque; 1km after crossing bridge, left into Urbanización Dominio El Santiscal; follow signs (carefully) to El Santiscal.

Francisca 'Paqui' Gallardo

tel	+34 956 708313
fax	+34 956 708268
e-mail	reservas@santiscal.com
web	www.santiscal.com

Hacienda Buena Suerte

Apartado 60, 11650 Villamartín, Cádiz

What a grand arrival! As you pass under the great portal and up the drive you feel the marriage of Andalucía's past — the great estates or *latifundia* — and its present — Judas trees, bougainvillaea, palm trees, whitewash and terracotta tiles. All this in the loveliest of settings: the gently rolling olive groves and wheat fields of the foothills of the Grazalema mountains. But the real star here is the horse. Groups of riders come to learn with owners Jean-Claude and Magda Dysli who are rarely out of the saddle, either teaching in the riding school or trekking in the hills with their guests. Non-riders are also welcome and there are lovely walks from the farm. The rooms, most of them in the converted granary, are large and simply furnished, decorated — naturally — with prints of horses and riders and with animal skins on the floors. You may find sweets on pillows or a candle in the corner. Meals, taken round the huge dining table, are global — everything from goulash to bouillabaisse to couscous, all with organic ingredients.

rooms	12 twins/doubles.
price	€ 88. VAT included.
meals	Lunch/dinner € 15.
closed	Rarely.
directions	From Ronda, C-339 Sevilla. At junc. with N-342, left for Jerez A-382. 7km before Villamartín, left at sign for El Bosque & Ubrique. Buena Suerte 1.5km on left.

Magda & Jean-Claude Dysli

tel	+34 956 231286
fax	+34 956 231275
e-mail	magda-dysli@smx.de
web	www.dysli.net

map 23   entry 244

Hostal Casa de las Piedras

Calle las Piedras 32, 11610 Grazalema, Cádiz

Grazalema is one of the most dazzling of Andalucía's mountain villages, clinging to grey and ochre cliffs and dominated by craggy peaks that are home to eagles and mountain goats. A special place with a special *hostal*, half of which is in a grand 300-year-old house (witness to the days when a thriving weaving industry made many a Grazalema fortune). Rooms vary in size, are full of family antiques and are loaded with charm. Bedrooms in the new half, built and decorated in traditional style, have their own bathrooms and central heating (temperatures can drop sharply during winter nights). Some have views across the terracotta roofs to the mountains beyond. Dishes range from tomato soup to venison with *salsa* in the lively restaurant. This is a base for walkers with a healthy appetite and breakfast is appropriately hearty. An unassuming and charming place whose owners understand the art of good old-fashioned inn-keeping.

rooms	32 doubles/singles.
price	€ 42. VAT included.
meals	Lunch/dinner approx. € 10.
closed	Rarely.
directions	From Ronda, C-339 Sevilla; after 14km, left to Grazalema. Enter main square, turn directly left up street beside Unicaja. Hotel 100m up on right.

Rafael & Katy Lirio Sánchez
tel +34 956 132014
fax +34 956 132014

El Antiguo Juzgado

Calle San Sebastian 15, 11330 Jimena de la Frontera, Cádiz

The perfect place for musicians to holiday: Peter and Monica Becko are musicians, and between them cover an impressive range of instruments. El Antiguo Juzgado was probably once a part of the church of Santa María whose tower stands alongside; it later became the local courthouse, hence the name. Of the five apartments (each named after a Spanish composer) the best are on the first floor, high-ceilinged with marvellous old doors and original 18th-century plasterwork. The constrastingly low ceilings of the attic apartment would not be for everyone. Rooms are decked out with durries, richly coloured bedspreads, books, country-style beds and chests and fully-equipped kitchens. Although we don't list many self-catering places, we happily include the Antiguo Juzgado because the Beckos provide you with all of the ingredients for a good breakfast. They also love guests to join in with their choral and instrumental get-togethers, their motto being *música sin fronteras*. Non-musicians would enjoy it here, too: the walking is marvellous and Jimena has some excellent restaurants. *Minimum two nights.*

rooms	5 apartments.
price	€90–€105; €260–€300 p.w.
meals	Self-catering.
closed	Rarely.
directions	In Jimena, up hill past Bar Cuenca. Opp. first shops, left into large parking beneath church. c/San Sebastian runs up hill to left of church. House on right.

Peter & Monica Becko

tel	+34 956 641317
fax	+34 956 640944
e-mail	becko@mercuryin.es
web	www.el-antiguo-juzgado.com

map 23   entry 246

Posada La Casa Grande

Fuentenueva 42, 11330 Jimena de la Frontera, Cádiz

One of the most impressive of Andalucía's *pueblos blancos*: Jimena's cluster of whitewashed houses fans out around a limestone crag topped by a Moorish castle. The two Toms (father and son) have lived here for many years. The restoration of this grand old village house took eight years and hats off to them for creating a hostelry that feels much more home than hotel. Pass through a flagged courtyard with an exuberant honeysuckle to find an enormous guest lounge; up another level to a reading room with hundreds of books. The base elements are those you expect in the south: waferbricks, tiled floors, potted palms, heavy old beams. We liked the bedrooms: clean and comfortable, and little matter that they share bathrooms. Breakfast is the only meal served but with a lively bar next door which serves the best *tapas* in the village (Tom would say "in Spain"!) you're off to a flying start and there are plenty of restaurants in the village. The mighty Atlantic is close by and the walking round here is fantastic: don't miss the climb up to the castle for an unbelievable sunset.

rooms	10: 5 doubles, 2 singles, 2 suites, 1 apartment for 8.
price	€34; single €29; suite €62; apartment €100. VAT included.
meals	Breakfast €5.
closed	February.
directions	From Málaga, N-340 Cádiz. Right via San Martín del Tesorillo for Ronda. In Jimena follow main street all way through village; last (sharp) right down to Casa Grande on right.

Oonagh Luke & Tom Andrésen-Gosselin
tel	+34 956 640578
fax	+34 956 640491
e-mail	tcag@eresmas.net
web	www.posadalacasagrande.com

Hostal El Anón

Calle Consuelo 34-40, 11330 Jimena de la Frontera, Cádiz

Five village houses and stables have been joined to make an organic whole of interconnecting levels and intimate terraces. It is a delicious little piece of authentic Spain. Suzanna is warm and very welcoming, has lived in Jimena for years; she knows the people and country like her own. She will disentangle the rich web of local history for you while organising horse-riding or advising on painting, birdwatching, walking and flora-spotting expeditions. The countryside has treasures galore for nature lovers: see it from the little rooftop swimming pool where the eye travels over the tile-topped village to Gibraltar. Dine – well – off spare ribs or *tapas* among geraniums on the terrace – or in the restaurant or bar. Enjoy the cool peace of the arched main courtyard and the exotic banana and custard-fruit trees, rejoice in the rich furnishings collected over the years (wall-hangings, paintings, sculptural bits and pieces) and the heavy beams and low ceilings of the old buildings. Rooms – and plumbing! – are basic, but come and soak up quantities of Spanishness in a wonderfully easy-going, cosmopolitan atmosphere.

rooms	12: 11 twins/doubles, 1 suite.
price	€52; single €31; suite €60. VAT included.
meals	Lunch/dinner €23 à la carte. VAT included.
closed	2 weeks in June & 2 weeks in November.
directions	From Málaga, N-340 Algeciras; at r'bout in Pueblo Nuevo de Guadiaro right for San Martín del Tesorillo & Jimena; in village centre left by taxi rank; 2nd right.

Gabriel Delgado & Suzanna Odell

tel	+34 956 640113
fax	+34 956 641110
e-mail	elanon@viautil.com

map 23   entry 248

Rancho Los Lobos

11339 Jimena de la Frontera, Cádiz

It's all about the great outdoors at Los Lobos, an old farmstead in a valley just outside the 'white' village of Jimena de la Fontera; these *de la frontera* villages once marked the boundary between Christian and Moorish Spain. Wolf and Esther came in the early Eighties and gradually converted a series of outbuildings to house their guests and their horses; riding is their first love. They will ensure that – if you wish it – you can saddle up and head out through old oak forests, stopping to swim (with your horse) in deep river pools. If you're not horsey choose between mountain-biking, hiking, tennis, swimming and Russian bowling; doing nothing is an option too. You eat in the old farm kitchen around bench tables – or across the courtyard in a larger dining room with a log fire in the colder months. Picnics can be prepared and dinner (after a sauna and an aperitif in the stable bar) combines Swiss and traditional Spanish food: wholesome rather than gourmet, and with paella on flamenco nights. Bedrooms are smallish, simply furnished with bright rugs and have small bath/shower rooms.

rooms	9: 8 doubles, 1 apartment for 2.
price	€60–€66; apartment €82. VAT included.
meals	Light lunches €4; dinner €17.
closed	Rarely.
directions	In Jimena, left at Bar Cuenca, then right past Guardia Civil building. Cross bridge, follow track to farm on right. Ask Wolf to send a map.

Wolf & Esther Zissler

tel	+34 956 640429
fax	+34 956 641180
e-mail	wolf@rancholoslobos.com
web	www.rancholoslobos.com

Cortijo El Papudo

11340 San Martín del Tesorillo, Málaga

The old farmstead of El Papudo lies in the fertile valley of the Guadiaro river. The area's exceptionally mild climate and its rich alluvial soils means that it has long been a place where fruit trees have flourished: everything from citrus to custard-fruit, avocados to pomegranates is grown here. And more recently a number of plant nurseries have sprung up; the Harveys have set up one of their own and it has become an obligatory shop-over for the coastal ex-pat community. They are, of course, highly knowledgeable about all things botanical and organise garden tours in Andalucía. Their own garden is a multi-coloured ode to southern flora, and laps up to the high, solid old *cortijo*, converted to a guest house not so very long ago. The original wooden ceilings give character to the bedrooms, which have Casablanca-style ceiling fans for the summer, and central heating for the colder months. All have views of the garden and across the farm to the surrounding citrus groves. The dining room is in the original kitchen and has a handsome flagged floor and a woodburner. *Contact the Harveys for details of their week-long garden tours.*

rooms	11 twins/doubles.
price	€ 64–€ 76; single € 42. VAT included.
meals	None available.
closed	Rarely.
directions	N–340 Málaga-Cádiz. After 3km, right for Benalmadena & Algeciras. At km134, right on C–514 for San Enrique & San Martin del Tesorillo. At km10, road bears left over Rio Guadiaro; before bridge, right for 2km, up hill & sharp left.

Michael & Vivien Harvey

tel	+34 952 854018
fax	+34 952 854018
e-mail	papudo@mercuryin.es

map 23   entry 250

Hotel Casablanca

Calle Teodoro de Molina 12, 29480 Gaucín, Málaga

Gaucín is one of Andalucía's most spectacular mountain villages. Its labyrinthine whitewashed streets huddle against a hillside beneath a Moorish castle; eagles wheel overhead, the views are glorious. The town lacked anywhere decent to stay until Mike and Sue – who once ran another of the delectable places included in this guide! – came across this grand old village house and created the hotel of their dreams. You too will soon fall under its spell. Pass through enormous wooden doors to emerge in the bar. Beyond is a walled garden where palms, magnolia and jacaranda lend colour and shade; a fountain murmurs beside the pool. Terraces on different levels look out across terracotta rooftops to the castle and all the way to the distant Rif mountains of Morocco; the sunsets from here are amazing! Most rooms have their own private terrace, and parquet or terracotta floors, good beds and bright colours in the bathrooms. Dine in at least once; the food is spicy and cosmopolitan, and follows the dictates of what's in season. The included breakfast is properly generous – a super place.

rooms	7 doubles/twins.
price	€72–€96; single €48. VAT included.
meals	Lunch/dinner €20 à la carte. VAT included.
closed	November-February.
directions	From Málaga N-340 for Algeciras. After Estepona right on MA-539 via Manilva to Gaucín (NOT Casares). Into centre to street of San Sebastián church; one way system right for Ronda; on left, signed.

Susan & Michael Dring
tel   +34 952 151019
fax   +34 95 2151019

La Almuña
Apartado 20, 29480 Gaucín, Málaga

The old farmstead sits high up on a mountainside beside ancient footpaths used in former days by smugglers and *bandaleros*; later, officers and their mounts would pass by en route from Gibraltar to Ronda. Views from the house's terrace are dreamlike; the eye reaches across the last foothills of the Sierra, all the way down to the coast and on to Africa. Diana's is a warm, happily shambolic home; she greets you with a big smile and always the offer of tea or something stronger. Her cooking is legendary in the area, and you will probably be dining in company. Much of her food has come from the estate and what doesn't is carefully chosen locally: you may be treated to smoked salmon, lamb, partridge or quail. Vegetables are fresh, herbs from the garden and wine always *à volonté*. Diana and her mother busily to and fro from kitchen to table; her Staffordshire bull terrier looks on. The drawing room is utterly homely; bedrooms a marriage of 'English country' and 'Spanish rustic'. Come to La Almuña to walk, talk and dine in congenial company. And there are horses next door, just waiting to be saddled for exploring this beautiful area.

rooms	7 doubles/twins.
price	€ 110; single € 55.
meals	Lunch/dinner € 30, by request only.
closed	Rarely.
directions	From Gaucín A-369 for Algeciras. At km44.8 marker, left at a white & ochre post at entrance; 2nd house to right behind cypress trees.

Diana Paget
tel   +34 952 151200
fax   +34 95 2151343

map 23   entry 252

El Nobo

Apartado 46, 29480 Gaucín, Málaga

Gaucín has long been popular among the more adventurous of the ex-pat community and the von Meisters live in one of the area's most gorgeous homes. Moorish courtyard, fountains, spectacular pool… you may have read about it in an interior design mag, its that sort of place. Hard to believe that 10 years ago a lowly farm building stood here. The position is amazing: from the shaded terrace you can see Gibraltar, the Strait and the mountains of Africa. The gardens are awash with colour and the house feels as if it has always been anchored to its rocky hillside. The drawing room is the most memorable space and pays full homage to that view-of-views thanks to enormous French windows: an enchanting spot at both breakfast and dinner. Sally's food is Good; she organises cookery courses and describes her culinary thing as "very Mediterranean". She uses lots of fish, whatever veg are in season and Tuffy's selection of wines is excellent. The bedrooms at El Nobo are comfortably flamboyant and Sally is a gregarious and entertaining hostess. A great place from which to escape the more dazzling delights of the Costa del Sol.

rooms	4: 1 double, 2 twins, 1 suite. 1 self-catering cottage for 2.
price	€ 112; suite € 120; cottage € 680 per week. VAT included.
meals	Dinner € 30 on request.
closed	July, August, Christmas, New Year.
directions	Málaga-Cádiz N-340; right to Manilva & on to Gaucín. Right opp. petrol station for 500m. Where 'La Fructosa' sign points left, sharp right downhill. 1km on left.

Sally & Christopher Von Meister
tel	+34 952 151303
fax	+34 952 117207
e-mail	info@elnobo.co.uk
web	www.elnobo.co.uk

El Gecko

Cañada Real del Tesoro, 29391 Estación de Cortes de la Frontera, Málaga

El Gecko (no, not that Spanish artist from Toledo) is a great name for a great place. Rachel used to work with her parents in the Casablanca in Gaucín; she seems to have inherited her parents' nose for a good spot – and their flair for hospitality. Her hotel is right next to the river in a sleepy hamlet, with a railway line that will take you to the gates of the Alhambra in no time. The bedrooms are large and decorated with care and flair by Rachel, using warm colours, Indian bedspreads and some good mirrors and prints. There are river views, and a riverside terrace where you can eat out. The restaurant is a big crowd-puller, and has earned the place a reputation for good food and friendly service. Rachel used to work in the wine trade and knows her stuff, so if you stay long enough you can explore her exclusively Spanish selection. Once here, you can't help but be aware that a lost tradition is being salvaged. The place was once an old station inn, serving the travellers who paused here on their journey; now, again, El Gecko opens its doors to those who, in the words of many a Sixties song, are just "passin' through". The British love it.

rooms	5: 3 doubles, 2 twins.	
price	€ 78. VAT included.	
meals	Lunch/dinner € 15.50.	
closed	January & February.	
directions	From Málaga, N-340 for Algeciras. Exit for Manilva & onto Gaucín. Right for Ronda, then left to Estación de Cortes de la Frontera. Hotel on left just before railway, signed.	

Rachel Dring

tel	+34 952 153315
fax	+34 952 153266
e-mail	elgecko@mercuryin.es
web	www.hotelelgecko.com

map 23   entry 254

Banu Rabbah

Sierra Bermeja s/n, 29490 Benarrabá, Málaga

Benarrabá is named after the Berber tribesman who first settled here with his family — the Banu Rabbah of the hotel's name. The hotel, built on the initiative of the local council, is in the capable hands of a group of six young people from the village. What makes this place special is its exhilarating position: almost 2,000 feet up with a magnificent sweep of mountain, white village and wooded hillsides. The building has a rather cumbersome design but wins points for its bedrooms with generous terraces. The hand-painted wooden beds, writing desks and the bright bedspreads add a merry note and their French windows bring in the light and the view. The restaurant, open to non-residents, features local produce: try the *saltavallao* (a hot gazpacho), with, perhaps, one of the local almond cakes for dessert. After dinner take a stroll through the village; you are unlikely to meet other foreigners here (unlike in neighbouring Gaucín). And if you're feeling more energetic, hike down to the Genal — route notes are provided — where you can swim in the summer months. Local legend has it that the Moors built a secret tunnel between here and Gaucín.

rooms	12 doubles/twins.
price	€ 41–€ 57.
meals	Breakfast € 3; half-board € 13.50; full-board € 21.
closed	Rarely.
directions	From Málaga N-340 for Cádiz. Then A-377 via Manilva to Gaucín. Here towards Ronda on A-369; after 4.5km, right to Benarrabá. Signed.

Jesús García

tel	+34 952 150288
fax	+34 952 150005
e-mail	hotel@hbenarraba.es
web	www.hbenarraba.es

Molino del Santo

Bda. Estación s/n, 29370 Benaoján, Málaga

Pauline and Andy moved south in search of the good life, and restored a century-old mill in a spectacular area of the Grazalema National Park. Water rushes past flower-filled terraces, under willows and fig trees and into the pool (heated for the cooler months). Rooms and restaurant wear local garb — terracotta tiles, beams, rustic chairs; the best rooms have private terraces. Fresh flowers are everywhere and the Molino's reputation for good Spanish food is established: most hotel guests are British but the Spanish flock in at weekends to enjoy local hams and sausages, rabbit and fish, and imaginative vegetarian cooking. Staff and owners are generous with advice on walks from the hotel. From the sleepy little station you can take a train to Ronda or, in the other direction, pass some of the loveliest 'white' villages of Andalucía. The Molino is one of the Sierra's most popular small hotels, and has been for more than a decade. It seems to get the balance just right between friendliness and efficiency and people come back again and again. Pay extra for a superior room with a terrace — and book in advance!

rooms	18: 15 doubles, 3 suites.
price	€ 76-€ 118; suites € 104-€ 136. VAT included. High season half-board € 168-€ 198.
meals	Lunch/dinner € 30-€ 40.
closed	Mid-November-mid-February.
directions	From Ronda, C-339/A-473 Sevilla; after km118 marker, left for Benaoján. After 10km, having crossed railway & river bridges, left to station & follow signs.

Pauline Elkin & Andy Chapell

tel	+34 952 167151
fax	+34 952 167327
e-mail	molino@logiccontrol.es
web	www.andalucia.com/molino

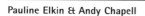

map 23   entry 256

Cortijo El Horcajo

Carretera Ronda-Zahara de la Sierra km. 95.5, Apdo. 149, 29400 Ronda, Málaga

The old farmstead of El Horcajo lies on the northern boundary of the Grazalema Natural Park; you reach it via a long track which snakes down to the bottom of a deep valley. This is every inch the classic Andalucían *cortijo*, where outbuildings are wrapped around a sheltered inner courtyard. This is partly designed not only for aesthetic appeal but also as a means of escaping the heat of the Andalucían summer. Things 'rustic' are prominent in cobble, beam, tile and ceramic. The large lounge, dining room and reception area are in the converted cattle byre; the original vaulting has been preserved and new windows opened to bring light into a rather dark space. Bedrooms are comfortable, if a little bare, and many of them have small terraces looking out to the hills. We liked the courtyard (patio) rooms, which are quieter than those above the restaurant. There are good walks close by and pretty Grazalema is just 20 minutes away by car. The housekeepers, 'Mari' and Bernabé, are friendly, and although their English is basic they make a huge effort.

rooms	24: 10 doubles, 14 suites.
price	€58–€95; single €49–€61, suite €66–€130.
meals	Lunch/dinner €14.71.
closed	Rarely.
directions	From Ronda, A-376 for Sevilla. After 15km, left for Grazalema on A-372. Don't take next left turn for Grazalema, continue towards Zahara & at km95.5 marker, left down track to farm.

Eduardo García Caparrós

tel	+34 952 184080
fax	+34 952 184171
e-mail	info@elhorcajo.com
web	www.elhorcajo.com

El Tejar

Calle Nacimiento 38, 29430 Montecorto, Málaga

El Tejar looks out from a hillside near to Ronda to a panorama of oak forest, almond groves and distant peaks. The house is the highest in the village and is made up of a deliciously labyrinthine series of spaces built on more than a dozen different levels. The decoration is stylish, intimate and southern: an open hearth, ochre washes and terracotta tiles impart a real *Andaluz* flavour while textiles and rugs collected in Asia, Africa and South America add spice and colour. There are masses of books and magazines, two friendly dogs and a well-stocked honesty bar. Bedrooms have a Moroccan feel with kilims, brightly woven blankets and photos of travels in distant lands; the views of the jagged outline of the Grazalema Sierra are sublime. Dinners, prepared by housekeeper Paqui, are Andalucían, wholesome and delicious and are served at a candlelit table; wine and conversation flow easily. Guy has written books on walking and can steer you towards the most enchanted, hidden corners of the Grazalema Park, with maps and route notes provided. *Special summer rental: rates on request. English, French, German, Spanish spoken.*

rooms	3: 2 twins/doubles, 1 suite.
price	€ 60; suite € 65. VAT inc. May, June, Sept, house rented £650 weekly.
meals	Breakfast € 4; dinner € 20, including wine. No meals Sat/Sun.
closed	May-Sept when house rented.
directions	Málaga-Cádiz N-340, then A-376 Ronda. Continue round Ronda on A-376. After 20km, right into Montecorto. At top of village via track through pines. Ask for 'la casa del inglés,' or call Guy if lost!

Guy Hunter-Watts

tel	+34 952 184053
fax	+34 952 184053
e-mail	eltejar@mercuryin.es
web	www.sawdays.co.uk

map 23   entry 258

La Fuente de la Higuera

Partido de los Frontones, 29400 Ronda, Málaga

Pom and Tina have travel in the blood; he chartered yachts, she worked for one of the big airlines. But then the magic of the Ronda mountains put them under its spell and they saw in this old mill a new dream: a luxurious retreat where good food, wine and company could ease away urban cares. Tina is the 'spark' — an enormously vivacious and likeable woman, she chose the furnishings and fabrics which give such panache to the rooms. Pom is born to the role of host: a raconteur by nature he has a dry humour born — perhaps — of many years in the UK. The conversion of this old mill has been accomplished with style by local craftsmen; good plastering and planked floors give the place a manicured and stylish look and make a nice change from the usual beam and terracotta. Indonesian beds, lamps, chairs and tables add a rich, exotic feel. The focus of the house is poolwards: beyond, groves of olives and the changing colours of the mountains make a great backdrop for your sundowner. At dinner, feast on local food and good wines. The staff are friendly and Pom will be around to share a yarn and/or a glass or two.

rooms	11: 3 doubles, 8 suites.
price	€130–€250; single €115; suite €160–€250.
meals	Dinner €27.
closed	15 January-February.
directions	From Málaga N-340, then m'way for Cádiz. Exit Ronda, then bypass Ronda on A-376 for Sevilla. Pass turning to Benaoján; right at sign for hotel. Under bridge, then left at 1st fork; over bridge; left after 200m.

Christina & Pom Piek

tel	+34 952 114355
fax	+34 952 114356
e-mail	info@hotellafuente.com
web	www.hotellafuente.com

La Goyesca
Calle Infantes 39, 29400 Ronda, Málaga

Don't be put off by the shabby entrance from the street to La Goyesca. You emerge in a magical inner courtyard full of plumbago, medlar, Virginia creeper, ferns, jasmine and a host of other plantery. New owners Javier Herrera Pérez and his wife arrived last year; teachers by profession, they have finally realised a long-held dream, to run a small hostelry in Andalucía. The building has a chequered history: it once housed a convent's garden, then became a small factory making quince jam, later it was a grain store... Rooms are wrapped around the patio, the hub of the place, and the decoration is rather 'Spanglish' (hand-painted dressers and bedside tables, geometric tiles in the bathrooms etc) but plans are afoot to introduce an Arabic theme. The rooms are warm and comfortable and, unusually for this town, they are quiet; you'll only hear the chirruping of the caged canaries. Hilltop Ronda is a delight and you are bang in the town's heart – the famous and magnificent bull ring, the oldest in Spain, is just around the corner. Visit out of season if you can.

rooms	7 doubles/twins/family.
price	€72–€90; single €48. VAT included.
meals	Restaurants nearby.
closed	Rarely.
directions	From Málaga, N-340 for Cádiz, then A-376 to Ronda. 1st right for Ronda; follow road through old town, cross bridge, pass bullring, then 1st right. Pass Hotel Polo; Hotel in 4th block on left.

Javier Herrera Pérez

tel	+34 952 190049
fax	+34 952 190657
e-mail	hotelgoyesca@ronda.net
web	www.ronda.net/usuar/hotelgoyesca/

map 23   entry 260

Hotel Polo

Mariano Soubirón 8, 29400 Ronda, Málaga

The Polo is one of Ronda's oldest hotels; the Puya family have been receiving guests here for nearly three decades. A sober, almost austere façade is softened with simple mouldings, and some of the tall stone-framed windows have authentic *cierros* (observation windows enclosed in decorative wrought-iron work). The elegant lines of the building are echoed inside where marble floors, antiques and deep sofas promise cool comfort. Brothers Javier and Rafael and sisters Blanca and Marta have taken over the family business and are warm, generous and welcoming. Bedrooms are large and light with a blue and white theme; some on the top floor have rooftop views to the mountains beyond; one has a bath with a view! The menu is very Spanish and the stuffed anchovies wonderful... Decoration, too, is thoroughly Spanish with wrought-iron bedheads and Mallorca-weave curtains; there is carpeting thoughout, mattresses are new and double-glazing cuts out the noise of the surrounding street life. In the lively and animated centre of Ronda, with a congenial bar and excellent restaurant, this is a genuine Andalucían experience.

rooms	36: 5 doubles, 29 twins, 2 singles.
price	€53–€69; single €33–€41.
meals	Breakfast 5; lunch/dinner €10–€13.
closed	Rarely.
directions	In centre of Ronda, near Plaza del Socorro. (Park in underground car park: special rates for hotel guests).

Rafael Puya
tel	+34 952 872447
fax	+34 952 872449
e-mail	hpolo@ronda.net

Alavera de los Baños

San Miguel s/n, 29400 Ronda, Málaga

A charming small hotel at the heart of the old Tanners Quarter — sheep-grazed pastures to one side, cobbled ascents to hilltop Ronda on the other. *A-la-vera de* means 'by the side of' — your hotel is right next to what was the first *hammam* (public baths) of the Moorish citadel. Christian and Inma are young, brimming with enthusiasm for their hotel and restaurant, and the nicest hosts imaginable. The brief to their architect was to create a building which was in keeping with the Hispano-Moorish elements of its surroundings: thus terracotta tiles, wafer bricks, keyhole arches without and, in the (smallish) bedrooms, a softly oriental feel: kilims, mosquito nets, colour washes of ochres, blue and yellow. Shower rooms are delightful. Do book one of the terrace rooms if you can; they lead to a little verdant garden and delicious pool. The dining room is flower-filled and candlelit, its eight-metre height cut across by an arched central walkway leading to the rooms at either end. Breakfasts are freshly different each day; dinners have a Moorish slant: lamb is the speciality and there is tasty veggie food too, much organically grown.

rooms	10 doubles/twins.
price	€ 70–€ 80; single € 50. VAT included.
meals	Dinner € 22.
closed	8 December–8 January.
directions	In Ronda, directly opp. Parador hotel, take c/Rosmario. Right at end & down hill to Fuente de los Ocho Caños. Here left, then 1st right to Arab Baths; hotel next door. Park here.

Christian Reichardt

tel	+34 952 879143
fax	+34 952 879143
e-mail	alavera@ctv.es
web	www.andalucia/alavera

map 23   entry 262

La Cazalla

Tajo del Abanico, Apartado de Correos 160, 29400 Ronda, Málaga

If you really want 'off the beaten track', make for this remote and lovely valley; spectacularly positioned at its head and built partly into the rock is La Cazalla. A Roman road once ran beside it – you can almost imagine legionaries trudging by. Today it is a place of astonishing greenness and peace, while the house, part Roman, part Arab, has been exquisitely restored by Maria. On the big terrace, with a cobalt-blue fountain and views to the Tajo del Abanico, shade is provided by vines and willows. Keep cool in the little spring water 'pool'. Everywhere there are fruit trees and the soothing sound of running water – even in the delightfully unusual sitting room, where natural rock walls and white paint contrast with rich kelims and piles of books. Bedrooms upstairs are airy and elegant. Each bathroom has an intriguing domed shower, each bedroom a pair of binoculars for watching birds and deer. Maria lives here with her son Rodrigo, who does the cooking – the three-course dinners are "always a surprise" and you are encouraged to say if there is anything you don't eat. There's also a small but good wine list. Worth the detour. *A Rusticae hotel.*

rooms	6: 5 doubles, 1 suite.
price	€ 102 (min. stay 2 nights); suite € 150 (min. stay 5 nights). VAT included.
meals	Dinner € 24.
closed	Rarely.
directions	From Ronda, C-369 for Algeciras. Pass 1st r'bout; at next r'bout, to right of road, avoid track for 'ermita' & take next right. Follow blue-painted marks on stones for 2.8km.

Maria Ruiz

tel	+34 952 114175
fax	+34 952 114175

El Molino, Hotel Rustico

2° Molino, Camino La Lobilla, 29680 Estepona, Málaga

The approach may be unpromising but the moment you enter you'll know the journey was worth it. El Molino is a converted 19th-century flour mill, surrounded by a profusion of oleanders, banana trees, pomegranates, avocados, persimmons, acacia... wonderful. A wooden gallery round two sides of the building gives the place the feel of a hacienda, and antique furniture, Casablanca fans and mosquito nets add to the Latin American effect. The Fischels have achieved an off-beat mix of the formal and the rustic which works really well. The baroque splendour of the great sitting room, with its antiques and paintings of Robert's ancestors, is softened by a chunky terracotta floor and beamed ceiling. And there's a similar mix of styles in the bedrooms, vast and comfortable. (Light sleepers beware: as elsewhere, country dogs are fond of starlight barking.) Anna is an artist and writer and she and Robert have a young daughter, Isabella — so, a good place for families, with lots of toys and a beach just down the road. Robert is the most genial of hosts and dining here is a memorable event, whether outside or in the cosy, subtly-lit dining room. *Multi-lingual hotel.*

rooms	4: 3 doubles, 1 twin.
price	From €90.
meals	Lunch/dinner €28.
closed	Christmas.
directions	From San Pedro into Estepona, right at 1st lights, uphill past Polideportivo Municipal (sports centre). At r'bout, left over N-340. After 1.5km, as road dips down to ford, take track on left for 250m to hotel.

Anna & Robert Fischel

tel	+34 952 791085
fax	+34 952 804346
e-mail	robert@estepona-molino.com
web	www.estepona-molino.com

map 23   entry 264

Albero Lodge

Tamesis 16, Urbanización Finca la Cancelada, 29689 Estepona, Málaga

A private villa reborn as a sophisticated small hotel. Trees stand sentinel in front of a modern, ochre-coloured exterior (*albero* is the sandy colour of the bull ring) giving it a ceremonious air. Indoors, the dining room, sitting room and bar (all interconnected spaces) are similarly formal. By contrast, the bedrooms are dramatically, triumphantly, individual. Each has been inspired by a different city — Florence, Deauville, Berlin, Dover, Ronda, Madras, Djerba, Fez and New York — each chicly decorated and furnished to match. Those with an eastern theme are especially effective. Linen and fittings are splendidly deluxe and every room has its own patio. The garden is similarly groomed and manicured, with palm trees and plumbago, hibiscus and jasmine and a delightful little pool, and there's a terrace dotted with colonial-style rattan furniture. Because the house is on a development of villas quite close to the N-340, you can hear traffic noise from outside; indoors, however, the sound insulation is good. The beach is a five-minute walk and Gibraltar a short drive to the west. You could even take a day trip to Morocco.

rooms	9 doubles.
price	€85–€155.
meals	Breakfast €7.
closed	Rarely.
directions	From Málaga, N-340 for Estepona. Exit after km164.5, signed Cambio de Sentido. Under bridge, left twice, right twice, past Park Beach. Hotel on right.

Anastasio Pérez Torres

tel	+34 952 880700
fax	+34 952 885238
e-mail	info@alberolodge.com
web	www.alberolodge.com

Breakers Lodge Hostal

Avenida Las Mimosas 189, Linda Vista Baja, 29678 San Pedro de Alcántara, Málaga

Although no longer the little fishing village of yore, San Pedro is one of the Costa villages that has managed to retain its Spanishness intact. This modern villa is in one of its residential areas on a quiet road leading straight down to the beach – perfect. Mark and Sharon have been in southern Spain for many years and, though widely travelled, would live nowhere else. You'll be greeted with a smile here; they are sociable, talkative types, but know that your privacy is precious. An electronic gate pulls shut behind you, reminding you that things have moved on since Laurie Lee arrived, fiddle in hand. Bedrooms are smartly furnished, with white cane furniture, beautifully padded headboards and matching drapes; some give onto the lovely little pool with palm tree at the back of the house. There is also a terraced area for sitting out with tea, or a beer. Meals are not normally available but give Sharon advance warning and her maid will come in and prepare you a paella. If not, walk into San Pedro and ask for Fernando's fish restaurant. You'll bless us for sending you there...

rooms	6 doubles/twins.
price	€ 78–€ 90.
meals	Not normally available.
closed	Rarely.
directions	From Málaga N-340 for Algeciras. Through San Pedro, under arch across road & exit shortly after for Benahavis. Back towards Málaga, under arch again & immed. right. House on right after 200m.

Sharon Knight

tel	+34 952 784780
fax	+34 952 784780
e-mail	breakers@mercuryin.es

map 23   entry 266

Amanhavis

Calle del Pilar 3, Benahavis, 29679 Marbella, Málaga

Benahavis is well-known to Costa residents for its string of restaurants which stretch all the way through the village. But it remains a pretty place and it certainly caught Burkhard Weber's eye when he came searching for the right place to set up his 'small-is-beautiful' hotel and eatery. Very soon after opening — less than two years ago — Amanhavis became popular with the Marbella set, thanks to what Burkhard calls his "creative Mediterranean cuisine". When designing the guest rooms, space was at a premium but he cleverly managed to fit nine around the hotel's ivy-clad inner courtyard where, in the warmer months, you dine by the central plunge pool. Bedrooms are a flight of decorative fantasy with themes which hark back to Spain's Golden Age: The Astonomer's Observatory, The Spice Trader's Caravan or The Philospher's Study, with decorative elements matching the theme. Satellite TV, safes and internet access speak of a more modern era. You are just five kilometres from the sea and all those golden beaches, and golfers are well looked after here: golf clubs abound.

rooms	9: 6 doubles/twins, 3 'de luxe' rooms.
price	€ 119-€ 179.
meals	Breakfast € 11. Dinner € 32.50. Restaurant closed Sunday & Monday.
closed	7-31 January.
directions	From Málaga, for Cádiz. Just past San Pedro, right for Benahavis. Hotel on far side of village, signed.

Leslie & Burkhard Weber

tel	+34 952 856026
fax	+34 952 856151
e-mail	info@amanhavis.com
web	www.amanhavis.com

La Posada del Ángel
Mesones 21, 29610 Ojén, Málaga

A mosaic angel welcomes you through a Moorish doorway tucked down a narrow street. You've arrived at La Posada del Angel, in the very heart of Ojén. It's hard to believe that a genuine Spanish village like this can still exist so close to the urban sprawl of the Costa del Sol but, miraculously, it does. And the *posada* is testimony to what can be achieved by a young couple with vision, dedication and flair. Carmen and Frank (she is Spanish and studied design, he is French) have transformed a row of five ruined houses into a delightful, Moorish-style little hotel. Each room and bathroom has a different theme and is decorated and furnished in vibrant colours with much wrought ironwork. There's a pleasant central patio and a bar where you can have afternoon tea or a sundowner before diving back into the village. Ojén's lure is irresistible: narrow streets converge on a square stocked with bars and places to eat. Visit the Ojén Caves, the 16th-century Church of the Incarnation and the Wine Museum. Ojén also has its place in the gastronomical history books: it was once famous for its *anise* liqueur.

rooms	17 doubles.
price	€ 67–€ 108. VAT included.
meals	Breakfast € 7.50. Food available at nearby Meson Laurente.
closed	Rarely.
directions	From Málaga, N–340 for Marbella. Exit km182, then A–355 to Ojén. Posada signed from south of village.

Carmen Calvo & Frank Thomas

tel	+34 952 881808
fax	+34 952 881810
e-mail	info@laposadadelangel.com
web	www.laposadadelangel.com

map 23   entry 268

El Oceano Hotel & Beach Club

Ctra. N-340 km 199, Urbanización Torrenueva, 29649 Mijas Costa, Málaga

El Oceano may not be particularly Spanish, but it is as luxurious as can be. Owners John and Lorraine have achieved their particular vision of paradise; if you wish to be pampered, you will be here. Wander around all day in a bathrobe if you like; at the end of the day – after an excellent dinner, good wine and a late-night swim – slip into a deeply comfortable bed. The rooms are decidedly ritzy, with an international feel. There's a hint of Florida about the sitting room/bar and a touch of Far Eastern exoticism in the curving pool, with its palm trees and thatched bar you can glide up to. The cuisine and wine list are international, too. Dine on lobster, Thai fish cakes or a generous steak to the classical tinkling of the background piano. In warm weather you dine on the wooden broadwalk overlooking the sea. Beyond the pool: a long sweep of sea front; the blue water shimmers, waves lap on the rocks and the beach feels as though it belongs to you. Considering how crowded this area is becoming, you are blissfully unaware of other development. What luxury!

rooms	18: 17 doubles, 1 twin.
price	€ 140–€ 240.
meals	Breakfast € 10–€ 12.50; lunch/dinner € 40 à la carte.
closed	Rarely.
directions	From Málaga, N-340 for Marbella. Exit Riviera del Sol. At r'bout, left under m'way, back onto N-340 for Fuengirola. After footbridge, 1st exit. Hotel on right.

John Palmer

tel	+34 952 587550
fax	+34 952 587637
e-mail	info@oceanohotel.com
web	www.oceanohotel.com

The Beach House

Urbanización El Chaparral, CN.340 km.203, 29648 Mijas Costa, Málaga

The sea's the thing. Just below the balustrade at the end of the pool, the Med splashes and sparkles: it's incredibly close. The position is arresting: you may be sandwiched between the devil (the busy N-340 coastal road) and the deep blue sea, but it's easy to forget the devil. In a previous life, the house was the ritzy villa of a wealthy Arab, then a B&B called Casa Aloha. Now Swedish Kjell and Olof – charming, friendly, immaculately dressed – have transformed it into a temple of design. They have created a remarkable impression of cool, studied simplicity and stark elegance – Japanese, minimalist, restful. Small details, such as a candle arrangement or a flower floating in a bowl by your bed, are handled in the same masterly way as the big effects. It is a unique creation, the sort of place that gets written up in the design magazines. Meticulous, but in no way clinical. And Kjell and Olof are very good hosts. Breakfast is a big buffet, usually eaten outside at attractive wooden tables and chairs. This is like staying in a beautiful villa, as close to the Med as you can get, with the lovely beaches of Fuengirola just a shake away.

rooms	9 doubles/twins.
price	€ 125-€ 175. VAT included.
meals	Good restaurants nearby.
closed	Rarely.
directions	From Málaga N-340 Cádiz & Algeciras. Do NOT branch onto A-7, keep on N-340; past km202, exit Cala de Mijas. Follow signs Fuengirola & Málaga back onto N-340. Keep hard right; past 1st footbridge, slip road to right. On right after 250m.

Kjell Sporrong & Olof Naslund

tel	+34 952 494540
fax	+34 952 494540
e-mail	info@beachhouse.nu
web	www.beachhouse.nu

map 24 entry 270

Finca Blake

Carretera de Mijas-Fuengirola km 2, 29650 Mijas, Málaga

Finca Blake lies just beneath Mijas, a village of narrow whitewashed streets just far enough back from the sea to have escaped the development that has left such scars on Spain's southern coast. It was built by one Major Blake, retired from the RAF; in 1961 his was the very first car in the village! The present owner, Amélie, is hospitable, multilingual and *sympa* and runs her B&B in the best tradition of *mi casa es tu casa*. She has nursed an already spectacular garden into something more precious still; sit and contemplate this botanical wonderland from the terrace which looks out to the glittering Med. Then return to one of Amélie's magical guest rooms. The antithesis of made-to-measure hotel rooms, these are filled with oil paintings, rugs, lamps and books, with new ceiling fans and own bathrooms inviting you to preen yourself with every imaginable 'aide-toilette'. Breakfast on the terrace, sip your tea (from Harrods or Fortnum's, no less), abandon yourself to the contemplation of the art, play a round of golf: there are so many courses around here you are spoiled for choice. You are also conveniently close to Malaga airport.

rooms	2 doubles; 1 cottage for 3.
price	Double/twin/cottage €78–€90. VAT and breakfast included.
meals	Restaurants in village.
closed	Rarely.
directions	From airport, A-7 Cádiz & Algeciras. Exit 213 Mijas & Fuengirola then A-387 for Mijas. Just after Restaurante Molino del Cura on right, Finca Blake is on left, with blue B&B sign. Ring bell to open gates.

Amélie Pommier

tel	+34 952 590401
fax	+34 952 590401
e-mail	fincablake@wanadoo.es
web	www.fincablake.com

La Fonda Hotel & Appartments

Calle Santo Domingo 7, 29639 Benalmádena Pueblo, Málaga

There *are* places on the Costa that have retained their identity and dignity through all those years of unbridled development. One of them is whitewashed, geranium-clad Benalmádena Pueblo; don't confuse it with Benalmádena Playa, best avoided. In a quiet street off the pretty main square, you are surprisingly near the airport. The Fonda was the creation of architect Cesar Manrique, known for his lifelong battle to show that old and new can work beautifully together. And this hotel and its neighbouring apartments are a hymn to the south; there are cool patios shaded by palms, potted aspidistras, geometric tiles, fountains, pebbled floors, the best set off by glimpses of the glittering sea. Hotel rooms are large, light, airy and marble-floored. Downstairs are wicker chairs and a shaded terrace. La Fonda's snack bar/restaurant doubles as a cookery school (closed during the summer, when the hotel gets busy): treat yourself to a good southern lunch at half the cost of elsewhere. Or wander along to the square and watch the night in with a plate of olives, a glass of sherry and the gaiety of Andalucían street-life.

rooms	26: 4 doubles, 18 twins, 4 singles. 26 self-catering apartments.
price	€ 60–€ 110; single € 44–€ 72. VAT included.
meals	Lunch/dinner € 20.
closed	Rarely.
directions	From Málaga airport, N-340 then A-7 Cádiz. Exit 223 for Benalmádena. Take 2nd exit at 1st r'bout, 2nd exit at next r'bout, 1st exit at 3rd r'bout. Park in village; lift up to hotel.

José Antonio García García
tel +34 952 568324
fax +34 95 2568273

map 24 entry 272

Santa Fe

Carretera de Monda km 3, Apartado 147, 29100 Coín, Málaga

Two young, enthusiastic and multi-lingual Dutch brothers have made a name for themselves since taking over at Santa Fe. Warden and Arjan's old farmhouse sits among the citrus groves of the Guadalhorce valley, to one side of the road from Marbella up to Coín (you can hear the rumble of traffic from the hotel). The transformation from farm to guest house has been faithful to local tradition; bedrooms – some small – have rustic furniture, terracotta floors (tiles fired with the dog-paw print bring good luck!) and colour-washed walls. The restaurant is popular with non-residents, too: guests are Spanish and Costa-cosmopolitan. A Belgian chef and an English sous-chef conjure up international delicacies such as spinach with langoustines, fillet steak with sherry, tomato and Serrano ham sauce, Dutch apple pie; there's a good selection of vegetarian dishes too. The dining room has a log fire in winter and the conservatory is cosy – but most of the year you dine beneath the old olive tree or the pool-side pergola. A casual, relaxed atmosphere reigns.

rooms	5 twins.
price	Twin €62; single €55. VAT included.
meals	Lunch/dinner €15–€25 à la carte. Closed Tuesday.
closed	2 weeks in November & 2 weeks in January/February.
directions	From Málaga, N-340 for Algeciras & Cádiz. About 1km after airport, A-366/C-344 to Coín. In Coín for Monda & Marbella. Santa Fe just outside Coín on right side of road.

Warden & Arjan van de Vrande

tel	+34 95 2452916
fax	+34 95 2453843
e-mail	info@santafe-hotel.com
web	www.santafe-hotel.com

El Castillo de Monda
29110 Monda, Málaga

What a position, high up above the village, reached by a series of steep switchbacks: the views from the hotel are magical, taking in the sweep of the Sierra Nevada and the Ronda mountains. The first fortifications were built on Monda's hilltop by the Moors in the 11th century, and this new hotel owes much to the Moorish tradition: there are fountains, wafer-bricked arches, ceramic tiles and much use of *muqarna*, the delicate stucco bas-relief which is the delight of the Alhambra Palace in Granada. But there are some English touches as well: a collection of watercolours of the English countryside suggest a certain nostalgia for Blighty. The main dining room evokes a medieval banqueting hall with its arches and flags, and the classical Andalucían mix spills over to bedrooms too: four-posters and Moorish arches, terracotta and snazzy fabrics, marbled and heated bathroom floors. Best of all is the wonderful terrace festooned with flora – sit out here at night with a post-dinner drink and watch the lights of the village twinkling below. Luxurious and fun. *Week-long relaxation skills courses available.*

rooms	29: 14 doubles, 4 twins, 11 suites.
price	€ 91–€ 160; single € 77–€ 114; suite € 156–€ 268. VAT included.
meals	Breakfast € 11.50; lunch/dinner € 24 set menu, € 55–€ 60 à la carte.
closed	Rarely.
directions	From Málaga N-340 for Cádiz & Algeciras. Shortly before Marbella (don't turn off N-340), right for Ojen & Coín. After 16km right into Monda; follow signs.

John Norris & Bruce Freestone

tel	+34 952 457142
fax	+34 952 457336
e-mail	monda@spa.es
web	www.costadelsol.spa.es/hotel/monda

map 23   entry 274

El Molino Santisteban
A366 km 52-53, 29108 Guaro, Málaga

Frits and Gisèle left Holland dreaming of warmer, more southern climes. It is easy to see how this old mill fitted that dream: it lies to one side of the lush valley cut through by the Río Grande, just half an hour from the coast, surrounded by willow, eucalyptus, citrus, rose and every kind of verdant climber. Olives were once milled here and the old mill race adds much life – for ears and eyes – to the pretty garden. The main building has the feel of a rather diminuitive hacienda; the six bedrooms give onto its sheltered inner patio where a fountain gurgles, and a wooden balcony wraps around its upper floor. The bedrooms are a good size, are dressed with mostly antique furniture and the nicest have French windows which look out across the river. Just across the way is the old mill itself which has become the breakfast room: you eat here round a long table on ornate leather-backed chairs that once graced a monastery. Your hosts are well-travelled, easy and cosmopolitan and speak near-perfect English. For those nights on which dinner is not served, there is a simple restaurant 50m off (you can park here too), and more sophisticated eateries down the road in Coín.

rooms	6 doubles/twins.
price	€54–€85; single €49. One-night supplement.
meals	Dinner €17–€20.
closed	December-March.
directions	From Málaga airport, N-340 for Torremolinos/Cádiz. After 200m right for Coin then Ronda on A-366/C-344. Hotel between km52 & km53 markers on right, just before Venta Gallardo.

Frits Blomsma & Gisèle Gerhardus
tel	+34 952 453748
fax	+34 952 453748
e-mail	info@hotelmolino.com
web	www.hotelmolino.com

Hotel Cerro de Híjar

Cerro de Híjar s/n, 29109 Tolox, Málaga

On a clear day you can see — well, if not forever, at least to the sea and the Sierra Nevada. It has a wonderful, remote position, this hotel, on a bluff 2,000 feet above sea level. (And in magnificent walking country, for you are on the eastern edge of the Sierra de las Nieves Natural Park.) From the ancient spa village of Tolox, follow the winding road up and up... The hotel is new but looks like a traditional hunting lodge and its three young managers have already stamped their personality upon it. There is a terrific sense of light and space throughout, enhanced by creamy stucco walls, bright rugs and attractive furniture; modern paintings and prints, some by Andalucía's best artists, hang on every wall. The bedrooms are large, comfortable, beautifully finished, dazzlingly clean. You'll eat and drink well here for Martín's cooking is inspired — traditional Andalucían with a modern touch. It's no surprise to learn that he used to work in the area's only Michelin-starred restaurant. He, Guillermo and Eugenio run the place in an eco-friendly manner, all three speak excellent English and are very friendly and welcoming. A place to remember.

rooms	18: 5 doubles, 9 twins, 4 suites.
price	€ 72–€ 84; suite € 84–€ 108.
meals	Lunch/dinner € 18–€ 27.
closed	Rarely.
directions	From Málaga, Cártama road. Filter right to Coín, then onto A-366 for Ronda. Left to Tolox, through village to Balneario (spa), then right up hill for 2.5km to hotel.

Guillermo Gonzalez

tel	+34 952 112111
fax	+34 952 710395
e-mail	cerro@cerrodehijar.com
web	www.cerrodehijar.com

map 23   entry 276

Hotel Posada del Canónigo
Calle Mesones 24, 29420 El Burgo, Málaga

Your arrival in the mountain village of El Burgo will be memorable: a splash of brilliant white amid the ochres and greys of the surrounding limestone massif. Little visited, it will give you as real a taste of Andalucían mountain life as can be found anywhere. This grand old village house is another good reason for coming. It is very much a family affair – 13 brothers and sisters helped restore and decorate! Bedrooms are simple with tiled floors, old bedsteads and lots of family things: prints, paintings and dried flowers have been lovingly arranged by María Reyes, one of the owners. It is all spotless and your charming hosts are proud of every last corner. There is a small dining room leading to a little patio where you breakfast – well – in the morning sun, and a newly opened *bodega*-style restaurant where just local dishes are on offer. Both sitting rooms have open hearths and exposed stonework and the whole place is uncannily quiet by Andalucían standards. Stay two nights to walk or let the owners take you riding in the virtually unknown National Park of the Sierra de la Nieves above Ronda – glorious.

rooms	12 twins/doubles.
price	€ 44–€ 70; single € 32–€ 37. VAT included.
meals	Lunch/dinner € 10.80. VAT included.
closed	24 December.
directions	From Torremolinos to Cártama then continue to Calea, Alozaina, Yunquera & El Burgo. Turn right into village & ask; hotel is next to San Agustín church.

Álvaro Pérez

tel	+34 952 160185
fax	+34 952 160185
e-mail	reservascanonigo@retemail.es
web	www.laposadadelcanonigo.com

Casa Piedra Vieja
Pueblo Perdido, 54321 Sierra Morena, Málaga

Push open the great door – or don't bother – and step straight through the grand portal onto a lush carpet of green, better and deeper by far than any shag pile you may have at home. The flower arrangements are as natural and impressive as anything attained by the professionals, and there are stunning shrubbery arrangements too. Richard Rogers eat your heart out – this is a house that actually 'fuses' with nature. Best of all: a lone pine that is the centre-piece of the open atrium. It is astonishing that all this was achieved centuries ago, long before the Spaniards threw the Moors out of Andalucía. Note the round-arched doors, intact despite the ravages of time and 'tiempo'. It was the Moors, of course, who created the remarkable irrigation system that still brings water burbling to the property; it is an oasis of greenery in the heart of an otherwise dry Sierra. Your hosts – an elderly couple who have spent a lifetime carefully ignoring the house – are rarely there. But we have been told that they are harmless and will now put your money to good use. Their next project will be the door...

rooms	1 open-plan.
price	From € 49.99.
meals	Dining al fresco.
closed	In bad weather.
directions	Given on booking.

Pedro & Clara Esperanza

tel	+34 (0)987 654321
fax	+34 (0)987 654322
e-mail	info@piedra-vieja.an
web	www.piedra-vieja.an

map 0   entry 278

Cortijo Jacaranda

Apdo. de Correos 279, 29500 Alora, Málaga

The problem with holidaying with young children is that few places answer your needs and theirs. The two ex-London families who run Cortijo Jacaranda go out of their way to help and even offer an airport pick-up and drop-off service. On their 16-acre farm in the hills – once the property of a doctor of natural medicine and an enthusiastic planter of rare trees – each of the two *casitas* has a little garden leading to a lovely shared swimming pool with a circular shallow area at one end. There's also a big terrace for sunbathing, purpose-built play areas, a gym and loads of other facilities… an idyllic set-up in this remote mountain setting. Twice-weekly family barbecues among the jacaranda trees are great fun – the cooking is done for you, should you wish – and your hosts are also happy to provide a courtesy babysitting service one evening a week, driving you to and from a local restaurant. They are a mine of information on the area and eager to share the pleasures of this particular corner of Spain. Skiing trips – a two-hour drive – can be arranged from January to April. *Minimum three-night stay.*

rooms	2 self-catering houses for 4; 1 apartment for 2.
price	House € 110–€ 120 p.p; apt € 75–€ 85 p.p.
meals	Breakfast € 5, picnic € 5, dinner € 10.
closed	Rarely.
directions	Málaga-Campillos A-357. After 25km, right to Alora. Pass village, over bridge. At Bar Los Caballos, right 1km, left past bus shelter 2km. Right fork, over stream bed, 2.7km to house.

Jeremy Henshaw
tel 0870 8010325
e-mail david@cortijojacaranda.com
web www.cortijojacaranda.com

Molino de las Pilas

Ctra. Vieja de Ronda s/n, 29327 Teba, Málaga

Could there be a link between this wild part of Andalucía and… Scotland? Surprisingly, yes. Above the old mill/farmhouse looms Teba Castle, scene of a fierce battle in 1331. Sir James Douglas, en route to the Holy Land with Robert the Bruce's heart in a casket, got caught up in a conflict with the Moors, and, to encourage his men, flung the casket and himself into the fray. He died but the casket was recovered and now lies peaceably in Melrose Abbey. Molino de las Pilas is less ancient. Built in 1882, it was in ruins when Pablo came across it and decided to restore; it took him three years. Simply but extremely comfortably furnished in an attractive rustic style, it has good beds and fine bathrooms. But what makes the inn unforgettable is the remarkable restaurant in the mill itself. All the old workings are still in place: great grindstones for mashing the olives, massive beamed press, huge *tintajas* set in the floor to store the oil. Equally remarkable is Paco's cooking: salads which are sheer delight, superb fish, fabulous marinaded partridge – brilliant cooking at amazingly reasonable prices. A truly special place.

rooms	6 doubles.
price	€ 60. VAT included.
meals	Lunch € 18 set menu, € 24 à la carte.
closed	Rarely.
directions	From Málaga, A-357 for Campillos. After Ardales, cross bridge at lake, then left at km11 to Teba (ignore 1st road to Ronda & Teba, signed at km19). After 6km, right at petrol station, up hill. Hotel signed to left after 1km.

Pablo Moreno Aragón

tel	+34 952 748622
fax	+34 952 748647
e-mail	info@molinodelaspilas.com
web	www.molinodelaspilas.com

map 23 entry 280

Cortijo Valverde

Ctra. Alora-Antequera km 35.5, 29500 Álora, Málaga

You are in a landscape of hills and rocky outcrops – rural Spain at its best. The 40 acres of land around Valverde are still farmed (fields of sunflowers, olive groves and citrus trees surround you) and the restored farmhouse has a traditional, rustic feel. In one direction, the house looks up at the Torcal; in the other, it has views of the Moorish castle and city walls of Alora, an ancient hill village still largely undiscovered by tourists. Eating here after a day's sightseeing is a delightful experience. (Do book.) Ron's excellent cooking makes full use of fresh produce brought in daily from the local market. After aperitifs on the terrace, try the grilled goat's cheese or flambéd prawns and relax in the pleasant dinner-party atmosphere: staying here is rather like being in the best kind of house party, with Ron and Moyra the warmest of hosts. Bedrooms are in their own *casitas*, each with walk-in shower and own terrace; furnishings and décor have an attractive simplicity, and are comfortable and stylish. There's a gorgeous pool, and, if you'd like to improve your Spanish, some intensive language courses are in the process of being set up.

rooms	7: 3 doubles, 4 twins.
price	€ 96.
meals	Lunch € 5 (snacks); dinner € 25.
closed	12 January-7 February.
directions	From Málaga, A-357 for Campillos, then A-343 to Alora. Don't go into village. Cross river up to T-junc. by Bar Los Caballos, then left for Valle de Abdaljis. Pass km35.5 & follow sign to right for Tierra Nueva. After 300m, sharp left up to hotel.

Moyra & Rod Cridland

tel	+34 952 112979
fax	+34 952 112979
e-mail	cortijovalverde@mercuryin.es
web	www.cortijovalverde.com

Casa Rural Domingo

Arroyo Cansino 4, 29500 Álora, Málaga

Domin and Cynthia once stayed at one of the small hotels we recommend in this book. They were so taken by the experience that they left Belgium, headed south and opened their own B&B. Meet them and you'll realise why they were bound to succeed: they are the friendliest of folk with a highly infectious *joie de vivre*. They were inspired when they chose the land where Casa Domingo would be built: high above Álora it has marvellous views of the eastern ranges of the Ronda Sierra. Guests can choose between B&B or self-catering apartments; our choice would be one of the B&B rooms: large, with comfortable beds, bright rugs and terracotta floors, and a mix of good contemporary furniture and antiques. Life in the warmer months centres on the poolside terrace and the atmosphere is relaxed; guests mingle easily, perhaps for a game of boules or tennis, or a barbecue. Domin and Cynthia don't cook but Álora is a few minutes away by car and has one particularly good restaurant. This would be a great place to spend time at the beginning or end of your holiday in Spain. Children are positively liked here, rather than tolerated.

rooms	5 twins/doubles. Also self-catering apartments.
price	€ 54–€ 60. VAT included.
meals	Restaurant nearby.
closed	December.
directions	Málaga airport, N-340 for Algeciras. After 500m, right for Churriana & Coín. 2nd r'bout, right to Cártama, then A-357 for Campillos. 16km on, right for Álora. At T-junc, right; then, after 200m, left. At next T-junc. track to farm, signed.

Domin & Cynthia Doms

tel	+34 952 119744
fax	+34 952 119744
e-mail	casadomingo@airtel.net
web	www.casaruraldomingo.com

map 24   entry 282

Hacienda San José

Buzón 59, Entrerrios, 29650 Mijas, Málaga

Hacienda San José lies far from the concrete buildings in what is known locally as 'Avocado Valley', between four golf courses on a hill with views to Mijas and the sea. Nikki opened one of the first small country hotels in Spain nearly 30 years ago; in this, her second venture, she and husband Pepe have created an immensely attractive, hugely comfortable and truly *Andaluz* hotel. Although the building is yet young, the smell of woodsmoke and beeswax, the terracotta floors, the high wooden ceilings and the many antiques give the place a much older feel. The exotic trees and plants in the garden also look suitably mature. Your bedroom is vast and contains every conceivable creature comfort: separate bath and shower, double sinks, underfloor heating (as throughout the house). Your hosts show great sensitivity in the way they treat guests, mindful of your intimacy yet there when you need them. Come for the riding, the golf or just to relax. This would also make a perfect winter break: Granada and Ronda are not too far, and this charmed corner of Andalucía just happens to have one of the mildest climates in Europe.

rooms	5 doubles/twins.
price	€ 140.
meals	Dinner € 18-€ 22.
closed	15 June-31 August.
directions	From Fuengirola for Marbella on N-340. In Cala de Mijas turn for La Cala Golf. At 1st r'bout right; at next fork right again for Entrerrios. 1.8km from here to hotel; signed.

Nikki & José García

tel	+34 952 119494
fax	+34 952 119494
e-mail	haciendasanjose@yahoo.co.uk

La Posada del Torcal

Carretera La Hoya-La Higuera, 29230 Villanueva de la Concepción, Málaga

The owners of Torcal lived on the coast before they discovered the harsh beauty of the mountains north of Málaga. The fruit of their conversion from Costa to Sierra is this fetching small hotel, a short drive from the Dalí-esque limestone formations of the Torcal Park. The hotel's base elements – tile, beam and woodwork – are true to local rustic tradition; inside and out feels thoroughly *Andaluz*. Bedrooms are dedicated to different Spanish artists, and the oils are copies of originals painted by Karen's brother. Many of the trimmings come from further afield – the beds, some brass, some Gothic, some four-poster, were shipped out from England. Open-plan bedrooms allow you to sip your drink from a corner bath yet not miss a second of the amazing views beyond. Underfloor heating warms in winter, Casablanca fans cool in summer. Many of the dishes on the menu are local/Spanish but there are a number of more familiar-sounding ones, too, and a good selection of wines and spirits. The swimming pool is heated all year round, and Michael, the manager, will point you in the right direction if walking – or horse-riding – is your thing.

rooms	10 doubles/twins.
price	€ 160–€ 180; single € 110.
meals	Lunch/dinner € 30 à la carte. VAT included.
closed	Rarely.
directions	Málaga N-331 Antequera, exit 148 for Casabermeja & Colmenar. In Casabermeja right for Almogía; next left to Villanueva de la Concepción. At top of village, left at junc.; after 1.5km right for La Joya & La Higuera. Hotel 3km on left.

Michael Soffe

tel	+34 952 031177
fax	+34 952 031006
e-mail	posadatorcal@codesat.net
web	www.eltorcal.com/posadatorcal

map 24   entry 284

Casa de Elrond

Barrio Seco s/n, 29230 Villanueva de la Concepción, Málaga

This is a favourite stopover in Andalucía and the reason we are such fans is that Mike and Una are such genuinely nice people. A friend and I were there on a walking holiday and Una made such a fuss of us that we were loath to leave. The mostly modern house is set back from a quiet road, surrounded by a carefully tended garden, and with an amazing view down towards the Mediterranean; don't miss sundown when range after range of mountains take on every imaginable hue of purple and blue. The three bedrooms lead off a small guest lounge where Mike, immensely practical, has added a woodburner. The bedrooms have modern pine furniture and duvets; one of them is large enough to sleep three. It's a perfect place for walkers: return after a day in the remarkable Torcal Park to one of Una's vegetarian suppers (be sure to let her know in advance – ingredients are market-fresh). You eat outdoors, of course, in the warmer months, and in the kitchen / diner the rest of the year. Dinner includes a house red but you're welcome to bring your own if you prefer. Excellent value: do give it a go.

rooms	3 doubles/twins.
price	€ 45-€ 62.
meals	Dinner on request € 12, includes half-litre of wine.
closed	Rarely.
directions	From Málaga N-340 for Antequera & Granada. At km241 marker, N-331 to Casabermeja & to Villanueva de la C. Here left at junc. House on right after 3km.

Mike & Una Cooper

tel	+34 952 754091
fax	+34 952 754091
e-mail	elrond@mercuryin.es

Arcadia Retreat

Antigua Venta de Santa María, 29150 Almogía, Málaga

A quiet mountain approach, a peach-coloured building by the side of the road. Inside, what a surprise... bedrooms with country-antique four-posters, sitting room with leather sofas, honeymoon suite with black-tiled bathroom, crisp white units and sunken tub. In short, a totally unexpected little hotel less than a half-hour's drive from the coast, with fine views of the Sierra del Hacho. A faint scent of incense gives the place a touch of the exotic, as does the Buddha statue in one of the bedrooms. The house is 300 years old and used to be run as a roadside restaurant — then Martina and Georgio took it over. She is Czech, he is Sardinian and they once lead high-powered lives in Covent Garden, a pressurized London existence they swapped for the Good Life in Andalucía. There is a certain cosmopolitan flair to the kitchen, but the Arcadia is best noted for its simple dishes like roast leg of lamb and fillet of duck with fruit. Georgio's *tiramisú* is special, too, and there's a good selection of wines. You eat in a pretty dining room with French windows opening onto a veranda and garden.

rooms	5: 2 doubles, 3 suites. 1 self-catering house for 6.
price	€ 50–€ 65; suite € 100. House € 400–€ 700 per week.
meals	Lunch € 5–€ 12; dinner € 25. Half-board € 20 p.p.
closed	Rarely.
directions	From Málaga, follow signs for Hospital & Avenida Carlos Haya. Continue through Puerto de la Torre, to Almogía. Hotel on left, 1km after village.

Georgio Melis

tel	+34 952 430598
fax	+34 952 430547
e-mail	arcadiaretreat@hotmail.com
web	www.arcadiaretreat.com

map 24   entry 286

Hotel Humaina

Parque Natural Montes de Málaga, Ctra de Colmenar s/n , 29013 Málaga

If your idea of hotel heaven is somewhere way, way off the beaten track then come here: Hotel Humaina is hidden deep in a forest of oak and pine, at the end of a mile and a half of steep track. It was a hunting lodge before being reborn as a small hotel; the area was popular with the shooting brigade, but its new status as a Natural Park means that the rabbit, foxes and hares that you see are more likely to be of this world than the next. What strikes you when you arrive is the utter tranquillity of the place and it seems fitting that the hotel's manager, Juan María, should greet you in such a gentle manner. The dining room and bedrooms are simply furnished with modern furniture and fittings – nothing special: their best feature is their peacefulness. The hotel's nicest room is the small lounge with chimney, full of books on the walking, flora and fauna of the area; set time aside to hike along the waymarked trail. This is an Eco-craft hotel: water is heated by solar energy, food comes from the kitchen garden. Do try the *plato de los montes* if you like fry-ups, followed by a glass of *vino de pasas*, the local (sweet) raisin wine.

rooms	13: 12 doubles, 1 suite.
price	€ 63–€ 69; suite €95–€ 107.
meals	Breakfast € 6; lunch/dinner € 18. Half-board € 21–€ 23; full-board € 31–€ 33.
closed	24 December.
directions	Málaga C-345 for Casabermeja: known as 'La Carretera de los Montes'. After 18km, left at signs for hotel. 2km of good track take you down to Humaina.

Juan María Luna

tel	+34 952 641025
fax	+34 952 640115
e-mail	info@hotelhumaina.es
web	www.hotelhumaina.es

Hotel Cortijo La Reina

Ctra. de Malaga-Colmenar km 549.5, 29013 Málaga

The road climbs to 3,000 feet before you reach La Reina. Hidden deep in the Montes de Málaga Park, it is not easy to find, but you won't forget your first sighting. At the front, it has the look of a hacienda; at the back, surrounded by cypress trees and olive groves, the building reminds one of Provence. Inside, the feel is more home than hotel. Beautifully finished wooden floors and ceilings give warmth and intimacy to stylish rooms; rugs, fireplaces and woodburning stoves add to the effect. (Only the taped music detracts.) Up the handsome wooden staircase with brass banister to bedrooms that are light and elegant, filled with every creature comfort and lovely paintings – they really do earn their four-star rating. Built as a *casa de recreo* by a Málaga doctor, the house has a magnificent view of the surrounding mountains. Manuel de Miguel and his staff take great pleasure in their guests' positive reaction to La Reina and do all they can to make your stay special. The walking in the area is good, too, starting with a number of marked routes through the estate itself. *Ask hotel to fax directions.*

rooms	12: 8 doubles, 1 twin, 1 single, 2 suites.
price	€ 150–€ 188; single € 113; suite € 225.
meals	Lunch/dinner € 30 à la carte.
closed	Rarely.
directions	Málaga N-340 Motril. Exit km244 Limonar. At r'bout, left under m'way, onto N-340 for Málaga. Exit km243 Ciudad Jardin; left opp. supermarket; left onto Málaga-Colmenar rd for 12km. At Venta El Detalle, track to hotel.

Manuel de Miguel

tel	+34 951 014000
fax	+34 951 014049
e-mail	info@cortijolareina.com
web	www.hotelcortijolareina.com

map 24   entry 288

Molino de Santillán

Ctra. de Macharaviaya km 3, Apdo. de Correos 101, 29730 Rincón de la Victoria, Málaga

Carlo Marchini, tired of the cut and thrust of business in Madrid, moved to the softer climes of Andalucía, bought an old farmhouse and, after years of restoration and planting, is now harvesting the fruits of his efforts. The building is inspired by the hacienda-style architecture of the New World; an arched patio opens at the southern end to catch the light and the view down to the sea. One of its wings is given over in its entirety to the restaurant, where many ingredients come straight from the farm gardens. Popular with guests are aubergines stuffed with hake and loin of pork in honey and apple sauce; there's a good paella, too, if you ask in advance. Both the arched terraced area looking seawards and the ochre-coloured dining room are attractive backdrops for a feast. Bedrooms feel properly Andalucían; stencilling and interesting colours add zest; there are Casablanca fans to keep the temperatures down and netting on windows to keep the mosquitoes at bay. Both Carlos and his daughter Adriana speak excellent English and are a winning combination. *A Rusticae hotel.*

rooms	10: 8 doubles, 2 suites.
price	€ 100–€ 120; single € 77–€ 99; suite € 142–€ 169.
meals	Breakfast € 9; lunch/dinner € 25.90.
closed	Rarely.
directions	From Málaga for Motril on N-340. Turn off for Macharaviaya & turn right at signs before you reach village. 1km of track to hotel.

Carlo Marchini

tel	+34 902 120240
fax	+34 952 400950
e-mail	msantillan@spa.es
web	www.hotel-msantillan.net

Hotel Paraíso del Mar

Prolongación de Carabeo 22, 29780 Nerja, Málaga

Nerja is one of the better-known resort towns of the Costa del Sol – hardly an auspicious beginning when searching for that 'special' hotel. But the Paraíso is just that. In a quieter corner of town, well away from the main drag of bars and restaurants, it stands at the edge of a cliff looking out to sea. The main house was built some 40 years ago by an English doctor; the other part is more recent and it has all been thoroughly revamped thanks to the hotel's charming young manager, Enrique. Most remarkable, perhaps, are the hotel's terraced gardens which drop down towards the beach: jasmine, palms, bougainvillaea, bananas, morning glory and a washingtonia give it an utterly southern air. Many guest rooms have a view and some their own terrace; ask for one of the quietest. They are large with mostly modern furniture and all the trimmings; some have jacuzzi baths, all have bathrobes and good towels. Beneath the hotel are a sauna and a hot-tub dug out of solid rock. It is all run on solar energy and could be just the place to recharge your batteries and still survive the *costa*.

rooms	17: 10 twins/doubles, 7 suites.
price	€ 53–€ 105; single € 47–€ 92; suite € 95–€ 125.
meals	Restaurants nearby.
closed	Mid-November–mid-December.
directions	From Málaga N-340 for Motril. Arriving in Nerja follow signs to Parador; the Paraíso del Mar is next door.

Enrique Caro Bernal

tel	+34 952 521621
fax	+34 952 522309
e-mail	info@hispanica-colint.es
web	www.hotelparaisodelmar.com

map 24   entry 290

Casa La Piedra

Plazoleta 14, 29754 Cómpeta, Málaga

Casa La Piedra is an old house in the heart of Cómpeta. This pretty white village is cradled by the Sierra de Tejeda and looks out across vine-covered hillsides to the Mediterranean: the moscatel grapes are used to make the sweet wine for which the village is famous. Accommodation here is self-catering but if you don't fancy preparing your meals there are masses of bars and restaurants a short walk away. The house has a wonderfully warm, organic feel, with simple, *Andaluz* décor and one huge roof terrace from which you can, at certain times of the year, see all the way to the Riff mountains of North Africa. The shared area of the house has an open fireplace (logs provided for winter guests) leading to an inner courtyard of jasmine and exotic plants. There are some delightfully unusual architectural features, a balustrade exposing two floor levels, beamed ceilings and terracotta floors, and the middle of the house has an open kitchen/dining room. Sandra is a reflexologist and aromatherapist, and will give you lots of local advice. *Minimum stay two nights. Linen, gas & electricity included. Call for weekly rates.*

rooms	4: 2 doubles, 1 twin, 1 single.
price	Twin/double € 60.
meals	Self-catering.
closed	Rarely.
directions	From Málaga airport towards Málaga, then almost immed. pick up signs Motril & Almería on N-340. Exit for Algarrobo. At r'bout, left for Algarrobo, Sayalonga & Cómpeta.

Sandra Irene Costello

tel	+34 952 516329
fax	+34 952 516329
e-mail	casa@2sandra.com
web	www.2sandra.com

La Posada Morisca

Loma de la Cruz s/n, Ctra. Montaña Frigiliana-Torrox, 29788 Frigiliana, Málaga

Simple comfort with stunning views. Sit on the little terrace outside your room, sip a glass of wine by the pool, gaze down to the distant Mediterranean... It is such a peaceful place to stay. The building gleams white and terracotta on the hillside, well away from the busy village. The inn is fairly new but traditional in style, with natural wood finishes. Sara, who runs it, is from Frigiliana and has always wanted to work in rural tourism; her warmth and charm add greatly to the welcoming atmosphere. There is a sense of gaiety and simplicity about the whole establishment, with its brightly coloured tiles, latticed wardrobes and woodburning stoves. Bedrooms have a country cottage feel. Meals are in the cosy, cream-walled dining room, or on the terrace; the cooking is Mediterranean and the choice of wines small but good. Try the local lamb or pork shoulder, and the excellent puddings; eating here won't break the bank. When your batteries are thoroughly recharged, visit nearby Nerja, where there's lots going on. Come in May or June and you will see the folk-dancing and the Pomeria of San Antonio. *A Rusticae hotel.*

rooms	12 twins/doubles.
price	€ 64–€ 77. VAT included.
meals	Breakfast € 3; lunch/dinner € 18.
closed	Rarely.
directions	From Málaga, N-340 for Motril. At Nerja, MA-105 to Frigiliana. Round bottom of village, then left at Taller los Cobos for Torrox. Hotel signed on left after 1.5km. Down steep track & bear left.

Sara Navas Sánchez

tel	+34 952 534151
fax	+34 952 534339
e-mail	info@laposadamorisca.com
web	www.laposadamorisca.com

map 24   entry 292

Hotel Rural Almazara

Los Tablazos 197, Ctra. Nerja-Frigiliana, 29788 Nerja, Málaga

There's a surprisingly rural feel to this hotel in the vibrant resort of Nerja, famous for its nightlife, beachside restaurants and caves. And despite the hotel's traditional appearance and the oil press (*almazera*) outside the front door, the building is brand new; it opened in summer 2002. After braving the beach or the shops, you'll find the beamed sitting room with its deep sofas a wonderful place in which to relax. Out on the terrace there's a swimming pool... another treat is the midnight-blue-and-terracotta 'cave' in the basement, with plunge pool, jacuzzi and sauna. In the dining room, which opens onto a long terrace in summer, you can watch the chef at work in the kitchen. The cooking here is truly creative – vegetable soup from local produce, angler fish served Arabic style, oxtail stew, duck. Wines are regional and very good. And a good night's sleep is guaranteed in the clean, well-equipped bedrooms, all air conditioned and beautifully quiet. José Antonio is a genial host and his staff are friendly and helpful. Take a copy of this guide with you and they will give you a 10% discount off the room price.

rooms	22: 21 doubles, 1 single.
price	€ 77–€ 112; single € 57–€ 76.
meals	Breakfast € 6.50; lunch/dinner € 20.
closed	Rarely.
directions	From Málaga, N-340 for Motril. At Nerja, MA-105 to Frigiliana. Hotel on right after 100m.

José Antonio Gómez Armijo

tel	+34 952 534200
fax	+34 952 534212
e-mail	info@hotelruralalmazara.com
web	www.hotelruralalmazara.com

Hotel La Tartana

Carretera de Málaga Km 308, 18697 La Herradura, Granada

This has always been a focal point for the people of La Herradura and never more so than now. Penny, Barry and Jo, who have taken it over, spent years on cruise ships catering for the rich and famous before coming to roost here. La Tartana is surrounded by mature trees and its arched entrance is swathed in a massive bougainvillaea. Though it's right by the road, which tends to be noisy first thing in the morning, there's an almost uninterrupted view of the sea, and a big terrace from which to enjoy it. The hotel is built, Granada-style, around a patio, with a fountain at the centre and rooms leading off. It has a mellow, established feel. The doors and beams come from an old convent and some of the furniture in the simply and comfortably equipped bedrooms is antique. Downstairs is a vaulted bar – a great place to get to know your friendly, relaxed hosts over a drink and an avocado dip before settling down to enjoy Jo's inspired cooking. The food, like the dining room, is colourful: Californian/Mexican cuisine with excellent salads – and there is a good and unusual selection of Navarra wines.

rooms	6 doubles.
price	€55–€79.
meals	Dinner €15.
closed	Rarely.
directions	From Málaga, N-340 for Motril. In La Herradura, 300m after km308 marker, hotel on left up steep slope.

Penny Jarret & Barry Branham

tel	+34 958 640535
fax	+34 958 640535
e-mail	hotellatartana@hotmail.com
web	www.hotellatartana.com

map 24   entry 294

La Casa de los Bates

Ctra Nacional 340, km 329.5 , Apartado de Correos 55, 18600 Motril, Granada

La Casa de los Bates dates from 1898: a bad year for Spain with the loss of its last American colony. But not a hint of depression in this flamboyant Italianate villa. It stands far enough back from the coastal highway for noise not to be a nuisance, and is surrounded by one of the most fabulous gardens in the south: such huge and exuberant palms, catalpas, magnolias and Atlas cedars to make a plant-lover's heart beat faster. Many of the trees and fishponds pre-date even the villa. When the Martín-Feriche family acquired the house it had long lain empty but thanks to careful restoration and the skill of an accomplished interior designer it is once again an elegant, beautifully furnished home-cum-hotel. Here are Deco lamps, marble floors, Japanese lacquered tables, screens and oils; a Bechstein piano, family photos and a harp; books, gilt mirrors and a butterfly collection. The mahogany table in the dining room sits up to 20. Give your charming, blue-blooded hosts enough warning and a candlelit dinner can be prepared. Bedrooms are as fabulous as you'd expect – this would be a fantastic venue for a really special occasion. *A Rusticae hotel.*

rooms	4: 3 twins/doubles, 1 suite.
price	€ 120; suite € 180.
meals	Dinner €25–€45 à la carte. VAT included. On request only.
closed	Rarely.
directions	From Málaga N-340 east. Pass Salobreña; after 2km you see large warehouses on right of 'Frutas de Cara'. Exit, then N-340 back for Salobreña; after 200m, right for house.

Borja Rodríguez Martín-Feriche

tel	+34 958 349495
fax	+34 958 349122
e-mail	borjar@jet.es
web	www.casadelosbates.com

El Cortijo del Pino

Fernán Núñez 2, La Loma, 18659 Albuñuelas, Granada

Although it is just a short drive from the Costa and only 30 minutes south of Granada, few people have heard of Albuñuelas. It is a fetching little place surrounded by citrus groves with wonderful walks along the rocky canyon which cuts south from the village. El Cortijo del Pino sits high on a bluff above and takes its name from the gargantuan 200-year-old Aleppo pine that stands sentinel over the house and valley. The sober lines of the building have an Italian feel and the sandy tones which soften the façade change with each passing hour. Perhaps it was these constant changes of light which attracted James Connel; he is a painter and his artist's eye, combined with his wife Antonia's flair for interior decoration, has helped create a gorgeous home-from-home for guests and friends. Bedrooms are big, beamed and terracotta-tiled with really comfortable beds and excellent bathrooms. And if you should feel inspired to grab a canvas and an easel you can make use of James's studio. Collectors be warned: you may be tempted to buy one!

rooms	5 doubles/twins.
price	€69; single €35.
meals	Restaurant close by.
closed	Rarely.
directions	From Málaga for Granada. Before Granada m'way to Motril, exit 153 for Albuñuelas. Opp. bus stop, right & follow steep road to house.

James Connel & Antonia Ruano

tel	+34 958 776257
fax	+34 958 776350
e-mail	cortijodelpino@eresmas.com

map 24   entry 296

El Molino del Puente

Puente de Durcal s/n, 18650 Durcal, Granada

The abundant water which runs off the high Sierras is the *raison d'être* for this old mill and it also explains its lush greenery and prolific birdlife. Dori and Francisco first established a cottage industry here making organic biscuits and jams; thanks to its success they have been able to convert the remainder of this rambling building into a small hotel and restaurant. As you would imagine, the sound of rushing water is never far away (you also hear cars crossing the bridge above – the motorway cuts down from Granada to the 'tropical coast'). Our favourite room is 102 which has a waterfall plummeting down just outside the window. All the bedrooms have warm colour washes, repro prints of the usual Impressionist stuff and smallish shower rooms. Because of the proximity of the river a first-floor room might be a wise choice during winter. The rather cavernous restaurant has only recently opened but it has already made a name for itself: the food is trad-Andaluz, the oven wood-fired, the fruits, vegetables, desserts and liqueurs home-made and home-grown. New for 2003: a pond and swimming pool.

rooms	9 twins/doubles.
price	€ 72; single occ. € 33; suite € 75. VAT included.
meals	Lunch/dinner € 18 à la carte.
closed	Rarely.
directions	From Motril, m'way north for Granada. Exit for Durcal/Cozvijar. Follow signs for Durcal. Just after crossing bridge, sharp right down hill.

María Dora Tello & Francisco Maroto

tel	+34 958 780731
fax	+34 958 781798
e-mail	biodurc@teleline.es
web	www.elmolinodelpuente.com

Hotel Palacio de Santa Inés

Cuesta de Santa Inés 9, 18010 Granada

Yards from the Plaza Nueva, off to the side of a quiet and leafy square at the heart of the Albaicin (the hill rising opposite the Alhambra was recently declared a World Heritage Site), is this 16th-century palace. The building came to be known as 'The House of the Eternal Father' after the frescoes that surround the inner patio – possibly the work of a pupil of Raphael. Above them, two storeys of wooden galleries lead to bedrooms and suites. These are the creation of owner Nicolás Garrido, whose love of antiques, modern art and interior design has been given free rein. His hotel, now managed by his daughter Ariadna, is southern and unique, though some rooms are small and ordinary. There are also some new, mostly split-level rooms (no. 36 has amazing views)... But hang the expense and book one of the suites with small terraces looking straight out to the Alhambra; ask for Morayma or Mirador de Daraxa or the Alhambra, which has a wonderful 16th-century *mudéjar* panelled ceiling. There's a large lounge which also has a *mudéjar* ceiling, a quiet retreat for musing over the wonders of the Alhambra.

rooms	35: 21 doubles; 10 twins; 4 suites.
price	€ 75–€ 100; suite € 120–€ 225.
meals	Breakfast € 8.
closed	Rarely.
directions	Into centre to Plaza Nueva; then Carrera del Darro and, by 1st bridge best to leave car, walk to hotel just up to left; someone from hotel can show you where to park. Or easier: any central public car park then taxi to hotel.

Nicolás Garrido Berategui

tel	+34 958 222362
fax	+34 958 222465
e-mail	sinespal@teleline.es
web	www.palaciosantaines.com

map 24 entry 298

Hotel Reina Cristina

Calle Tablas 4, 18002 Granada

The Reina Cristina is a big 19th-century townhouse, close to the cathedral and the bustling, pedestrianised Bib-Rambla square. The hotel sits comfortably astride time past and time present, quite able to please the most demanding of modern travellers. Make sure you get one of the larger rooms; they're set round a cool courtyard with a neo-*mudéjar* ceiling, a fountain, geometric tiles, aspidistras and marble columns – all of it utterly in sympathy with tradition and climate. In one corner is a reproduction of the painting depicting the rendition of Granada. The downstairs dining room has the original Art Deco fittings and a series of photos from the period when Spain's most revered poet, Garcia Lorca (he spent his last night here) was around. Make sure you eat at least once at the Cristina whose Rincón de Lorca restaurant was recently voted the top hotel eatery in town. It serves a mix of local dishes and those "we create ourselves", and the wines have been intelligently selected and honestly priced. There are also excellent *tapas* in the café as well as home-made cakes. A favourite Granada address.

rooms	43 doubles/twins.
price	€66–€280; single €55–€99.
meals	Breakfast €7. Lunch/dinner €22, à la carte €35.
closed	Rarely.
directions	From A-92 exit 131 onto Mendez Nuñez which becomes Avenida Fuentenueva. Just before Hotel Granada Center, right into Melchor Almagro which becomes Carril del Picón. Left at end into c/Tablas. Hotel on left.

Federico Jiménez González

tel	+34 958 253211
fax	+34 958 255728
e-mail	clientes@hotelreinacristina.com
web	www.hotelreinacristina.com

Hostal Suecia

Calle Molinos (Huerta de los Angeles) 8, 18009 Granada

Hostal Suecia is hidden away at the end of a quiet little street at the foot of the Alhambra hill. It seems hard to believe that you're in the centre of the city and just a few hundred yards from one of Europe's architectural wonders. The Suecia is most seductive too, every inch a southern house with terracotta roof tiles, arched windows and an old Sharon-fruit tree (pictured) in the front. But don't get the idea that the Suecia pretends to anything fancy: inside the feel is of a family home. There is a pretty sitting room downstairs, a tiny breakfast room up above and bedrooms which vary in size and comfort, like those of your own house. The beds are comfortable, the rooms are spotless. Come for the most peaceful spot in town, the rooftop terrace (no better place to read *Tales from the Alhambra*) and leisurely breakfasts. Or relax in the nearby *plaza*, Campo del Príncipe, where you can sit in a café and think of the generations who have flitted across this lively square.

rooms	11 twins/doubles.
price	€ 43. VAT included.
meals	Breakfast € 4.
closed	Rarely.
directions	Entering Granada follow signs for Alhambra via 'Ronda Sur'. Near Alhambra Palace Hotel, down Antequerela Baja which becomes Carril de San Cecilio. At bottom right into c/Molinos. After 30m, right under arch to Suecia. If lost pay taxi to guide you.

Mari–Carmen Cerdan Mejías

tel	+34 958 225044
fax	+34 958 225044

map 24 entry 300

Hotel Carmen de Santa Inés

Placeta Porras 7, 18010 Granada

Such a deliciously intimate hotel — it has almost the feel of a B&B — right in the heart of one of Granada's most beautiful quarters. Push aside the heavy studded door and enter a small flagged patio, with tinkling fountain, potted aspidistra and deep sofas. Marble columns still support the old beams and, off to one end, beyond another fine old door... a small formal garden with roses, a lemon tree, a vine, goldfish and a view up to the Alhambra. It is the most romantic spot imaginable for breakfast, and a blissful place to relax at any time of day. Climb the marble stair and pass the tiny chapel to your rooms; even those on the small side will delight. Or you can opt for a suite — El Mirador is the loveliest, with its own private terrace — but we liked all the rooms with their potpourri of antique and modern art, fine fabrics and lovely tiles. Breakfast on cooler days in the honeycomb-tiled dining room where there are just three tables; later wander the Albaicín's maze of streets and discover the bars, restaurants and tea places. It is a fabulous place to wander at dusk. One of our favourite little hotels.

rooms	9: 7 doubles, 2 twins.
price	€ 100–€ 195; single € 75.
meals	Breakfast € 8.
closed	Rarely.
directions	Go to sister hotel, El Palacio de Santa Inés (entry 298): staff will park car & accompany you to hotel. Easier still, park in Parking San Agustín & take a taxi.

Nicolás Garrido Berastegui

tel	+34 958 226380
fax	+34 958 224404
e-mail	sinescar@teleline.es

Hotel Casa Morisca

Cuesta de la Victoria 9, 18010 Granada

Imagine yourself outside a tall, balconied, 15th-century house on the south-facing slopes of the Albaycín. The street drops steeply away and opposite, beyond the Darro Gorge, towers the Alhambra. You are in the old Moorish quarter of Granada and the house Casa Morisca is an exquisite example of the old style. Rescued from terminal decay and restored by Carlos, its architect owner, it won the Europa Nostra prize: it's not hard to see why. A heavy door leads from the street to a galleried inner courtyard, where slender pilasters, wafer-brick columns, delicate mouldings and a pool create an air of serenity and space. The same subtle mastery of effect is apparent throughout. In one of the beautiful bedrooms you can lie on the bed and espy the Alhambra in a specially angled bathroom mirror. Another, with astonishing views, has been turned into the most romantic of eyries. A third boasts a magnificent *mudéjar* ceiling, stripped of its plaster shroud… On a more prosaic note, the eateries of Acera del Darro are just yards away – or you can climb the labyrinthine streets to the restaurants of Plaza San Miguel Bajo and rub shoulders with the Granadinos.

rooms	14: 4 doubles, 8 twins, 2 suites.
price	€ 111-€ 190.
meals	Breakfast €9.
closed	Rarely.
directions	Granada orbital m'way, exit c/Recogidas. In centre, c/Reyes Católicos to Plaza Nueva. Left through barrier (ring hotel) into narrow street (Acera del Darro). Cuesta de la Victoria on left.

María Jesús Candenas & Carlos Sánchez

tel	+34 958 221100
fax	+34 958 215796
e-mail	info@hotelcasamorisca.com
web	www.hotelcasamorisca.com

map 24 entry 302

Casa del Capitel Nazarí

Cuesta Aceituneros 6, 18010 Granada, Granada

At the heart of this restored 16th-century *palazete* is a superb Granadino patio. Half a dozen slender marble columns, two of which are Roman, surround the distinctively patterned pebble-mosaic; there's also an exquisite Nasrid carved capital, from which the hotel takes its name. Some of the house's original carved wooden ceilings are still in place, too. Look skywards and you'll see the encircling galleries of the floors above, giving access to the bedrooms: the effect is one of austere elegance. The rooms are small but very well-finished and furnished, with a warm, intimate feel. Breakfast is at glass-topped tables in the little dining room; in summer you spill into the courtyard. No dinners here, but Mari-Luz, the vivacious manageress, will be delighted to recommend restaurants, *tapas* bars, even Moroccan tea-houses, where you can eat out. This is the latest of the Albaycín's ancient houses to be converted into a hotel and it makes a quiet and comfortable place to stay in Granada's oldest quarter. The position is wonderful — just 200m from the Plaza Nueva and a 20-minute walk up the wooded Alhambra hill to the palace entrance.

rooms	17: 9 doubles, 8 twins.
price	€ 79; single € 69.
meals	Breakfast € 6. Restaurants and tapas bars nearby.
closed	Rarely.
directions	Don't attempt to drive here! Park as close to Plaza Nueva as possible (car park next to cathedral) & take taxi to bottom of Cuesta Aceituneros.

Angel Pinto

tel	+34 958 215260
fax	+34 958 215806
e-mail	info@hotelcasacapitel.com
web	www.hotelcasacapitel.com

Alojamiento Rural El Molino

Avenida González Robles 16, 18400 Orgiva, Granada

Wander round the weekly market to see how colourful and creative this multi-ethnic community is. Orgiva is the New Age capital of Andalucía and El Molino is just off its busy main street. It may all seem a touch frenetic but once past El Molino's heavy grille and into its inner patio, peace reigns. Esteban is a relaxed and friendly host, who ran this old olive mill as a bar before turning it into a *turismo rural*. Though it's not truly rural, terracotta floors, massive beams and palms do give an authentic Andalucían feel. There is a delicious smell of wood throughout the high-ceilinged rooms and the antiques are intriguing; one wardrobe was a confessional! Breakfast is a truly excellent spread and for much of the year is served on the patio by the fig tree. And in the heat of the day you can float in the small, jacuzzi-style pool, staring up at a deep blue Andalucían sky. This lush, exuberant area, put on the map by Chris Stewart's *Driving Over Lemons*, offers some great walks: take advantage of the GR7 long-distance footpath which traverses the southern flank of the Sierra Nevada, or explore the remoter villages of the Alpujarra.

rooms	5: 2 doubles, 3 twins.
price	€ 60. VAT included.
meals	Restaurants nearby.
closed	Rarely.
directions	From Málaga, N-340 for Motril, then N-323 for Granada. Exit Lanjarón, then N-322 to Orgiva. El Molino on right just before 1st set of lights.

Esteban Palenciano

tel	+34 646 616628
e-mail	elmolino@turinet.net

map 24 entry 304

Hotel Rural El Montañero

Carretera Orgiva-Pitres s/n, 18410 Carataunas, Granada

El Montañero is an unexciting building at first sight: it sits just off to one side of the road which leads up to the high Alpujarra with large plastic signs announcing your arrival. But if you want an active holiday consider staying here. On offer are guided walks, horse-riding, canoeing, scuba-diving (just three-quarters of an hour gets you down to the Med and Enrique is a qualified teacher) and mountain biking for the really energetic. Bedrooms, which give onto a central lounge, are functional rather than memorable, simply furnished with bright bedspreads of local weave and with small bathrooms. Ask for one with views over the valley. The restaurant-cum-bar looks out across a long rectangular pool that runs the length of the building, and Enrique's kitchen produces a mix of traditional Andalucían and Moroccan-inspired dishes and good vegetarian food. We leave the last word to two readers who recommended the place to us: "Friendly owners, good food, all very reasonably priced," said one; "we'll be back" promised another. *Alternative therapies can be arranged.*

rooms	7 doubles. 1 self-catering apartment for 2.
price	€36-€47; single €23-€31; apartment €43-€58.
meals	Lunch/dinner €15.
closed	November.
directions	From Granada towards Motril, then left on A-348 via Lanjarón; just before Orgiva, left for Carataunas. Hotel on right immed. after entrance to village.

Enrique de la Monja & Carolina Pavageau

tel	+34 958 787528
fax	+34 958 787528
e-mail	edelamonja@terra.es
web	www.hotelmontanero.com

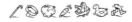

Albergue de Mecina

La Fuente s/n, 18416 Mecina Fondales, Granada

The walking here is wonderful and this small, modern hotel would be a great place to return to after a day of trail-bashing. It looks out across Guadalfeo valley; read more about the area and its people in Chris Stewart's delightful *Driving Over Lemons*. In spite of a puzzlingly large reception area, the hotel has a cosy, inviting feel; best of all is the dining room which has dark chestnut beams, cheery curtain fabrics and naïve paintings. In winter a fire burns in the hearth. If you don't need to worry about cholesterol try the *plato alujarreño*, a sort of glorified fry-up: it has several local variants but will certainly include spicy black-pudding and 'poor-man's potatoes' fried in olive oil with sweet green peppers. Bedrooms are medium to large, as clean as can be, and have an attractive choice of fabric; insist on one with a view. All are centrally heated, well furnished and great value, and the staff here are very kind. The hamlet of Mecina Fondales sits high on the Sierra Nevada, a cluster of whitewashed houses with the flat slate roofs and rounded chimney stacks which give the villages of the Alpujarra their unmistakable identity.

rooms	21 twins/doubles.
price	€ 55–€ 84; single € 44.
meals	Breakfast € 5.5; lunch/dinner € 12 set menu, € 17.50–€ 20 à la carte.
closed	Rarely.
directions	From Granada, N-323 for Motril, then C-333 through Lanjarón. Before Orgiva, Pampaneira road to Pitres. 1km before village, right for Mecina. At top of village, to right.

Victor Fernández

tel	+34 958 766254
fax	+34 958 766255
e-mail	victor@hoteldemecina.com
web	www.ctv.es/alpujarr

map 25   entry 306

Los Tinaos

Calle Parras s/n, 18412 Bubión, Granada

The apartments of Los Tinaos have been built on terraces at the bottom of Bubión in local style: slate walls, flat-topped roofs and rounded chimney stacks with potted geraniums in brilliant contrast to whitewashed walls. What lifts these new, simple, self-catering houses into the 'special' bracket is the beauty of their position, close to the village church and looking out over terraced groves of cherry, pear and apple all the way to the Contraviesa Sierra; on a clear day you can make out passing ships in the Mediterranean. Each house has an open-plan sitting, dining and kitchen area giving onto a small terrace – a wonderful spot for meals and sundowners. They have open hearths, workaday pine furniture, smallish bedrooms and bathrooms; the locally-woven curtains and bedspreads add a welcome splash of colour. You are well away from the lively village centre and won't hear much apart from the murmur of the Poqueira river and the tolling of the church bells. Wood is supplied in winter for a small charge and Isabel and José (they own a gift shop opposite Los Tinaos) will advise on what to do and see.

rooms	12 apartments.
price	Apartment for 2, €54; apartment for 4, €57; apartment for 6, €80. VAT included.
meals	Self-catering.
closed	Rarely.
directions	Motril-Granada on N-323. Exit Vélez Benaudalla. Here to Orgiva, there right to Bubión. Enter village, left into c/Lavadero. After 25m 1st (sharp) turning to left; at small fountain right to Los Tinaos.

Isabel Puga Salguero

tel	+34 958 763217
fax	+34 958 763192
e-mail	info@lostinaos.com
web	www.lostinaos.com

Alquería de Morayma
A348 Cádiar-Torvizcón, 18440 Cádiar, Granada

Mariano and his family built this small hotel entirely in the local vernacular and have created a series of rooms and buildings which have the feel of an Alpujarran village. The main farmstead and the individual houses (one in the old chapel) are set amid olive groves, vineyards and vegetable plots, all of it farmed organically. Decoration is in the same vein as the architecture: old brass bedsteads, bright Alpujarra bed covers, marble-topped dressers, grilled windows, old paintings, and a large collection of photographs of a different age. Each room differs from the next, each feels warm and cared-for. The food, too, is a celebration of things local: olive oil and tomato, fennel, wild capers, goat's cheese, thick stews and *migas* (semolina cakes to accompany tomatoes and peppers or fish). Organic wine comes from Morayma's *bodega*. There is wonderful walking, the chance to see olives being milled during the winter and you could even join in with the grape harvest or the sausage-making! Mariano hopes that guests leaving La Morayma do so with a deeper understanding of the traditions of these high mountain villages.

rooms	18 doubles/twins.
price	€ 49–€ 55; single € 37–€ 44; apartment € 59.
meals	Breakfast € 2; lunch/dinner set menu € 11–€ 15.
closed	Rarely.
directions	From Granada N-323 south for Motril, then A-348 via Lanjarón, Órgiva & Torvizcón. 2km before Cádiar, signed to left.

Mariano Cruz Fajardo

tel	+34 958 343221
fax	+34 958 343221
e-mail	alqueria@alqueriamorayma.com
web	www.alqueriamorayma.com

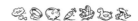

map 25   entry 308

Sierra y Mar
Calle Albaycín 16, 18416 Ferreirola, Granada

Take the blue door for paradise: enter a sunny, shady, flowery, leafy walled garden, a magic world apart. Mention breakfast: you will eat a minor feast under the spreading mulberry tree. This is a gorgeous place run by two delightful northerners (Italian and Danish) who know and love their adopted country; they are relaxed, intelligent and 'green'. They have converted and extended an old Alpujarran house with total respect for its origins; they like things simple, the emphasis being on the natural treasures that surround them. The house is furnished with old rural pieces, lovely materials for curtains and bedcovers, all in good simple taste. Fear not, there are modern bathrooms and central heating! José (Giuseppe) and Inger organise walking tours: there is a beautiful half-day circular walk which begins and ends at the house. Head out to the nearby villages for meals – there is a marvellous family-run restaurant within walking distance and two vegetarian restaurants nearby. The atmosphere at Sierra y Mar is easy-going and your hosts know the Alpujarras like few others. A wholly special B&B; book well in advance. *Minimum stay two nights.*

rooms	9 doubles/twins.
price	€48; single €28. VAT included.
meals	Kitchen for guests. Restaurants nearby.
closed	Rarely.
directions	From Granada N-323, for Motril, then C-333. Before Orgiva turn to Pampaneira. Before Pitres right for Mecina & Ferreirola. From Málaga, on E-15; before Motril, N-323 for Granada. Cross small bridge after Vélez Benaudalla for Orgiva.

Inger Norgaard & Giuseppe Heiss

tel	+34 958 766171
fax	+34 958 857367
e-mail	sierraymar@hotmail.com
web	www.sierraymar.com

Las Terrazas de la Alpujarra

Plaza del Sol 7, 18412 Bubión, Granada

You are high up in the Alpujarra, so high that on a clear day you can see down to the coast, across the Mediterranean and all the way to Africa. Las Terrazas, as the name implies, stands on a terraced hillside on the southern edge of Bubión. You enter via the quietest bar in Spain: this is the only place, monasteries and churches apart, where we have ever seen a 'Silence Please' sign on the wall. Here you breakfast – and, unusually, for a simple place like this, the menu includes cheeses and cold sausage. No other meals are served but there are plenty of eating places in the village. The rooms are nothing fancy but with their terracotta floors, locally-woven blankets and framed photographs they do have a simple charm; though smallish, they are remarkably good value, especially those with their own terrace. You can self-cater here too. Your hosts, the kindest of folk, have a number of mountain bikes and will happily help you plan your expeditions on two wheels – or two feet.

rooms	20 doubles. 3 self-catering apartments (sleep 2, 4 & 6); 2 houses (sleep 10 & 20).
price	€24. Apartment €37–€72; house €120–€180.
meals	Restaurants in village.
closed	7 January-7 February.
directions	From Granada N-323 for Motril; C-333 through Lanjarón; just before Orgiva take road to Pampaneira, then left to Bubión. In village on left.

Francisco Puga Salguero

tel	+34 958 763252
fax	+34 958 763034
web	www.terrazasalpujarra.com

map 25   entry 310

Hotel La Fragua

San Antonio 4, 18417 Trévelez, Granada

Just to the south of the towering peak of Mulhacén (at 3,481m, the highest in the Sierra Nevada), Trevélez is one of the prettiest villages of the Alpujarra. You climb steeply up to the middle of the village to find La Fragua, divided between two old village houses and next to the town hall. In one building is the friendly little bar, and above, an eagle's nest of a pine-clad dining room with a terrific view across the flat rooftops — a wonderful place to sit and gaze between courses. The food is like the place: simple and authentic. The locally-cured ham is utterly delicious and whatever you do, leave some space for one of the home-made puddings. A few yards along the narrow street is the second house where you'll find your rooms: no fussy extras here, just terracotta floors, timbered ceilings and comfy beds. Up above is a roof terrace with tables and the same heavenly view. Your host, Antonio, knows walkers and their ways and will gladly help you plan your hikes. Discover the Alpujarra before everyone else does!

rooms	14 doubles/twins.
price	€30–€50; single €20.
meals	Breakfast €2.50; lunch/dinner €9 set menu, €12–€15 à la carte. VAT included.
closed	10 January–10 February.
directions	From Granada N-323 for Motril; C-333 through Lanjarón; just before Orgiva take road to Trevélez. In village ask for 'barrio medio'; park in Plaza Las Pulgas. House next to Town Hall.

Antonio y Miguel Espinosa González

tel	+34 958 858626
fax	+34 958 858614
e-mail	fragua@navegalia.com

Hotel Los Bérchules

Carretera de Bérchules 20, 18451 Bérchules, Granada

I was lucky to come across Los Bérchules when walking in the area. It was all that I wanted: cosy, inexpensive, with good food, wine and a genuine welcome from Alejandro and his mother Wendy. The hotel sits just beneath the village of Bérchules, 1,322m above sea level – approximately the same height as the summit of Ben Nevis. Things are on a human scale here: there is a small, pine-clad bar-cum-lounge with a hearth and a small collection of walking guides and novels, then a beamed dining room where you choose between the (wonderfully cheap) *menú del día* or à la carte. If you enjoy rabbit then be sure to try Wendy's paella. Guest bedrooms are simply furnished with bright Alpujarra-weave curtains and blankets and the central heating is a boon during the colder months. The long-distance footpath which runs the length of the southern flank of the Sierra Nevada passes right beside the hotel; Wendy knows many other paths and will even run you to and from your walks. This is a hostelry which proves that 'special' is not synonymous with 'grand'.

rooms	13: 10 doubles, 3 singles.
price	€36–€49; single €24–€36. VAT included.
meals	Breakfast €3.50; lunch/dinner €7 set menu, €20 à la carte.
closed	Rarely.
directions	From Málaga, east on N-340. Pass Motril, then left to Albuñol. Just after Albuñol, right on GR-433 to Cádiar, then towards Mecina, then left to Bérchules. Hotel on left at village entrance.

Alejandro Tamborero

tel	+34 958 852530
fax	+34 958 769000
e-mail	hot.berchules@interbook.net
web	www.hotelberchules.com

map 25   entry 312

El Rincón de Yegen

Camino de Gerald Brennan, 18460 Yegen, Granada

Yegen is the village where Gerald Brennan came to live in the 1920s: required reading before, during or after your stay here is his *South from Granada*. Getting here is much easier than in Brennan's day, and although the 21st century has caught up with the villages of the Alpujarra, there is still beauty here in great measure. The recently-built hotel fits well with its older neighbours: local slate, beam and bamboo have been used throughout. Agustín is a trained cook who likes reworking local dishes in a more "modern" (read 'lighter') way. His onion and goat's cheese tart makes a heavenly starter and his braised lamb with grapes is excellent. Bedrooms are to the back of the restaurant, built high to catch the views from the hotel's 3,500-foot perch – they are large, with loads of space, pine furniture, bright bedspreads, shining floor tiles. It's all as spick and span as can be, and you'll appreciate the underfloor heating if you're here in the winter. If you prefer self-catering, the apartments have all you need and more.

rooms	4 twins/doubles. 3 self-catering cottages for 4.
price	€ 36–€ 60; single € 24. Cottage € 330 per week. VAT included.
meals	Breakfast € 4; lunch/dinner € 10 set menu, € 10–€ 16 à la carte. No meals on Tuesday.
closed	Rarely.
directions	Málaga N-340 Motril & Almería. Exit La Rábita & Albuñol; via Cádiar & Mecina Bombarón to Yegen. Signed left in village.

Agustín & Mari-Carmen Rodríguez

tel	+34 958 851270
fax	+34 958 851270

Casa Rural Las Chimeneas

Calle Amargura 6, 18493 Mairena, Granada

Mairena lies at the eastern end of Sierra Nevada, one of the first of the Alpujarran villages that you encounter from the high pass of La Ragua; it has barely changed since the advent of tourism. David and Emma are keen walkers and many of their guests come to explore the little-trodden paths which radiate from the village. The old house has been restored with particular sensitivity; you feel good the moment you enter the guest sitting/dining room. It is a beautiful, light, high-ceilinged room with rocking chairs around a hearth, potted aspidistra, masses of books and views across the terraced hillside beneath Mairena. A plant-filled terrace with a tiny plunge pool shares the same view – you can glimpse North Africa on a clear day! Guest bedrooms feel as special as the shared space, delightfully furnished with old dressers, antique beds (but modern mattresses) and plants. Bathrooms, too, are attractive. Dinner and breakfast are eaten *en famille* and the spirit of Las Chimeneas is relaxed and friendly. A perfect place for a long, restful stay. *No smoking.*

rooms	6 twins/doubles. 3 self-catering studio apartments.
price	€ 50–€ 60; single € 30–€ 40; suite € 60. Apts. € 60–€ 90 per night (€ 300–€ 500 per week). VAT incl.
meals	Packed lunch € 5; dinner € 15. VAT included.
closed	Rarely.
directions	From Laroles, 2nd right into Mairena by willows. Park in square; down narrow street at south-east corner; 100m to house.

David & Emma Illsley

tel	+34 958 760352
fax	+34 958 760004
e-mail	dillsley@moebius.es
web	www.moebius.es/contourlines

map 25   entry 314

Refugio de Nevada

Carretera de Mairena s/n, 18493 Laroles, Granada

More proof: small *is* beautiful. The Refugio de Nevada opened less than five years ago but it has a growing number of old faithfuls. The building makes much use, inside and out, of local slate – entirely in keeping with traditional Alpujarran architecture – and it sits well among the older village houses of Laroles. The lounge/bar area is a perfectly cosy spot and the restaurant even more so: here are half a dozen tables, crocheted lace curtains, cut flowers, rush-seated chairs and old prints of Granada. The bedrooms have the same quiet intimacy about them: beams and terracotta, chimneys in the studios (open-plan with a lounge area), feather duvets, and simple wooden tables and chairs. They aren't enormous but it all works perfectly. They are light, too: the hotel faces south so the maximum sunlight is captured. Rooms and food are reasonably priced, the set menu particularly so. Try the roast goat with garlic and perhaps some wild asparagus as a starter. This is a hotel of very human dimensions, the staff are young and friendly, and the Alpujarras are waiting to be walked. Book a winter stay and hunker down by a crackling fire.

rooms	12: 10 doubles, 2 studios.
price	€43; single €33; studio €45–€56. VAT included.
meals	Breakfast €3; lunch/dinner €9 set menu, €14 à la carte. VAT included.
closed	Rarely.
directions	From Granada A-92 to Guadix, then right for El Puerto de La Ragua & continue to Laroles. Signed to right as you reach village.

Victor M. Fernández Garcés

tel	+34 958 760320
fax	+34 958 760338
e-mail	alpujarr@ctv.es
web	www.ctv.es/alpujarr

Los Omeyas
Calle Encarnación 17, 14003 Córdoba

You couldn't hope to find a better positioned hotel than Los Omeyas, in a plexus of mystic alleys just yards to the east of the great Mezquita in the old Jewish quarter, beyond dozens of souvenir shops... one of Andalucía's most alluring urban sites. The building is in harmony with much older neighbours; the whitewashed façade, with its wrought-iron balconies and wooden shutters, is classic Cordoban architecture. And so too within, where a small patio gives access to bedrooms on two levels. The design may seem a little theatrical – the Mezquita-style arches in reception, the marble staircase – but then we are in the larger-than-life south. Marble floors and whitewashed walls are the perfect foil for the summer heat and the whole hotel is as clean as the newest pin. There's air conditioning, too. Do opt for the newest rooms (201-210) if you are a light sleeper. This is a small, functional hotel that belongs more in the 'safe' than the 'remarkable' category – and a few of the bathrooms are very small – but the location is superb.

rooms	40 doubles/twins.
price	€ 52–€ 64; single € 34–€ 40.
meals	Breakfast € 3.50.
closed	Rarely.
directions	Entering Córdoba follow signs for centre, then Mezquita. In a street just off north-east corner of the Mezquita. Nearest parking by Alcázar de los Reyes Católicos.

Juan de la Rubia Villalba

tel	+34 957 492267/492199
fax	+34 957 491659
e-mail	hotelomeyas@hotmail.com

map 18   entry 316

Hotel Los Abetos del Maestre Escuela

Avda. San José de Calasanz Km 2.8, 14012 Córdoba

Los Abetos is in a quiet residential area to the north of the city, just at the foot of the Sierra Morena and a 10-minute drive from the centre. The 200-year-old hotel, named after a famous schoolmaster who once took up residence here, stands among palm and cypress trees; these and the hotel's pink and white façade give it a distinctly colonial air. There is a peaceful pebbled courtyard with wicker chairs for sitting out on and other equally attractive spots beneath the palms. The restaurant and lounge have much less of a period feel: the hotel was renovated with business folk in mind and seminars and banquets are often held here. The guest rooms have had a recent refurb: we preferred those with views across the estate towards Córdoba which come with Provençal-style furniture and modern tiled floors. In spite of the muzak and a 'hotelly' feel, this is a good place to stay if you want to be just out of town. The Jewish quarter and the Mezquita are an easily-arranged taxi ride away and there is a beautiful swimming pool discreetly sculpted into the terraced gardens.

rooms	36: 33 doubles, 3 singles.
price	€69–€89; single €50–€68.
meals	Breakfast €4.80–€7.50; lunch/dinner €13.
closed	Rarely.
directions	From Madrid, 1st exit for Córdoba: 'Córdoba Norte'. Follow this road round town's eastern & then northern edges; soon see signs for hotel.

Rafael Jurado Diáz

tel	+34 957 767063
fax	+34 957 282175
e-mail	hotelabetos@teleline.es

Hotel Zuhayra

Calle Mirador 10, 14870 Zuheros , Córdoba

The rather monolithic structure of the hotel might at first have you wondering. But do visit this small village which lies at the heart of the natural wilderness of the Subbetica Park – Zuheros is quintessentially Andalucían and its houses hug the hillside beneath the old castle. Up above, the greys and ochres of the mountains; below, mile after mile of silver-green olive groves. Two gentle-mannered brothers and their wives manage the hotel and they are exceptionally kind hosts. Zuhayra's downstairs café-cum-bar is vast but climb up to the first floor to find a cosier dining room where local specialities include partridge, *clavillina* (thick stew served with a fried egg) and delicious *remojón* (potato, onion and pepper salad with oranges). Wonderful bread, too, from the local bakers. Bedrooms are functional rather than memorable: modern pine, new curtains and bed covers, hot-air heating and really comfy beds; bathrooms are surprisingly plush. Second-floor rooms have the best views. Footpaths radiate out from Zuheros; there are cave paintings at The Cave of the Bats just outside the village and Córdoba is an hour's drive.

rooms	18 doubles/twins.
price	€ 42–€ 52.
meals	Lunch/dinner € 11 set menu; € 16–€ 20 à la carte.
closed	Rarely.
directions	From Málaga for Córdoba on N-331; just past Lucena, right to Cabra. On towards Dona Mencia, then right for Luque & Zuheros. Here through village to Castillo (castle); in same street, 200m down hill.

Juan Carlos Ábalos Guerrero

tel	+34 957 694693
fax	+34 957 694702
e-mail	hotelzuhayra@zuheros.com
web	www.zuheros.com

map 18   entry 318

Cortijo La Haza

Adelantado 119, 14978 Iznajar, Córdoba

An old farmhouse lost in the olive belt that stretches from here north and eastwards across nearly half of Andalucía. If you like olive groves (it helps) and little-known corners of Spain, stay here; even better, use it as a base for your visit to the Alhambra in Granada and the Mezquita in Cordoba, both reachable by car. Tim and Keith, quiet and friendly, left teaching and catering (professions which share the strain of having to keep an eye on lots of different things at once!) to set up in this remote spot. Thanks to the wonders of the internet, they already had a houseful when we visited. The renovation is new, but the 'rustic' feel of a traditional Andalucian *cortijo* has been beautifully preserved: walls have a rough render, bedsteads are of wrought iron and older country pieces have been restored. Bedrooms have Egyptian cotton sheets, fluffy towels and their own bath or shower rooms. The five-tabled dining room is cosy, but in good weather you will spill out into the courtyard. Food is honestly priced, and draws on Keith's long experience as a chef, with vegetarians well catered for. Quiet, remote, friendly... and with a pool with a spectacular view.

rooms	5: 3 doubles, 2 twins.
price	€67. Single occ. €57.
meals	Dinner €15.
closed	Rarely.
directions	From Málaga airport, N-340 for Málaga (Antequera). Then N-331 & A-359 for Granada. After 24km, exit 1 onto A-333 for Iznajar. After km55 marker, left on CV-174 for 100m, left by small school for 2.6km. Signed to right.

Tim Holt & Keith Tennyson

tel	+34 605 489052
e-mail	info@cortijolahaza.com
web	www.cortijolahaza.com

Hospedería Fuentenueva

Paseo Arca del Agua s/n, 23440 Baeza, Jaén

There is a good reason for Fuentenueva's rather forbidding façade: it was a women's prison. Both sexes are now welcome – unshackled to boot. Under the aegis of the town council it has been converted into an open, airy, friendly hotel run by a co-operative of five enthusiastic young professionals. Inside, the arches and vistas, the marble floors, the tinkling fountain and the neo-Moorish cupola create impressions of space and gentle cool. Exhibitions of works by local artists and craftsmen are held in the salons. Bedrooms are mostly large and light with modern, locally-built furniture and fittings, bright bedcovers and plush bathrooms. On summer evenings drink in the outside bar in the shadow of the old prison tower, then dine on the patio on local fish specialities. When all the windows are opened in the morning, the characteristic scent of high-quality olive oil drifts in and envelops you. Visit unsung Baeza (guided tours daily, in English), revel in her exuberant Renaissance palaces and richly endowed churches and don't miss the cathedral's silver monstrance (hidden behind St Peter…). Fuentenueva is a great place to serve time!

rooms	12 twins/doubles.
price	€ 69; single € 40.
meals	Lunch/dinner € 12 set menu, € 20 à la carte.
closed	Rarely.
directions	From Granada N-323 to just before Jaén, then N-321 to Baeza. On far side of Baeza on left as you leave, in direction of Úbeda.

Victor Rodríguez

tel	+34 953 743100
fax	+34 953 743200
e-mail	info@fuentenueva.com
web	www.fuentenueva.com

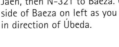

map 19 entry 320

Maria de Molina

Plaza del Ayuntamiento s/n, 23400 Úbeda, Jaén

Úbeda is one of Andalucía's most beautiful towns; a wander through its old quarter at dusk feels like a step back in time. You will come upon a number of grand old houses, built by descendants of the Christian knights who were given land in the city by King Fernando 'el Santo' following the Reconquest from the Moors. The very heart of the town is an imposing Renaissance square and its finest *palacete* (small palace) has recently been converted into a small, coquettish and very comfortable hotel. The building is wrapped round an inner courtyard, to one side of which is an enormous dining room that seats up to 600; you, however, dine in a smaller, more intimate one, or in the fountain-graced patio when its warm. Although miles from the sea the restaurant serves very good fresh fish – as well as the roast meats for which the area is known. Bedrooms are excellent, each individually decorated with repro antiques, warm colour washes and beautiful lamps, cushions, linen and prints. Staff are attentive and charming. This hotel is already making waves and we recommend it wholeheartedly.

rooms	20: 18 twins/doubles, 2 suites. 3 apartments.
price	€ 70–€ 92; single € 45–€ 63; suite € 92–€ 122; apartment € 61–€ 133.
meals	Breakfast € 6. Half-board € 17.25; full-board € 31.50.
closed	Rarely.
directions	In Úbeda, follow signs for 'Centro Histórico'. Hotel next to Town Hall (Ayuntamiento) & Plaza Vázquez de Molina. Signed.

Juan Navarro López

tel	+34 953 795356
fax	+34 953 793694
e-mail	hotelmm@hotel-maria-de-molina.com
web	www.hotel-maria-de-molina.com

Palacio de la Rambla

Plaza del Marques 1, 23400 Úbeda, Jaén

The old towns of Úbeda and Baeza are often missed as travellers hurry between Madrid and the Costa, yet they are two of the brightest jewels in the crown of Spanish Renaissance architecture. At the heart of old Úbeda, the exquisite Palacio de la Rambla dates from this period and has never left the Orozco family. You enter through an ornate Corinthian-columned portal into the main patio; colonnaded on two levels, ivy-covered and with delicately carved lozenges and heraldry, its sheer opulence is a surprise. Lounge, dining room and bedrooms are a perfect match for their setting: antique beds, chests, lamps, claw-footed bath tubs, oil paintings of religious themes and, of course, family portraits. Native terracotta is softened by *estera* matting. You will be served a full Andalucían breakfast: eggs, toast with olive oil, fresh orange juice, a glass of chilled water in summer, lace-edged napkins. Palacio de la Rambla has a long tradition of regal welcoming; King Alfonso XIII stayed here when he was in town. *A Rusticae hotel.*

rooms	8: 7 twins/doubles, 1 suite.
price	€ 99; single € 72; suite € 111.
meals	Restaurants nearby.
closed	15 July–15 August.
directions	From Madrid south on N–IV. At km292 marker, N–322 to Úbeda. There, follow 'Centro Ciudad' until Palace is in front of you, between c/Ancha & c/Rastro, opposite cafetería La Paloma.

Elena Meneses de Orozco

tel	+34 953 750196
fax	+34 953 750267

map 19   entry 322

Molino La Farraga

Calle Camino de la Hoz s/n, Apartado de Correos 1, 23470 Cazorla, Jaén

La Farraga is unforgettable, one of the brightest stars in the places-to-stay firmament! The setting is one of great beauty: a deeply verdant river valley just beneath the rocky crests of the Cazorla mountains. This 200-year-old mill's gardens are an Ode to Water — it is everywhere, in ponds, channels, races and falls. The gardens were planted by an English botanist, nurtured for years by an amiable American and now tended by the kindliest Spanish woman you could hope to meet. Nieves left her native Canary Islands for this corner of paradise and visitors here can revel in simple comfort, wholesome food and buckets of caring; it's no surprise to learn she was once a nurse. A delicious waft of linseed oil pervades the house. The architecture is an organic, interlocking puzzle of stairways, corners, niches and turns, and the bedrooms are perfect: some have fireplaces, another a small terrace, and all are spotlessly clean. The price of your room includes a generous breakfast and don't miss dinner: it's a friendly, relaxed affair, often organic and served around one big table in winter — or on a gorgeous riverside terrace on summer nights.

rooms	8: 7 doubles, 1 suite.
price	€64–€90; single €34; suite €75. VAT included.
meals	Meals available.
closed	15 December–15 February.
directions	In Cazorla, signs for Ruinas de Santa María. Here, pass between ruined church & Cueva de Juan Pedro retaurant towards 'Castillo'. Park on left by sign for La Farraga. Cross river (on foot), house on right after 100m.

Nieves Santana Martín

tel	+34 953 721249
fax	+34 953 721249
e-mail	farraga@teleline.es
web	www.molinolafarraga.com

Hotel La Finca Mercedes

Ctra de la Sierra km 1, 23476 La Iruela, Jaén

La Iruela is a tiny village just outside Cazorla on the road leading up to the Natural Park of the same name. Its crowning glory is the castle-fortress which was built by the Templars; slog up to the top for an amazing view. La Finca Mercedes is just outside the village, a simple roadside hotel and restaurant that takes its name from its gregarious and charming owner who is helped by her two young daughters. Although you are just next to the road there is little passing traffic and rooms and restaurant are on the far side of the building. The dining room is as cosy as a Cotswold pub, even in winter (it can get cold here) when a fire burns in the corner hearth throughout the day. The food is simple, regional, flavourful and good value. So too are the bedrooms, medium-sized with good bathrooms, simple pine furniture and wonderful views across the olive groves which surround the village; nothing is fussy but nothing is missing, either. The Castillo family has just completed a further six bedrooms at Cortijo Berfalá which you reach in just five minutes down a very steep track. A great place to stay for walkers.

rooms	9 doubles/singles/suites.
price	€33–€42; single €30; suite €36.
meals	Breakfast €3.31; lunch/dinner €8 set menu, €14 à la carte.
closed	Rarely.
directions	From Cazorla, follow road up into village centre; at large square, left for La Iruela. Follow road round bottom of La Iruela: Finca just to left after approx. 1km. Signed.

Mercedes Castillo Matilla

tel	+34 953 721087
e-mail	info@lafincamercedes.com

map 19   entry 324

Hotel Family

Calle La Lomilla s/n, 04149 Agua Amarga, Almería

Gentle-mannered Frenchman René Salmeron came to Agua Amarga on holiday and, instantly seduced by what was then a little-known fishing village, dreamed of coming to live and work here. And here he is, running this simple whitewashed *hostal* and restaurant just behind one of the area's most seductive beaches, and making new friends A bumpy track leads you to the building which has recently acquired a second floor. Downstairs and up, rooms are simply furnished with all-wooden furniture and thick, Alpujarran blankets as bedspreads; rooms at the front have sea views. In the rather kitsch courtyard restaurant (covered in winter) you can expect to eat well; René's food is "Mediterranean with a French touch" and his home-made pâté makes a delicious starter. There are decent breakfasts with home-made jams, yogurt and fruit, or tortillas if you prefer. Do stay at least a couple of nights and explore the nearby Cabo de Gata National Park: the walking is wonderful. Even if Agua Amarga is more developed than when René first came, it remains an enchanting spot.

rooms	9 doubles/twins.
price	€45–€85; single €40–€80.
meals	Lunch/dinner €16 (lunch weekends only).
closed	1 November–15 December.
directions	From N-344 exit 494 Venta del Pobre & Carboneras. On for Carboneras, then right for Agua Amarga. Signed to right in village.

Marc Bellavoir

tel	+34 950 138014
fax	+34 950 138070
e-mail	riovall@teleline.es

Casa Geminis

Ctra Mojácar-Turre, 04638 Mojácar, Almería

Mojácar, a pretty white hill village just back from the Med, was discovered in the Sixties by a group of painters. Anywhere you set up your easel was a cameo view of a narrow street, a flower-filled balcony or perfect little square. Tourists later flocked to the coast, but the village has retained its charm. Nowadays you are best visiting 'out of hours' so why not stay at this palm- and oleander-graced villa just a couple of miles up the road? The Howard-Adys are great entertainers, legendary among their many friends for their hospitality. Eileen is a great cook while Geoff has an eye for what looks right in décor, design and presentation. Dinners are of four courses and include wine and coffee; your hosts enjoy these eat-togethers as much as their guests. There are just two guest bedrooms, each with its own entrance; they have bright duvet covers and curtains, rattan chairs and a host of electrical extras like TVs, hairdryers, fridges, teas-mades and even an iron. The one at the back looks out to the mountains. There's also a lovely pool... and should you prefer a day on the beach, a picnic hamper can be prepared. Just ask.

rooms	2 twins/doubles.
price	€ 54–€ 66.
meals	Lunch/dinner € 21, wine & coffee included.
closed	Rarely.
directions	South on N-340/E-15, exit 520 signed Los Gallardos, Turre & Mojácar. Follow signs for Mojácar via Turre. House on right shortly before Mojácar, next to Delfos Bar.

Geoff & Eileen Howard-Ady

tel	+34 950 478013
e-mail	geha@computronx.com

map 25   entry 326

Finca Listonero

Cortijo Grande, 04639 Turre, Almería

Lovers of desert landscapes, their barrenness, aridity and sense of eternity, will be rewarded at the Finca Listonero with its wraparound views of the Sierra Cabrera. For the sybaritic, this sensitively extended pink (original colour) farmhouse has all the luxuries. David and Graeme, cultured and gourmet Anglo-Australians, have lavished huge care on this conversion. Bougainvillaea defies the dry sierra with every flower; the delightful dining and drawing rooms, the fern-filled atrium, the antiques and the *objets* impose grandeur on lowly origins. Each guest room uses a different colour theme; double doors open onto a terrace; they all have their own bathrooms and cooling fans. Breakfast is an easy-going occasion while dinner – which you must book in advance, and don't expect to eat until late – is definitely a serious matter with a mix of regional and international dishes (ingredients from the garden, fish delivered fresh from the port), great home-made English puds and a good selection of wines. There is walking for the hardy in the cooler months, you are not far from the sea, and horse-riding can be arranged.

rooms	5 doubles/twins.
price	€75–€85; single €55–€65.
meals	Dinner €28.
closed	Rarely.
directions	From N-340/E-15 exit 520 for Turre & Mojácar. 3km on, right through entrance to Cortijo Grande. Finca on right after 3.5 km, signed.

Graeme Gibson & David Rice

tel	+34 950 479094
fax	+34 950 479094

Casa de Huespedes Cortijo del Faz

Apartado 1075, 04638 Mojácar, Almería

Spaghetti-western country – this desert landscape with its sense of wilderness is fine riding country too. The farmstead stands among date palms, yucca and jacaranda on a bluff overlooking the plain; to the south are the Cabrera mountains where you may glimpse foxes, eagles, hoopoes and rollers, even the occasional wild boar. The house was slowly crumbling when Londoners John and Val bought it in 1984 and began the laborious task of restoration. Accommodation is in the cottage and you can self-cater if you wish; if you opt for B&B, you come to the house to eat. The cottage has been converted from an outbuilding and is simply furnished, with two bedrooms (if only one is occupied, the other will not be let), a sitting room with a fireplace and plenty of books, and a kitchen area. Do treat yourself to lunch or dinner here: in her London life, Val was a professional cook and she serves wonderful local and international food. An *al fresco* dinner on the terrace by the pool is something to remember, and John and Val are the most welcoming and unobtrusive of hosts. It's a short drive down the valley to Mojácar and the sea. *A no-smoking house.*

rooms	1 cottage for 4.
price	B&B € 54–€ 66 (not July/August); self-catering € 320–€ 720 p.w.
meals	Lunch/dinner € 21.
closed	Rarely.
directions	From Almería, N-340/E-15 for Murcia. Exit 520 Turre & Mojácar. Before Mojácar, 100m before km2, left. Keep to main track. After 500m, right up steep hill. House ahead, 2nd track on left, round low wall to gate.

John Cairns

tel	+34 950 478926
fax	+34 950 478926
e-mail	johncairns@inicia.es
web	www.inicia.es/de/johncairns

map 25   entry 328

Mamabels

Calle Embajadores 5, Mojácar Pueblo, 04638 Mojácar, Almería

Tourists — and artists — discovered the charms of this clifftop village long, long ago: it has become extremely popular yet it keeps its identity still. Juan Carlos and his mother Isabel Aznar ('Mamabel') greet you with big smiles. Their small, homely guesthouse has gradually been rebuilt and added to since Isabel first came, 40 years ago. The house is delightfully organic with stairways leading up and down and each room is different from the next. They are prettily decorated and have a feminine feel; no. 1 is the grandest with its canopied bed, antique table and many knick-knacks, yet still no hint of 'hotel'. All of them are charming and we particularly recommend one of those with a terrace looking down to the glittering sea. There is a cosy little dining room where there are stacks of paintings by Mamabel's husband, hand-painted chairs and really good food with a Mediterranean flavour. If you head out for dinner there is lots of choice in the village. And a word of advice: when you arrive, drop your luggage at the hotel first, then look for a parking space.

rooms	10: 9 doubles/twins, 1 'special' room.
price	€55–€75; 'special' room €85–€90.
meals	Breakfast €6; dinner €17 set menu, €25 à la carte.
closed	Rarely.
directions	From Almería, N-340/E15 for Murcia; exit 520 Turre & Mojácar. Up into village of Mojácar, signed to right, then left just before main square; 100m to hotel.

Isabel & Juan Carlos Raths Aznar

tel	+34 950 472448
fax	+34 950 472448
e-mail	hotel@mamabels.com
web	www.mamabels.com

Hostal Mirador del Castillo
Mojácar Pueblo, 04638 Mojácar, Almería

Its local advertising slogan is *el punto mas alto* ('the highest point') and that it certainly is. There was once a fortified castle up here on top of the hill; it was rebuilt in the 1960s as a private home and a venue for concerts and music festivals. The modern interpretation of a Moorish fortification may leave something to be desired – 1960s architecture has a lot to answer for – but don't be put off: this is a marvellous spot. There are all-round views of the village, the valley, the mountains and the sea. *And* an enchanting walled garden. The bedrooms are well and simply furnished and the whole atmosphere of the place is relaxed and happy. Juan, the manager, is an excellent cook. Specialities are paellas or shellfish prepared over a wood fire in the garden, fish baked in salt and vegetarian buffets. Light food is also available all day in the Café Bar. In summer there are jazz concerts outside among the palm trees and the flowering shrubs; in winter, chamber music is played in the salon. A large party can rent bedrooms, salon and suite, plus solarium, kitchen and pool, as a separate self-contained unit in the summer – with or without cook.

rooms	5: 4 doubles, 1 suite.
price	€42–€52; suite €66. Entire house €120–€300.
meals	Breakfast €5; lunch/dinner €10 a la carte.
closed	Rarely.
directions	From Almería, N-340/E-15 for Murcia. Exit 520 for Turre & Mojácar. At top of village, left fork at intersection, then 1st left after 'Arnes Cuero' shop. House signed.

Juan Cecilio Cano

tel	+34 950 473022
fax	+34 950 473022
e-mail	info@elcastillomojacar.com
web	www.elcastillomojacar.com

map 25   entry 330

Hotel Tikar

Ctra. Garrucha - Vera s/n, 04630 Garrucha, Almería

Don't worry that the Tikar is a few blocks from the busy beach and next to a main road – just step through the door. This is not only a hotel, but an art gallery and restaurant too – run with immense warmth and charm by Beatriz and Sean. The jolly colour scheme – blue, sienna and white – is offset by dark parquet floors and teak furniture, and modern paintings (for sale) hang everywhere, even in the bedrooms, which are large and extremely comfortable. Children are welcomed and well catered for, too: Beatriz and Sean have two small sons of their own. Relax on the rooftop terrace, listen to the sea, take a dip in the (little) pool. But the main reason for the hotel's success is the Restaurant Azul; it has a devoted local following. There's a list of over 75 interesting wines – Sean knows his stuff – and the cuisine is innovative and sophisticated, a mix of Californian (fish, vegetables, light sauces) and Spanish. There are plenty of vegetarian dishes too. Garrucha, though not the prettiest of fishing ports, has an authentic Spanish feel and the lively afternoon fish market is well worth witnessing.

rooms	6: 1 double, 5 twins.
price	€54–€98.
meals	Dinner €19.50.
closed	Rarely.
directions	From N-340/E-15, exit 534 for Garrucha. Pass Vera & continue round outskirts of Garrucha. Straight on at r'bout. Hotel on right.

Beatriz Gallego & Sean McMahon

tel	+34 950 617131
fax	+34 950 617132
e-mail	hoteltikar@hoteltikar.com
web	www.hoteltikar.com

Las Almendras

Bda. Los Herreras s/n, 04271 Lubrín, Almería

You approach Las Almendras down the proverbial long and winding road, past marble quarries and through barren land… just as you begin to wonder whether the drive is worth it, bingo! Into view comes the restored Andalucían goat farm, 100 years old and charming with it, sitting in its remote pocket of land beneath the Filabres mountains. There are a sun terrace, a mountain water plunge pool and a chicken coup in the garden, tomatoes and herbs popping up among the flowers, bird- and cicada-song in the air. Apricots, lemon trees and the odd prickly pear surround the barbecue area; olive and almond groves stretch beyond. In the cottage for guests you share a sitting room, a small kitchen area for making tea and coffee, and an honesty bar – a nice touch. Bedrooms are whitewashed and simply furnished, and the Blue Room has a double bed perfectly positioned for mountain-gazing. There is also a room in the house given over to a museum, which displays the original farm marriage bed (from which who knows how many heirs have sprung) along with local artefacts. New owners have just taken over this delightful place.

rooms	4 doubles/twins.
price	€ 55; single € 40. VAT included.
meals	Lunch € 7.50; dinner € 17.50.
closed	Rarely.
directions	From Almería, N-340 for Huercal. Left at Sorbas for Lubrín on Ruta Valle del Fonte. Pass Lubrín to La Rambla Aljibe, then left for Albanchez, through Los Dioses & Los Herreras. 50m past sign, left for house.

Oliver & Helen Robinson

tel	+34 950 528587
e-mail	oliver_helen_robinson@hotmail.com
web	www.lasalmendras.com

map 25   entry 332

BALEARICS &
CANARY ISLANDS

"Consistency is the last refuge of the unimaginative."
OSCAR WILDE (ATTRIB.)

La Colina

Ctra Ibiza a Santa Eulalia km 10, 07840 Santa Eulalia del Río, Ibiza

A stylish place with a huge heart – and well-priced rooms and food. Ellen Trauffer visited the area 16 years ago and was inspired to create a small country hotel. Tourism at the time was on the decline, yet she was determined to get things right. She has succeeded: seven out of 10 visits to this 400-year-old farmhouse are repeat bookings. Ellen went for comfort rather than superfluous luxury – don't expect a TV in your room but do expect a beautifully furnished, light and spotlessly clean living space, with lovely bathrooms. The organic, almost minimalist cut of house and rooms is in the true tradition of Ibizan architecture, and the pool is gorgeous. Unlike the restaurants of other hotels of the 'pack-them-in' variety, La Colina's is for guests only. It is has an intimate feel, and although the food is from the international recipe book nearly all ingredients – fish, meat, fruit and veg – arrive fresh from the market. Breakfast is a big buffet spread and the muesli a delicious import from Ellen's native Switzerland. Once a week she gets all of her guests together and takes them out to a local restaurant!

rooms	12 suites/doubles/singles.
price	€ 64–€ 92; single € 44–€ 60; suite € 108–€ 180. VAT included.
meals	Dinner € 21. VAT included.
closed	Mid-November-mid-December.
directions	From Ibiza towards Santa Eulalia. After 10km on right-hand side right by Swiss flag. Up track to La Colina.

Ellen Trauffer

tel	+34 971 332767
fax	+34 971 332767
e-mail	ellen@lacolina-ibiza.ch
web	www.lacolina-ibiza.ch

map 26   entry 333

Les Terrasses

Ctra. de Santa Eulària km 1, Apartado 1235, 07800 Ibiza, Ibiza

Françoise Pialoux has crafted, planted and furnished a remarkable vision in this hidden corner of Ibiza. She is an immensely likeable, vivacious woman and her character infuses every corner of Les Terrasses. The farm stands alone on a knoll in the island's centre surrounded by terraces of fruit trees and exotic plants. In the sitting room there are deep sofas, lace curtains, books and a piano; hammocks await in the shade outside and two exquisite pools, one of them heated, are hidden away behind stands of bamboo. The bedrooms are on different levels, some in the main house and others in the converted outbuildings. No two are alike and nearly all the well-known design mags have run articles on them. The vibrant colours, hand-embroidered bedspreads, bamboo-shaded terraces, open hearths, candelabras, wooden and terracotta floors are a photographer's dream. Choose where and when you'd like to breakfast – by one of the two pools, in the house or in your room. Stay for dinner, too: fish is usually a strong feature. But do book well in advance to be sure of a room; there is no better place to unwind.

rooms	9: 7 doubles, 1 twin, 1 suite.
price	€ 132–€ 179; single € 102–€ 126; suite € 175–€ 218.
meals	Lunch € 20; dinner € 30.
closed	15 November–February.
directions	From Ibiza for Santa Eulària; after 9km on right, at blue-painted rock, right; up track, farm on left.

Françoise Pialoux

tel	+34 971 332643
fax	+34 971 338978
e-mail	lesterrasses@interbook.net
web	www.lesterrasses.net

Mofarés

Avenida Capdellá s/n, Apartado de Correos 17, 07184 Calvía, Mallorca

Antonio and his daughter are relaxed and charming and it is a delight to stay with them on their farm. The fine house and cluster of outbuildings stand in a semi-rural area amid neatly tended groves of almond and carob — to the rear of the *finca* you can forget entirely about encroaching modernity. Life here looks inward, to a paved central patio where exotic plants offset the dazzling lime-washed walls. Antonio has brilliantly succeeded in creating comfort in a historical setting; he'll eagerly show you the old olive mill, the bakery and his collection of agricultural instruments in the stables. Although they no longer do dinner, you can profit from Antonio's love of wine and choose a bottle from the cellar on an honesty basis, and there's a great little 'groggery' in the wine press room with its vaulted ceiling. At breakfast Antonio has a simple rule-of-thumb: you have whatever you like. Bedrooms (more like suites) vary in size and shape; all are pleasant, with elegant repro Mallorcan beds, *yengo* weave curtains and bedspreads, and the usual creature comforts.

rooms	9 doubles/twins/family.
price	€ 135–€ 169, single € 113. VAT included.
meals	None available.
closed	5 November–5 February.
directions	From Palma for Andratx; exit Palma Nova. Here to Calvía, then road for Capdellá. On right, 700m after Calvía.

Antonio Rotger

tel	+34 971 670242
fax	+34 971 670071
e-mail	info@mofares.com
web	www.mofares.com

map 26   entry 335

Es Passarell

2a Vuelta No. 117, 07200 Felanitx, Mallorca

Far from the madding crowds of the beach resorts, Es Passarell is testimony to the boundless energy of María Dolores ('Lola') who saw in these old stones a vision of better things. Outbuildings were converted, gardens were planted: you approach this isolated farm through a swathe of colour made up of palm and vine, honeysuckle and geranium, almond, fig and citrus. No two bedrooms are alike and size and configuration follow the dictates of the old farm buildings. Choose between house, apartment, suite or double room, between self-catering and catered-for. It's all been converted and decorated with a designer's touch; the mix of antique furnishing and modern art feels good and you can understand why some of Europe's most prestigious magazines have featured the place. There are bright rugs, dried flowers, unusual angles, intimate terraces for *al fresco* thinking and a delicious whiff of the linseed used to treat beam and tile. Breakfast is buffet and big, there are gourmet dinners twice-weekly (Monday's is meat-based, on Friday, salmon is the main theme) and the cellar is stocked with well-priced and delicious Spanish and Portuguese wines. *A Rusticae hotel.*

rooms	4 doubles. 6 self-catering apartments.
price	€65-€110; apartment €90-€145.
meals	Lunch/dinner €12, à la carte €25.
closed	Rarely.
directions	From Llucmajor to Porreres; here, towards Felanitx. Between km2 & km3 markers, at sharp bend, right; after 2.5km, house on right, signed.

María Dolores Suberviola Alberdi

tel	+34 971 183091
fax	+34 971 183091

Son Mercadal

Camino de Son Pau s/n, Apartado de Correos 52, 07260 Porreres, Mallorca

If you are looking for a peaceful setting, a blissfully comfortable bed, good food and kind hosts, look no further. It is just four years since the Ripoll family welcomed their first guests to their beautifully restored and renovated farmhouse, where every last corner has been carefully considered. The house is a 'painting', as the Spanish would say, a measured still life of things old and rustic. José's son, Toni, a graphic designer by profession, is responsible for the decoration and his artistic eye has created a warm and harmonious mood throughout. Most of the beautiful antique pieces were already in the family: the grandfather clock, piano, old washstands, a complete Art Deco bedroom set, the engravings of Mallorca. And the food is of the best the island has to offer: Toni is keen for you to try the local specialities. At breakfast you are fêted with local sausage, cheeses, eggs from the farm and wonderful bread; at dinner with a *tumbet* perhaps (the local meat-and-veg delicacy), and, from the *bodega*, a selection of the island's very best wines. Much of what graces your table is straight from the farm.

rooms	7 doubles/twins.
price	€ 99; single € 75.
meals	Lunch/dinner € 18 on request.
closed	Rarely.
directions	From Palma towards Santyani. Here, on far side of town, left to Porreres. Here towards Campos. After approx. 1.5km left at sign Son Mercadal & Son Pau. 2km of track to house.

José Roig Ripoll

tel	+34 971 181307
fax	+34 971 181307
e-mail	son.mercadal@todoesp.es
web	www.son-mercadal.com

map 26   entry 337

Leon de Sineu

Carrer dels Bous 129, 07510 Sineu, Mallorca

Sineu, mellow in the sunlight, is one of the oldest small towns and slap in the middle of the island. People come here for the fabulous farmers' market on Wednesdays, and have been doing so ever since it was established in 1214. Sineu's bars and restaurants are another lure. The Leon has a lovely symmetrical façade and a cobbled garden on many levels; it is fresh, clean and welcoming. A large arch spans the entrance hall, beyond which is the Winter Room, a large covered terrace where one can sit and admire the surprisingly large garden. The bedrooms, opening off a staircase of almost Parisian splendour of tiles and wrought-iron balustrade, are a comfortable mix of antique dark wooden beds, the odd Moroccan ornament or rug, and simple white walls. Senora Gálmez Arbona is welcoming, and manages to recreate the atmosphere of a Mallorcan home. The food is something they are proud of here: the Leon is one of the best restaurants in town (yet not the most expensive). You will be served a traditional Mallorcan breakfast of cheeses, salami, patés, eggs, fruits and cake – just the thing before you don your bikini and head for the beach.

rooms	8: 3 doubles, 3 twins, 1 single, 1 suite.
price	€ 115–€ 155; single € 90; suite € 162. VAT included.
meals	Lunch (snacks and salads); dinner € 22–€ 27. VAT included.
closed	20 November–20 December.
directions	Head for town centre. Hotel signed.

Francisca Gálmez Arbona

tel	+34 971 520211
fax	+34 971 855058
e-mail	reservas@hotel-leondesineu.com
web	www.hotel-leondesineu.com

Scott's Hotel

Plaza de la Iglesia, 07350 Binissalem, Mallorca

Whatever the reputation of a hotel, experience doesn't always equate to expectation. Not so at Scott's. Your genial, immensely cosmopolitan hosts have created a stylish and intimate small hotel from a grand seigniorial townhouse in the centre of old Binissalem; you'll be very well looked after and blissfully comfortable. To this end enormous beds were handmade in England, goosedown pillows brought from Germany, Percale sheets from New York. "Pretty came second," says George, but pretty Scott's most certainly is and a night here is an experience to remember. Suites have any number of exquisite decorative touches and the feel is fresh, light and elegant; here an 18th-century Japanese print, there a grandfather clock, perhaps a Bokhara rug or a *chaise longue*. Breakfast in the gorgeous patio-courtyard at any time you like and dine in the hotel's new little bistro nearby: candles, damask, fresh flowers and Gershwin tinkling in the background, and simple but sumptuous food. And buy a copy of George's novel, a whodunnit whose action takes place right here: its called *The Bloody Bokhara*!

rooms	17 twins/doubles/suites.
price	€ 175–€ 205; single € 131–€ 154; suite € 235–€ 270.
meals	Dinner € 20 set menu, € 32 à la carte.
closed	Rarely.
directions	From airport towards Palma, then PM-27 for Inca & Alcudia. Exit km17 for Binissalem. Hotel next to church, signed by discreet brass plaque beside entrance.

George Scott

tel	+34 971 870100
fax	+34 971 870267
e-mail	reserve@scottshotel.com
web	www.scottshotel.com

map 26   entry 339

Son Porró

Diseminados Poligono 3°, Parcela 223, 07144 Costitx, Mallorca

You are at the heart of the Plá, the vast plain which lies in the lee of the great Tramuntana range. The area has a unique beauty with ancient farmhouses and equally ancient groves of fig and almond. Son Porró's stone walls look old, too; the house, however, is brand new. It owes its existence to Pilar Sánchez, who greets you as she would an old friend: nothing is too much trouble and when guests arrive unavoidably late she'll cook a meal at midnight. Her bedrooms are large, functional, extremely comfortable; some lead off a quiet, jasmine-filled courtyard to the back of the house, others are in two stone-built houses in a lemon and almond grove that lies just beyond the lovely pool. In Son Porró's vast lounge the bright Mallorcan *lenguas*-weave fabric of the curtains adds zest; black leather sofas feel rather more sombre. What really makes this place special are Pilar's lunches and dinners, and the barbecues out on the patio. She tailors her cooking to suit her guests and uses ingredients from the local markets. And friends of hers can take you out on a guided walk or ride.

rooms	8: 4 doubles, 2 apartments for 4, 4 suites. 1 house for 6.
price	€96–€120; suites €126–€150. House from €210. VAT included.
meals	Lunch/dinner €15.
closed	Rarely.
directions	From Palma towards Alcudia on m'way. Exit for Inca & at 2nd r'bout follow signs for Sineu. Son Porró signed on right after 9km.

Pilar Sánchez Escribano
tel +34 971 182013
fax +34 971 182012

C'an Reus

Carrer de l'Auba 26, 07109 Fornalutx, Mallorca

Few villages in southern Europe have quite such a heart-stopping natural setting. Fornalutx is in the middle of Mallorca's rumpled spine, sandwiched between the craggy loveliness of the Puig Major and the Puig del'Ofre. Artists, sculptors and writers discovered the village long ago – and the tourists followed – but the place has kept its identity. C'an Reus is at the bottom of the village, built by a returning emigrant – with none of the ostentatiousness that some of the so-called *casas de Indianos* are wont to display. A light and elegant house, it feels a million miles from the poorer parts of Palma where Tomeu used to work as a social worker; he is the kindest of hosts with a deep knowledge of his native Mallorca. The bedrooms are to die for with their original tiled floors, wonderful beds and linen, antique dressers and perhaps an old print of the Sierra. Breakfast is a feast: local cheeses and sausages, home-made marmalades and tarts for you to feast upon as you gaze at that view-of-views from the steeply terraced garden. Tomeu is keen that you experience the very best of Mallorca; the home-from-home that he has created is just that.

rooms	6 doubles/twins.
price	€ 122–€ 154. VAT included.
meals	Not available.
closed	Rarely.
directions	Round Palma on Via Cintura (ring-road) then exit for Soller. Through (toll) tunnel & round Soller for Puerto de Soller. At 2nd r'bout, right at signs for Fornalutx. Park in village & walk to hotel; C'an Reus is in lowest street in village.

Tomeu Arbona
tel	+34 971 631174
fax	+34 971 631174

map 26   entry 341

Can Furiós

Camí Vell de Binibona 11, 07314 Binibona-Caimari, Mallorca

Can Furiós is one of the most upmarket of Mallorca's small hotels and in just three years has established a reputation for both its rooms and its food. It is in the tiny hamlet of Binibona on the sheltered eastern flank of the Tramuntana Sierra. Terraced gardens with palm, olive and citrus trees have been beautifully sculpted round the swimming pool and the main building, parts of which date back to the Moorish period. Amazing to think that there was just a ruin here five years ago — the building pays homage to the skill of local masons. The restaurant is in what was once the farm's almond press. Formally dressed tables and chairs are as you'd expect, given the prices on the menu, and the food is excellent with fresh seafood the house speciality. Rooms are in the main house and the suites are in what were the farmworkers' cottages: they are rather luxurious with their oriental rugs on tiled floors, best English mattresses and four-posters whose drapes match those of the windows. Open yours to catch the scent of rosemary and jasmine on the breeze. *The hotel does not accept children.*

rooms	7: 3 doubles, 4 suites.
price	€ 102/€ 162; single € 87–€ 138; suite € 132–€ 242.
meals	Breakfast € 16; lunch € 15–€ 30, dinner € 45.
closed	January & February.
directions	At Moscari church, left & follow road towards mountains. After approx. 1km at a fork, go right. Over next x-roads & on for 1km to Binibona; hotel ahead.

John Hughes

tel	+34 971 515751
fax	+34 971 875366
e-mail	info@can-furios.com
web	www.can-furios.com

Son Siurana

Ctra Palma-Mallorca km 45, 07400 Alcudia, Mallorca

The Roselló family has been in residence at Son Siurana for over 200 years and the latest two generations have given the estate a new lease of life as a luxurious rural retreat. Although you are close to Pollensa Port and Alcudia, the mansion house is deeply rural, surrounded by more than 100 hectares of fig and almond groves and sheep-grazed pastures. The main house is a long, low and graceful stone building with doors and windows highlighted by lighter-coloured *marés* surrounds. Life in summer centres around a large terrace with woodburning stove which looks onto a pool sculpted in among the rocks. Beyond, the estate has ancient pines, lakes and a vegetable and herb garden which supplies Siurana's kitchen: guests can pick their favourite vegetables. You stay in one of eight stylish self-catering cottages which have been slotted into the farm's outbuildings. The beautiful rooms have hand-painted tiles, terracotta or wooden floors, good modern furniture and antiques – perfect for the design mag photographers who have flocked to write about the place. Breakfast is served in the main house, on the terrace or in your cottage. *A Rusticae hotel.*

rooms	1 suite. 5 self-catering houses for 2; 1 house for 4; 2 apartments for 4.
price	Suite € 105–€ 138; apartment & house € 114–€ 225.
meals	Breakfast € 10; dinner € 24 (Tuesday & Thursday only).
closed	Rarely.
directions	From Palma towards Alcudia. Left for Son Siurana opp. km45.

Montse Roselló

tel	+34 971 549662
fax	+34 971 549788
e-mail	info@sonsiurana.com
web	www.sonsiurana.com

map 26   entry 343

Hotel Fínca Son Gener

Carretera Artà-Son Servera, Apartado de Correos 136, 07550 Son Servera, Mallorca

A few years ago this 18th-century farmhouse in the quiet north-east of the island, far from the bronzing crowds, lay in ruins. But a minor miracle has been worked thanks to an architect-designer of immense sensitivity and creativity. When you first see the building you are struck by its luminosity with the white *marés* stone of its façade, framed between the greenery of the surrounding lawns and the blue of the sky. The interior of Son Gener is a celebration of light and form, too: nothing in excess, just carefully selected sculptures and sofas, plants, tables and lamps that seem to create a backdrop for the walls and the structure of the building. It is both relaxing and uplifting, and the same holds for the bedrooms – all are suites with their own terraces – where every corner, lamp, tap or vase seems at one with the spirit of the place. You breakfast overlooking the peaceful gardens which have as much beauty and composure as the rest of the house. If you like understated elegance, that Japanese way of saying so much with such simplicity, then you will love Son Gener.

rooms	10 junior suites.
price	€230. VAT included.
meals	Lunchtime snacks; dinner €30. VAT included. Restaurant closed Tuesday.
closed	1 December-15 January.
directions	From Palma to Manacor. There on for Artá. Through Sant Llorenc; 2km before reaching Artá right on 403-1. Signed on left after 3km.

Angelika Senger
tel	+34 971 183612
fax	+34 971 183591
web	www.fincasongener.com

Alcaufar Vell

Ctra de Cala Alcaufar km 7,3, 07710 Sant Lluís, Menorca

The house is old. In 1773 the present building was wrapped around a 14th-century Moorish tower; six generations of Jaume's family have lived here. An entry in Alcaufar Vell's guest book reads: "We came for one night and then booked for four, we stayed for eleven… need we say more?". Places to stay are rather like friends; you get to know them gradually and however much you plan things, you should let your heart decide the ones you choose to keep. There is a lot of heart in the family home which María Angel and her son Jaume run in the best Spanish tradition of *mi casa es tu casa*. There are three guest lounges, one with a vast inglenook. Not a TV in sight, instead books, old farm instruments and a delicious feel of uncluttered comfort. The dining room is grander with beautiful blue and white stucco and Art Nouveau floor tiles. At breakfast feast on fruit and honey from the farm, local sausage and bread from a wood-fired oven as you gaze out to the sparkling sea. At dinner try the best of what the Menorcan cookery book has to offer before retiring to your bedroom which is every bit as enchanting as the rest of this magical place.

rooms	6: 3 twins/doubles, 3 suites.
price	€ 138–€ 174. VAT included.
meals	Dinner € 18. VAT included.
closed	December–January.
directions	From airport towards Maó, then to Sant Lluís. Just before Sant Lluís turn for Cala Alcaufar. Pass turning for Punta Prima then 2nd turning to right. Signed.

Jaume de Febrer

tel	+34 971 151874
fax	+34 971 151492
e-mail	hotel@alcaufarvell.com
web	www.alcaufarvell.com

map 26   entry 345

Biniarroca Hotel

Camí Vell 57, 07710 Sant Lluís, Menorca

Biniarroca once was a working farm; now, although parts of the building date back to the 16th century, the place is 21st-century-smart – thanks to five years of restoration work by its English owners. Sheelagh, a designer, used to run a guest house on the island; Lindsay is a painter and you'll see her light-filled creations on display in the hotel's antique-filled lounges. Thanks to their combined artistic nous, the hotel has taken root on this flat tract of land which leads down to Menorca's southern coast. A solitary palm stands sentinel over the cobbled courtyard; off to one side is a pool with a shaded terrace where plumbago and bougainvillaea are already softening the façade of the beautiful *marés* limestone. Each bedroom's decoration is different, all come with extra-large beds, antiques and oils and full optional extras. We marginally preferred those in the old stables for their extra privacy. You'll also remember the hotel for its elegant Mediterranean food: the fish, of course, is excellent, and most vegetables are organic and come fresh from the farm gardens. The silence at night is enchanting.

rooms	16: 13 doubles, 3 suites.
price	€ 108–€ 198; suite € 200–€ 280. VAT included.
meals	Light lunches € 18; dinner € 30 à la carte.
closed	November–February.
directions	From airport towards Maó, then to Sant Lluís. Here, follow signs for Alcaufar, then 1st left for Es Castell. Biniarroca signed on left after 2km.

Lindsay Mullen & Sheelagh Ratcliffe

tel	+34 971 150059
fax	+34 971 151250
e-mail	hotel@biniarroca.com
web	www.biniarroca.com

Hotel San Roque

Esteban de Ponte 32, 38450 Garachico, Tenerife

Ravishing – the brochure alone will lure you straight to the Canaries. The old mansion has been transformed – with magic and good taste. Wood and steel, geometric shapes and warm, earthy colours have been introduced with a flourish. Nothing is overdone; all is muted, bold and interesting. White-covered beds may float on a sea of dark-polished timber, a modern rug on the floor, a vast painting behind the bed. Each of the rooms is different, all good-looking, with more than a passing nod to 1930s design. If you don't love every minimalist detail your eye will be drawn to something that is, quite simply, breathtaking – like the courtyard, transformed by its all-round wooden balcony and ochre walls into an outside room with white armchairs, potted plants and soaring steel sculpture. Puritans will be unsettled for there are far too many opportunities for decadence: sauna, pool, music, tennis, food to long for and breakfast as late as you want. Garachico is, apparently, an insider 'tip': ancient and intimate. Mountains and sea; there is everything, and nothing, to do.

rooms	20: 16 doubles, 4 suites.
price	€ 175-€ 228; suite € 259-€ 312.
meals	Light lunch € 10; dinner € 25.
closed	Rarely.
directions	From southern airport m'way past Santa Cruz, La Laguna & Puerto de la Cruz. On past San Juan de la Rambla & Icod de los Viños to Garachico. Here, 4th left into cobbled street, then 1st left. Hotel on right.

Familia Carayon

tel	+34 922 133435
fax	+34 922 133406
e-mail	info@hotelsanroque.com
web	www.hotelsanroque.com

map 22   entry 347

WHAT'S IN THE BACK OF THE BOOK? ...

USEFUL VOCABULARY

Before arriving

Do you have a room free tonight?
¿Tiene una habitación libre para hoy?

How much does it cost?
¿Cuánto cuesta?

We'll be arriving at about 7pm.
Vamos a llegar sobre las siete.

We're lost.
Estámos perdidos.

We'll be arriving late.
Vamos a llegar tarde.

We're in the 'La Giralda' bar in…
Estámos en bar 'La Giralda' en …

Do you have animals?
¿Tienen animales?

I'm allergic to cats/dogs.
Tengo alergía a los gatos/los perros.

We'd like to have dinner.
Queremos cenar.

On arrival

Hello! I'm Mr/Mrs Sawday.
¡Hóla! Soy Señor/Señora Sawday.

We found your name in this book.
Le hemos encontrado en este libro.

Where can we leave the car?
¿Dónde podemos dejar el coche?

Do you have a car park?
¿Tiene aparcamento propio?

Could you help us with our bags?
¿Podría ayudarnos con las maletas?

Could I put this food/drink in your fridge?
¿Podría dejar esta comida/bebida en su nevera?

Could I heat up a baby's bottle?
¿Podría calentar este biberón?

Can you put an extra bed in our room?
¿Es posible darnos una cama supletoria?

How much extra will that be?
Cuánto más costará?

USEFUL VOCABULARY

Things you need/that go wrong

Do you have an extra pillow/blanket?
¿Podría dejarnos otra almohada/manta?

A light bulb needs replacing.
Es necesario cambiar una bombilla.

The heating isn't on.
No está encendida la calefacción.

Can you show us how the air-conditioning works?
¿Nos puede enseñar como funciona el aire?

We have a problem with the plumbing.
Tenemos un problema de fontanería.

The room smells.
Nuestra habitación huele mal.

Do you have a quieter room?
¿Tiene una habitación más tranquila?

Please could you ask the man in the room next door to stop singing!
¡Dígale al hombre de al lado que deje de cantar!

Where can I hang these wet clothes?
¿Dónde puedo colgar esta ropa mojada?

Where can I dry these wet boots?
¿Dónde puedo secar estas botas?

Could we have some soap, please?
¿Hay jabón por favor?

Could we have some hot water please?
¿Podría darnos agua caliente, por favor?

Do you have an aspirin?
¿Tendría una aspirina?

Could you turn the volume down?
¿Podría bajar un poco el volumen?

How the house/hotel works

When does breakfast begin?
¿A partir de qué hora dan el desayuno?

We'd like to order some drinks.
Queremos tomar algo.

Can the children play in the garden?
¿Pueden jugar fuera los niños?

Can we leave the children with you?
¿Podemos dejar los niños con vosotros?

USEFUL VOCABULARY

Can we eat breakfast in our room?
¿Es posible desayunar en nuestra habitación?

Local information

Where can we get some petrol?
¿Dónde hay una gasolinera?

Where can we find a garage to fix our car?
¿Dónde hay un taller de coches?

How far is the nearest shop?
¿Dónde está la tienda más cerca?

We need a doctor.
Necesitamos un médico.

Where is the nearest chemist's?
¿Dónde está la farmacía más cerca?

Where is there a police station?
¿Dónde está la comisaría?

Can you recommend a good restaurant?
¿Podría recomendar un buen restaurante?

Where is the nearest cash dispenser?
¿Dónde hay un cajero automático?

Can you recommend a nice walk?
¿Podría recomendar algun paseo bonito?

Do you know of any local festivities?
¿Hay alguna fiesta local en estos dias?

On leaving

What time must we vacate our room?
¿A qué hora tenemos que dejar libre nuestra habitación?

We'd like to pay the bill.
Queremos pagar.

How much do we owe you?
¿Cuánto le debemos?

We hope to be back.
Esperamos volver.

We've really enjoyed our stay.
Nos ha gustado mucho nuestra estancia.

This is a wonderful place.
Este es un lugar maravilloso.

Eating in/or out

Could we eat outside, please?
¿Podemos comer fuera?

USEFUL VOCABULARY

What is today's set menu?
¿Qué tienen hoy de menú?

What do you recommmend?
¿Qué es lo que recomienda usted?

What's that person eating?
¿Qué está comiendo aquel hombre?

We'd like something with no meat in it.
Queremos comer algo que no tenga nada de carne.

What vegetarian dishes do you have?
¿Qué platos vegetarianas hay?

We'd like to see the wine list.
Queremos la lista de vinos, por favor.

This food is cold!
¡Esta comida está fría!

Do you have some salt/pepper?
¿Hay sal/pimienta?

Where is there a good tapas bar?
¿Dónde hay un bar con buenas tapas?

Which tapas do you have?
¿Qué tapas hay?

We'd like a plateful of that one.
Una media ración de aquella, por favor.

A plate of that one, there.
Una ración de aquella, allí.

Please keep the change.
La vuelta es para usted.

Where are the toilets?
¿Dónde están los servicios?

The toilet is locked.
El servicio está cerrado con llave.

It was a delicious meal.
Estaba muy rica la comida.

I'd like a white/black coffee.
Un café con leche/un café solo.

We'd like some tea, please.
Quisieramos tomar un té, por favor.

WHAT IS ALASTAIR SAWDAY PUBLISHING?

Fifteen or more of us work in converted barns on a farm near Bristol, close enough to the city for a bicycle ride and far enough for a silence broken only by horses and the occasional passage of a tractor. Some editors work in the countries they write about, e.g. France; others work from the UK but are based outside the office. We enjoy each other's company, celebrate every event possible, and work in an easy-going but committed environment.

These books owe their style and mood to Alastair's miscellaneous career and his interest in the community and the environment. He has taught overseas, worked with refugees, run development projects abroad, founded a travel company and several environmental organisations. There has been a slightly mad streak evident throughout, not least in his driving of a waste-paper-collection lorry for a year, the manning of stalls at jumble sales and the pursuit of causes long before they were considered sane.

These books owe their style and mood to Alastair's miscellaneous career and his interest in the community and the environment

Back to the travel company: trying to take his clients to eat and sleep in places that were not owned by corporations and assorted bandits he found dozens of very special places in France – farms, châteaux etc – a list that grew into the first book, *French Bed and Breakfast*. It was a celebration of 'real' places to stay and the remarkable people who run them.

The publishing company grew from that first and rather whimsical French book. It started as a mild crusade, and there it stays – full of 'attitude', and the more appealing for it. For we still celebrate the unusual, the beautiful, the individual. We are passionate about rejecting the banal, the ugly, the pompous and the indifferent and we are passionate too about 'real' food. Alastair is a trustee of the Soil Association and keen to promote organic growing and consuming by owners and visitors.

It is a source of deep pleasure to us to know that there are many thousands of people who share our views. We are by no means alone in trumpeting the virtues of resisting the destruction and uniformity of so much of our culture – and the cultures of other nations, too.

We run a company in which people and values matter. We love to hear of new friendships between those in the book and those using it, and to know that there are many people – among them farmers – who have been enabled to pursue their decent lives thanks to the extra income our books bring them.

ALASTAIR SAWDAY'S

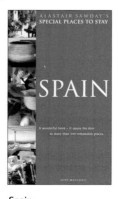

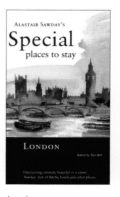

**British Hotels,
Inns & Other Places**
Edition 4   £12.99

British Bed & Breakfast
Edition 7   £14.99

British Holiday Homes
Edition 1   £9.99

**Bed & Breakfast for
Garden Lovers**
Edition 2   £14.99

French Bed & Breakfast
Edition 8   £15.99

Paris Hotels
Edition 4   £9.99

Spain
Edition 5   £13.99

Ireland
Edition 4   £12.99

London
Edition 1   £9.99

SPECIAL PLACES TO STAY SERIES

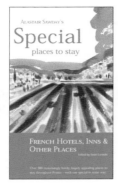

**French Hotels, Inns &
Other Places**
Edition 2   £11.95

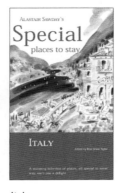

Italy
Edition 2   £11.95

French Holiday Homes
Edition 1   £11.99

Portugal
Edition 1   £8.95

THE LITTLE EARTH BOOK

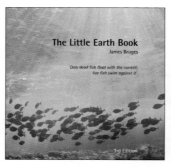

The Little Earth Book
James Bruges

'Only dead fish float with the current; live fish swim against it'.

3rd Edition

Over 30,000 copies sold.

A fascinating read. The earth is now desperately vulnerable; so are we. Original, stimulating short essays about what is going wrong with our planet, and about the greatest challenge of our century: how to save the Earth for us all. It is succinct, yet intellectually credible, well-referenced, wry yet deadly serious.

Researched and written by a Bristol architect, James Bruges, The Little Earth Book is a clarion call to action, a stimulating collection of short essays on today's most important environmental concerns, from global warming and poisoned food to unfettered economic growth, Third World debt, genes and 'superbugs'. Undogmatic but sure-footed, the style is light, explaining complex issues with easy language, illustrations and cartoons. Ideas are developed chapter by chapter, yet each one stands alone. It is an easy browse.

The Little Earth Book provides hope, with new ideas and examples of people swimming against the current, for bold ideas that work in practice. It is a book as important as it is original. Learn about the issues and join the most important debate of this century.

Did you know?

- If everyone adopted the Western lifestyle we would need five earths to support us.
- In 50 years the US has — with intensive pesticide use — doubled the amount of crops lost to pests.
- Environmental disasters have already created more than 80 MILLION refugees.

www.littleearth.co.uk

THE LITTLE FOOD BOOK

The Little Food Book
An explosive account of the food we eat today

Craig Sams

Our own livelihoods are at risk — from the food we eat. Original, stimulating, mini-essays about what is wrong with our food today, and about the greatest challenge of the new century: how to produce enough food without further damaging our health, the environment and vulnerable countries. Written by Craig Sams, Chairman of the Soil Association, it is concise, deeply informative and an important contribution to the great food debate. Just like The Little Earth Book, this is pithy, yet intellectually credible, wry yet deadly serious.

- A brilliant and easy-to-read synthesis of complex subjects
- Pertinent — food is a daily issue — organics, genetically-modified crops, farming practices, healthy eating
- Especially timely — the decline of the rural economy, foot and mouth, changes to the Commom Agricultural Policy
- Compact size — an excellent Christmas present or stocking filler.

Extracts from book:

"In the UK alone 25,000,000 kilos of pesticides are sprayed on food every year."

"In 2001 the World Trade Organisation fined the EU $120 million for suggesting that US meat imports should label the presence of hormone residues."

"Aspartame is a neurotoxin that probably causes as much brain damage as mobile phone use."

"300,000 Americans a year die of obesity."

"Research indicates that monosodium glutimate is a contributing factor in Alzheimer's disease."

"Globally, the market for organic food in 2001 exceeded $20 billion."

There is room for optimism — but you need to read this engrossing little book first!

WWW.SPECIALPLACESTOSTAY.COM

Britain

France

Ireland

Italy

Portugal

Spain...

all in one place!

On the unfathomable and often unnavigable sea of internet accommodation pages, those who have discovered **www.specialplacestostay.com** have found it to be an island of reliability. Not only will you find a database full of trustworthy, up-to-date information about all our Special Places to Stay across Europe, but also:

- Links to the web sites of all of the places from the series
- Colourful, clickable, interactive maps to help you find the right place
- The facility to make most bookings by e-mail –
  even if you don't have e-mail yourself
- Online purchasing of our books, securely and cheaply
- Regular, exclusive special offers on titles from the series
- The latest news about future editions, new titles and new places

The site is constantly evolving and is frequently updated, providing news, updates and special features that won't appear anywhere else but in our window on the worldwide web.

Russell Wilkinson, Web Producer
website@specialplacestostay.com

If you'd like to receive news and updates about our books by e-mail, send a message to **newsletter@specialplacestostay.com**

ORDER FORM UK

All these Special Places to Stay books and The Little Earth Book and The Little Food Book are available in major bookshops or you may order them direct. Post and packaging are FREE.

		Price	No. copies
French Bed & Breakfast	Edition 8	£15.99	
French Hotels, Inns and other places	Edition 2	£11.99	
French Holiday Homes	Edition 1	£11.99	
Paris Hotels	Edition 4	£9.99	
British Bed & Breakfast	Edition 7	£14.99	
British Hotels, Inns and other places	Edition 4	£12.99	
Bed & Breakfast for Garden Lovers	Edition 2	£14.99	
British Holiday Homes	Edition 1	£9.99	
London	Edition 1	£9.99	
Ireland	Edition 4	£12.99	
Spain	Edition 5	£13.99	
Portugal	Edition 2	£9.99	
Italy	Edition 2	£11.95	
The Little Earth Book	Edition 3	£6.99	
The Little Food Book	Edition 1	£6.99	
Please make cheques payable to Alastair Sawday Publishing	Total £		

Please send cheques to: Alastair Sawday Publishing, The Home Farm Stables, Barrow Gurney, Bristol BS48 3RW. For credit card orders call 01275 464891 or order directly from our website www.specialplacestostay.com

Title _____ First name _____

Surname _____

Address _____

_____

_____

Postcode _____

Tel _____

If you do not wish to receive mail from other like-minded companies, please tick here ☐

If you would prefer not to receive information about special offers on our books, please tick here ☐

SP5

ORDER FORM USA

All these books are available at your local bookstore, or you may order direct. Allow two to three weeks for delivery.

		Price	No. copies
Portugal	Edition 1	$14.95	
Ireland	Edition 4	$17.95	
French Bed & Breakfast	Edition 8	$19.95	
Paris Hotels	Edition 4	$14.95	
British Holiday Homes	Edition 1	$14.95	
British Hotels, Inns and other places	Edition 4	$17.95	
French Hotels, Inns and other places	Edition 2	$19.95	
British Bed & Breakfast	Edition 7	$19.95	
London	Edition 1	$12.95	
Italy	Edition 2	$17.95	
French Holiday Homes	Edition 1	$17.95	
	Total $		

Shipping in the continental USA: $3.95 for one book, $4.95 for two books, $5.95 for three or more books. Outside continental USA, call (800) 243-0495 for prices. For delivery to AK, CA, CO, CT, FL, GA, IL, IN, KS, MI, MN, MO, NE, NM, NC, OK, SC, TN, TX, VA, and WA, please add appropriate sales tax.

Please make checks payable to: **Total $**
The Globe Pequot Press

To order by phone with MasterCard or Visa: (800) 243-0495, 9am to 5pm EST; by fax: (800) 820-2329, 24 hours; through our web site: www.globe-pequot.com; or by mail: The Globe Pequot Press, P.O. Box 480, Guilford, CT 06437

Date

Name

Address

Town

State

Zip code

Tel

Fax

REPORT FORM

Comments on
existing entries
and new
discoveries

If you have any comments on entries in this guide, please let us
have them. If you have a favourite house, hotel, inn or other
new discovery, not just in Spain, please let us know about it.

Book title: _____

Entry no: _____ Edition no: _____

New
recommendation: _____

Country: _____

Name of property: _____

Address: _____

_____

_____

Postcode: _____

Tel: _____

Date of stay: _____

Comments: _____

_____

_____

From: _____

Address: _____

_____

_____

Postcode: _____

Tel: _____

Please send the completed form to:

Alastair Sawday Publishing,
The Home Farm Stables, Barrow Gurney, Bristol BS48 3RW
or go to www.specialplacestostay.com and click on 'contact'.

Thank you.

BOOKING FORM

Atencion de:
To:
_____

Date:
_____

Estimado Señor/Estimada Señora,

Le(s) rogamos de hacernos una reserva en nombre de:
Please make the following booking for (name):

_____

Para	noche(s)	Llegando día:	mes	año
For	night(s)	Arriving: day	month	year
	Saliendo día:	mes año		
	Leaving:	day	month	year

Necesitamos   habitacíon(es):
We would like   rooms, arranged as follows:
_____

Doble
Double bed   Twin beds
_____

Triple   Individual
Triple   Single
_____

Tipo Suite   Apartamento   ou autre
Suite   Apartment   or other
_____

Requeriremos también la cena:	Si	No	Para	persona(s)
We will also be requiring dinner	yes	no	for	person(s)

Les rogamos de enviarnos la confirmacíon de esta reserva a la siguiente dirección:

Please could you send us confirmation of our reservation to the address below (esta misma hoja o una fotocopia de la misma con su firma nos valdrá).

(this form or a photocopy of it with your signature could be used).

Nombre: **Name:**
_____

Dirección: **Address:**
_____

_____

Tel No: E-mail:
_____

Fax No:
_____

QUICK REFERENCE INDICES

WHEELCHAIR

These owners have told us that they have facilities suitable for people in wheelchairs. It is essential that you confirm what is available.

Galicia • 3 • 5 • 8 • 9 •12 • 13 • 15 • 16 • 18 • 21 • 22 • 23 • 24 • 27 • 29 • 37 • Asturias & Cantabria • 48 • 50 • 51 • 52 • 55 • 60 • Basque Country • 64 • Navarra - La Rioja • 74 • 76 • Aragón • 87 • 97 • Catalonia • 107 • 111 • 120 • 124 • 135 • Castilla - Leon • 145 • 150 • 151 • 152 • 154 • 158 • Castilla - La Mancha • 161 • 162 • 165 • 174 • Madrid • 176 • 179 • Levante • 180 • 182 • Extremadura • 198 • 203 • Andalucía • 211 • 215 • 218 • 220 • 223 • 229 • 231 • 232 • 240 • 250 • 252 • 257 • 260 • 264 • 269 • 276 • 287 • 288 • 289 • 297 • 298 • 299 • 302 • 304 • 306 • 315 • 318 • 321 • 325 • 327 • 331 • Balearics • 336 • 337 • 338 • 345 • 346 •

WINE

A selection of places of particular interest to wine buffs.

Galicia 12 • 15 • 21• 22 • 24 • 25 • 28 • Asturias & Cantabria • 32 • 48 • 49 • 54 • 56 • 58 • 63 • Basque Country • 67 • 71 • 72 • Navarra - La Rioja • 74 • 76 • 77 • Aragón • 80 • 84 • 87 • 89 • 92 • 94 • 95 • 98 • Catalonia • 102 • 106 • 107 •111 • 119 • 123• 128 • 129 • 131 • Castilla - Leon • 134 • 138 • 153 • 154 • 156 • Castilla - La Mancha • 161• 175 • Madrid • 177 • Levante • 184 • 191• 192• Extremadura • 199 • 204 • 205 • Andalucía • 217 • 218 • 224 • 227 • 231 • 252 • 253 • 254 • 258 • 259 • 263 • 268 • 269 • 284 • 286 • 287 • 291 • 292 • 293 • 294 • 308 • 312 • 326 • 327 • 331 • Balearics • 335 • 336 •337

QUICK REFERENCE INDICES

WALKING

The following places have good walks close by and owners who are knowledgeable about them.

QUICK REFERENCE INDICES

GREAT VALUE

The following places offer rooms at € 50 or less (excluding breakfast) for two in high season.

Galicia • 1 • 2 • 3 • 4 • 8 • 9 • 13 • 14 • 15 • 17 • 23 • 24 • 28 • Asturias & Cantabria • 33 • 34 • 35 • 38 • 43 • 46 • 49 • 51 • 52 • 55 • 56 • 59 • 61 • Basque Country • 65 • 66 • 67 • 70 • Aragón • 81 • 82 • 84 • 85 • 86 • 88 • 90 • 91 • 93• 94 • Catalonia • 100 • 101 • 102 • 109 • 112 • 117 • 118 • 128 • Castilla - Leon • 136 • 137 • 139 • 140 • 144 • 146 • 153 • Castilla - La Mancha • 166 • 168 • 169 • Levante • 180 • 182 • 186 • 187 • 188 • 191 • Extremadura • 201 • 207 • Andalucía • 226 • 230 • 240 • 241 • 245 • 247 • 255 • 277 • 285 • 286 • 300 • 305 • 308 • 309 • 310 • 311 • 312 • 313 • 314 • 315 • 318 • 324 • 325 • 330

RUSTICAE

These places are members of the Rusticae association.

Galicia • 5 • 12 • 20 • 22 • Asturias & Cantabria • 32 • 34 • 47 • 48 • 50 • 58 • 62 • 63 • Navarra - La Rioja • 74 • 76 • 77 • Aragón • 83 • 86 • 97 • Catalonia • 107 • 118 • 125 • Castilla - Leon • 133 • 138 • 149 • 154 • 158 • Castilla - La Mancha • 160 • 162 • 163 • 169 • 170 • 171 • 172 • 174 • 175 • Madrid • 179 • Levante • 193 • Extremadura • 196 • 199 • 205 • Andalucía • 211 • 216 • 238 • 243 • 263• 289 • 292 • 295 • 322 • Balearics • 336 • 343

QUICK REFERENCE INDICES

PAZOS DE GALICIA

These places belong to the Pazos de Galicia association.

Galicia • 2 • 3 • 5 • 6 • 8 • 9 • 10 • 14 • 15 • 16 • 19 • 21 • 23 • 26 • 27 • 28 • 29

RIDING

These are places where riding can be arranged, often with the owners and using their horses.

Asturias & Cantabria • 49 • 52 • Catalonia • 117 • 118 • Levante • 190 • Andalucía • 217 • 228 • 244 • 249 • 277 • 283 • 328

INDEX BY PROPERTY NAME

INDEX BY PROPERTY NAME

INDEX BY PROPERTY NAME

INDEX BY PROPERTY NAME

INDEX BY PLACE NAME

INDEX BY PLACE NAME

INDEX BY PLACE NAME

INDEX BY PLACE NAME

EXPLANATION OF SYMBOLS

Treat each one as a guide rather than a statement of fact and check important points when booking.

Full and approved wheelchair facilities for at least one bedroom and bathroom and access to all ground-floor common areas.

Ground-floor bedrooms for people of limited mobility.

Smoking restrictions exist usually, but not always, in the dining room and some bedrooms. Check when booking.

Pets are welcome but may have to sleep in an outbuilding or your car. Check when booking.

Payment by cash or cheques only.

Vegetarians catered for with advance warning. All hosts can cater for vegetarians at breakfast.

Most, but not necessarily all, ingredients are organic, organically grown, home-grown or locally grown.

Your hosts speak English, whether perfectly or not.

Swimming pool on the premises.

You can borrow or hire bikes.

Good hiking nearby.

Air conditioning in bedrooms. It may be a centrally-operated system or individual apparatus.

These properties are uninspected at the time of going to press:
8, 15, 16, 19, 28, 41, 96, 184, 189

EXCHANGE RATE TABLE

Euro€	US$	£ Sterling
1	1.01	0.64
5	5.05	3.20
7	7.07	4.48
10	10.10	6.40
15	15.15	9.60
20	20.20	12.80
30	30.30	19.20
40	40.40	25.60
50	50.50	32.00

December 2002